S0-BWQ-932

Freud

TEACHES

Psychotherapy

Other Books by Richard D. Chessick

How Psychotherapy Heals

Why Psychotherapists Fail

The Technique and Practice of Intensive Psychotherapy

Agonie: Diary of a Twentieth-Century Man

Great Ideas in Psychotherapy

Intensive Psychotherapy of the Borderline Patient

Freud *TEACHES* *Psychotherapy*

RICHARD D. CHESSICK, M.D., Ph.D.
Professor of Psychiatry, Northwestern University, Evanston, Illinois; Adjunct Professor of Philosophy, Loyola University of Chicago

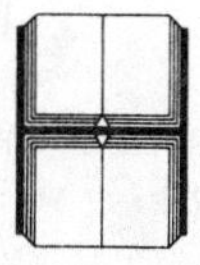

HACKETT PUBLISHING COMPANY
Indianapolis • Cambridge

Printed in the United States of America
First printing

Library of Congress Catalog Card Number 79-84334

ISBN 0-915144-63-8

For further information, please address
Hackett Publishing Company, Inc.
Box 55573, Indianapolis, Indiana 46205

Jacket design by Laszlo J. Balogh
Interior design by James N. Rogers

TO EDITH AND GEORGE FRIEDMAN

In appreciation for your kind and generous actions over the past thirty years

σωφρονεῖν ἀρετὴ μεγίστη
καὶ σοφίη ἀληθέα λέγειν
καὶ ποιεῖν κατὰ φύσιν ἐπαΐοντας.

. . . Heraclitus (ὁ Σκοτεινός)*

*See p. 4.

Contents

PART IV: UNFINISHED DEBATES

Acknowledgements

The author wishes to express special appreciation to the faculty members of the Department of Psychiatry at Northwestern University and of the Departments of Psychology and Philosophy at California Western University for their many comments and suggestions concerning the manuscript of this book. During the years of preparation of this work, the continued support and encouragement of Dr. John Shedd Schweppe and many others from the Institute for Living, Winnetka, Illinois, and the helpful suggestions of Dr. Franklin Walker, Director of Residency Training, Department of Psychiatry, Indiana University School of Medicine, are gratefully acknowledged. I also deeply appreciate the many special kindnesses I have experienced from Dr. Harold Visotsky, Chairman, Department of Psychiatry, Northwestern University, and Dr. Stanley Lesse, President, Association for the Advancement of Psychotherapy, in providing the atmosphere required for the sustained effort necessary to produce the manuscript.

Further acknowledgment is gratefully given to residents in the Department of Psychiatry at Northwestern University and to doctoral candidates in the Department of Pastoral Counselling, Garrett Theological Seminary, who, over the past several years, have attended my seminars and participated in discussions and criticisms of the various ideas expressed in this book and of portions of the manuscript, both individually and in group interactions. Their appreciation of my teaching has also sustained and encouraged me during the writing and research.

Ms. Betty Grudzien provided invaluable assistance in the library work involved; Ms. Wanda Sauerman worked long and hard to type the manuscript. I thank them sincerely and also Mr. James Newell Rogers for his editorial help in the preparation of the final manuscript, and in seeing the book through final proofs.

Introduction

This book explores and utilizes Freud's unparalleled genius in discovering, practicing, and describing the art and craft of intensive psychotherapy, for the purpose of teaching modern psychotherapists. His dedicated attitude and untiring endeavors, as they emerge in his writing, should also serve as a model to student and clinician alike. It is our ethical obligation to imitate Freud's deep devotion to understanding his patients and facing the truth—no matter how painful—and to offer our patients, as he did, the best technique and practice of intensive psychotherapy of which we are capable.

I hope this book will in addition counteract a most unfortunate current trend in the training of psychotherapists and in psychiatric residency-training programs—a trend away from reading the works of Freud himself. No substitute for or précis of Freud's work provides the flavor and atmosphere of his therapeutic approach or reveals the ambience of his psychotherapeutic sessions. Freud's contributions to the practice of *psychotherapy* are often neglected because we focus on his role as the discoverer and proponent of formal psychoanalysis. We should never forget that in his practice, he conducted himself fundamentally as a physician engaged in the treatment of emotionally disturbed patients.

This book is not primarily about psychoanalysis—it is about intensive psychotherapy. For besides founding psychoanalysis, Freud was an intuitive master of psychotherapeutic healing. The emphasis in the book is on *useful clinical concepts* and current unsettled debates that every psychotherapist is forced to confront. No writing has superseded the value of Freud's clinical reports and many helpful suggestions for the technique and practice of intensive psychotherapy, a discipline derived from the more basic and precisely defined procedure of formal psychoanalysis.

Indeed, just as Whitehead pointed out that all Western philosophy is a series of footnotes to Plato, all subsequent clinical writing on the technique and practice of intensive psychotherapy represents a series of footnotes—and usually minor footnotes—to the work of Freud. Each chapter in this book will utilize references from the twenty-four volumes of the *Standard Edition* of the Complete Psychological Works of Sigmund Freud published by the Hogarth Press, and will discuss the material from Freud's many publications that is pertinent to the current technique and practice of intensive psychotherapy. This material is considerably supplemented by my discussions and elaborations and is illustrated further by specific clinical examples and vignettes from my personal experience.

To understand Freud it is necessary to keep in mind the intellectual climate of his time. Trosman (Gedo and Pollock 1976) presents an excellent survey of the cultural influences on Freud's development. He explains that Freud in his prescientific days was already exposed to a wide cultural and humanistic tradition: "Through an interest in German literature and particularly in the writings of Goethe, he became conversant with the tradition of Romanticism and its regard for the irrational and unconscious." Freud responded to the romantic concern with the powers of nature, Goethe's views, and the *naturphilosophie* of the German philosopher Schelling with its one-sided attitude of repudiation of rationality and reason, not with philosophy but with an interest in observation. According to Trosman, Vienna provided an environment which encouraged an openness and acceptance of learning and innovation. Trosman concludes, "His early political aspirations encouraged an attitude of independence and an unwillingness to bow to authority, and the Jewish tradition provided the strength to tolerate prejudice and opposition. His classical education provided a complex substratum against which universals concerning the human mind could be tested." Freud may be thought of as blending the two broad movements in the history of Western thought, Romanticism and Classicism, in the sense in which, according to Trosman, "psychoanalysis attempts to find order in chaos, synthesis among conflicting irrational forces, integration and self-knowledge in the place of warded off unconscious impulses."

In 1925 Freud explained that in his youth he had felt an overpowering need to understand something of the riddles of the world in which we live and perhaps even to contribute something to their solution. He also later (1926E;20:253) wrote, "After forty-one years of medical activity my self-knowledge tells me that I have never really been a doctor in the proper sense. I became a doctor through being compelled to deviate from my original purpose; and the triumph of my life lies in my having, after a long and roundabout journey, found my way back to my earliest path." This is a truly amazing statement from someone who spent the first twenty years of his professional life in a meticulous study of neuroanatomy, neurophysiology, and clinical neurology.

By pursuing an empirical investigation of psychic reality, he attempted to move from the intuitive understanding of people, an understanding displayed by famous philosophers and authors in the past, to an application of the methods of science to psychic phenomena. Miller et al. (Gedo and

Pollock 1976) point out that "In Charcot, he found a living model whom he could follow into the endeavor of bringing man's psychological vicissitudes into the realm of scientific investigation. In this way, Freud's decade of scientific preparation could be wedded to his natural humanistic bent. in the service of establishing an entirely novel area of intellectual life, that of a *scientific* introspective psychology."

Holt (1975) presents an outstanding introduction on the subject of reading Freud. He calls our attention to the pervasive, unresolved tension in Freud's writings between two antithetical images of man. First, there is the prevailing image of man conveyed by the humanities, in which man is seen as both an animal and a creature with aspirations to divinity, thus having a dual nature. Each human being is seen as unique even though all are members of the same species. Each person is worthy to be respected, helped if in trouble, and encouraged to live up to the extent of his capacities. In this tradition, man is seen as a creature of longings and a producer and processor of subjective meanings, including the need to find his life meaningful. The complexity of human sexual love as compared to that of the animals is stressed, and man is viewed as an intensely social creature whose life becomes abnormal if it is not immersed in a web of relationships to other people. Man is not static but always changing—"developing and declining, evolving and devolving. His most important unconscious motives derive from experiences in childhood—the child is father to the man." Thus man is seen as both the active master of his own fate and the plaything of his passions.

By contrast, the school of Brücke and Helmholtz presents the mechanistic image of man as a proper subject of natural science, no different from any other object in the universe. In this view the differences among men are scientifically negligible, and man is fundamentally motivated by the automatic tendency of his nervous system to keep itself in an unstimulated state. Values and meanings are left out of this scientific investigation and consciousness is an epiphenomenon of trivial interest compared to the busy activities of the nervous system. Man's behavior is strictly determined by his past history, and free will is a fallacious illusion; the processes "sentimentally known as love are nothing more than disguises and transformations of the sexual instincts, or, more precisely, its energy." Thus relationships as such are not real and other people are objects and important insofar as they provide stimuli that set the psychic apparatus in motion, leading to a reduction of internal tensions.

Freud's magnificent literary style obscures this fundamental, unresolved tension—one found even today in the conflict between behavioral psychotherapy and psychodynamic psychotherapy. Thus Holt warns us to beware of lifting Freud's statements out of context for polemical purposes and advises us not to take Freud's extreme formulations literally but rather to treat them as his way of calling attention to a point. Inconsistencies, figurative language, and fuzzy definitions which change over a period of time are unavoidable in this situation.* A tendency to assert that proof of something has been established beyond doubt, an overfondness of dichotomies, and the tremendous persuasiveness of Freud's literary style go together; but Holt explains, "Don't let yourself be so offended by Freud's lapses from methodological purity that you dismiss him altogether. Almost any reader can learn an enormous lot from Freud if he will listen carefully and sympathetically and not take his pronouncements too seriously." To return to reading Freud again and again over many years provides one, as does every great work of Western civilization, with renewed insights and repeated intellectual and aesthetic excitement.

The intensity of the tension in Freud's conception of man is reflected throughout the history of Western thought. For example, the Greek philosopher Heraclitus (circa 500 B.C.) suffered from a similar tension: he constantly and ill-humoredly complained that men were not listening to what is really significant, and earned the epithet "the obscure" by introducing into his writing a deliberate ambiguity—to force concentration. The fragment (facing p. vii) from Heraclitus is usually translated: *Balanced thinking is the greatest excellence most characteristically human, and wisdom consists of saying the truth and acting in accordance with nature, listening hard [to it].*

Following the thought of Heidegger, as in his *Early Greek Thinking* (Harper & Row, 1975), I suggest a different translation: *Balanced thinking is the greatest excellence most characteristically human, and what is really significant comes to pass when we let unconcealment lie before us and bring forth what is immediately present-at-hand along the lines of self-disclosure, paying attention in a condition in which we may be struck hard by it.*

One aspect of Freud's genius was to transcend and complement the usual scientific, mechanistic conception of man by a return to the attuned, intuitive, free-floating attention of the Greek thinkers at the dawn of philosophy.

RICHARD D. CHESSICK, M.D., Ph.D.
Evanston, Illinois

*For those readers who are unfamiliar with psychiatric terms, an excellent glossary is available from the American Psychiatric Association, Publications Office, 1700 Eighteenth Street, N.W., Washington, D.C. 20009. A more technical but very useful and important glossary of psychoanalytic terms and concepts is available from the American Psychoanalytic Association, 1 East 57th Street, New York, N.Y. 10022.

When a child is born, his first years pass unnoticed in the joys and activities of infancy. As he grows older and begins to become a man, then the doors of the world open and he comes into touch with his fellows. For the first time notice is taken of him, and people think they can see the germs of the virtues and vices of his maturity taking shape.

That, if I am not mistaken, is a great error.

Go back; look at the baby in his mother's arms; see how the outside world is first reflected in the still hazy mirror of his mind; consider the first examples that strike his attention; listen to the first words that awaken his dormant powers of thought; and finally take notice of the first struggles he has to endure. Only then will you understand the origin or the prejudices, habits, and passions which are to dominate his life. The whole man is there, if one may put it so, in the cradle.

. . . Alexis De Tocqueville, *Democracy in America*

Part I

FIRST GREAT DISCOVERIES: THE PSYCHOANALYTIC PSYCHOTHERAPIST

I have not always been a psychotherapist. Like other neuropathologists, I was trained to employ local diagnoses and electro-prognosis, and it still strikes me myself as strange that the case histories I write should read like short stories and that, as one might say, they lack the serious stamp of science. I must console myself with the reflection that the nature of the subject is evidently responsible for this, rather than any preference of my own. The fact is that local diagnosis and electrical reactions lead nowhere in the study of hysteria, whereas a detailed description of mental processes such as we are accustomed to find in the works of imaginative writers enables me, with the use of a few psychological formulas, to obtain at least some kind of insight into the course of that affection.

Sigmund Freud, *Studies on Hysteria* (1895D;2:160)

Freud, age thirty-five, in 1891. MARY EVANS / SIGMUND FREUD COPYRIGHTS.

1

FREUD'S EARLY STRUGGLE

Sigmund Freud was born in Freiberg, Moravia, in 1856. At four he moved to Vienna only to leave there after the Nazi occupation in February 1938. He was saved from being murdered by the Nazis through the intervention of influential friends, and left for England, where he died in London on September 23, 1939, at the age of eighty-three, three weeks after the onset of World War II.

He came from a Jewish background and retained his sense of Jewish identity throughout his life, although he did not actively practice the Jewish religion. He suffered from anti-Semitism all his life and could never forgive his father for what he felt was cowardice in the face of prejudice. When he was ten or twelve years old, his father told him how once in his youth, as he was walking in the street, a gentile passed by and threw his father's cap in the mud, saying "Jew, get off the sidewalk!" Sigmund asked his father what he did then, and Jacob Freud replied, "I went to the road and picked it up."

Much has been made of Sigmund Freud's Jewish background. The most extreme view is that of Bakan (1965), who insists that the Jewish traditional cabalistic mystical doctrine had an important influence on the development of Freud's theories. A more modest view agrees with Freud's attribution to his Jewish origin of his capacity to not let himself be influenced by the opinions of the majority. Ellenberger (1970) adds that his readiness to believe that he was rejected was also influenced by his Jewish origin.

I think that a much better explanation of Freud's continual sense of being isolated and rejected is given by Holt (1975), who reminds us that "Freud operated always from the exposed and lonely situation of private practice." Freud's precious professorship did not carry either salary or tenure and, as Holt pointed out, "Freud might have been less of a fighter in his writing if he had worked from the protective security of an academic position." Only those who try to create from the exposed and lonely situation of private practice can understand the importance of this point.

The best brief overview of Freud's life and thought (among innumerable such publications) is the chapter "Sigmund Freud and Psychoanalysis" in

Ellenberger (1970). It is interesting that, as Ellenberger points out, "The difficulty in writing about Freud stems from the profusion of the literature about him, and from the fact that a legend had grown around him, which makes the task of an objective biographer exceedingly laborious and unrewarding. Behind this mountain of factual and legendary material are wide gaps in our knowledge of his life and personality."

The first three years of Freud's life were spent in Freiberg, Moravia, a little town with a picturesque landscape. This was followed by a year in Leipzig and then a settling of the Freud family in Vienna, in February 1860. Almost nothing is really known about Freud's early childhood except that his father, a not-very-successful businessman, changed his place of residence in Vienna several times between 1860 and 1865.

Freud began his medical studies in 1873 and received his degree in 1881, eight years later. The most important early influence on him was Ernst Brücke (1819–1892), adopted by Freud as his venerated teacher, and a rigid, authoritarian Prussian. Together with Helmholtz, Dubois-Reymond, Ludwig, and a few others, Brücke rejected any kind of vitalism or finalism in science. He insisted on striving to reduce psychological processes to physiological laws and physiological processes to physical and chemical laws.

During his work in Brücke's institute, Freud met Josef Breuer (1842–1925), a well-known and highly respected physician who became an older and rather fatherly friend, helping him in later years with substantial loans of money. In 1882 he suddenly left Brücke's laboratory, where he had worked for six years, and turned without enthusiasm to the career of a practicing physician, a shift probably related to his engagement during that year to Martha Bernays. As was the custom of the time, a long engagement entailing separation and assiduous correspondence resulted. It is clear that Freud had resolved to make a brilliant discovery so that his slow and arduous career as a practicing physician would be accelerated and he could attain financial security and marry. In 1883 he experimented on himself and others with a supposedly harmless substance called cocaine, and in 1884 he published a paper greatly praising the drug. It was a colleague, however, who discovered the value of cocaine as a surface anesthetic, and it was the colleague who acquired the sudden fame that Freud desired. Jones (1953) mentions that Freud's pushing of cocaine already gained him a reputation of being rather rash in his judgments.

In 1885, as a result of the intervention of Brücke and Meynert—a famous brain anatomist with whom Freud also studied for a short time—Freud received a traveling grant to study in Paris at the Salpêtrière with Charcot. What can the practicing psychotherapist learn from this? Freud regarded his experience at the Salpêtrière under the influence of Charcot as a turning point in his intellectual development. When he arrived in Paris,

Freud's chosen concern was the anatomy of the nervous system; when he left, his mind was filled with the problems of hysteria and hypnotism. From October 1885 to March 1886, at around the age of 30, Freud turned his back on organic neurology—primarily because of the discovery in Charcot's clinic that the symptoms of emotional disorders could be removed, altered, and substituted by psychological methods alone. This of course is the *fundamental hypothesis* of the practice of intensive psychotherapy. It was Freud's lifelong task to develop to the best of his ability the clinical practice of altering the symptoms of mental disorders by purely psychological techniques and to establish the principles of this clinical discipline, a basic science that he named psychoanalysis.

Volume 1 of the *Standard Edition* contains prepsychoanalytic publications and unpublished drafts from this period. The first thing that can be learned from this early material is the remarkable influence that a fine teacher can have on the development of a serious student. The description of his experience with Charcot has great literary beauty and the depiction of Charcot as a teacher is worthy of emulation today by those who would attempt to train others. It is no wonder that Ellenberger describes Freud's meeting with Charcot as "an existential encounter," even though it lasted for less than four months.

Freud in 1886 describes Charcot at work, openly surrounded by his assistants as well as by foreign physicians, of which Freud was just one. "He seemed, as it were, to be working with us, to be thinking aloud and expecting to have objections raised by his pupils" (1956A;1:10). Anyone who wished to ask a question or contribute to the discussion was welcome and no comment was left unnoticed by Charcot. Freud was impressed by the informality of the discussion and the way in which everyone was treated on an equal and polite footing; he remarks that this informality came as a surprise to foreign visitors and made it easy for even the most timid to take part in Charcot's work. Freud observed his method: Charcot would first be undecided in the face of some new and difficult manifestation of illness and then apparently work and think out loud in order to demonstrate how he arrived at an understanding. He was especially impressed that Charcot never grew tired of looking at the same phenomenon until his repeated and unbiased efforts allowed him to reach a correct view of its meaning. Years later, in his autobiography, Freud (1925D;20:3ff) mentions this as the most important methodological rule that he learned from Charcot. Freud was also impressed with the "complete sincerity" of Charcot. It might be added that Charcot was a rather theatrical individual who, in the way of many great teachers, was able to maintain a high level of interest and excitement in his seminars.

Freud returned to Vienna and in 1886 presented a paper on male hysteria before the distinguished medical society, The Imperial Society of Physicians. The paper, received with incredulity and hostility, was the starting point of Freud's lifelong, open feud with the Viennese medical world and the world of physicians in general. Ellenberger makes a convincing case that the hostile reception was in substantial part caused by Freud's overenthusiastic attributions to Charcot of what were the views and discoveries of other authors and of his narcissistic need to make a famous discovery and come into the Viennese limelight, especially after the narrow miss with his work on cocaine.

In the ten years that followed, Freud struggled to raise his family and build up his private practice, first in neurological work and then in the new psychology that he created. Not only did he start out in 1886 with the usual handicap of a young doctor with debts and few private patients, but from the very beginning there seems to have been an atmosphere of isolation and distrust fostered by his unsuccessful presentation to the society of physicians and by their scorn of his uncritical enthusiasm for cocaine, which of course was soon discovered to have addicting properties. He also broke with his supporter Meynert and became involved in an acrimonious quarrel with him in 1889. During this period he remained friendly with Breuer, who sent him patients.

Freud allegedly enjoyed a happy marriage; he was able to work very hard and gradually develop his reputation as a neurologist. He had six children and moved in 1891 into the famous apartment at Bergasse 19 (Engelman 1976), where he stayed until 1938. In these unpretentious quarters [which I visited and found to be surprisingly small in contrast to the greatness of Freud's psychological vision (Chessick 1977*a*)] Freud worked from early morning to late at night six days a week, but took three months of summer vacation spent traveling, sometimes without his wife.

The important point is that in the ten years from 1886 to 1896 he made an overwhelming transition from neurology based on the work of Charcot, to his own system of psychotherapy. The two major events in this transition are Freud's relationship with Fliess, involving first Freud's neurotic disturbances and self-analysis, and Freud's work at first with Breuer and then alone in discovering and elaborating the basic concepts of psychoanalysis.

Freud explained that like every other foreigner in a similar position, he left the Salpêtrière as Charcot's unqualified admirer. In the presence of such a fine teacher it is easy to see how Freud became fascinated by the clinical phenomena of hysteria and hypnotism that added so much drama to Charcot's demonstrations and lectures. Since that time many others, after discovering Freud's writings or under an inspiring teacher, have had a similar experience in moving from the field of organic neurology to the field of psychodynamic psychiatry. This also happened to me.*

Freud's first book, *On Aphasia* (discussed in detail in a later chapter), was published in 1891 and dedicated to Breuer. It is not included in the *Standard Edition* of Freud's works, but it does show him at the age of thirty-five as an experienced neurologist with an outstanding literary style. As one might expect of Freud, in place of minute localizing schemas to explain aphasia, he introduced a quite different *functional* explanation based on the Hughlings Jackson doctrine of "disinvolution," according to which more recently acquired or less important capacities suffered earlier than more fundamental ones. Jones (1953) sees this functional explanation as a stage in Freud's emancipation from the more mechanical aspects of the Helmholtz School in which he had been brought up in the laboratory of Brücke. The explanation includes severe criticism of Meynert's theory that ideas and memories are to be pictured as attached to various brain cells. The book sold 257 copies after nine years and was obviously not a success. The book that brought Freud his reputation as a neurologist was published in 1891 with his friend Dr. Oscar Rie, and dealt with unilateral paralysis of children. This and other work on cerebral palsy and his neuroanatomical research established Freud's neurological reputation. It should be remembered that by 1893 he had established this reputation as a competent neurologist on the basis of about twenty years of work.

As we go through the many pages of the first volume of the *Standard Edition*, we witness Freud's intensive intellectual struggle with a series of theoretical concepts in trying to explain the various clinical phenomena of hysteria, neurasthenia, depression, obsessive-compulsive neurosis, anxiety, and even paranoia. Over and over he grapples with complex theoretical problems, adopting one explanation and then discarding it for another. Even a cursory reading of this material demonstrates the extreme difficulty of attaching diagnostic labels to patients in the field of psychotherapy, a confusion in psychiatric nosology which continues to this day.

What emerges with compelling clarity in his famous letters to Fliess (Freud 1950A;1:175ff) is the paramount importance of Freud's self-analysis. Thus in the teaching and learning of psychotherapy, the *first* principle for success lies in the importance of the opportunity to identify with outstand-

*I began as a medical student doing research during elective and vacation periods on the histochemistry of the nervous system. In this field I published a number of papers; but, due to the influence of Dr. N. S. Apter, an outstanding teacher of psychodynamic psychiatry (and my earlier personal discovery of the writings of Freud under the famous "Hutchins plan" at the University of Chicago), I shifted my interest to the field of intensive psychotherapy. Such teachers are becoming rare in medical schools today; from time to time I receive moving letters from medical students who have read my books and approached the department of psychiatry in their medical school only to be told that the era of biological psychiatry is at hand and to forget about psychotherapy and psychodynamics.

ing teachers and clinicians, and the *second* principle rests on the intensive psychotherapy of the psychotherapist. It was only after his own thorough self-analysis, and in spite of the obvious defects that such a procedure entailed, that Freud was able to arrive at a deeper understanding of the phenomena of mental disorders and to devise a more profound technique than hypnotism and suggestion for their treatment.

It has become my increasingly firm conviction that no one should practice intensive psychotherapy without first undergoing *a thorough intensive psychotherapy* of his or her own. The question often arises, How much psychotherapy? As a rule-of-thumb, I advise students to limit their treatment of patients to a frequency of one time per week *less* than that of their own intensive psychotherapy. Thus a psychotherapist who has successfully completed a twice-a-week personal treatment will protect himself and tend to stay out of trouble with destructive countertransference and clinical confusion if he sees his patients once weekly; patients who need greater frequency of treatment should be sent to others.

For example, a young doctoral candidate who had just finished his dissertation came to me, because his supervisor had become ill, for a few supervisory sessions near the end of his schooling. The candidate was personable, successful, and well thought of. He had been approved for graduation and was about to take a post as a psychotherapist in an important clinic.

He presented himself with tact and dignity and showed no evidence of psychopathology. He reported on two female patients whom he had been seeing and casually mentioned that the second of the two constantly complained because he started her sessions late. The admitted reason for this was that he had a tendency to keep the first of the two female patients for extra time; he attributed the second patient's complaining to her personal psychopathology and was attempting to interpret it to her. The doctoral candidate had received about a year of once-a-week psychotherapy but had terminated treatment at the end of the year because both therapist and patient agreed that there was "little further to talk about." After a cursory description of each patient, he launched into a complex metapsychological description of what he regarded to be their psychodynamics and psychopathology. I had to stop him because I could not fix in my mind any superficial physical description of either; they seemed fused together in my head and were only intellectual abstractions as he presented them.

In the second supervisory session, the candidate attempted to go into greater depth regarding the psychodynamics of the patients. Finally, I insisted that he give me a detailed superficial, empirical, clinical description of each patient. It immediately became apparent that the first patient was beautiful and seductive whereas the second patient was dumpy and unattractive. In spite of his repeated efforts to return to psychodynamic descriptions, I insisted that the candidate dwell on his emotional reactions to each patient. He finally blurted out that he had many fantasies of sexual intercourse with the first patient. It was most difficult for him to let the first patient go at the end of her session and only with reluctance did he face the unattractive patient.

Although I attempted to explain in every possible fashion how this preoccupation with sexual fantasies about the first patient might profoundly affect his treatment of both patients, the candidate really did not grasp what I was trying to say and tended to slide over the subject. At my suggestion that perhaps some further psychotherapy would be indicated for him, he agreed that perhaps "some day" he might consider it. He finished his schooling and to my knowledge is now operating as a clinician.

Over years of supervising residents and various students, many episodes of this nature could be reported. Even experienced supervisors are sometimes amazed when an advanced student brings tense countertransference reactions into the very first evaluation interview—reactions of such a transparent nature that it is incomprehensible how they could be overlooked by the candidate. The only protection for the patient against such countertransference is to insist that the candidate see patients on an infrequent basis, if his own treatment has been infrequent, in order to minimize intense development of emotional misalliances with patients (Langs 1975). This is only a very weak protection.

In case the reader feels that only beginning students can experience this, Greenson (1967) describes an outstanding example of a candidate at a psychoanalytic institute who was unable to empathize with a patient's concern over her seriously ill infant. Treatment ended abruptly with the patient telling the candidate that he was sicker than she was. Although Greenson quotes the candidate as agreeing to his need for further treatment, he does not inform us whether the candidate *actually went for it*; my experience has been that it is very difficult to get students to re-enter treatment once they have found a way to "finish" what they consider to be their "training psychotherapy."

Wilhelm Fliess, an ear and nose specialist in Berlin, was the author of a number of theories involving the correspondence between the nasal mucosa and the genitals, bisexuality, and the existence in each individual of a double periodicity with a feminine and masculine cycle of twenty-eight to twenty-three days, respectively. A friendship developed by 1892, during which Freud in his isolation used Fliess as a touchstone to correspond about his new ideas and theories. In one way the famous letters to Fliess are a kind of diary; but there is no question that the friendship and the emotional interaction with Fliess was supportive and therapeutic for Freud also, which is something one does *not* obtain from a diary. As with Charcot, Freud tended to enthusiastically overexaggerate his friend's abilities and theories, calling him "the healer into whose hands one confidently entrusts one's life." In fact, Fliess, in contrast to Charcot, was mediocre in every way.

At the beginning of 1894, Freud suffered from heart symptoms, and on Fliess's advice stopped smoking for fourteen months until he could stand it no longer. From July 1895 up to the death of his father on October 23, 1896, he published with Breuer *Studies On Hysteria*, broke off his relationship with Breuer, and worked on the unfinished "Project For a Scientific Psychology," which is the last item in the first volume of the *Standard Edition* (1950A;1:283–387).

Freud's cardiac problem was marked by an arrhythmia and some chest discomfort, but Fliess's diagnosis of nicotine poisoning was wrong, since abstention and then smoking a few cigars seemed to make no difference. There is no evidence that Freud's twenty cigars a day had any effect on his heart; the malady seems to have been purely psychogenic in origin. The subsequent break with Fliess is attributed to a number of circumstances involving, first, Freud's partly successful self-analysis (Kohut 1977), and second, their basic disagreement on scientific matters, in which Freud could not accept Fliess's numerology and Fliess could not accept Freud's dynamic etiological findings in the psychoneuroses.

One must keep in mind that Freud and Fliess had much in common in their life situation. Both were young medical specialists, both were from the Jewish middle class, both were concerned with establishing a practice, and both were preoccupied with maintaining and raising a family—although Fliess had an easier time of it because he married a wealthy woman and was more successful than Freud in his Berlin practice. Both men were educated in the humanities and so could understand each other's allusions to classical and modern literature. Fliess was also influenced by the Helmholtz School; his Christmas present to Freud in 1898 consisted of two volumes of Helmholtz's lectures.

Freud's extreme dependency on Fliess, up to the age of forty-five, is described by Jones (1953) as having the appearance of delayed adolescence and is marked by Freud's inordinate overestimation of Fliess. The basis of this attachment seems related to Freud's separation from Breuer. Fliess, in contrast to Breuer, was quite preoccupied with sexual problems, although in a curiously mysterious and numerological way. He was much more willing to speculate and explore forbidden territory than the older and conservative Breuer, and he was faithfully willing to listen to Freud's accounts of his various findings and theoretical explanations and to pass judgment on them. Freud often wrote to Fliess more than once a week, and they had frequent personal meetings for a day or two. I agree with Jones that Fliess served essentially as psychological encouragement (mirroring) at a time when Freud was suffering personally and wrestling with his discoveries.

The letters to Fliess show that for about a year after his father's death, Freud brooded day and night in a psychoneurosis which seems to have had depressive, obsessive, and hysterical components. Interpretation of this malady seems to depend essentially on a critic's general feeling about Freud and his work, with his adversaries contending that it shows he was severely ill and his writing simply the expression of neurosis, and his rather uncritical followers (such as Jones) claiming that his self-analysis was a heroic feat without precedence, never to be performed again.

I agree with Ellenberger (1970) that this self-analysis was part of a creative illness reaching its resolution with the publication of *The Interpretation of Dreams* in 1900:

> A creative illness succeeds a period of intense preoccupation with an idea and a search for a certain truth. It is a polymorphous condition that can take the shape of depression, neurosis, psychosomatic ailments, or even psychosis. . . . Throughout the illness the subject never loses the thread of his dominating preoccupation. It is often compatible with normal professional activity and family life. But even if he keeps to his social activities, he is almost entirely absorbed with himself. He suffers from feelings of utter isolation, even when he has a mentor who guides him through the ordeal. . . . The termination is often rapid and marked by a phase of exhilaration. The subject emerges from his ordeal with a permanent transformation in his personality and the conviction that he has discovered a great truth or a new spiritual world (Ellenberger 1970, pp. 447–448).

Freud made a point of spending two or three months in the country every summer, even during the years when he was not doing well financially. For climatic reasons long summer holidays were the custom in Vienna, but Freud recognized this as a necessity rather than a luxury. As Jones (1953) points out, "Freud found early that the strain of the work of intensive psychotherapy was such that without an ample period for recuperation its quality would surely deteriorate."

In addition to his sensible precaution of taking ample vacation time in spite of the financial losses incurred, Freud also had at least one passionate hobby—antiquities. This seems to have gratified both his aesthetic needs (he detested music) and his abiding interest in the sources of civilization. Like his vacations, the hobby also represented a financial extravagance; he was able to make himself only occasional presents of various archeological objects. Clearly, Freud's attitude toward money was a mature one, and in fact he insisted that wealth brings little happiness, since money is not primarily involved in childhood wishes.

We have gone a long way from this attitude in our present civilization.

In a previous publication (1969) I have discussed vanity and greed in the life of the psychotherapist. Generally speaking Freud had more insight into the greed problem of psychotherapists than he did into vanity; it remained for later pioneers to investigate the nature of narcissism in greater depth.

Perhaps the most dramatic description of the problem of life in private practice with respect to money is presented by Saul (1958), who deplores the current emphasis on the equation stating that the more hours that the analyst works, the more money that he makes. The average therapist is in middle life with wife and children and perhaps even in debt because of his training. He is insecure about filling his time and not sure when a patient finishes treatment whether the next available hour will be filled promptly by another patient: "Therefore he works all the hours he can and risks slipping into the mire of equating hours and income. Of course, this equation is true, but if not properly balanced and separated, the result is entrapment and slavery." Thus the therapist cannot take time for lunch because the time represents a lost fee, and he cannot take a day off or vacation for similar reasons. Saul calls this "the dance of the hours" in which the therapy hour becomes too intimately associated with the therapist's receptive needs. Thus "Time off is no longer a legitimate, wholesome respite from work, the satisfaction of his proper receptive needs; it has become a frustration of his receptive needs because he is not receiving, in the form of money, when he is not working. . . . He is pushed in the same direction by the pressures of a money-civilization in which money is a means to security, pleasure, prestige, romance—well-nigh everything" (p. 22).

Saul makes the solution sound easy, but it is not. Basically it requires maturity in the therapist's wife as well as in himself. An income less than that of most physicians must be expected for the intensive psychotherapist. Still, working with no more than six or seven patients a day to avoid fatigue, and allowing for breaks for meetings, illnesses, and vacations, the psychotherapist can make a reasonable income and have a nice life "if he and his wife are not greedy."

The wholesomeness of the therapist is a very important subject. Sociability among friends, where there is normal, nonstructured interaction and physical exercise on a daily basis, are absolutely essential to the mental and physical hygiene of the psychotherapist.

Many authors have discussed an epidemic of depression, depressive equivalents, and suicide in physicians, especially psychiatrists, in the age group of 45 to 55. In the case of psychiatrists attempts have been made to connect this to the unusually great professional identity problem of psychiatrists in their residencies and later in their mid-career crises. The gnawing sense of dissatisfaction and impatience, the feeling of being boxed in, doubts about our choice of profession, and doubts about our very life style were termed "destination sickness" at the 1976 meeting of the American Psychiatric Association (Rosen 1973, 1976). The problem of destination sickness is related rather to our sense of self, which forms as the consequence of transformations of narcissism—and which therefore, may be disturbed either by initial developmental deficiencies or eroded by the vicissitudes of living.

Every human being is forced by the ambiguity of existence to make two fundamental choices—choices that Kierkegaard called "criterionless choices" or "leaps." We cannot avoid these choices; their very nature will have a profound effect on the way each individual lives his life, and on the healthy or pathological state of the spiritual aspect of the human mind. These choices are: (1) either we declare the human situation to be utterly absurd and hopeless and just try to make the best of it on a day-to-day basis, or we look for a further dimension, or depth, or ground, to human existence that makes more sense out of it, supports it, and brings order and fulfillment to it; (2) either there is a force in the human mind that drives man, in spite of his limitations, to bump up repeatedly against the limits of pure reason, as Kant put it, and to constantly strive to transcend the self and make contact with something outside of and greater than the self—a force which makes man unique among the animals—or there is no such force and we are strictly physico-chemical entities with inherent and conditioned behavior patterns exactly like all other animal species.

These choices have special meaning to every psychotherapist because not only do they affect, as in the case of all humans, the personal life of the therapist; they also seriously affect his approach to his patients and the psychic field (Chessick 1971) that he has to offer them. Furthermore, because these problems and choices cannot be avoided in the dialectic of long-term psychotherapy, the therapist is forced to think about them.

There is general agreement that the rate of suicide among physicians is significantly higher than that of the general population. Steppacher and Mausner (1974) indicate that below age 45, women physicians are at the highest risk; whereas over 45, male physicians show a higher suicide rate than women. Most authors agree that the rate increases with age and that married physicians are the least prone to suicide, as compared with bachelors, widowers, and especially divorced physicians. Ross (1975) presents preliminary data from the American Psychiatric Association Task Force on Suicide Prevention and reminds us that in the United States suicide causes more physician deaths than do automobile accidents, plane crashes, drownings, and homicides combined. He reviews the literature extensively and reports a high incidence of psychopathology, alcoholism, drug addiction, and most of all, depression, in physicians who commit suicide.

Green et al. (1976) describe the problem of drug addiction among physicians and point out that the median age of onset of addiction in their series was 43 years. Many authors have reported and discussed the tragic problem of the middle-aged physician as alcoholic or drug addict. Furthermore, Ross (1975) explains, "Among physicians who committed suicide, colleagues have noticed a change in behavior, an increasing indecisiveness, disorganization, and depression for two to four months preceding suicide."

The question of whether psychiatrists have a significantly higher rate of suicide than other physicians is not settled. Several contradictory studies have been published and methodological problems have left the question unanswered. Physicians hostile to psychiatrists have jumped at the chance to use some published reports to attack the psychiatric profession; Rosen (1973) from the Langley Porter Clinic has eloquently and maturely addressed such critics.

Kelly (1973), and Pasnau and Russell (1975, also Russell et al. 1975) surveyed suicide in psychiatric residents. They found no higher incidence than for residents in other specialties, and no difference among males, females, minorities, or foreigners. Detailed analysis of five cases of suicide demonstrates that all the residents were intelligent, motivated, sensitive, and ranked high in their class. This fits the description by Ross (1975) of the suicide-prone physician: "graduated at or near the top of high prestige medical school class, and now he practices a peripheral specialty associated with chronic problems where satisfactions are difficult and laggard."

We can help the psychiatrist to reintroduce quality, as I have described it elsewhere (1969), into the physician's life. We must urge him to find the leisure for keeping up with and contributing to medicine, for expanding his soul (Chessick 1978) through the transcendent beauty of art and music, and for contemplation of human life in terms of first principles; that is, for what is true, what is good, and what is valuable. Gilbert Highet (1976), one of the inspiring teachers of our time, puts it this way:

> Wholeness of the mind and spirit is not a quality conferred on us by nature or by God. It is like health, virtue, and knowledge. Man has the capacity to attain it; but to achieve it depends on his own efforts. . . . That is the lesson that the great books above almost all other possessions of the human spirit, are designed to teach. It is not possible to study them—beginning with Homer and the Bible and coming down to the magnificent novels of yesterday (*War and Peace*) and of today (*Doctor Faustus*)—without realizing, first, the existence of permanent moral and intellectual standards; second, the difficulty of maintaining them in one's own life; and, third, the necessity of preserving them against their chief enemies, folly and barbarism (pp. 16, 33–34).

Clearly, a firm sense of self and the mature capacity for love and intimacy with others are indispensable foundations for protecting us against the chronic drain of our psychiatric work. In a recent book (1976) I have described the death of a middle-aged psychiatrist, from coronary artery disease, as a result of neglect of these factors. Intensive psychotherapy is mandatory to enhance these capacities within us, and common sense ought to force us to seek such therapy both as a protection in training and later on in life.

Not enough has been done to reduce the isolation of the practicing psychiatrist and to provide an atmosphere where self-esteem is not reduced but rather enhanced by the decision to seek further personal psychotherapy. Channels for consultation with colleagues are not sufficiently open and little has been provided to educate the family of the psychiatrist to the fact that psychiatrists also are human and at times must be strongly urged by those around them to get help. Exactly contrary to the popular misconception, it is the psychiatrist who seeks help for himself by consultation and further psychotherapy who shows best his capacity to help his patients; the psychiatrist who denies his needs and pretends to be self-sufficient may temporarily impress those around him but actually is showing weakness rather than strength. Support from colleagues and loved ones is vital in helping the psychiatrist deal with the narcissistic problems involved in seeking help and consultation.

We have a special obligation to residents in training; we clearly already know how to reduce the number of breakdowns and suicides by residents. Kelly (1973) suggests such measures as psychological testing and psychiatric interviewing at the time of selection; sensitive individual supervision; early explicit discussion of the stress residents will experience and of suicidal thoughts as well as innumerable other reactions, thoughts, and phantasies that may plague the resident under stress; periodic evaluation of emotional development during training; and prompt recognition of crisis situations and referral for treatment—preferably without financial burden to the resident.

In addition Kelly poses the question, "What can be done during the years of residency to prepare the psychiatrist to cope more readily with personal depletion and distress throughout the years following formal training, when he will be fully engrossed in his practice, carrying the burden of his patients' fears, angers, and self-loathings and separated from close personal contact with understanding colleagues?" Up to the present we have failed to address ourselves to this question and to recognize its great importance.

2

IDENTITY OF THE PSYCHOTHERAPIST

By 1913 Freud was considering the question of nonmedical psychotherapists. Although the bulk of his argument in favor of the subject was presented twenty years later in *The Question of Lay Analysis* (Freud 1926E; 20:179ff), his brief introduction to Pfister's book on psychoanalytic method already contains a memorable quote (Freud 1913B;12:331) on the subject:

> The practice of psychoanalysis calls much less for medical training than for psychological instruction and a free human outlook. . . . The educator and the pastoral worker are bound by the standards of their profession to exercise the same consideration, care, and restraint as are usually practiced by the doctor, and apart from this their association with young people perhaps makes them better fitted to understand these young people's mental life. But in both cases the only guarantee of the harmless application of the analytic procedure must depend on the personality of the analyst.

In *An Autobiographical Study* (1925D;20:8) Freud points out, "Neither at that time, nor indeed in my later life, did I feel any particular predilection for the career of a doctor. I was moved, rather, by a sort of curiosity, which was, however, directed more towards human concerns than towards natural objects; nor had I grasped the importance of observation as one of the best means of gratifying it." On the other hand, he warns us that anyone who wants to make a living from the treatment of nervous patients must clearly be able to do something to help them. And he reminds us that the "art of interpretation" requires tact and practice. Freud makes much of his insistence that psychoanalysis should be treated like any other science and he objects to philosophy proper, which he claims to have carefully avoided. He wants psychoanalysis to be "serious scientific work carried on at a high level."

Freud complained because *The Question of Lay Analysis* (1926E; 20:179ff) was published in America in the same volume as his autobiography; because of that the autobiography was eclipsed since the entire volume received the title *The Question of Lay Analysis*. Actually the two works do belong very much together, especially since Freud's remarks in the autobiography about not really wanting to be a doctor are expanded in the postscript to *The Question of Lay Analysis*. Here Freud remarks that the triumph of his life lies in having "after a long and roundabout journey" found his way back to the earliest path which was "an overpowering need to understand something of the riddles of the world in which we live and perhaps even to contribute something to their solution."

Freud states unequivocally that medical training produces a one-sided attitude which must be actually overcome by the person's wishes to become a psychotherapist in order to help the medical psychotherapist "resist the temptation to flirt with endocrinology and the autonomic nervous system, when what is needed is an apprehension of psychological facts with the help of a framework of psychological concepts" (1926E;20:257).

In his book on lay analysis, one of his most eloquent efforts, he argues strongly against the notion that a psychoanalyst must be first a physician, thereby taking a firm position on one of the thorniest and most controversial issues facing the field of psychotherapy. The book also contains a remarkable literary conception, consisting of a dialogue between Freud and a so-called Impartial Person, in which, in his lightest style, Freud introduces the impartial person to the practice of psychoanalysis in a nontechnical way, for the purpose of demonstrating that medical training is really unnecessary.

The aim of psychoanalytic psychotherapy is beautifully expressed:

> By encouraging the patient to disregard his resistances to telling us these things, we are educating his ego to overcome its inclination towards attempts at flight and to tolerate an approach to what is repressed. In the end, if the situation of repression can be successfully reproduced in his memory, his compliance will be brilliantly rewarded. The whole difference between his age then and now works in his favour; and the thing from which his childish ego fled in terror will often seem to his adult and strengthened ego no more than child's play (1926E;20:205).

What are the issues involved in the question of lay analysis? I believe the problem is actually more difficult today because of the advent of psychopharmacology than it was in Freud's time. First of all, Freud agrees that the initial work of evaluation should include a thorough investigation by a physician who should be a psychiatrist, as the dangers of overlooking any organic condition which is being expressed by mental symptoms are obvious. Furthermore, the psychiatrist must be available for medical consultation whenever any organic symptoms appear in the treatment. It seems impossible to quarrel with this—yet lay analysts practicing today generally do *not* make it a rule to have a psychiatrist involved in their initial work-up of a patient. I have never been able to find any kind of reasonable argument that would excuse exposing patients to such a risk.

This subject brings up the entire issue of moral responsibility. Freud emphasizes that the complete honesty demanded from the patient puts a "grave moral responsibility" on the therapist as well, but he argues that the ethics of other professions such as psychology, ministry, and social work all stress the same moral responsibility to patients or clients as do medical ethics. In this day and age of malpractice suits one would be hard put to argue that the professional ethics of the physician are above or more stringent than those of psychologists or ministers or social workers; and clearly, the issue of moral responsibility rests on the personal treatment of the psychotherapist. That is to say, the best protection of the patient against being exploited by the therapist is the thorough, intensive psychotherapy of the therapist. Personal integrity is not developed by professional training, but is rather a function of emotional maturity. As Saul (1958) puts it, "The child lives on in the analyst as in every one else; only one expects the child to be a little less fractious, unruly and disruptive in those whose profession it is to help others in life's journey."

Thus the crucial issue in determining whether a layman (nonphysician) should practice psychotherapy, in my opinion, rests on the adequacy of the intensive psychotherapy or psychoanalysis of the layman. As Freud points out, "The work is hard, the responsibility great." The second cornerstone of qualification to practice intensive psychotherapy is the training that the therapist has received. Freud writes, "anyone who has passed through such a course of instruction, who has been analysed himself, who has mastered what can be taught today of the psychology of the unconscious, who is at home in the science of sexual life, who has learnt the delicate technique of psychoanalysis, the art of interpretation, of fighting resistances and of handling the transference—anyone who has accomplished all this *is no longer a layman in the field of psychoanalysis*" (1926E;20:228). Conversely, no one should practice intensive psychotherapy, whether or not they are physicians, who has not received a long, arduous training. I have outlined in detail the kind of training I think necessary for the practice of intensive psychotherapy in another book (Chessick 1971).

As Freud explains, the power of professional feeling makes it very difficult for physicians to accept lay analysts. This feeling involves the physician's wish to remain alive to the medical profession, with the identity that the physician has carefully developed in his medical training, in addition to the well-earned competitive advantage. The lay therapists who are enemies of the medical profession stress the economics of this situation, but those who are physicians realize there is an extremely important identity problem involved here. This identity problem today pervades the entire field of psychiatry as well as psychotherapy.

The resident in psychiatry suffers acutely from his sense of isolation from other medical colleagues and is the continual butt of jokes and ostracism from residents in all other fields of medicine. This is true, even with the advent of psychopharmacology, because physicians in all other fields simply do not wish to deal with mental disorders. Even within the psychiatric profession itself a sharp dichotomy exists between those psychiatrists who wish to take a primarily psychological approach to mental disorders and those psychiatrists who wish to approach mental disorders within an increasingly biological orientation—the very orientation that Freud warned must be corrected after medical training if one is to become an intensive psychotherapist. This leaves the psychotherapist ostracized by the rest of the medical profession and under continual attack from the members of the psychiatric profession who disagree with his approach; those who are certified psychoanalysts have the security of the psychoanalytic associations to help them with their identity problem, but those who are not are forced to go it alone.

The hard truth must be faced that *a different curriculum* is necessary for those who will work primarily with mental phenomena utilizing the method of introspection and empathy, as I have described it in my book on the training of psychiatrists who wish to be psychotherapists (Chessick 1971). As Freud puts it, "The experience of an analyst lies in another world, with other phenomena and other laws" (p. 247). Thus the great mass of what is taught in medical schools is of no use to the psychotherapist for his purposes and is, according to Freud, the hard way of preparing to be a psychoanalyst.

I think this is not so true for the intensive psychotherapist, especially because of the current advent of psychopharmacology and its common use as an adjunct in psychotherapy. In a substantial number of intensive psychotherapy cases, psychopharmacological agents are employed from time to time; if they are not used in the proper fashion the patients are either deprived of something they ought to have or are endangered needlessly. Those lay therapists I know and admire have familiarized themselves with the indications for these medications and have developed a close working relationship with psychiatrists to help them when such indications arise; but here again we have nothing but the personal integrity of the lay therapist to depend on in his frequent search for psychiatric consultation.

The lay therapist remains in one sense a second-class psychotherapist, because he cannot judge the use of psychopharmocological agents and is not aware of the possible manifestations of neurologic and other organic disorders that may present themselves in the mental sphere. On the other hand, many cases can be adequately treated by the lay psychotherapist, the most obvious of which are cases needing brief therapy or crisis intervention.

Furthermore, there is no reason to believe that a well-trained and properly treated lay therapist could not do long-term intensive psychotherapy, provided he developed the proper consulting relationship with a psychiatrist and providing the cases are properly chosen. The importance of continuing to train psychiatrists who are also experts in long-term intensive psychotherapy should be evident from this discussion, since not only do they have the basic responsibility to treat patients of a most difficult kind, but also they are necessary to guide and supervise well-qualified lay therapists and to participate in their proper training. The attempt of the fanatical fringe of the American Psychiatric Association to remove all cases requiring long-term intensive psychotherapy from the responsibility of the psychiatrist and to dump all psychotherapy into the lap of lay therapists, can only be described as a potential disaster for the patients and an inexcusable flight from responsibility to society. To redefine mental illnes in order to avoid this responsibility is not honest.

Because of the poor training and the even worse personal psychotherapy that goes on in the career of the professional of many disciplines, a problem remains which ought to be resolved with amity instead of quarrels filled with professional jealousy as well as economic competition. The result of this unfortunate current situation is that psychiatrists—especially psychiatrists who are intensive psychotherapists—are not making the contribution to the training and supervision of lay therapists which would be in the best interest of the patients. The disciplines quarrel and compete rather than cooperate, and the patient is the loser.

Although Freud's teaching on this subject is just as pertinent today as it was when he wrote *The Question of Lay Analysis* in 1926, it still remains largely ignored. The psychiatrists, because of their intradisciplinary identity problems, ignore the fact that lay therapists are here to stay and therefore it would obviously be most sensible to cooperate and offer them opportunities for training, as Freud points out. The lay therapists, on the other hand, due to narcissistic problems refuse in any sense to be considered second class and therefore avoid psychiatric supervision and consultation—thus endangering their patients. In this age of psychopharmocology and highly complex medical diagnostic techniques, the lay therapist can no longer justify the practice of intensive psychotherapy without a close relationship to a consulting psychiatrist. The psychiatrists can neither justify nor ignore their obligation to the training and supervision of desperately needed lay therapists. The reader will note, therefore, that I am taking a position akin to that of Jones (1957), which is essentially a middle position with a condemnation of fanatics on both sides: "a plague on both your houses." In no way, however, does this affect my unalterable opposition to *all* forms of so-called "touchy-feely" or "primary process" psychotherapy regardless of by whom it is performed and for what excuses; this was certainly also Freud's point of view!

The last item in the first volume of the *Standard Edition* represents Freud's final and unsuccessful effort to remain in the realm of organic neurology and medicine. He calls it "Psychology for Neurologists" or *Project for a Scientific Psychology* (1950A;1:283ff); it represents a brilliant failure of great historical interest and is coming under considerable scholarly study. He dashed it off in two or three weeks, left it unfinished, and criticized it severely at the time of writing. Even more interesting, later in life he seems to have forgotten it, and when in his old age he was presented with it he did his best to destroy it.

Although the ideas expressed in *Project for a Scientific Psychology* reemerged strongly in many of his later metapsychological theories, what is significant for us here is how these ideas represent his final attempt to maintain psychodynamics (or as he called it, depth-psychology) as a neurological science and his realization that this was impossible. This brings us, as it did Freud, to the painfully hard and frank realization that the practitioner of intensive psychotherapy cannot consider himself as engaged in the practice of general medicine in the commonly used sense of this term. He is not applying the results of basic laboratory research to the amelioration of organic disturbances in the human body, and there is an unbridgeable gap between the work he does and the usual approach in the medical specialties. The basic science of intensive psychotherapy resides in the discoveries from the clinical practice of psychoanalysis (such as that of the phenomena of transference). The application of these discoveries to the treatment of many disorders by intensive psychotherapy is the essence of our task. Therefore, there is no general acceptance of intensive psychotherapy as a specialty of medical practice even among some psychiatrists.

The intensive psychotherapist, like Freud, will have to endure a certain isolation from the mainstream of medical practice no matter how hard he tries to integrate his work with other physicians. This isolation means that nonphysicians will feel justified in engaging in the practice of intensive psychotherapy, and indeed many of them have the potential or the capacity to do excellent work. This leads to blurring the boundaries in the public mind between the "doctor" who is a Ph.D. and the "doctor" who is an M.D. when both are engaged in the practice of psychotherapy.

Since the basic science on which intensive psychotherapy rests does not have the customary firm laboratory foundation that one finds in the sciences behind other specialties in medical practice, it is comparatively easy for emotionally disturbed psychotherapists to rationalize their exploitation of patients and their hostile retaliation and other acting out of every sort of unethical behavior. The only protection we can afford to the patient in this situation is careful training and personal psychotherapy of the psychotherapist as well as the establishment of basic guidelines and principles for the technique and practice of psychotherapy (see Chessick 1969,1971,1974).

The most serious problem in this area occurs for the psychotherapist who is a physician. Even in training he soon comes to learn that specialists in other medical fields do not consider him a legitimate "doctor," and he experiences the derision and isolation this entails. This represents an assault on his identity as well as a chronic wounding on top of the inevitable narcissistic wounding involved in making mistakes as one learns any discipline (Chessick 1971a). The way in which the intensive psychotherapist resolves these problems has a *profound effect* on the kind of psychotherapist and psychiatrist he becomes.

For example, Dr. A was an eminent biological psychiatrist, always at the forefront of the attacks on intensive psychotherapy and psychodynamics. He lectured repeatedly during a long and prominent professional life, urging the formal separation of all intensive psychotherapy from the discipline of psychiatry and the limitation of psychiatric treatment to those disorders which respond in a brief period to pharmacologic and other techniques. Investigation of his past revealed that as a young physician he wished to specialize in psychiatry but because of financial difficulty had to accept a high-paying residency in a large state hospital system. At that time, all residents were poor and were expected to be so, but some large county and state institutions paid a somewhat better stipend. Dr. A explained that soon after he had begun his residency, he received a few lectures on schizophrenia, was given the keys to a ward of seventy-five to one hundred patients, and was then ordered to assume the total responsibility for their care. As the only physician on the ward, in the days before the antipsychotic drugs, he literally was placed in a situation of bedlam, assisted only by a few untrained male attendants recruited from nearby farms.

The anxieties in the situation were overwhelming and Dr. A suffered an emotional breakdown. He went to a nearby city and consulted a poorly trained psychoanalyst who immediately placed him on the couch and advised him to free-associate—I remind you that this was many years ago. Needless to say Dr. A's anxiety worsened and in a few weeks he became transiently psychotic so that his treatment had to stop. He reintegrated spontaneously, left the residency, and resumed the practice of general medicine in a large hospital where he began to treat emotional problems with "medicines." Although he never became board-certified as a psychiatrist, he immersed himself in biological work and remained an undying enemy of psychodynamics and psychoanalysis. The return to general practice brought him considerable support from his medical colleagues in the other specialties and enabled him to form a firm sense of identity which protected him throughout his life.

There is no better description of the anxieties encountered in facing the plethora of dramatic phenomena in mental disorders and attempting to apply the principles of psychodynamics, than in the first volume of the *Standard Edition*. The outcome in Freud's case was very successful, but he was a genius. The outcome in the case of lesser mortals can often be disastrous—personally and for the hostility and destructiveness toward our field that may result. This problem is unfortunately accentuated by the tendency of some psychoanalysts to sequester themselves in "institutes," and it is only recently that the introduction of psychoanalysts as teachers as well as courses in psychoanalysis have become a more common practice in some university programs. It remains to be seen whether it is not already too late.

Medical students must be educated so that *early-level training* produces a greater awareness of the vital importance of psychological factors both in the production and treatment of emotional disorders. The urgency of this matter is not yet sufficiently appreciated; even the American Psychiatric Association is seriously splintered at the present time between those who see a complete return to the practice of general medicine as a solution to the identity crisis in psychiatry and those who have the conviction that intensive psychotherapy is a very important subspecialty in psychiatry.

Kris (1954), in his introduction to the first published edition of Freud's letters to Fliess, explains that "Freud's friendship with Fliess filled the gap left by his estrangement from Breuer and provided a substitute for a friendship and intellectual relationship that had ceased to be viable." Although Fliess was important to Freud in the development of his theories and his self-analysis, the transition from neurologist to psychologist actually occurred somewhat earlier, during what Jones calls the "Breuer period," from 1882 to 1894. Only after his self-analysis had taught him to realize the crucial significance of the past history of the individual, did Freud become aware that Fliess's attempt to explain neurotic conflict by a pseudobiological "periodicity" meant shackling the dynamic thinking of psychoanalysis. These pseudobiological explanations tend to recur over and over again in the recent history of psychiatry.

The final phase of Freud's transition from neurologist to psychologist is marked by his explaining neurotic phenomena on the basis of the individual's past history without reference to neuroanatomy or neurophysiology. The *Project for a Scientific Psychology*, written during his early studies of hysteria, marked Freud's last effort to synthesize psychology and the anatomy of the brain; "Not until after his self-analysis, when he was able completely to fuse the dynamic and genetic points of view, did Freud succeed in establishing the distance between the physiological and psychological approaches" (Kris 1954). It is this distancing upon which our entire conviction about psychodynamic psychiatry and intensive psychotherapy stands or falls.

Every student, especially if he is a physician, must undergo a similar kind of evolution in his training and thinking if he is to become an intensive psychotherapist. The resident faces a crucial triad of difficulties: (a) the development of his identity as a psychotherapist; (b) the anxiety attendant upon the development of psychological mindedness; and (c) the need to develop conviction about the meaningfulness of psychodynamics and long-term psychotherapy. How the resident resolves these difficulties is crucial to his entire professional future. Not only is there a need for the beginning resident to move away from the physiological model but he *must* mourn his systemized and controlling medical styles, painstakingly developed over recent years; he *must* suffer tension and depression; and he *must* struggle to comprehend the unknown inside himself as well as that around him and in his patients.

This identity problem is confounded by many factors. The training environment requires the resident to have capacities for empathic understanding and behavioral observation which he has not developed. Brody (1969) points out that developing the identity of "psychotherapist" threatens loss of the physician's professional mantle of social responsibility and authority. Like Freud, he also mentions the irrelevance for the psychiatrist of so much learned at arduous cost during medical school. Many authors have described the increasing sense of alienation the psychiatric resident feels from his fellow residents in other specialties as their development progresses.

The tremendous anxiety problem of the resident has been mentioned in the literature, but it has not received the attention it deserves. D'Zmura (1964) has discussed the interference with learning that undue levels of anxiety in the student produces. This anxiety is often increased by the usual experience of the resident in the first year where he is assigned the most pathologic and the most difficult patients that psychiatry has to offer. Between the resident's lack of experience and the serious pathology of his case load, not very many of his patients in long-term intensive therapy are going to respond successfully.

Halleck (1962) mentions that it is rare for a resident to have more than one or two patients who have materially improved in long-term intensive treatment. In fact, many residency programs do not even offer the opportunity for long-term treatment in the training program. Semrad (1969), for example, delineates three phases in the psychotherapy of the psychotic person. These are restitution of ego function, resumption of ordinary life, and finally "analysis of the vulnerable ego." It is obvious that the resident rarely has much experience with the third phase, which involves several years of therapeutic work. Therefore, the resident is in the embarrassing position of having to take the conviction of the supervisor on faith—a faith which is threatened by the resident's repeated failures and distresses in his work with severely pathologic or chronic patients, efforts which are rarely buttressed by therapeutic success.

From the training point of view, Gaskill and Norton (1968) present an excellent summary of what is desired. Taking psychoanalytic theory as the basic form of reference, the dyadic therapeutic relationship is conceived of as the primary model of the clinical psychiatrist:

> Fundamental to this is an increasing awareness and understanding of the dynamic unconscious and intrapsychic conflict as it relates to the patient and the therapist. . . . Knowledge of the intricacies and complexities of this relationship with all of its theoretical and therapeutic implications and unknowns is the unique tool of the psychiatrist of both today and the future (p. 9).

It is obvious that the crucial triad of anxiety-producing problems interferes with the attainment of these goals. Semrad (1969) summarizes these areas of interference as (a) personal emotional burdens, (b) ignorance and inexperience, (c) the need for omnipotence and omniscience, (d) distress with instincts, (e) countertransference, and (f) the relative lack of empathy.

If these areas of interference are not attended to with deliberate intent on the part of the training staff, three serious dangers are present. The most obvious of these will be the development of a psychiatrist who is mediocre or worse. A second is that the beginner will constrict himself in a narcissistic, self-limiting fashion. Such an individual tends to go his own way and becomes at that point unteachable. He makes a closure in his points of view too early—a closure based not on training and experience but manifesting instead the rigid characteristics of a flight from anxiety.

Perhaps the most dangerous resolution, because it is so subtle and easy to rationalize, is what Ornstein (1968) described as "uncritical eclecticism." This can take many forms (for example, a premature immersion in community psychiatry, administrative work, or somatic therapies) and results in a psychiatrist who is a jack-of-all-trades, master of none, with a fuzzy identity, and who tends to resemble an "as-if" personality (Deutsch 1965). Everyone who has supervised residents has met these individuals, who represent, as Ornstein points out, a serious pedagogic failure. Thus, the shift toward eclecticism and the disappointment in psychodynamics and psychotherapy are *symptoms that the training program is defective.*

Freud's greatest and most magnificent exposition of psychoanalysis is contained in his *Introductory Lectures on Psychoanalysis* (1916X;15–16). The first two parts of this work remain the best introduction to the concept of psychodynamics and the unconscious mind ever written, but in the Introduction Freud points out that there is only one practical method for learning psychoanalysis: "One learns psychoanalysis on oneself, by studying one's own personality. . . . One advances much further if one is analyzed oneself by a practised analyst and experiences the effect of analysis on one's own self, making use of the opportunity of picking up the subtler technique of the process from one's analyst. This excellent method is, of course, applicable only to a single person and never to a whole lecture-room of students together" (1916X;15:19).

Of the several volumes of Freud's correspondence (Meng and E. Freud 1963; E. Freud 1960; Kris 1954; McGuire 1974), *The Freud-Jung Letters* (McGuire 1974) are the most painful and poignant to read. One is impressed with Freud's repeated efforts to be reasonable and to try to empathize with Jung's position. Jung's deep ambivalence runs throughout the letters, combining a worship of Freud with an intense rivalry and admitted ambition. Freud's dedication to the psychoanalytic movement stands starkly against Jung's wish for public acclaim and money. Freud's towering greatness and determination borders on the neurotic in his demand for rapid responses to his letters and his identification with Moses: "If I am Moses, then you are Joshua and will take possession of the promised land of psychiatry, which I shall only be able to glimpse from afar."

The prescience of Mrs. Jung about the coming break, and Freud's rejection of her warnings on this issue, contrasts with his warmth to her in her personal difficulties. It is interesting to follow the tedious cross-analysis of these pioneers, sitting on a ship headed for the United States, and analyzing each other's dreams and mistakes, and the irritations and narcissistic wounds this must have stored up in them. The Freud–Jung correspondence set a precedence for the current acrimony and *ad hominem* arguments which still plague the whole field of psychiatry.

One cannot evade the issue however; Jung's change in libido theory *had* to be rejected by Freud, because Jung watered down psychoanalysis to abstract meaninglessness and threw out the very essence of Freud's clinical discoveries. Jung still deserves today a psychoanalytically oriented expositor to cull out from his innumerable volumes what is clinically useful and what tends to degenerate into amateur metaphysics and abstract speculations. He really gave Freud no choice. Another issue that lurks in the background is Jung's anti-Semitism and wish for social "respectability"; his cooperation with the Nazis in later years is well known. Freud's determination to hold his beleaguered psychoanalytic movement together against all odds in spite of repeated defections is truly remarkable and a tribute to his energy and strength of character.

Three essays appearing together in volume 14 of the *Standard Edition* deal with the famous issue of Freud's alleged pessimism and are fascinating for the psychotherapist. The first two were written around March and April of 1915, some six months after the outbreak of World War I; the third, "On Transience" (1916A), was written in November of the same year. In the first two, published as "Thoughts for the Times on War and Death" (1915B), Freud outlined the terrible disillusionment of war. This disillusionment is based on the obvious retrogression from the level of ethics and civilization we had hoped to have reached permanently.

Freud philosophically reminds us that such disillusionment is not altogether justified, since we have never risen so high as we believed in the first place. He points out, "If we are to be judged by our unconscious wishful impulses, we ourselves are, like primeval man, a gang of murderers" (p. 297). He concludes rather sadly, in keeping with the times, "If you want to endure life, prepare yourself for death" (p. 300). A few months later after great inner perturbation, Freud shows, in the essay "On Transience," his understanding of the mourning process engendered by the destruction of civilization in the war, and he concludes optimistically, "When once the mourning is over, it will be found that our high opinion of the riches of civilization has lost nothing from our discovery of their fragility. We shall build up again all that war has destroyed, and perhaps on firmer ground and more lastingly than before" (p. 307). The basically optimistic and resilient strength of Freud's personality, a strength to be tested in his long and tortuous bout with cancer, already shows itself in this interesting series of essays. The short essay "On Transience" has an almost lyric beauty, and reminds one of Rachmaninoff's composing of his famous second piano concerto, written on his recovery from melancholia.

One wonders if at the end of his life in *Moses and Monotheism* (1939A; 13:3ff), Freud was talking about himself when he discussed, in section II B (pp. 107–111), how a great man influences his fellow men. He stresses two ways in which this influence takes place: "By his personality and by the idea which he puts forward." He sees the decisiveness of thought, strength of will, and energy of action in a great man as part of the picture of a father. Above all stands the autonomy and the independence of the great man. Thus he is impressed with Pharaoh Akhenaten and reminds us that Breasted calls this Pharaoh "the first individual in human history." In chapter 19 of the present book, "Transcendence," I discuss in more detail Freud's feeling of identification with Moses, especially at the end of his life, as he was about to leave Vienna. This final identification, of course, has more to do with Freud's personal life and background than with any problems involved in the identity of the psychotherapist.

We turn now to a careful examination of Freud's thought, organized on the suggestion by Graves (1971): "an understanding of the way in which a theory was actually conceived and developed is essential for an understanding of its content, rationale, function, and modus operandi, as well as the hopes which its users have of possible future accomplishments" (p. 40). Graves also reminds us "that the truly interesting scientific theories are not those whose principles are fixed, static, and codified, but those which are constantly being modified and added to in an effort to achieve a more perfect correspondence with reality" (p. 35).

3

THE CLINICAL CORNERSTONES OF FREUD'S APPROACH

One is sometimes asked where to begin reading about Freud's theories. As one might expect, the best place to begin reading about Freud's theories is in Freud himself. I suggest the *Five Lectures on Psychoanalysis* (1910A; 11:3ff). These lectures, which were delivered extempore, represent a marvelous preliminary introduction to Freud's approach and also display Freud as a talented teacher and lecturer.

In the third lecture there is no better review of objections to psychoanalysis than that presented on one page by Freud. Psychotherapy must be learned just as the techniques of histology or surgery, writes Freud. Innumerable judgments on the subject are made by people who know nothing about it and do not employ it. We still see again and again today, even in psychiatric meetings, manifestations of what Freud eloquently described:

> Psychoanalysis is seeking to bring to conscious recognition the things in mental life which are repressed; and everyone who forms a judgment on it is himself a human being, who possesses similar repressions and may perhaps be maintaining them with difficulty. They are therefore bound to call up the same resistance in him as in our patients; and that resistance finds it easy to disguise itself as an intellectual rejection and to bring up arguments like those which we ward off in our patients by means of the fundamental rule of psychoanalysis (p. 39).

Conviction about the validity of Freud's basic concepts rests primarily on following the same route that was followed by Freud, beginning with the study of one's own dreams in one's own treatment. The practicing psychotherapist must maintain a continual study of his own dreams for his entire professional lifetime. Freud recommends that the second step is to experience the transference in one's own intensive psychotherapy and then to carry out psychotherapeutic treatment and observe for oneself the workings of the transference in one's patients. Thus only personal experience of these phenomena can establish the deep sense of conviction in the psychoanalytic orientation to psychotherapy.

Another easy or fruitful place to begin the study of Freud is the twelfth chapter of the *Psychopathology of Everyday Life* (1901B;6:239–279). This volume, which contains innumerable clinical examples and repeatedly illustrates Freud's approach, gives a glimpse of his meticulous attention to detail on a day-to-day basis, with the rich reward that such attention brings. It also establishes the scientific and philosophical premises on which Freud's entire system is built.

Recently a patient of mine discovered that her husband had fifteen loaded rifles in a locked cabinet. This discovery occurred when he shot one of their pets because it soiled the carpet while she was away at a friend's house. She was under considerable pressure from me to deal with this problem and try to get these guns removed from the premises. She appeared at one of her regular sessions five minutes late and casually mentioned that she had misjudged the time because she was chatting with the babysitter before coming to her session. The patient, who had been in therapy for some time, anticipated the next question—as to whether she could think of any association to her coming late—by mentioning that she felt the pressure from me to deal with this extremely unpleasant situation with her husband. After a long pause her next thought was, "I wonder what will be the next problem or pressure I will have to deal with." She then noted that she tended to be late to her Thursday sessions, which occurred in the office at my home, but was rarely late in her Saturday session at my office in the professional building. After a long pause I asked her to associate to her last sentence about my home. The association was that I live here. This finally led to a considerable discussion of her hidden wish to live here and her wish to be married to me instead of the husband with whom she is having so much trouble. In this absolutely typical clinical vignette one can see the rich reward of investigating the psychopathology of everyday life, especially if it can be done in noncondemnatory fashion with the patient.

The most common beginner's error is to confront and demand from the patient an explanation or series of associations for innumerable minute errors, an encounter experienced by the patient as an assault. It is the properly timed and tactful, continuing investigation of parapraxes and dreams that constitutes part of the day-to-day practice of intensive psychotherapy, and that repeatedly opens new vistas of investigation—often just at times when it seems that the current material of the patient's reality has become exhausted.

In 1901 Freud at the age of forty-five had reached maturity and had embarked upon an almost unbelievable flurry of intellectual productivity. In terms of publication, *The Interpretation of Dreams* marks the beginning of this period; but *The Psychopathology of Everyday Life*, *Jokes and their Relation to the Unconscious*, and *Three Essays on the Theory of Sexuality*, were all written earlier, between 1897 and 1900. Furthermore, they seem to have been written more or less simultaneously. Freud kept the manuscripts of the book on jokes and the three essays side by side on separate tables and went from table to table while he worked on them.

In *The Psychopathology of Everyday Life*, the little daily failings, the inoffensive aberrations of the normal person, are carefully described and studied in a detailed manner so as to create a link between the psychology of the normal man and the so-called neurotic, revealing common roots and uncertain boundaries. The purpose is clearly stated by Freud himself in a footnote added in 1924 (1901B;6:272): "This book is of an entirely popular character; it merely aims, by an accumulation of examples, at paving the way for the necessary assumption of *unconscious yet operative* mental processes, and it avoids all theoretical considerations on the nature of this unconscious." It is Freud's thesis that in all instances known as parapraxes, including the forgetting of names, words and intentions, slips of the tongue, slips of the pen, misreadings, bungles, and what are called "symptomatic" actions—where chance or accident or inattention are thought to reign—there is actually an unconscious operative impulse or intention. He writes (1901B;6:239), "*Certainly seemingly unintentional performances prove, if psycho-analytic methods of investigation are applied to them, to have valid motives and to be determined by motives unknown to consciousness.*"

In order to be included in the class of phenomena called parapraxes, certain conditions must be fulfilled: the phenomenon must not exceed certain dimensions which are judged to be in the limit of the normal; it must be in the nature of momentary and temporary disturbance, and we are tempted to explain it by chance or inattentiveness if we perceive it at all; we must not be aware in ourselves of any motive for it.

The unconscious or hidden motives that produce the parapraxes need not express a person's repressed and most secret wishes, although they may. These intentions may have expressed themselves to the person just before their expression in a parapraxis; they may be known to the person by a knowledge of which he has had no recent awareness; or they may be not known to the person and vigorously denied. The common factor is the intention having been to some degree forced back so that the parapraxes are explained as the outcome of a *compromise* between a conscious intention and an unconscious contrary intention. The significance of the parapraxis lies with the disturbing intention and, as this disturbing intention draws closer to the truly repressed, we get a distinction between the manifest and the latent disturbing intention, as illustrated in the clinical vignette at the beginning of this chapter. In our clinical work we must be careful not to be satisfied with an easily recovered manifest disturbing intention, but if possible to try to pursue the material to find a link to a more significant and secret latent disturbing intention in important parapraxes.

It is necessary to point out that the study of parapraxes in clinical work can be badly abused. Freud remarks that a slip of the tougue "has a cheering effect" during the clinical work when it serves as a means of providing the therapist with a confirmation that may be very welcome to him "if he is engaged in a dispute with the patient." There are two constructive situations in which this observation is correct. The most ideal is when an interpretation is made and in the process of rejecting it the patient makes a slip of the tongue which the patient himself notices and interprets as a confirmation of the interpretation, often with a chuckle that indicates a high level of observing ego function and a sense of humor. Second best, as Freud points out, is when the therapist calls the attention of the patient to the slip and this leads, without much dispute, to understanding and acceptance of interpretation by the patient.

The destructive situation is in the development of a dispute where the therapist attempts to use slips and errors as evidence in a debate to *force* a patient to accept an interpretation. I believe that Freud in the earlier days of his clinical work actually did this; he was not at all reluctant to demand and insist in a forceful and authoritative way that the patient accept his interpretation as correct. Kohut (1977) points out that Freud's early "cures" were largely a function of his narcissistic investment in the correctness of his theories, and that his earliest descriptions of therapy often point more to the problems in the practice of psychotherapy than to formal psychoanalysis.

I believe it is unwise to try to "ram home" interpretations to patients or to debate with patients over the meaning of parapraxes, and I agree with Menninger (1958) that this is an invariable mark of countertransference. It is perhaps useless to discuss Freud's countertransference problems, but this is certainly a countertransference problem in the ordinary psychotherapist. Minor slips and errors may be interpreted during psychotherapy—but if the interpretations are rejected a mental note should be made of this and it is best to move on to other material. The kind of parapraxes most useful for interpretation in psychotherapy are repeated ones, such as always coming two minutes late, and so on, where it is impossible for the patient to insist that there is no meaning involved since the parapraxis occurs with such a consistent pattern. Although parapraxes may provide a source of humor in the therapy, another danger signal of countertransference occurs if the therapist feels victorious or jubilant when a patient has finally admitted to the validity of an interpretation on the basis of a parapraxis or anything else; this may be a clue to unresolved narcissistic problems in the therapist.

Freud's theory of parapraxes is really remarkable in many ways. For example, he even held that in cases of fatigue or sickness or alcoholic states there is still some psychologic meaning to be found in the particular mistakes that are made—he presents a completely thoroughgoing postulate of psychic determinism. Even though a circulatory disorder in the brain might distort a person's speech and actions, the nature of the distortion still reflects some unconscious motivation. Mistakes can be interpreted just like dreams, and the same processes of repression, inhibition, displacement, condensation, and concealment can be expected to be at work beneath the mistake, just as they are in the dreams. Even the "arbitrary" selection of a number is explained in this fashion.

In solving the meaning of parapraxes and symptomatic acts Freud advises us that "It often happens that a dream which proves refractory during an attempt to solve it the next day will allow its secret to be wrested from it a week or a month later, after a real change has come about in the meantime and has reduced contending psychical values. The same applies to the solving of parapraxes and symptomatic acts." More ominously, Freud suggests that the readiness to believe in a different explanation of parapraxes "is obviously a manifestation of the same mental forces which produced the secret and which therefore also devote themselves to preserving it and resist its elucidation" (1901B;6:269–70).

This opinion leads to the dangerous possibility that Freud's system is circular, for anyone who disagrees with his interpretation of a phenomenon can be accused of suffering from resistance. As a sample of the danger of this, one can take his discussion of *déjà vu* and *déjà raconté* in the same reference cited. Freud believes these phenomena to be similar, but this is quite debatable, for *déjà vu* phenomena can be elicited by stimulating specific areas of the cerebral cortex. We are led into a thorny mind–brain problem if we try somehow to interpret the meaning of such phenomena in purely psychological terms. *Déjà raconté*, as it occurs in psychotherapy, is very much pertinent to our work. This refers to the illusion of having already reported something of special interest when that something comes up, and the patient maintains that he has already recounted certain material to the therapist. How do we deal with this? Freud (1900B;6:268) states, "The physician is however sure of the contrary and is as a rule able to convince the patient of his error. The explanation of this interesting parapraxis is probably that the patient has felt an urge to communicate this information and intended to do so, but has failed to carry it into effect, and that he now takes the memory of the former as a substitute for the latter, the carrying out of his intention."

Other explanations of this parapraxis are possible without one's being accused of manifesting resistance. Freud's explanation is important and sometimes it is correct; equally possible is that the therapist *forgot* the material—again an indication of countertransference. A dispute then may ensue in which the patient backs down and accepts the therapist's interpretation. This event can have an ominous effect on the therapeutic alliance, and can also be an acting-out in the transference where the patient has to accept passively any aggression from the authoritative parent. In situations where the patient insists that he has mentioned something to the therapist and the therapist is equally certain that no such material has been brought up before, the best approach in psychotherapy is to declare to the patient that an honest difference of opinion exists in the situation. The patient is urged to discuss the material and an effort is made to see if such material could have been defended against by the *déjà raconté* phenomenon As before, if this happens many times, it will soon become clear in the psychotherapy who is doing the forgetting, and why.

The clinical cornerstone of Freud's approach lies in the postulate that in dreams, parapraxes, chance actions, and neurotic symptoms, "the phenomena can trace back to incompletely suppressed psychical material, which, although pushed away by consciousness, has nevertheless not been robbed of all capacity for expressing itself" (p. 279). All these phenomena share common features—the repression of impulses, substitute formations, compromises, and the dividing of the conscious and unconscious into various psychical systems—leading to the implication that psychoanalysis provides a science of the mind equally indispensable for understanding normal as well as abnormal people, both as individuals and in groups. The philosophical premise at the basis of this approach is the insistence on the extent of determinism in mental life—an emphasis on the degree to which the principle of determinism operates in every psychic phenomenon. This premise can safely by called the most relentless and deep-seated philosophical conviction of Sigmund Freud.

This conviction led Freud to immersion in some murky problems in the age-old philosophic dispute .between free will and determinism.* For instance, as Freud points out, many people contest the assumption of complete psychical determinism by appealing to a special feeling of conviction that there is a free will. His answer is that such a feeling manifests itself not in the great and important decisions of the individual—"On these occasions the feeling that we have is rather one of psychical compulsion, and we are glad to invoke it in our behalf"—and on these major decisions he quotes Martin Luther's famous declaration "Here I stand: I can do no other." It is only with regard to the unimportant and indifferent decisions that we claim we could just as well have acted otherwise, and that we have acted of our free will. Freud dodges the problem by claiming it is not necessary to

*See Basch (1978) for a recent attempt to resolve this problem in Freud's thought by the use of "semantics, cybernetics, and general systems theory."

dispute the right to the feeling of conviction or having a free will. Having our minor decisions made for us from the unconscious is still consistent with such a feeling.

It is a curious fact that Freud held two related beliefs with apparently equal enthusiasm. On the one hand, he believed that every psychic phenomenon was strictly and rigidly determined—in fact overdetermined—by unconscious motive forces. On the other hand, he believed completely in external chance, and that when apparently accidental events occurred in reality—anything from an earthquake to a minor chance happening—no divine plan or divine force motivated these events. Indeed, he regarded such a belief as superstition based on an outward projection of the feeling which belongs within, in the philosophical tradition of Feuerbach. Even as early as 1901, in *The Psychopathology of Everyday Life*, Freud maintains that the religious view of the world is "nothing but psychology projected into the external world." As I will elaborate in later chapters, his method was to explain all religion as myths which should be transformed from metaphysics into metapsychology [the first published appearance of the word metapsychology, not used again for fourteen years until the essay "The Unconscious" (1915E;14:181fn.)]. We can see from this how Freud's conviction of psychic determinism led to the cornerstone of his entire approach, and how his equally fervid conviction in chance external reality led to his relentless denial of all kinds of religion and theology. To avoid a common error, the student should keep in mind that Freud clearly distinguished between a determined causality stemming from the past, and a fatalism—in which he did not believe—which pre-established the future (Slochowor 1975).

In *The Psychopathology of Everyday Life* an important contribution is made to the understanding of paranoia. The paranoid patient holds the opposite from the normal viewpoint about parapraxes and so-called accidental behavior, in that he insists that everything he observes in other people is of vital significance and can be interpreted. In that sense he recognizes something that escapes the normal person, and Freud realized even this early that there is a core of truth in paranoid delusions. Unfortunately, because of his psychopathology, the paranoid patient selectively perceives these truths and weaves them into an interpretative pattern that presents a projection to meet his own psychic needs; for this reason the superior perception of the paranoid patient is rendered useless.*

Jokes and Their Relation to the Unconscious (Freud 1905C;8:3ff) not

* Freud's first major statement on paranoia occurred in "Further Remarks on the Neuro-psychoses of Defense" (1896B;3:174) in which the concept of projection is presented for the first time. This reference, and the comments in *The Psychopathology of Everyday Life*, are the first of a series of Freud's writings on paranoia. A complete list may be easily found in the subject index at the back of the abstracts of the *Standard Edition* (Rothgeb 1973).

only constitutes Freud's major contribution to the subject of aesthetics—a contribution which is peripheral for our purposes—but also extends his application of his theories to the phenomena of everyday life. This is probably the least read of Freud's works. One reason for this is the confusing mixture of theory and clinical examples—a mixture which makes for difficult reading; in addition, the writing is closely reasoned and needs considerable concentration to appreciate. The book on jokes could be considered a transitional work because Freud moves away from the relatively mechanical model of the mind which he has been using and into more highly theoretical discussions; at times here he still treats concepts like psychic energy and the release of psychic energy as though they were descriptions of observable phenomena.

For a variety of reasons, however, the subject of jokes is worth our clinical attention. Freud notes that the characteristics and the effects of jokes are linked with certain forms of expression involving condensation, displacement, and indirect representation—processes similar to the dream work. Thus in his theory there is a relationship of the formation of jokes to the formation of dreams, and the unconscious is involved in both. Jokes are formed as a preconscious thought is given over for a moment to unconscious revision, and the outcome of this is at once grasped by conscious perception. According to Freud, dreams serve predominantly for the avoidance of unpleasure and jokes for the attainment of pleasure—and all our mental activities converge in these two aims.

Especially important for psychotherapists is the fact, as Freud recognized, that jokes are social process. For example, the motive force for the production of innocent jokes may be an ambitious urge to show one's cleverness or to display one's self. This is very important, and the division of jokes into innocent jokes representing the need to show one's cleverness and what Freud calls tendentious jokes that have primarily a hostile or aggressive purpose is extremely important in the everyday practice of psychotherapy. Freud further divides tendentious jokes into the hostile joke (serving the purpose of aggressiveness, satire, or defense) or the obscene joke (serving the purpose of exposure)—but the basic motivation in both cases is aggressive.

Thus in psychotherapy we are likely to be confronted with three kinds of jokes; those which are motivated to display the cleverness of the joker; the obscene joke; and the directly hostile joke—with both of the latter based on aggressive motives. In each case the patient's joke may be accompanied by more or less of a demand that the therapist laugh along with the patient, and with the rationalization that the joke is being presented as a gift to the therapist to offer a little pleasure to break up the tedious work of intensive psychotherapy.

In my experience the most common presentation of a joke in psychotherapy occurs when patients have been reading the *New Yorker* or other cartoon or joke-carrying magazines in my waiting room; as I open the door to the waiting room to begin the session they show me this or that cartoon with a chuckle. Although it is perfectly reasonable to respond with the expected polite chuckle, the therapist should treat the matter as the initial communication of the hour, often signaling the red thread behind the material of the hour, as described by Saul (1958). During the presidential campaign of 1976, for example, several patients began the session by showing me with a chuckle a *New Yorker* cartoon in which a family is engaged in a bitter fist fight in their living room. A political discussion had apparently degenerated into such a battle. The aggressive ramifications of displaying such a joke at the beginning of the session were obvious, often to the point of being interpreted by the patients a moment or two after they began their session.

A common side-motivation to the telling of jokes is the wish to be liked by the therapist through a process of providing him with pleasure. Such a wish, which may be conscious, often hides a variety of feelings of hostility and insecurity. Equally common is the wish for a mirroring appreciation from the therapist of the patient's exhibit of cleverness and entertaining performance.

The subject of jokes also tells us a great deal about the psychotherapist. For example, the therapist who responds to a pleasant joke with stony-faced silence is giving one kind of message about himself to a patient; the therapist who responds with obvious laughter and pleasure at a joke which involves degradation of ethnic groups or pornographic exposure of women, as Freud describes it, is giving another kind of message about himself. Thus, just as the therapist learns about the patient through jokes which appear in the psychotherapy, the patient learns a great deal about the therapist. The best approach to a patient's jokes is a natural one—chuckling at those which seem funny and not chuckling at those that do not or at those which seem offensive. The joke material should be treated like any other material in the session; if the patient protests that the joke has no meaning it is not necessary to enter a dispute with the patient since further material will invariably be on the same theme as the joke, if the therapist is patient and does not contaminate the material by narcissistic efforts to prove something to the patient.

Perhaps most important clinically is the issue of therapists who need to tell jokes to their patients, or who need to make puns or be sarcastic. A similar division of motivations can be made in understanding the countertransference of psychotherapists who tell jokes to their patients. The so-called innocent jokes represent a need on the part of the therapist to appear clever and to exhibit himself. Hostile or pornographic jokes, or engaging in sarcasm toward the patient, clearly represent a very aggressive countertransference reaction to the patient.

In my clinical experience the most common cause of the tendency to become sarcastic with a patient is as a reaction to the patient's narcissism. Narcissistic patients treat the therapist as a selfobject who has no independent existence of his own (Kohut 1971). The two typical reactions to being used as a selfobject in this fashion are boredom and retaliatory sarcasm. It is thus diagnostically useful for the therapist—if he finds himself becoming bored or sleepy by the material or if he notices sarcasm in his comments to the patient or in his thoughts about his patient—to conclude that he is probably dealing with an intensely narcissistic relationship in which the patient is perceiving him only as an extension of the patient's self. Needless to say, sarcastic retaliation for such a relationship is never therapeutic since the patient is in his own way communicating to the therapist the very difficulty for which he hopes to be helped, and retaliation easily destroys the psychotherapy.

A second common situation, in which the therapist tells jokes to the patient, occurs when there is insufficient gratification in the therapist's personal life and the patient is exploited either as a friend with whom to share pleasure or as a punching bag to discharge the therapist's private aggressions.

It does not follow from this that the therapist should never tell the patient a joke or engage in a humorous interchange. This would be a stiffly wooden and unnatural relationship in a situation where two human beings are together for a long period of time. Sometimes, telling a joke or an anecdote illuminates an interpretation in a way that the patient can understand; and the art of therapy, just as the art of any effective communication, is in knowing how to present material that can be grasped clearly by the other person. However, I cannot imagine any situation in which tendentious jokes are necessary to effective psychotherapeutic work; thus, the therapist who finds himself sarcastic to a patient or sharing hostile or degrading jokes should carefully analyze his countertransference to find the motivations.

In *The Psychopathology of Everyday Life* (1901B;6:43–52) Freud returns to the subject of childhood memories and screen memories. He points out that in the so-called earliest childhood memories, we possess not the genuine memory but a later revision of it. This revision is subjected to influences of a variety of later psychic forces, and thus memories presented by patients as early childhood memories acquire the same significance as screen memories. This explains why a person's earliest childhood memories frequently seem to have preserved what is indifferent and unimportant, and why some seem even odd and unintelligible. The usual processes of condensation and displacement with respect to both time and place are at work here just as in the formation of dreams. Freud explains, "The indifferent memories of childhood owe their existence to a process of displacement: they are substitutes, in (mnemic) reproduction, for other impressions which are really significant" (p. 43).

The indifferent memories reported owe their preservation to an associative relation between their content and another memory which is repressed—in this sense they are screen memories. Similarly, mistakes in recollection cannot be attributed to simply a treacherous memory, for motives are present which make the distortion and the displacement of the experience necessary: "Strong forces from later life have been at work on the capacity of childhood experiences for being remembered—probably the same forces which are responsible for our having become so far removed in general from understanding our years of childhood" (p. 47).

Even in the early paper "Screen Memories" (1899A;3:301ff) Freud distinguished between the simpler type of screen memory in which the preserved memory is but a part of a more significant whole which has been repressed, and a more complex type in which the memory is a construction in which a certain event of early childhood has been combined with a repressed event of adolescence. The earlier memory is not necessarily untrue but is a harmless substitute for the later, unacceptable memory.

Ellenberger (1970) summarizes the basic working model that Freud used in his explanation of dreams, screen memories, parapraxes, jokes, and neurotic symptoms. Both a simple and a more complex model is employed, and it is necessary for the clinician to keep these models in mind as a guide to his day-to-day work. In the simple model an unconscious, unacceptable tendency receives its expression, in the conscious mind or in conscious behavior, through a process of compromise formation; through this compromise formation it escapes the process of repression. The weaker the repression, the more directly the unacceptable tendency expresses itself in conscious thought or behavior, and the less deciphering is necessary.

In the more complex model, there are, so to speak, two floors in the unconscious mind. The lower floor constitutes the basic childhood infantile sexual wishes and memories. Unconscious tendencies of all sorts that express themselves in dreams, parapraxes, symptoms, jokes, and screen memories are connected by association to such childhood and infantile wishes and memories. Therefore, the process of analyzing conscious material and behavior leads first to the understanding of unconscious interfering tendencies and thence to the deeply buried associated infantile sexual wishes and childhood memories.

One of the most crucial questions that arises from Freud's attempt to extend his investigations to the psychopathology of everyday life and thus to provide an investigation of normal human phenomena, is whether or not

Freud has overrated the notion of an unconscious mind. The whole premise of so-called third-force psychology (Goble 1970) stands on this issue. For example, Goldstein (1971) insists that overrating the unconscious mind was Freud's fundamental error. In Goldstein's view, and in the view of third-force psychologists, the jump from the mentally disturbed to the relatively normal individual is a qualitative and not simply a quantitative jump. In the mentally disturbed, conflicting forces arising out of the unconscious send the patient on a detour in life which can only be understood by an investigation of the unconscious. On the other hand, in the normal individual it is important to take into account the whole drive toward actualization of the organism, a drive in which conscious phenomena and goals must be more accepted as fundamental motivating forces.

The obvious danger of this view lies in its attractiveness as a way of avoiding facing the power of the unconscious in everybody, sick or well. Furthermore, such a view involves one in serious terminological and conceptual confusion, and is far more complex than it appears on the surface. The reader must decide whether or not the third-force psychology represents a step forward or an escape from facing the truth about man; the decision will profoundly affect one's therapeutic practices.

4

BREUER AND FREUD STUDY HYSTERIA

From December 1880 to June 1882, Dr. Josef Breuer (1842–1925), a well-known and highly reputed physician in Vienna, treated Fraulein "Anna O." for what was generally accepted as a classical case of hysteria. The patient was an intelligent girl of twenty-one who had developed a large variety of symptoms in connection with her father's fatal illness, including paralysis of the limbs, disturbances of sight and speech, inability to eat, a distressing nervous cough, and the presence of two distinct states of consciousness—one rather normal and the other "naughty" and troublesome. To Breuer's great astonishment, on one occasion when she related the details of the first appearance of one of her innumerable symptoms, this resulted in its complete disappearance. The patient realized the value of her discovery and continued with the same procedure of relating the details of the first appearance of a symptom, calling this procedure "the talking cure" or "chimney sweeping." For more than a year, Breuer devoted hours every day to this patient, supplementing the chimney sweeping by artificial hypnosis; the chimney sweeping took place in the evening, and artificial hypnosis took place in the morning, a process Breuer named catharsis.

Breuer developed a strong countertransference to this patient and became so engrossed that his wife became jealous, unhappy, and morose. Breuer felt guilty and decided to bring the treatment to an end. He announced this to Anna O., by this time much better, and that same evening he was fetched back to find her in a terrible state, apparently as ill as ever. In addition, the patient, who according to him had appeared to be asexual and never made any allusions to such a forbidden topic throughout the treatment, was now in the throes of an hysterical childbirth, the logical termination of an imagined pregnancy that had been invisibly developing in response to Breuer's treatment. Breuer calmed her by hypnosis and in a state of shock fled the house. He left for Venice the next day with his wife, to spend a second honeymoon, which resulted in the conception of a daughter (who sixty years later committed suicide in New York). The forty-year-old Breuer wanted no more of the chimney sweeping treatment and left the field to Freud.

Jones (1953) relates that Anna O. later became institutionalized and inflamed the heart of the psychiatrist in charge of the institution. She was then taken to live with her mother and later became the first social worker in Germany, founding a periodical as well as institutes for training students. She never married, remained very religious, and gave her life to women's causes and work for children. One must keep this in mind in assessing the depth of the psychopathology of Anna O., who has sometimes been labeled schizophrenic.

On November 18, 1882, Breuer told Freud about the case; it made a deep impression on him. He discussed it with Charcot but failed to arouse his interest. Anna O. and Freud's experiences with Charcot demonstrated that "whatever the unknown neurological basis of hysteria might be, the symptoms themselves could be both treated and abolished by ideas alone. They had a psychogenic origin. This opened the door to a medical motive for investigating the psychology of patients, with all the ramifying results that the past half century has shown. It put psychology itself on a totally different footing from its previous academic one" (Jones 1953, p. 227).

In *Studies on Hysteria*, one observes the gradual evolution of the method of free association from Breuer's original hypnotic and cathartic procedures. The development of this method was essentially an effort to free the therapist from the need to hypnotize patients, which was often extremely difficult. A crucial demonstration of the difference between Freud and Breuer occurred during this period when a patient suddenly flung her arms around Freud's neck—"an unexpected *contretemps* fortunately remedied by the entrance of a servant" (p. 242). Rather than retreating, Freud regarded this problem of the erotic transference as one of scientific interest and recognized its great importance in the psychotherapy of hysteria.

We now appreciate situations in which the erotic transference arises unrelated to hysteria and that an erotic transference is not necessarily even undesirable. For example, the oldest patient I have ever treated, a seventy-eight-year-old lady with a depression, unexpectedly and suddenly threw her arms around me at the end of the therapy and told me lovingly how, although she understood very little of the "nonsense" I was saying, my presence made her feel better because I reminded her of her deceased son. This surprising event, coming at the end of the patient's treatment for depression (which had been entirely successful and was carried out over fifteen years ago without the benefit of drugs) was a startling experience for a young psychotherapist. Due to the patient's age there was no countertransference difficulty; but the event was a striking demonstration of the power of a personal relationship between the patient and the physician to influence therapeutic improvement. My experience has been that often the true intensity of the erotic transference does not appear, as in Breuer's case, until the termination of the psychotherapy.

Freud's efforts to proceed with cases such as Fraulein Elisabeth von R. were encouraged, even though she could not be hypnotized, by the French neurologist Bernheim's remark that things experienced in hypnosis were only *apparently* forgotten afterwards and that they could at any time be brought into recollection if only the physician insisted forcibly enough that the patient knew them. Freud's genius made the extrapolation that this should be equally true for the forgotten memories in hysteria. Fraulein Elisabeth von R. was the first patient treated by his "concentration technique," which later became the method of psychoanalysis. At this point it consisted of much urging, forehead-pressing, and questioning. On one historic occasion, the patient reproved Freud for interrupting her flow of thought by his questions. Again Freud's genius showed itself; by being willing to *listen to the patient* and follow the lead given by her, he made another step toward free association.

It is hard to comprehend today the difficulties involved for this turn-of-the-century Viennese physician, who occupied a totally respected and authoritative position, in allowing himself to be led toward his discoveries by his neurotic patients. *It was the beginning recognition of the requirement for patience and meticulous attention to detail needed for the successful practice of psychotherapy, as well as a demonstration of the importance of being able to refrain from an authoritative medical stance with one's patients, when the therapy requires such restraint.*

In the summer of 1894, Freud's cooperation with Breuer came to an end, for personal reasons and over Breuer's disagreement with Freud as to whether sexual disturbances in childhood were essential factors in the etiology of neuroses. Although Freud's first book, *On Aphasia*, was dedicated to Breuer, the relationship cooled until there was nothing left of twenty years of cooperation, friendship, and mutual interest (Balogh 1971). As the relationship with Breuer disintegrated, the relationship with Fliess gained a corresponding intensity.

When Breuer, who was fourteen years older than Freud, died in 1925, Freud wrote a warm obituary acknowledging him as "a man of rich and universal gifts" even though, according to Roazen (1975), the friendship in later years had developed, at least on Freud's part, into an intense loathing. It is difficult to evaluate the validity of this report. Part of Freud's problem with Breuer was due to Freud's personality, for Freud often felt that those who were not wholly with him in his theories were against him, and he did not hide his feelings.

This attitude gains significance for the psychotherapist as we gradually realize that Freud's basic orientation as a psychotherapist was that of a passionate investigator and teacher. Roazen (1975) puts it very strongly:

> To Freud, patients were "students" for whom the analyst was a 'guide.' The analytic process was itself an educative activity; psychoanalysis sought to educate the ego. . . . Freud thought that in all analyses points would arise at which the analyst had to act as a model for his patients and sometimes directly as a teacher. But he cautioned against indiscriminate instruction: 'The patient should be educated to liberate and fulfill his own nature, not to resemble ourselves' (p. 18).

Freud's strength as a writer and a psychologist rested on his ability to appeal to the hearts of all men. Examine yourself, said Freud; look within your own depths, and see whether what is true for me is true for you too. This kind of challenge tends to make strong allies but many outspoken enemies.

Studies on Hysteria (Freud 1895D;2:21ff) is a neglected gold mine for the psychotherapist. I cannot imagine a more appropriate starting point for those who wish to learn about psychotherapy or to deepen their historical and technical understanding of the process of psychotherapy. This book should be mandatory reading for all students of intensive psychotherapy. It literally enables us to observe Freud developing his techniques and is loaded with clinical insights of current value. It contains some model case histories, is easy to read, and is beautifully written. In addition, this work is usually regarded as the historical starting point of psychoanalysis. The term "psychoanalysis" was first used by Freud in a paper published in French, in March 1896.

Breuer's patient Anna O. demonstrated and overcame the first obstacle to the scientific examination of the human mind. This obstacle, the amnesia characteristic of the hysterical patient, led Breuer and Freud to the realization that an unconscious series of mental processes lay behind the conscious mind and that, clearly, some special instrument would have to be developed to get at such processes. Freud himself explains the inadequacy of hypnotic suggestion as such an instrument—with many patients of little use at all. He describes how he gradually developed the system of free association, at first with the occasional use of pressure on the forehead. The attempt to get the patient to free-associate raised the next obstacle—the patient's resistance to the treatment. Freud's decision not to shout down or force away this resistance but rather to investigate it like other mental phenomena led him directly to the whole field of psychoanalysis.

It is of interest that the central theoretical assumption in *Studies on Hysteria* is expressed in the principle of constancy: that the human mind tries to keep the quantity of excitation constant. This principle accounts for the clinical necessity for abreacting affect and the pathogenic results of affect.

The idea of "cathexis" (which first appears in this work), that the whole or part of the mental apparatus carries charges of energy, is presupposed by the principle of constancy. The concept of psychic energy, which is still controversial today (Peterfreund 1971), represents the beginning of metapsychology. I hasten to add that by 1905 Freud finally and explicitly repudiated all intention of using the term "cathexis" in any but a psychological sense, and abandoned all attempts at equating neuronal tracts or special neurons with paths of mental associations.

Gedo et al. (1976) did a careful study of the differing methodologies of Breuer and Freud in *Studies on Hysteria* and reached the conclusion that the book has been neglected because of "the difficulty of culling the scientific logic from this monumental volume supersaturated with new concepts." Gedo et al. "reduced" the book to a series of statements classified according to a schema borrowed from Waelder (Gedo et al. 1976, p. 172) and paraphrased as follows:

1. *The data of observation.* Facts of conscious life, derivatives from the unconscious, and their configurations
2. *Clinical interpretations.* Interconnections among the data of observation and their relationships with other behavior
3. *Clinical generalizations.* Statements about a particular type of category such as sex, an age group, a symptom, a disease, etc.
4. *Clinical theory.* Concepts implicit in clinical interpretations or logically derived from them such as repression, defense, etc.
5. *Metapsychology.* More abstract concepts, such as cathexis, psychic energy, etc.
6. *The author's philosophy or Weltanschaung.* For example, scientific humanism

This classification is an excellent starting point for the evaluation of any of Freud's writing or, indeed, any writing on psychotherapy, and I urge the reader to keep it in mind. Note especially that, "The data of observation we call 'lower-level' statements; clinical interpretations and generalizations we place at the middle level of abstractions, while clinical theories and metapsychological propositions are at the highest levels" (p. 172).

Gedo et al. (1976) conclude that no statements of the authors' philosophy appear in *Studies on Hysteria* and that the entire book contains only three metapsychological propositions: (1) the brain works with a varying but limited amount of energy: (2) there is tendency to keep intracerebral excitation constant; and (3) psychic forces operate in dynamic interrelationships.

What emerges with the most compelling clarity from the Gedo et al. study is the difference in methods used by Freud and Breuer. Thus Breuer displayed considerable talent and creative ability in building hypotheses based on deductive reasoning, but the kind of hypotheses developed did not lend themselves to furthur clinical testing and remained a kind of speculative superstructure. "Freud, on the other hand, clearly subjected his inspirational hunches to thorough inductive revision in the light of the clinical evidence available to him. In other words, the internally consistent evolution of psychoanalysis was a process which took place exclusively within Freud's mind" (p. 168). These authors, although they give much credit to Breuer, were impressed by "the tightness of Freud's inductive thinking and his restraint in refusing to outdistance his evidence, as Breuer consistently did" (p. 183).

Of course, the essential difference was that Freud was able to persist in the face of internal conflicts stirred up by his discoveries, while Breuer withdrew. As we shall see in the next chapters, "Freud's great and extraordinary achievement was his capacity to extend the range of psychological observation to include not only his patients but also himself" (p. 204).

Turning directly to an examination of *Studies on Hysteria* (Freud 1895D; 2:21ff), the basic clinical discovery of Breuer, and Freud was that each individual hysterical symptom "immediately and permanently disappeared when we had succeeded in bringing clearly to light the memory of the event by which it was provoked and in arousing its accompanying affect, and when the patient had described that event in the greatest possible detail and had put the affect into words" (p. 6).

The first important clinical fact in the book is "Recollection without affect almost invariably produces no result" (p. 6). So much for the argument that psychotherapy is merely an intellectual process. Reading these marvelous case histories quickly reveals the emotion-laden interactions between the patient and the physician. For example, notice Breuer's remark that Anna O. would never begin to talk "until she had satisfied herself of my identity by carefully feeling my hands" (p. 30). Breuer mentions later that the talking cure could not be carried out by anyone but him.

Considerable argument (Reichard 1956) exists as to whether some of the cases in this book are really hysterics, schizophrenics, or borderline patients —an argument that I regard as rather unfruitful because it seems to rest mainly on semantic debate about patients we cannot examine personally at this time. At any rate it is clear that these patients are all substantially emotionally disturbed; they are not bored ladies who have nothing better to do than to pass away the time in psychoanalysis. The procedure was designed and developed to help seriously emotionally disturbed individuals, and the importance of touching, feeling, and being held appears almost at once. Hollender (1969, 1970, 1970*a*) has discussed at length the need of such patients to be held and I have reviewed the subject in my book, *Intensive Psychotherapy of the Borderline Patient* (1977). The kinds of difficulty the psychotherapist can get into when he gives in to this need of patients to be held—even holding hands—is nowhere better illustrated than in what happened between Breuer and Fraulein Anna O.

Reichard (1956) divides the cases in *Studies on Hysteria* into two schizophrenic patients and three hysterical patients. She claims that Anna O. and Emmy von N. were schizophrenic because they had fixed, bizarre, and horrifying hallucinations with a pan-neurosis, a family riddled with pathology, conflicts which were mainly pregenital in origin, various psychotic symptoms, and were hospitalized at times. The other three cases have less severe family pathology, fewer symptoms, and more lasting cures.

Reichard's definition of hysterical neurosis is:

> Hysteria is a neurosis showing a minimal degree of ego defect and is characterized by conversion symptoms, which are limited to changes in physical functions that represent solutions of unconscious sexual conflicts derived from the phallic or genital levels of psychosexual development and expressive of unresolved oedipal incestuous wishes (p. 160).

By this definition Lucy R., Katharina, and Elisabeth von R. seem to be classical cases of hysteria, whereas Anna O. and Emmy von N. are not, although all five patients suffered from conversions which were the original basis of the diagnosis of hysteria. Whether Anna O. and Emmy von N. were schizophrenics suffering from a psychosis at the time of treatment (Reichard 1956) or borderline patients (Chessick 1977) is highly debatable. One must keep in mind that flamboyant hysterical symptomatology is much less common today, and patients manifesting such symptoms tend to be diagnosed as schizophrenics with hysterical features.

Also revealing is the remark by Breuer about just how ill-tempered and malicious Anna O. could become, especially when he was away from her. The rage, hatred, and need for revenge in the hysteric and especially in the borderline patient has also been discussed at length. Here is a clinical example:

> Mrs. B. was an attractive young woman in her twenties whose chief complaint was frigidity. This frigidity consisted of the absolute inability to become aroused or to experience orgasm under any circumstances with her husband or her previous boyfriends. She was an attractive modern young woman who was apparently genuinely concerned that she was missing something important in life. She went first to a

psychoanalyst who recommended a formal psychoanalysis and began with her on the couch four times a week. This lasted two weeks, for by the time the second week had passed the patient was in a total rage at the psychoanalyst because she "could not bear" not being allowed to see him, and at the "difference in power" as she perceived it in the psychoanalytic situation; the idea that he could see her while she could not see him, and the idea that she had to say everything that came to her mind while he said very little were absolutely intolerable to her. She terminated the treatment.

Since she was clearly unsuitable for formal psychoanalysis he referred her to me. The patient then engaged in a sitting-up psychotherapy twice weekly which lasted for seven years and ended successfully in her achievement of satisfactory orgasms with her husband. The essence of the treatment consisted of seven years of the patient raging at me in the transference. This began in the most intense manner, accompanied by diarrhea before and after the sessions, and a general temper tantrum and raging of every possible kind and description at the slightest indication that I had any kind of control or power over her. For example, the end of each session was often characterized by her leaving the treatment a minute or two early and slamming the door, because she could not tolerate the fact that she had to leave at the time appointed by me when the session was due to conclude.

The patient exhibited a clear-cut example of an extreme narcissistic rage, and over the years this rage was abreacted and gradually abated itself until the patient began to have orgasms in intercourse. Actually there was little direct discussion of sexuality in the treatment; the discussions focused on her rage and need to control, her fear of vulnerability, and above all, her fear of losing control—especially to a man.

The patient was raised by a cold, unfeeling mother and a father who encouraged her to climb on his lap and reach out for affectionate caresses; when she did he would scratch her with his whiskers, tease her, poke, and pinch her. He often woke the patient in the morning by pulling off her bedclothes and pinching her bare buttocks. The father used many other forms of teasing cruelty to ward off his own sexual and sadistic desires toward his daughters. A profound diasppointment in both parents produced the patient's chronic narcissistic rage. The gradual working-through of her narcissistic problems and

> catharsis of rage, in a situation which at least she could barely tolerate, enabled the normal developmental forces to take over once more.

In Breuer's situation, as he points out, he was faced at times by a malicious hysteric, "refractory, lazy, disagreeable, and ill-natured." He explains how her "true character," the opposite of all these, reappeared after the various abreaction sessions. There is no question that profound narcissistic rage is an important, if not the most important, element in borderline cases and severe hysterias.

This extremely difficult nosological problem—What do we mean by severe hysterias?—still rages today. We are reminded by Lazare (1971) that Freud's early cases dealt with symptoms—blindness, convulsions, contractures, and disturbances in sensation. "Character traits often associated with hysteria, such as increased excitability, instability of mood, and suggestibility, were mentioned only in passing." Hysteria is here used as a diagnostic term for these various symptoms of psychological—not neurological—origin, believed related to disturbed sexuality.

Returning to *Studies on Hysteria*, Freud's case of Emmy von N. introduces us to the method of free association; one might say that again the patient led the way: "It is as though she had adopted my procedure and was making use of our conversation, apparently unconstrained and guided by chance, as a supplement to her hypnosis (p. 56). Patients often guide us when we have gone in the wrong direction, if we are willing and able to listen to them.

The term "conversion" is used in this case history (although it was first introduced elsewhere). The meaning of the term—by which Freud signified "the transformation of psychical excitation into chronic somatic symptoms, which is so characteristic of hysteria"—still remains mysterious, and indeed many authors still speak of the "mysterious leap from the mind to the body." Furthermore, the question of whether conversion is to be restricted more or less to cases of hysteria, or exists throughout the realm of psychopathology, remains a matter of debate (Rangell 1959). Certainly the ubiquitous presence and the unpredictable shifts of conversion symptoms form one of the most dramatic manifestations in the realm of psychopathology, and the removal of conversion symptoms by the use of hypnosis or barbiturates is often convincing demonstration to beginners of the influence of mental processes on body phenomena.

Today, florid conversion symptoms are rarely found away from rural communities. The disappearance of dramatic classical conversion symptoms seems to be related to the growing sophistication about sexuality in our society and to the acceptance of the sexual needs of women. Perhaps the preponderance of florid conversion symptoms among nineteenth-century women can partly be blamed for Freud's chauvinistic comment about "the moral seriousness with which she viewed her duties, her intelligence and energy, which were no less than a man's." This unfortunate disparagement of women, as we shall see in later chapters, occurs from time to time throughout Freud's work and is due partly to his Victorian mentality and partly to the then-prevailing theory that hysteria involved some kind of degeneracy or inferiority in the nervous system, a theory which Freud gradually abandoned. In spite of this bias, it does not logically follow that all Freud's views or discoveries are to be rejected; his material must be judged on the basis of clinical experience and logical consistency.

The third case, Lucy R., was treated entirely without the use of hypnotism and represents the application of the forehead-pressuring technique. The case illustrates the notion that an idea is "intentionally repressed" from consciousness, forcing an accumulation of excitation which, being cut off from psychical association, "finds its way all the more easily along the wrong path to a somatic innervation." The basis for the repression is the feeling of unpleasure, "the incompatibility between the single idea that is to be repressed and the dominant mass of ideas constituting the ego. The repressed idea takes its revenge, however, by becoming pathogenic" *(Studies on Hysteria*, p. 116). This is the basis of the whole notion of psychodynamics. (Notice the metaphorical and poetic language; in the fourth case, of Katharina, Freud's literary genius soars into an almost pure poetic short-story.)

It follows from the premise quoted above that the therapeutic goal is to compel the split-off ideas to unite once more with the conscious stream of thought, and Freud remarks that "strangely enough" success does not run *pari passu* with the amount of work done—only when the last piece of work was completed did recovery suddenly take place. This phenomenon introduces another important clinical problem in that it is not possible to predict by an algebraic formula the relationship of the rate of recovery and the bringing of unconscious ideation to the conscious mind. Very often patients appear to improve in quantum jumps after long, tedious plateaus of work.

The final case in the book (Elisabeth von R.) deals above all with the problem of psychogenic pain and the clinical distinction between the patient's description of psychogenic pain and other forms of pain. The hysteric shows the well-known facial indifference and cheerfulness while giving an indefinite description of the severe pain. These descriptions are all the more surprising in their indefiniteness because the patient is often intelligent. In contrast, a patient suffering from organically based pains usually describes them definitely and calmly. "He will say, for instance, that they are shooting pains, that they occur at certain intervals, that they extend from this place to that and that they seem to him to be brought on by one thing or another" (p. 136). Hypochondriacal pain, which is more characteristic of the narcissistic neuroses, as described by a patient gives the impression of his

> being engaged on a difficult task to which his strength is quite unequal. His features are strained and distorted as though under the influence of a distressing affect. His voice grows more shrill and he struggles to find a means of expression. He rejects any description of his pains proposed by the physician, even though it may turn out afterwards to have been unquestionably apt. He is clearly of the opinion that language is too poor to find words for his sensations and that those sensations are something unique and previously unknown, of which it would be quite impossible to give an exhaustive description. For this reason he never tires of constantly adding fresh details, and when he is obliged to break off he is sure to be left with the conviction that he has not succeeded in making himself understood by the physician (p. 136).

No better description can be found of pain in the narcissistic neuroses as a symptom of the impending fragmentation of the sense of self (Kohut 1971).

The procedure of clearing away pathogenic psychical material layer-by-layer is compared to the technique of excavating a buried city. At the same time that this archeologic work was going on, however, Freud contributed a considerable amount of encouragement, persuasion, and authoritative instruction. He took it for granted, at this point, that such behavior on the part of the physician is *essential* to the treatment. "For instance, I sent her to visit her sister's grave, and I encouraged her to go to a party at which she might once more come across the friend of her youth" (p. 149).

Freud also did a considerable amount of consoling and soothing. In his efforts to develop a scientific theory of psychotherapy he tends to de-emphasize this sort of empathetic, intuitive material. Perhaps he simply and modestly assumed that the physicianly vocation (Stone 1961) of the therapist would always be present in any doctor–patient relationship. For example, when it occurred to Elisabeth that her sister's husband would be free if her sister died and she could then marry him, the period that followed "was a hard one for the physician." Freud deals with the shattering effect on the patient of the recovery of this unacceptable and therefore repressed idea by "two pieces" of consolation in the best tradition of pastoral counselling: "that we are not responsible for our feelings, and that her behavior, the fact that she had fallen ill in these circumstances, was sufficient evidence of her moral character" (p. 157). There is an interesting contrast between Freud's consciously "dry" presentation of interpretations, and his shift to soothing, physicianly behavior when the patient is upset.

The cases presented convinced Freud that in hysteria two separate psychic groups are formed; one is intolerable to the adult conscious; the other is repressed by the ego to preserve harmony; the mechanism of conversion, which Freud confesses he cannot explain, is used to spare psychic pain by substituting physical pain. The resistance to the treatment springs from and is proportional to the repressing force that holds the unacceptable ideas in the unconscious mind. Again the tendency to keep excitation constant, the principle of constancy, is assumed behind this explanation.

Freud could be very authoritative; for example, he insists, because he is convinced of the trustworthiness of his technique, that *something* must occur to the patient when she is asked to say what comes to her mind. We still use this technique today. The section of *Studies on Hysteria* entitled "The Psychotherapy of Hysteria" depicts psychotherapy as a laborious and a time-consuming procedure for the physician and presupposes both his "great interest in psychological happenings" and "personal concern for the patients as well."

The clinical problems of defense and resistance are again taken up. For example, regarding situations where an idea is brought to the conscious and the patient tries to disown it even after its return: "Something has occurred to me now, but you obviously put it into my head," or "I know what you expect me to answer. Of course you believe I've thought this or that." Freud answers, "In all such cases, I remain unshakably firm. I avoid entering into any of these distinctions but explain to the patient that they are only forms of his resistance and pretexts raised by it against reproducing this particular memory, which we must recognize in spite of all this" (p. 280). Thus *the most important clinical problem* in intensive psychotherapy is to overcome the continual resistance.

Freud asks, in a magnificent passage, about the techniques we have at our disposal for overcoming this continual resistance. His answer, which deserves careful study, is that the available techniques are few "but they include almost all those by which one man can ordinarily exert a psychical influence on another."

Freud first counsels patience, since resistance can only be resolved "slowly and by degrees." Then he advises explanation and informing the patient about the "marvelous world of psychical processes" to make the patient into a collaborator and to "induce him to regard himself with the objective interest of an investigator." The strongest method, however, is persuasion by various means, in which one does one's best "as an elucidator, as a teacher, as the representative of a freer or superior view of the world, as a father-confessor who gives absolution, as it were, by a continuance of his sympathy and respect after the confession has been made." Here is where it becomes impossible to state psychotherapeutic process in formulae since one is limited by the "capacity of one's own personality and by the amount of sympathy that one can feel for the particular case" (pp. 282–3). In addition Freud emphasizes directly

> the personal influence of the physician, which we can seldom do without, and in a number of cases the latter alone is in a position to remove the resistance. The situation here is no different than what it is elsewhere in medicine and there is no therapeutic procedure of which one may say that it can do entirely without the co-operation of this personal factor (p. 283).

The essence of the treatment in intensive, psychoanalytically informed psychotherapy is to cause the resistance to melt. We begin, as he explains, at the periphery of the psychical structure and we work gradually, through the procedure of getting the patient to talk down to a deeper and deeper understanding of what has happened. Of trying to penetrate directly to the nucleus of the pathogenic organization, even if we ourselves could guess it, "the patient would not know what to do with the explanation offered to him and would not be psychologically changed by it."

In his attempt to describe the process of psychotherapy, Freud uses a number of similes which he recognizes as having only a limited resemblance to his subject and which moreover "are incompatible with one another." Although this method throws light "from different directions on a highly complicated topic which has never yet been represented," an unfortunate side effect is that these similes have from time to time been taken too seriously and concretely by later authors. This has produced confusion and contradiction in post-Freudian writing. In later chapters we will see the appearance of these similes and literary allusions throughout our examination of Freud's work.

There comes a moment "when the treatment takes hold of the patient; it grips his interest, and thenceforward his general condition becomes more and more dependent on the state of the work" (p. 298). The abundant causal connections and the multiple determination of symptoms are described by Freud, and the procedure works in such a way that if mistakes are made in interpretations, the context will later on tell us to reject them because the material will have become inconsistent.

The subject of the failure of the psychotherapeutic technique is first raised in this work. Freud approaches the topic in the same manner he approaches everything else—to study objectively what has happened. He concentrates on disturbances of the patient's relation to the physician—"the worst obstacle that we can come across." There may be a personal estrangement if, for example, the patient feels neglected or too little appreciated or insulted, or if she has heard unfavorable comments on the physician or the method of treatment. The patient may be seized by a dread of becoming too dependent on the physician; and, most important, the patient may become frightened by finding she is transferring onto the figure of the physician the distressing ideas which arise from the content of the analysis.

Freud here raises for the first time the issue of *transference* as a false connection in which the unacceptable wish first appears linked to the person of the physician. The result of this is a mésalliance or "false connection." It is part of the greatness of Freud to have been able whenever he had been "similarly involved personally, to presume that a transference and a false connection have once more taken place," rather than to have been fooled into believing that the patient had "really" developed personal feelings for him because he was "really" so wonderful or handsome or marvelous. Freud adds, "Strangely enough, the patient is deceived afresh every time this is repeated" (p. 303).

Freud's humility as a scientific investigator is nowhere better illustrated than in this brief discussion of transference. His humility is evident when he answers the patient's objection that since he cannot alter the circumstances and events of the patient's life, what kind of help does he have to offer? Freud (p. 305) replies that "much will be gained if we succeed in transforming your hysterical misery into common unhappiness. With a mental life that has been restored to health you will be better armed against that unhappiness"—and this is all that Freud can promise.

Freud compares the technique of "cathartic psychotherapy" with surgical intervention, not so much for the purpose of the removal of what is pathological as for "the establishment of conditions that are more likely to lead the course of the process in the direction of recovery." This is most important to understanding Freud's basic orientation, which is essentially quite a modest one and which differentiates his approach from the various other authoritative, directive, and organic approaches to the neuroses. Essentially in cathartic psychotherapy the conditions are established by the psychotherapist, through the arrangements of the treatment and the removal of the resistances, for the patient to take part in the healing process and gradually take it over, going forward to ever-increasing levels of complexity and maturity (Chessick 1974).

5

EARLY PSYCHOANALYTIC HYPOTHESES

An examination of Freud's early psychoanalytic publications from 1893 to 1899 is of interest in the understanding of hypothesis formation and hypothesis change in the field of intensive psychotherapy. In Freud's early theories, the notion of a traumatic event in the Charcot–Breuer tradition as the precipitating cause of the psychoneurosis is retained, and discussion of the predisposition to neurosis is somewhat vague. The importance of sexuality is a basic revolutionary contribution.

In 1895 Freud made an attempt to distinguish the "actual neuroses," which are thought of as resulting from current factors causing "damming up" of libido due to blocked or inadequate forms of sexual discharge, from the "transference neuroses" which, like hysteria, are based on unacceptable sexual thoughts and memories from the past; thus the famous quotation "hysterics suffer mainly from reminiscences." More specifically (Freud 1896C;3:189ff), no hysteria arises from a single experience but is a matter of a series of experiences and so is "overdetermined"; these experiences take place in early childhood and are sexual in nature; an incredibly complicated chain of associations leads to the memories of these significant experiences. Ideas associated with these unacceptable reminiscences call forth a "defense" on the part of the ego, writes Freud in this early work, and he continues by borrowing the philosopher–psychologist Herbart's notion of the "thrusting" of an idea outside of the conscious.

Wollheim (1971) points out that Freud attended the seminars of the famous philosopher–psychologist Franz Brentano, probably most well known for his influence on Husserl. Brentano contended that every mental state or condition can be analyzed into two components: (a) an idea, which gives the mental state its object or what it is directed upon; and (b) its charge of affect, which gives its measure of strength or efficacy. Thus ideas with high charges of affect, which are unacceptable to the conscious mind, produce a defensive reaction in which idea and affect are separated and expressed in disguised manners. In hysteria the vital factor is "conversion" (Freud 1894A;3:49), defined as the transformation of affect or excitation into some bodily manifestation, while in the obsessional neuroses both idea and affect are expressed but are totally separated from each other and pursue divergent paths. For example, the affect attaches itself to another idea while the original idea remains weak and unnoticed in the consciousness. These basic principles are elaborated in various ways in the early publications.

In the early hypotheses Freud firmly insisted that a traumatic sexual experience in childhood was at the basis of all the defense psychoneuroses; this is the so-called "seduction theory" of the psychoneuroses. The shift from the seduction hypothesis to an understanding of the importance of infantile fantasies and how they attain a psychic reality of their own was the great turning point in the development of a viable scientific theory of psychotherapy, and was contingent upon Freud's self-analysis. This shift is dramatically described in Freud's (1950A;1:175ff) letters to Fliess.

The realization that his seduction theory was leading him into an absurd and improbable explanation led Freud to a bewilderment and depression that was only resolved by his self-analysis. Here again Freud's courage and willingness to persevere in his exploration are remarkable. In the summer and fall of 1897, his self-analysis revealed the essential features of the Oedipus complex; by 1898 he was at work on the first draft of *The Interpretation of Dreams*, written in final form in 1899, the year in which, according to Kris (1954), he discovered that dreams were the royal road to the unconscious mind and in which he united the study of dreams with the clinical questions of the neuroses.

As Jones (1953) explains, "It was the awful truth that most—not all—of the seductions in childhood which his patients had revealed, and about which he had built his whole theory of hysteria, had never occurred. It was a turning point in his scientific career, and it tested his integrity, courage, and psychological insight to the full. Now he had to prove whether his psychological method on which he had founded everything was trustworthy or not. It was at this moment that Freud rose to his full stature" (p. 265). Jones sees 1897 as the acme of Freud's life, in which the first understanding of infantile sexual fantasies and the importance and explanation of dreams were achieved.

Sadow et al. (1968) convincingly contend that the seduction hypothesis was formulated on the basis of a defensive projection of blame for infantile sexuality onto parental figures. When Freud succeeded in becoming aware of his own sexual wishes by means of his self-analysis, he was able to correct his error and arrive at a universal hypothesis of the role of the Oedipus complex. This emphasizes in a spectacular way the most important feature of the honest and dedicated day-to-day practice of intensive psychotherapy. As the psychotherapist, on the basis of his own prior and thorough psychotherapeutic treatment, continues with his own perpetual analysis of his countertransference reactions, he gains further understanding of his patients and is able continually to revise his hypotheses about the meaning of patient material. Thus even Freud, according to Jones (1953) "never ceased to analyse himself, devoting the last half hour of his day to that purpose."

A properly conducted intensive psychotherapy is marked by a continuing revision of our hypothesis about our patients, on the basis of patient material and our self-analysis of the countertransference that such material produces. When properly conducted it is a meticulous scientific process very much in the spirit of scientific investigation as described by Popper (1965), as I have discussed it in detail in *Great Ideas in Psychotherapy* (Chessick 1977*a*):

In his autobiography Popper (Schilpp 1974) writes:

> But it seems to me that what is essential to "creative" or "inventive" thinking is a combination of intense interest in some problem (and thus a readiness to try and try again) with highly critical thinking; with a readiness to attack even those presuppositions which for less critical thought determine the limits of the range from which trials (conjectures) are selected; with an imaginative freedom that allows us to see so far unsuspected sources of error: possible prejudices in need of critical examination (vol. 1, p. 37).

What a fine characterization of the attitude in the psychotherapist that generates successful interpretations!

The correct application of Popper's methods to the use of interpretations in psychotherapy, and the notion of the psychotherapist in intensive uncovering psychotherapy as primarily a *puzzle solver*—in the sense of functioning as an accessory ego to the patient's observing ego—is central to the crucial conception of the analytically oriented psychotherapist, even as delineated by Freud himself. The differences with Popper come primarily at what he calls—correctly—a metascientific level, in which he attempts to apply his theories in a rather dogmatic fashion to the accumulation of *all* knowledge; for the purposes of the practicing psychotherapist this is an issue of secondary relevance.

The point is that Popper's basic schemata are uniquely applicable to the understanding of the progress of knowledge in the individual psychotherapy of the patient. In this process the creative intuition of the therapist, based on empathic perception, produces hypotheses about psychodynamic explanations, which are then subjected to testing by presenting them to the patient and observing the patient's reaction, which either corroborates or tends to refute or falsify the hypotheses. The process leads to an elimination of error and the formulation of new hypotheses which, although they may incorporate some aspects of the early hypotheses, are closer to the truth and a deeper level of understanding.

Thus the new and correct interpretations permit us to move deeper into an approximation of the basic truths about the patient; even a failure of an earlier hypothesis or interpretation teaches us something new about where the difficulties lie, and helps us to formulate a more active and deeper interpretation of hypothesis.

It is not even necessary to review the well-known patient's responses which serve the practicing psychotherapist as either corroborations or refutations of his interpretations (or conjectures)—that is, the error elimination process—since these responses are presented in any standard textbook such as that by Langs (1974, vol. 2). The experienced psychotherapist who has a thorough knowledge of his countertransference usually has little difficulty in deciding whether a given interpretation has correctly made its mark, or for some reason is incorrect and is being rejected by the patient. Only the most inexperienced neophyte attempts to hammer an interpretation down a patient's throat without accepting the possibility that the interpretation may simply be wrong. This is a matter for the personal treatment and training of the therapist, but again need not concern us here since we are talking about psychotherapy as practiced by the experienced therapist.

It is this approximation process, when clearly understood, that forms the basis of understanding a patient and works consistently with Freud's notion of therapy as peeling off the layers of an onion. Popper's basic schemata give us a chance to formulate this notion in a specific and exact terminology.

On the other hand, such formulations run us into the difficulty that is presented by Bohr's principle of *complementarity*, in which this neat procedure breaks down at a certain level because of the multiple possible ways of interpreting the same data. Thus some data may be lost through the approach the therapist takes. To minimize loss of data the therapist has to be prepared to take at least two approaches—that of scientific understanding and that of humanistic imagination. In this way Popper's delineation of scientific procedure can be fit optimally into an understanding of the therapy process; however, his basic philosophical preconceptions about science and non-science confuse this orientation, and have given rise to great debate among various philosophers as to what science is and what science does—a question essentially unanswered in any satisfactory manner as of the present date.

Let us turn directly now to certain of the papers that are still relevant in volume 3 of the *Standard Edition*. The first major paper in the volume, a lecture "On the Psychical Mechanism of Hysterical Phenomena" (Freud 1893H;3:26ff), reviews some of the early psychoanalytic hypotheses. The traumatic event and its resistance to recall necessitate hypnosis; the connection between the event and the hysterical phenomena may be simple or have a symbolic relation, as seen in dreams. There may be several "partial traumas," that is, any experience which calls up distressing affect, with the symptoms disappearing on being "talked out." This is known as abreaction, *in which language is experienced as a substitute for action.*

The term "repression" is first used here but as meaning a deliberate act of exclusion from conscious thoughts. Freud postulates the existence of ideas marked by great intensity of feeling but cut off from the rest of consciousness. The essence of the therapy is to get rid of the idea's affect which "was, so to say, 'strangulated'," a principle which remains one of the pillars of psychotherapeutic effect to the present day. Even in the case of Emmy von N. in *Studies on Hysteria*, Freud already recognized that suggestion and abreaction are not enough, and he already demonstrated the need to analyze down to causes in a deterministic way—only then, he felt can one use the abreaction technique successfully.

As already mentioned in the previous chapter, the undoing of repression or the removal of resistance was, from the beginning, considered the central task of psychoanalytic psychotherapy. This requirement has a particularly eloquent expression in the *Minutes of the Vienna Psychoanalytic Society* (Nunberg and Federn 1962, vol. 1, pp. 100–102), where Freud is noted by Rank as adding, "There is only one power which can remove the resistances, the transference. The patient is compelled to give up his resistances to *please us.* Our cures are cures of love. . . . The vicissitudes of the transference decide the success of the treatment." Freud regarded transference as affording a chance to produce a permanent change in the patient, whereas he calls hypnosis "nothing but a clever trick." Freud regarded the notions of resistance and transference as the conceptual hallmarks of psychoanalysis.

We come next to two papers in which Freud first gave public expression to many of his major hypotheses: "The Neuro-psychoses of Defense" (1894A;3:43ff) and "Further Remarks on the Neuro-psychoses of Defense" (1896B;3:159ff). The former paper is more famous, for Freud's originality of thought. He makes a major therapeutic point in his metapsychologically unsatisfactory explanation (at this point in his development) that in any repression the *affect* is repressed, not so much the idea. Thus in a sense, the purpose of repression is to make a "weak idea" out of a strong one, based on the key point that the "sum of excitation" present in the psychic functions can be increased, decreased, displaced, or discharged. These processes form the nucleus of the psychic mechanism of the neuroses, which at that time Freud thought had to do with repressing memories of highly affectually charged childhood traumata.

In the second paper, an analysis of a case of chronic paranoia is presented, and the term "projection" is first used and illustrated as a defense.

The notion of symptoms as representing compromise formations is presented; the symptom in a neurosis is explained as a partial discharge in a way acceptable to the conscious mind. I would especially recommend the paper on "The Neuro-psychoses of Defense" and part III of "Further Remarks on the Neuro-psychoses of Defense" for discussion in a basic seminar on psychopathology. They remain pertinent examples of clinical case-presentation and attempts at understanding, based on the theory of repression or defense that Freud called "the cornerstone on which the whole structure of psychoanalysis rests." They also outline the more controversial metapsychological concept of *the quota of affect*, a manifestation of the "sum of excitation," as well as the notion of cathexis, which will be discussed later and which forms an important concept in Freud's effort to keep psychoanalysis parallel to "scientific" Newtonian physics.

To aid the reader in studying the early psychoanalytic hypotheses it is useful to outline Freud's concept of the factors which cause neuroses, and Freud's nosological system (1898) based on the "conversion theory" of anxiety. According to Freud, a neurosis has multiple causation which involves:

(a) hereditary disposition;

(b) specific cause—factors without which the neurosis cannot occur: these are sexual and the classification depends on them as will be explained in the nosology;

(c) contributory or ancillary causes—any other factors which may or may not be present and contribute toward overloading the nervous system;

(d) an exciting or releasing cause: the traumatic events immediately followed by the appearance of the neurosis.

This formulation represents Freud in transition from a neurological to a purely psychological understanding of the neuroses. The specific cause determines more than anything the type of neurosis; whether a neurotic illness occurs at all depends on the total load on the nervous system in relation to its capacity to carry this load.

The classification based on this formulation is:

(a) ACTUAL NEUROSES (due to organic causes)
   1. Neurasthenia proper—due to inadequate "abnormal" discharge of sexual excitation, e.g. masturbation.
   2. Anxiety neurosis—due to blockage of sexual discharge and deflection into morbid anxiety, e.g., abstinence or coitus interruptus.

(b) TRANSFERENCE NEUROSES ("psychoneuroses")
   1. Hysteria—due to childhood sexual traumata of a passive nature, imposed on the child quite early.

2. Obsessive–compulsive neuroses (including phobias)—due to the above plus later a superimposed, more pleasant aggressive sexual activity in childhood.

(c) NARCISSISTIC NEUROSES
1. Depression
2. Paraphrenia (a term Freud preferred, loosely representing schizophrenia—see pp. 103–104 below)

Section I of the paper "On the Grounds for Detaching a Particular Syndrome from Neurasthenia Under the Description 'Anxiety Neurosis'"(Freud 1895B;3:91-99) contains an outstanding clinical description of the anxiety neurosis as it is retained in present day nosology! The curious concept of neurasthenia was given prominence by the American neurologist G. M. Beard (1839–1883); it disappeared from the first edition (DSM–I) of the Diagnostic and Statistical Manual of Mental Disorders, issued by the American Psychiatric Association, and then reappeared in the second edition of this manual. In DSM–II neurasthenic neurosis is differentiated from anxiety neurosis. It is characterized by "complaints of chronic weakness, easy fatigability, and sometimes exhaustion." Beard's description of the typical symptoms of neurasthenia included "spinal irritation" and dyspepsia with flatulence and constipation. Freud clearly differentiates the anxiety neuroses, and when DSM–II separates out the psychophysiological disorders and depressive neuroses, it is unclear what is left for neurasthenic neurosis! DSM–III deliberately moves entirely away from all this.

Although most of the papers in volume 3 of the *Standard Edition* are based on the generally discarded conversion theory of anxiety, in which Freud believed that libido, here defined as sexual excitement, was converted directly into anxiety if the normal discharge was blocked—one major clinical paper in this volume is still relevant and mandatory reading for anyone engaged in the practice of intensive psychotherapy. This is the paper "Screen Memories" (1899A;3:301ff). A screen memory is a recollection whose value lies in the fact that it represents, in the reported memory of impressions and thoughts of a later date, events—which are associated either by symbolic or other links—from an earlier date in the person's life. (This subject has already been discussed in the latter part of chapter 3.) Curiously, the autobiographical screen memory described by Freud in this paper works in an opposite direction—one in which an early memory is used as a screen for later events; this kind of screen memory has not often been mentioned in the psychiatric literature.

Freud's screen-memory paper implies the importance of asking patients for their earliest memories, the content of which is usually referred back to the period between the ages of two and four. The most frequent content of the earliest memories is some occasions of fear, shame, physical pain, and important events such as illnesses, deaths, fires, the births of brothers or sisters, and so on. Such memories must be regarded as disguised representations of more fundamental psychological interactions with significant people in the past, or even better, as representations of the atmosphere of early childhood. As such they are important clues to what will be forthcoming in the transference and in the uncovering of significant childhood interactions and events.

Freud points out that we are so accustomed to not remembering the impressions of childhood that we are inclined to explain this hiatus as a self-evident consequence of the rudimentary character of the mental activities of children. He continues, "Actually, however, a normally developed child of three or four already exhibits an enormous amount of highly organized mental functioning in the comparisons and inferences which he makes and in the expression of his feelings; and there is no obvious reason why amnesia should overtake these psychical acts, which carry no less weight than those of a later age" (p. 304). The notion of displaced affect is used to explain the fact that many people produce earliest recollections of childhood that are apparently concerned with everyday and indifferent "events" which could not produce any emotional affect even in children. In fact, some of these so-called childhood memories may be of "events" that never happened at all!

Thus Freud at the age of forty-three gives us a hint of what is now to follow in 1900—his major work, *The Interpretation of Dreams*, based primarily on his own self-analysis. A screen memory holds its value as a memory not due to its own content but to the relation of its existence between that content and some other content that has been repressed. A hint that we are dealing with a screen memory occurs whenever in a memory the subject himself appears in this way as an object among other objects, since "this contrast between the acting and the recollecting ego may be taken as evidence that the original impression has been worked over." It may even be questioned whether we have any memories at all *from* our childhood; memories *relating to* our childhood may be all that we possess. Thus the so-called childhood memories were actually formed later, and a number of motives, having no concern with historical accuracy, had a part in forming them, as well as in the selection of memories themselves, explains Freud.

It is a working rule of thumb among experienced clinicians that the earliest memories, along with the first dreams related in psychotherapy, contain the nucleus of the psychodynamic conflict that has generated the emotional disorder. Of course it may take years of intensive psychotherapy to perceive correctly and interpret the hidden content and nuclear conflicts in this material. It is, however, wise to make notes of the earliest memories and first dreams as they are reported, and to refer back repeatedly to them during the course of the treatment as an overall guide while one is immersed in the specific material at any given period of the treatment.

Two early papers in volume 7 of the *Standard Edition* still represent an excellent starting point in the seemingly endless debate on the legitimacy of the art and craft of psychotherapy. They should be assigned as part of any first-year residency reading list. The paper "Psychical Treatment" (1950B;7:282ff) should be read first. Freud presents a cogent argument for the legitimacy of mental treatment by the use of words as important media—in fact the most important media—by which one man seeks to bring his influence to bear on another. The historical background of mental treatment and the legitimacy of including treatment of the so-called functional disorders and hypochondriases in the practice of medicine are presented. This debate continues today, even in the American Psychiatric Association, I am sorry to report.

At the same time, Freud admits that all the mental influences which have proved effective in curing illnesses "have something incalculable about them." Freud recognizes that the problem of the regularity of therapeutic results achieved by psychical treatment is a function of the individual nature of the personalities of the subjects, with their variety of mental differences. Even at this early date he stresses the importance of the patient finding a doctor who is suitable for his disorder. He explains that if the right of a patient to make a free choice of his doctor were suspended, "an important precondition for influencing him mentally would be abolished." He also recognizes the limitations of personal involvement placed upon the physician who attempts to treat mental disorders. These limitations have not been properly observed in the current practices of some schools of psychotherapy; Freud gives a timely warning of the effect of transgressing these obvious limitations, on the life of the patient as well as the personal life of the physician.

In the paper "On Psychotherapy" (1905A;7:256ff) Freud points out that all physicians are continually practicing psychotherapy whether they want to or not, and clearly it is a disadvantage not to keep a check on it, administer it in doses, and intensify it as needed. He asks: "Is it not then a justifiable endeavour on the part of a physician to seek to obtain command of this factor, to use it with a purpose, and to direct and strengthen it? This and nothing else is what scientific psychotherapy proposes" (p. 259). He reminds us of the famous dictum that certain diseases are not cured by the drug but by the physician; that is to say, by the personality of the physician inasmuch as through this personality he exerts a mental influence. He warns us that scientific psychotherapy, which involves searching for the origins of a mental illness and removing its manifestations, is not an easy task which can be practiced offhand, and indeed it makes great demands "upon the patient as well as upon the physician. From the patient it requires perfect sincerity—a sacrifice in itself; it absorbs time and is therefore also costly; for the physician it is no less time-absorbing, and the technique that he must study and practice is fairly laborious" (p. 261).

The most important point in these early papers is that severe emotional disorders cause no less serious suffering than any of the dreaded major organic diseases. Therefore, psychoanalytically informed psychotherapy "was created through and for the treatment of patients permanently unfit for existence, and its triumph has been that it has made a satisfactorily large number of these permanently *fit* for existence" (p. 263).

It is indeed difficult to understand the objections of many physicians even today, as it was in 1905, to the inclusion of intensive psychotherapy among legitimate medical procedures. It is true that, because of the varying personalities of physicians and patients and the variety of disorders that patients develop, it is hard to establish good results with statistical regularity; yet there is no question that for many patients suffering from chronic characterological and emotional disorders, intensive psychotherapy is the best treatment available and they will seek it out. If psychiatrists do not provide this form of treatment while observing the ethical limitations on the medical principles of protecting the patient and attempting to help the patient as scientifically as possible, charlatans of every possible description will move into the breach, as is already happening, and exploit patients without mercy.

Freud's wrath at physicians who attacked psychotherapy without knowing anything about it, and his insistence that such attacks were based on personal resistances, is just as pertinent today as it was in 1905. The refusal of organized medicine generally to accept intensive psychotherapy as a legitimate medical technique has made it easier for third-party-payment business organizations to evade the obligation of helping patients with mental illness, and for untrained charlatans to take advantage of the suffering of the emotionally ill. Psychotherapy carries serious responsibilities and is a craft, which, like surgery, must be learned meticulously through arduous training; abandoning the mentally ill to charlatans in the field is analogous to the old tradition of allowing barbers to perform surgery.

Part II

CLINICAL PROBLEMS

Freud's values were not primarily health values. He believed in the intrinsic desirability of knowing as much as possible: he was—through the convergence and mutual reinforcement of the dominant world view of his time and some personal preferences (no doubt determined by experiences in early life) which transformed that scientific world view into his personal categorical imperative, his personal religion—intransigently committed to the task of knowing the truth, facing the truth, seeing reality clearly.

H. Kohut (1977), The Restoration of the Self (p. 64)

6

NOSOLOGICAL ISSUES

Sexuality. Most authors agree that along with *The Interpretation of Dreams*, Freud's *Three Essays on the Theory of Sexuality* (1905D;7:125ff) represents his greatest work. Essentially, the three essays present a continuation of his nosological considerations based on the sexual etiology of psychogenic disorders, as already begun in his earlier papers. Although this is a famous and important work, it is beyond the purposes of the present clinical book to present metapsychological details of Freud's basic libido theory as it was set down in the three essays and later contributions. Those who wish a thorough review of the subject are referred to Nagera (1969). A brief review of some of the salient concepts of Freud's libido theory is to be found in chapter 2 of *The Technique and Practice of Intensive Psychotherapy* (Chessick 1974); Freud's views on sexuality are reviewed in many standard textbooks, for example, Brenner (1973).

Here I will concentrate on the clinical aspects of the three essays. The first essay classifies sexual deviations according to object and aim, points out the basic bisexuality of humans, and identifies the relationship between perversion and the normal varieties of sexuality. It contains the famous statement that neurosis is the opposite or negative of perversion, in the sense that the impulses acted out by the pervert are the strongly repressed fantasies at the basis of the neuroses.

Infantile sexuality is discussed in the second essay and the famous erogenous zones and phases of development are delineated. In later editions details of infantile sexual theories and the concept of the "primal scene" (in which the child observes parental intercourse) were added. The third essay, "The Transformations of Puberty," describes the great struggle that the child has to go through in order to reach mature sexual development. Freud depicts in these three essays an epic struggle for maturity and health, in which the child is inescapably engaged from the dawn of life. As Robert (1966) points out, each time the child has to adapt himself to a new state he has to renounce the old one, and his life's happiness depends largely on the way he resolves the various primitive conflicts, a battle in which he has to fight essentially alone:

> Just as he can mature only by gradually freeing himself from the objects he has loved, so he can reach his full intellectual development only by separating his curiosity from the sexuality which first aroused it and transferring it to the multiple objects in the world. Puberty is only the last of these stages, in which development goes by fits and starts and at the cost of painful sacrifices. . . . Thinking about this slow evolution, which is in danger of being diverted by so many obstacles, one is inclined to be amazed that individuals can successfully negotiate all the stages without too many accidents and become balanced people capable of loving and freely realizing their potentialities of action and thought (p. 197).

The good clinician will ask at this point, What are the kinds of evidence on which Freud's libido theory is based? The most important evidence comes from Freud's work with neurotics, in which he again and again uncovered by his method the infantile sexual forces at the root of the psychoneuroses. A converse approach provides a second form of evidence, for the fact that we cannot obtain conscious memories of childhood sexuality in hysterics, due to the burial of those memories through amnesia, shows the importance of infantile sexuality, which should appear naturally as part of the ordinary memories of infancy. Both these types of evidence are presumptive and depend primarily upon the method of Freud.

Direct evidence is also provided by two major clinical phenomena. The first of these is the re-emergence of infantile sexual longings focused in the transference; the second comes from the direct analysis of children. For example, psychoanalysts accepted the case of Little Hans (1909B;10:3ff) as the first confirmation of Freud's theory of infantile sexuality obtained by direct observation of a child.

Hans, a five-year-old boy, suddenly refused to go into the street, alone or accompanied, because he was afraid of horses. His unwillingness to leave the house, where he seemed contented, happy, and fear-free, was an attempt to avoid his feelings of fear. In many such cases, similar inhibitions of activity result from phobias but are only secondary to the phobia and have nothing to do with its structure. This is important to remember because there is no advantage in trying to treat such inhibitions, as is frequently done. These inhibitions are most frequently observed in regard to attending school or playing with other children. Rather than simply trying to treat the inhibition, it is more important to try to understand the phobia underlying it, if at all possible. The model for all psychoanalytic therapy of phobias in children is Freud's analysis of Hans's case. Guided by the material produced by the boy, although Freud observed him directly only once, the "analysis" followed definite steps as it proceeded from one level to another.

The fear of horses consisted of two parts—a fear that a horse might fall down and a fear that a horse might bite him. The boy recognized and could discuss the former with greater clarity and ease than he could the latter, which actually contained the essential nucleus of the phobia. It should be noted that there is a reality element to the fear of a horse-bite. Horses do bite, but such occurrences are so infrequent that a child usually does not consider them.

Hans's two fears were projected expressions of a conflict in the boy's feelings: he was jealous of and hostile toward the father and toward his younger sister and wished that he could bite them both and that they would both fall down—or die. This aggressive hostility resulted from his strong attachment to his mother, which made him desire to possess her wholly himself without having to share her with anyone, to obtain from her, in addition to all the physical manifestations of love and tenderness he already had, all that she gave to his two rivals.

Hans feared these hostile feelings for two reasons. First, he was afraid that if his father knew about these hostile wishes, he would become angry. Being bigger and stronger, he would then inflict on Hans by way of punishment the same misfortune as the boy wished on him. Second, he loved his father and knew that if he injured or killed him, he would not have any father to love him. In the face of the fear of injury at his father's hands and loss of his loving care, he attempted to repress his hostile feelings and was successful in that they did not seem to exist toward the father but only in a confused fantasy about horses.

Freud felt it was necessary first to discuss with the boy the facts of the situation, facts which were available from the observations made and reported by the parents before the phobia developed. The boy was afraid of horses—at first lest they fall down and later, and somewhat more justifiably, lest they bite him. At Freud's suggestion, Hans's father told him that the reason he was so afraid of horses was that he was so preoccupied with penises; that he felt that he had no right to be so preoccupied; that he was too fond of his mother, wanted to be with her all the time, and particularly wanted to be taken into her bed. Since it was felt that the aim of his desire to be taken into his mother's bed was to see her penis, and since this aim had to be taken away, he was also told that a girl does not have a penis—a fact Hans had refused to accept for several years.

The boy reacted to the first part of this interpretation by becoming interested in looking at horses from a distance; to the last part by a slight improvement in his phobia but with a vigorous denial that what his father said was true. It seemed evident that this vigorous denial was a protective measure, since to admit that a girl has no penis would shatter his self-confidence and mean that his mother's castration threat (actually made by her against Hans's masturbation) might really be carried out.

This situation was followed by a dream which presented further material, since it revealed that he was afraid his mother would not like him because his penis was too small. The dream also expressed a desire to do something forbidden. The forbidden thing was, of course, his longing for his mother, which he felt had been forbidden by his father. The real situation—that he was afraid not of horses but of his father because he, Hans, loved his mother so much—was discussed with him by Freud on his single visit, in the company of his father. Hans reacted to the discussion by bringing out clearly his ambivalent reaction to his father and in addition another fear: that his father would leave him. The ambivalence was based on a conflict of two impulses: fear of his father and fear for his father's safety; that is, he felt hostile toward him, yet loved him and did not want to lose him as a result of the hostility.

After this was discussed with him he began to abreact some of his feelings. Although still afraid of horses, he began to play-pretend he was a horse. Here he was beginning to identify himself with his father. The material now changed. He began to express his conscious disgust with his now unconscious but formerly conscious desire to be so intimate with his mother as to be able to see her move her bowels; he then brought up one of his two earlier fears, that of the horse falling down. This was associated with a fear of defecation, as interest in seeing the feces falling—a concern lest his mother let him fall at his birth (pointing to his infantile theories about birth), and a wish that his mother would drop his younger sister into the bath and let her drown. Here again was the fear of his hostile wish against his rival.

The discussion of this new material allowed him to express verbally certain sadistic wishes to beat and tease horses. These wishes seemed to be better tolerated by him when directed toward the mother and were partly the expression of an obscure, sadistic desire for the mother, but they were really directed toward his father and were an expression of a clear impulse to revenge himself on him. There was also the motive of revenge against his mother, for he began to wish to have a child of his own and to wish that his mother would not have one. He became intrigued with the question as to whether people liked or did not like having children. The basis for this concern was, of course, the question as to whether people liked or did not like moving their bowels.

Satisfied on this account, he began to fantasize that he had a large family which he would look after as his mother had looked after him. In this fantasy he compensated for his unsatisfied passive longing to be fondled by his mother by an active longing to fondle others. He then solved his conflict over his jealous rivalry with his father by fantasizing that he would marry his mother and then his father would be his grandfather, and by dreaming that his father could not castrate him for his hostility but instead would give him a bigger and better penis. After he produced these ideas his phobia disappeared and his relationships with his parents became normal.

Freud calls attention to three important points. First, Hans's anxiety dared show itself boldly in a phobia because he had been brought up by understanding parents; hence, the anxiety situation was not too severely complicated by a guilty conscience or a fear of punishment. Second, the turning point of the case—the beginning of the entrance of unconscious material into consciousness—came with the interpretation given to the boy that he was afraid of his father because he cherished jealous and hostile wishes against him. The boy's realization that his father knew this and yet was not angry allowed him to produce his unconscious thoughts and fantasies. Third, the motive for the illness—the gain the boy obtained by his unwillingness to leave the house—allowed him to stay with his mother and thus gave him an excuse to avoid the conflict between his affection for and his hostility toward his father. This point—the excuse for avoiding conflict—is highly important, as it often appears as a marked resistance to treatment and may necessitate lengthy discussion with the child during the course of treatment.

The case of Hans illustrates the application of Freud's theories of infantile sexuality in clinical situations. The symptoms of neuroses develop as a converted expression of impulses which in a broader sense might be designated as perverse if they could manifest themselves directly in purely conscious fantasies and acts. The polymorphous perverse disposition is the primitive and universal disposition of the human sexual impulse, from which normal sexual behavior develops as a consequence of maturation, organic changes, and psychic repression. At this point in his work, Freud conceived libido as a quantum of sexual energy arising from all over the body; the psychic representative of this is ego libido. Libido is accessible to study only when invested in objects; libido can be given, removed, suspended, or invested in the self. In psychotherapy we study the vicissitudes of libido in the individual's life history and via the transference.

In the third essay, on the transformations of puberty, Freud presents his theory of the more complex and difficult psychosexual development of females and uses this theory to explain why females are more prone to hysteria than are males. I will not review the controversial issue of female sexual development here since I have already done so in a previous book (Chessick 1977*a*). A clinician should never forget Freud's point in this essay: that sublimation enables strong excitations arising from particular sources of sexuality to find an outlet and use in other fields, so that an increase in psychical efficiency results from a disposition which in itself may threaten the adequate functioning of the personality.

Because Freud was a marvelous writer, rare among scientists in clarity and style, the best place to study his libido theory is the three essays on sexuality—rather than trying to struggle through condensed abstractions of his work; even an aesthetic literary reward awaits the reader who studies Freud directly. [An appendix to the three essays in the *Standard Edition* (p. 244–5) provides a complete list of Freud's writings dealing predominantly or largely with sexuality. Philosophical aspects of the libido theory are found in the third essay, section 3 (1905D;7:217–218.]

Precipitating Factors. A brief paper by Freud (1912C;12:229ff) emphasizes the clinical search for the precipitating factors in any neurosis. In this paper he attempts to classify the various ways in which a person may become afflicted with a neurosis. (For some reason this classification has not been thoroughly investigated.)

There are several ways in which reality can become unbearable, leading to the onset of a neurosis. Neurosis may appear simply as the result of a more-or-less sudden libidinal privation, that is, from severe external frustration. In these situations, given the proper predisposition, the libido turns away from reality and toward the life of fantasy, "in which it creates new wishful structures and revives the traces of earlier, forgotten ones" (p. 232). This process revives the repressed infantile desires which are incompatible with the subject's present-day individuality, leading to a conflict. The conflict is resolved by the formation of symptoms which represent compromises and often carry punishment as well as substitutive gratification.

A neurosis may also be precipitated by an individual's failure to adapt to reality and fulfill its demands. This is a consequence of internal inflexibility in which the person is unable to change in order to meet fresh demands from reality. The consequence is frustration and the same chain of events as described previously.

Yet another precipitation of neurosis results from an inhibition in development. Freud's example of this concerns people who collapse after leaving the irresponsible age of childhood because their libido has never left its infantile fixations—a common and important clinical problem.

Finally, a fourth precipitant involves people who have met successfully with fresh demands of reality and who have been previously healthy, but now suffer from a purely internal, organically determined change in the psychic economy such as may occur at puberty or the climacteric. For example, in puberty the sudden upsurge of the instinctual drives can overwhelm the immature ego, which is then forced to move in a regressive direction.

It should be clear that this is a very important clinical paper; the strategy for psychotherapy will depend in an important way on the therapist's assessment of the factors involved in the onset of the emotional illness. This again emphasizes the importance of taking a *careful history* at the beginning of any psychotherapy procedure and requires a meticulous scientific assessment of the various factors, internal and external, with which the patient's ego constantly has to deal throughout the changing circumstances of human life.

Character. One of Freud's favorite theories concerns the injurious influence of civilization when it dedicates itself to the harmful suppression of the sexual life of civilized peoples, as first put forth in a brief paper in 1908 (1908D;9:179ff). A fascinating aspect of this paper is Freud's review of statements by other authors about the injurious effect of "modern" civilization, statements taken from various writings prior to 1908. In contrast to these superficial studies, Freud's theory explains that civilization is built up on the suppression of instincts, both aggressive and sexual. This suppression places extraordinarily large amounts of force at the disposal of civilized activity, and thus the aim of these instincts is displaced without materially diminishing the intensity of the drive. Freud explains, "This capacity to exchange its originally sexual aim for another one, which is no longer sexual but which is psychically related to the first aim, is called the capacity for *sublimation*. . . . The original strength of the sexual instinct probably varies in each individual; certainly the proportion of it which is suitable for sublimation varies" (p. 187). This theme was taken up later in a very famous book (Freud 1930A;21:59ff).

One of Freud's most famous papers, "Character and Anal Erotism" (1908B;9:168ff), was greeted with jeers and disbelief on all sides when it was published. Nevertheless, it represents a very important beginning contribution to the subject of personality disorders. The theme is very simple. Freud proposes that the character traits of orderliness, parsimony, and obstinacy are to be regarded as the "first and most constant results of the sublimation of anal erotism." This leads to the major general thesis, "We can at any rate lay down a formula for the way in which character in its final shape is formed out of the constituent instincts: the permanent character-traits are either unchanged prolongations of the original instincts, or sublimations of those instincts, or reaction-formations against them" (p. 175).

Freud did not leave many accounts of the nature of the formation of character. A discussion of sublimation may be found in the "Three Essays" but it adds little to what has already been quoted previously. Freud believed that "The processes of the formation of character are more obscure and less accessible to analysis than neurotic ones" (1913I;12:323). His main discussion of the subject is in the first half of chapter III of *The Ego and the Id* (1923B;19:28ff), a discussion which is essentially repeated in lecture 32 of the *New Introductory Lectures* (1933A;22:81–111). Here he discusses the role of introjection or identification in the formation of character, as a consequence of having to give up a sexual object primarily during the resolution of the Oedipus complex. Further confusion is introduced by his introduction of the phrase "the character of the ego." At any rate, not only does the character of the ego become "a precipitate of abandoned object-cathexes" in which these identifications or introjections play an important role in the building of character; but the formation of the ego ideal by identification with the parent of the same sex as an heir to the resolution of the Oedipus complex is described by Freud as the most important identification of all.

This view explains the concept of multiple personality, in which different identifications seize the consciousness. Even if a subject has not reached this stage there obviously may remain the problem of conflicts among the various identifications, in which the ego crumbles if the identifications are too numerous, powerful, and incompatible with one another. To summarize, Freud (1933A;22:91) writes,

> We have already made out a little of what it is that creates character. First and foremost there is the incorporation of the former parental agency as a super-ego, which is no doubt its most important and decisive portion, and, further, identifications with the two parents of the later period and with other influential figures, and similar identifications formed as precipitates of abandoned object-relations. And we may now add as contributions to the construction of character which are never absent the reaction-formations which the ego acquires—to begin with in making its repressions and later, by a more normal method, when it rejects unwished-for instinctual impulses.

The treatment of personality disorders or disorders of character has become increasingly important in our time as the sexual revolution may have reduced the number of classical sexual psychoneuroses. Today's treatments are time-consuming and difficult, and some psychiatrists have attempted to legislate such disorders out of existence by simply dropping them from the manual of mental disorders or relegating their treatment to psychologists or social workers. To me this is analogous to arguing that because the treatment of cancer is lengthy and expensive and often not completely satisfactory, physicians should not use up their valuable time in working with such patients. In the same vein, insurance companies should not be expected to pay or compensate for lengthy and expensive treatment of malignancy since this raises the insurance rates for everybody. The etiology of cancer is obscure and in most cases difficult to ascertain; why not relabel these diseases as "difficulties in cellular metabolism" and relegate their treatment to physiologists or biochemists? Calling cancer or character disorder by a different name does not change the amount of suffering, pain, and unhappiness caused by these disorders; both groups of disorders can be fatal, both groups of disorders have multiple etiology often with numerous factors contributing to the development of an individual case, and both groups of disorders present frightened human beings who are living a life characterized by pain and suffering.

"Some Character-types Met with in Psychoanalytic Work" (1916D;14:310ff) presents one of Freud's rare papers on character traits and their formation. He avoids broad general statements and instead chooses three particular types of character traits that he came across in his work. The first of these Freud labeled "Exceptions" and as an example he presents Shakespeare's Richard III. Much of the unreasonable and furious behavior of such people is founded on their secretly cherishing the belief that they are exceptions to the rule that society demands a certain level of conduct from everybody. Today we know (Chessick 1977) that such patients are suffering from severe narcissistic disorders as manifested by a sense of entitlement and a disavowal of the restrictions placed on ordinary human beings. Freud's example was right on the target, for he felt that such cases suffered unjustly in childhood from some ill-treatment or accident; indeed Richard III suffered the tremendous narcissistic blow of being born in a deformed state, so that "Dogs bark at me as I halt by them." His narcissistic rage and subsequent attempts at revenge should be well known; I assume the great plays of Shakespeare are familiar territory for every practicing psychotherapist, since Shakespeare was the greatest psychologist who ever lived, the acknowledged master even of Freud.

The second two types of characters are better known to the general public. Those "wrecked by success" such as Lady Macbeth collapse upon attaining their ambitions, because the attainment of the success is associated with a forbidden infantile wish which may be toyed with or strived after but not actually gratified. "Criminals from a sense of guilt" are cases where a criminal act has been committed in order to provoke a punishment. This would alleviate some unbearable sense of guilt arising from deeper unconscious sources, and also allow the patient to practice behavior that forms a rationalized ground for the displacement of the guilt. Freud remarks that Nietzsche in *Thus Spoke Zarathustra* gave broad hints of the same mechanism in his section entitled "The Pale Criminal" (discussed in Chessick 1977*a*).

In *Herzog* (1964) Bellow explains "To haunt the past like this—to love the dead! Moses warned himself not to yield so greatly to this temptation, this peculiar weakness of his character. He was a depressive. Depressives cannot surrender childhood—not even the pains of childhood." This great novel almost paraphrases a passage in the first lecture on psychoanalysis given by Freud in the United States in 1909 (1910A;11:16–17), in which he explains how neurotics not only remember painful experiences of the remote past, but still cling to them emotionally: "They cannot get free of the past and for its sake they neglect what is real and immediate. This fixation of mental life to pathogenic traumas is one of the most significant and practically important characteristics of neurosis."

Thus one of the basic premises of psychoanalytically informed psychotherapy maintains that a vital treatment goal is to enable the patient to separate emotionally from his or her past, to allow the past to sink into obscurity and to lose its influence on the patient's current life. This process offers a continuing barometer of the patient's progress in psychotherapy as we watch the patient's reactions to people mature, and as we experience the changes in the transference. It is also important in nosology, for a successful psychoanalytically-informed nosology must distinguish among the disorders in terms of the developmental vicissitudes. For those who worry about whether the past can ever be understood correctly Freud, in discussing the case of Little Hans, reminds us (1909B;10:122), "In an analysis, however, a thing which has not been understood inevitably reappears; like an unlaid ghost, it cannot rest until the mystery has been solved and the spell broken."

Anxiety. In his innovative *Inhibitions, Symptoms and Anxiety* (1926D; 20:77ff), a work that Freud had some difficulty in binding together in one theme, he presents his so-called signal theory of anxiety, which is vitally important in understanding the formation, diagnosis, and treatment of neurotic and character disorders. The significance of this theory requires clinicians to go over this work rather carefully.

In the first section Freud points out that "inhibition" represents a simple lowering or restriction of function, whereas "symptom" occurs when a function "has undergone some unusual change or when a new phenomenon has arisen out of it" (p. 87). As clinicians we frequently see both inhibitions and symptoms in our patients. This work reverses the early theory of Freud which insisted that inhibitions lead to anxiety. Freud now contends that anxiety motivates the ego to inhibit or repress (with subsequent symptom-formation) when there is a conflict with the id, a conflict with the superego, or problems within the ego itself leading to impoverishment of energy. An example of the latter is seen when the ego is involved in a particularly difficult psychical task such as in the process of grief or mourning, during which other ego functions are generally inhibited out of the impoverishment of energy. Inhibition is the expression of a restriction of an ego-function, whereas symptoms arise due to the failure of repression.

Section II deals with the process of symptom formation, in which a symptom is viewed as the behavioral, affective, or somatic manifestation of a defense. Among the famous mechanisms of defense elaborated by Anna Freud (1946) and others, repression has a central and basic role in all neurotic symptom formations. Where does the ego get the power to repress? How can it forbid the gratification of an instinct by inhibiting or deflecting? Freud's answer is that this process arises from the intimate relationship between the perceptual system and the ego. Thus when the ego is opposed to an instinctual process in the id, "it has only to give a *signal of unpleasure* in order to attain its object with the aid of that almost omnipotent institution, the pleasure principle" (p. 92). According to Freud, the ego withdraws energy cathected to the instinct that is to be repressed, and uses this energy for the purpose of releasing unpleasure—which Freud equates with the feeling of anxiety. This unpleasure then mobilizes psychic functions along the pleasure principle and sets the ego's mechanisms of defense into action.

If the ego successfully represses the instinct we learn nothing; we find out about this repression only from those cases in which the repression has more or less failed. In the event of failure of the repression, a substitute formation occurs, very much reduced, displaced, and inhibited, and which is no longer clearly recognizable as a satisfaction. This is a symptom. Thus a symptom is a sign of, and a substitute for, an instinctual satisfaction which has been forbidden direct gratification—it is a consequence of the process of repression. As Freud conceives of it, the ego, in its close connection with the perceptual system, perceives and wards off internal and external dangers in the same fashion. When it perceives an unacceptable instinct in the id it gives a signal of unpleasure (felt as anxiety) in order to enlist the aid of the pleasure principle in overpowering the id.

In section III, Freud explains that the ego is the organized portion of the id: because of this, when the ego tries to suppress an instinct, the remainder of the id—which is not organized—does not come to the rescue of the endangered part and grapple with the ego, at least initially.

Freud then explains, in a discussion of very great importance to clinicians, how the ego must subsequently struggle with the symptoms that have now been formed. Thus "The initial act of repression is followed by a tedious or interminable sequel in which the struggle against the instinctual impulse is prolonged into a struggle against the symptom" (p. 98). The very nature of the ego obliges it to attempt to organize and synthesize all the aspects of the personality, and therefore it finds it necessary to use every possible method to incorporate the symptoms into the organization of the personality and prevent them from remaining isolated. It makes an adaptation to the symptom.

For example, if the presence of a symptom entails the impairment of a capacity, this defect can be used to appease the sueperego or to refuse some claim from the external world. "In this way the symptom gradually comes to be the representative of important interests; it is found to be useful in asserting the position of the self and becomes more and more closely merged with the ego and more and more indespensable to it" (p. 99). The clinical point here is that when the therapist tries subsequently to help the ego and deal with the symptom, he finds that these "conciliatory bonds" between the ego and the symptom operate on the side of the resistance and are very difficult to separate. For example, in obsessional symptoms and even in paranoia the symptoms may become very valuable to the ego, leading to success in certain types of work and affording narcissistic gratification—forms of secondary gain from an illness. Therefore, Freud regards the attitude of the ego toward symptoms as both friendly in its effort to integrate the symptoms into the personality and unfriendly in the continuing direction of repression of the basic forbidden instinct.

Section IV, which is rather tortuous for the practicing clinician, essentially contains Freud's repudiation of his old theory of anxiety and again emphasizes the notion that the source of anxiety is energy borrowed from instinctual drives, energy then used by the ego to give a signal of unpleasure as explained previously. The concept of actual neuroses (described before in chapter 5) is never abandoned by Freud; his new theory of anxiety simply sidesteps this type of neurosis. Subsequent authors have repeatedly pointed out the ambiguity in this situation (Compton 1972, 1972*a*; Waelder 1967).

Section V explains how, as an emotional disorder progresses, the instinctual forces in a symbolic way gain the upper hand through a spread of the neuroses. Freud conceives of this phenomenon as a ceaseless struggle being waged against that which is repressed, a struggle in which the repressing forces steadily lose ground. Freud describes a familiar clinical picture in the obsessional neuroses, in which symptoms that once stood for a restriction of the ego come to represent satisfactions due to the ego's inclination to synthesis as described; the eventual result is an extremely restricted ego which is reduced to seeking satisfaction in the symptoms. The final outcome, familiar to clinicians, is that in every decision in certain spheres of living the ego finds itself almost as strongly impelled from one side as from the other and cannot decide, with a resulting paralysis of will. More and more spheres of living become drawn into the conflict as the disorder progresses.

At the time it was believed that this problem was of special importance in obsessive-compulsive neuroses, because the instincts involved were thought to be more primitive and thus quantitatively stronger; an equally reasonable viewpoint, and one closer to my clinical experience, is that the ego in obsessive-compulsive neuroses is relatively weak and closer to the borderline disorders than other forms of neuroses. I have observed a number of schizophrenic breakdowns resolve themselves under the influence of psychotherapy into obsessive-compulsive neurotic disorders of varying degrees of severity. Sullivan (1956) discusses the relationship of obsessionalism and schizophrenia at length—but from the interpersonal point of view.

Section VI describes some of the mechanisms of defense and leads logically to Anna Freud's (1946) famous book on the subject. It is hardly necessary to add at this point that every practicing psychotherapist must be thoroughly familiar with this book and all the standard mechanisms of defense as they are described in every textbook (for example Brenner 1973). I would like however to caution the therapist against an increasingly common error in dealing with this subject. The mechanisms of defense are called into play by the failure of repression on the part of the ego against an instinctual drive; they have nothing directly to do with interpersonal relationships and social transactions! Those who discuss "games" or defenses in interpersonal relationships or social transactions are not employing the psychoanalytic orientation to understanding human beings, an orientation based on the empathic perception of *intrapsychic* phenomena.

Section VII proposes the famous signal theory of anxiety, in which anxiety is conceived of as a signal by the ego of a situation of danger, and subsequently obviated by the ego's doing something to avoid that situation or to withdraw from it. Symptoms are the ultimate result of attempting to avoid the danger situation emerging from within, whose presence was originally signaled by the generation of anxiety.

Readers of Freud may well be confused by the fact that he uses the concept of regression in several different ways: for example (1) "temporal" regression, defined as returning to earlier reaction patterns or to temporally earlier modes of psychic functioning; (2) "formal" regression, involving a change from the use of general and abstract symbols and signs such as words to visual imagery as in dreams; and (3) "topographical" regression, representing a change from organized secondary process thought and behavior to primary process thought. [A thorough discussion of this difficult subject is presented by Arlow and Brenner (1964).]

In section VIII, anxiety itself is analyzed into three components: (1) a specific unpleasurable quality or tension as felt with an unpleasurable character which "seems to have a note of its own"; (2) fairly definite physical sensations usually involving the heart or respiration, symptoms which Freud calls "acts of discharge"; and (3), perceptions of physiologic discomfort which differentiate anxiety from similar states such as mourning and pain. Freud's differentiation of unpleasure and anxiety is never very convincingly established.

In this section, considerable discussion occurs about the prototype of the anxiety experience and Rank's birth-trauma theory, which is obsolete today. For the clinician what is important is Freud's contention that anxiety cannot be experienced until at least a rudimentary ego exists—which immediately obviates Rank's theory. As the rudimentary ego comes into being, the infant learns that the mother relieves the danger of a growing tension due to need, against which the infant alone is helpless. The infant learns from experience that the mother satisfies these needs and avoids danger for the infant. When the infant has found that the mother can put an end to this danger, the fear is displaced from the danger of being overwhelmed by need-tensions to the danger of the loss of the mother. Thus "It is the absence of the mother that is now the danger; and as soon as that danger arises the infant gives the signal of anxiety, before the dreaded economic situation has set in. This change constitutes a first great step forward in the provision made by the infant for self-preservation, and at the same time represents a transition from the automatic and involuntary fresh appearance of anxiety to the intentional reproduction of anxiety as a signal of danger" (p. 138).

Section IX defines defenses as an attempt at flight from an instinctual danger and attempts to describe the kinds of dangers experienced at various phases of development. In the final section, X, Freud delineates three factors that create the conditions under which the forces of the mind are pitted against one another: the long period of helplessness during child development; inferred biogenetic factors having to do with human prehistory; and a psychological factor wherein the ego is obliged to guard against certain instinctual impulses in the id and to treat them as dangers, while at the same time, it is intimately bound up with the id and therefore, "can only fend off an instinctual danger by restricting its own organization and by acquiescing in the formation of symptoms in exchange for having impaired the instinct" (p. 156).

The "Addenda" to this work contains a classification of five varieties of resistance, most useful for clinicians: (1) The first variety arises from repression, in which the ego resists the uncovering of the repressed unacceptable ideation. (2) Transference resistance represents a form of resistance to remembering, in which a repetition of the relationship to early significant figures in the transference is substituted for the remembering of these relationships. (3) Resistance arises as a consequence of the gain of illness (discussed above), for the ego has synthesized the symptoms into a functioning personality and achieved a certain secondary gain from the symptoms, a gain which it attempts to retain. (4) The sense of guilt over the repressed instinctual drive and the need for punishment resists any success of the treatment, and is termed superego resistance by Freud. (5) Freud labels the final form of resistance as "resistance of the unconscious," which seems to me closely related to the transference resistance. It is extremely important and has to do with the compulsion to repeat, necessitating a long period of working through in any intensive psychotherapy (this will be discussed in greater detail in the present book in chapter 12 on transference and countertransference). Freud's most important discussions of "resistance of the unconscious" are found in his papers "Remembering, Repeating and Working-through (1914G;12:146ff) and "Analysis Terminable and Interminable" (1937C;23:211ff). Every clinician must be continuously aware of these five varieties of resistance as they appear in the day-to-day practice of intensive psychotherapy.

The philosophy of science behind Freud's theory of the formation of symptoms presented here has been opened recently to serious question. As Waelder (1967) points out, the notion of the ego's activities in this theory is fundamentally teleological: it explains psychic activities in terms of the purposes they serve. Waelder explains, "It is a close relative of Aristotle's *entelechy*, the pre-existing form which guides the development of plant or animal according to nature; or a relative of the medieval physician's *vis medicatrix naturae*, the healing power of nature" (pp. 13–14). This subject will be discussed in detail in the final section of the present book.

In *An Outline of Psychoanalysis* (1940;23:141ff), written thirteen years later, Freud pushes his teleologic description of the ego to its final extreme: goal-directed or teleological expressions abound in that late work. This again illustrates the unresolved tension in Freud's thought, as pointed out in the introduction and first chapter of the present book, between a humanistic and vitalistic explanation of phenomena and a mechanistic and deterministic orientation. On the other hand, it is certainly true that, as Waelder points out, "The revision of the theory of (neurotic) anxiety and the realization of a variety of defense mechanisms have born rich fruit and have changed the outlook and practice of psychoanalysis" (pp. 34–35).

Freud's notion of actual neuroses, viewing anxiety in these cases as a consequence of dammed-up libido, has been discarded by most psychoanalysts, but there is an interesting revival of this theory in an attempt to explain manic-depressive illness as an actual neurosis (Wolpert 1975). A complete description of the psychoanalytic theory of anxiety from its beginnings to the present day is presented in detail by Compton (1972, 1972*a*). He notes Freud's lack of discussion about anxiety in the psychoses and suggests that psychotic anxiety might possibly be a type of response different from neurotic anxiety. Reviewing experimental work, he feels that Freud is confirmed in argument that no experience of fear or anxiety is possible before ego nuclei have formed around three to six months of age. Further work is clearly necessary to resolve the ambiguity in Freud's anxiety theory; some contributions have attempted to dispel this ambiguity by sweeping assumptions leading to further obfuscations; others have sharpened up the theory here and there, but without adding much of fundamental importance for the practice of intensive psychotherapy.

An exception to this is the contribution of Loewenstein (1964), who suggests that *intra*systemic conflict may also result in anxiety based on a threatened loss of control of the ego's own function. Hartmann, Kris, and Loewenstein have suggested that the ego does not differentiate from the id but that both develop from a common undifferentiated matrix. Their work on the concept of ego autonomy and its various implications has been summarized previously (Chessick 1977), and has basic ramifications for the practice of intensive psychotherapy. Recent advances on Freud's hierarchy-of-danger situations typical in various developmental phases have been summarized by Gedo and Goldberg (1973).

Nosology. In Freud's outstanding description of the development of a neurosis presented in the *Introductory Lectures on Psychoanalysis* (1916X; 16:243ff) he reminds us repeatedly that neurotics are anchored in their past. They search about in the history of their life until they find a period in which there was some kind of happiness, even if they have to go back as far as the time when they were infants in arms (as they remember it or as they imagine it from later notions and hints). This anchoring in the past and the search for early infantile kinds of satisfactions collides with the adult censorship and leads to symptom formation.

Freedman et al. (1976) present an interesting table (p. 1082) developed from an early edition of Freud's collected papers in which the four famous case histories are compared in terms of the psychoneurotic reactions in the childhood of the patients. Dora, Little Hans, "The Rat Man," and "The Wolf-Man" are compared with respect to family history, childhood symptoms, and alleged etiologic experiences. Those interested in child psychotherapy will find this table especially interesting.

Gedo and Goldberg (1973) have also brought Freud's models of mental functioning up to date and integrated the discoveries of Kohut (1971). By this synthetic work, which is very difficult and technical, a nosological structure of the emotional disorders can be constructed, with important ramifications for the understanding and treatment of mental disorders. The first phase of development, the autistic and oral libido phase, is best understood on the reflex arc model as given in chapter VII of *The Interpretation of Dreams* (Freud 1900A;5:509–622). The experienced danger of this phase is traumatic overstimulation, and narcissism is primary. Hallucinatory omnipotence is the sense of reality; and the typical defense is automatic avoidance, described by Freud as primal repression. Patients in this phase are in a traumatic or panic state and need medication and need-gratification or pacification as treatment. The unpleasure principle—to avoid unpleasure—is the regulatory principle of mental functioning.

This phase ends with the achievement of cognitive self object differentiation at roughly six to eight months of age.

The second phase of oral and anal attachments of the libido exhibits a characteristic danger of separation, or the loss of the object or its love. The grandiose self and idealized parent imago are invested with narcissism, and reality is tested by magical gestures and words. Typical defenses are what I would call intrusion and extrusion; in other words, massive projection plus externalization, and introjection. Psychotic disintegration is characteristic of this phase, and repetitive behavior to restore self-cohesion occurs along the principle of self-definition. The treatment in this phase is identification with the therapist and his reliable self. Unification is achieved by utilizing the therapist and his setting as the transitional object.

By three to four years of age a consolidation of the cohesive sense of self occurs, and the Oedipus complex begins; grandiosity is confined to the phallus and the phallic phase begins. Due to jealousy and hostility in the Oedipus complex, castration is the significant anxiety and phallic narcissism prevails. The omnipotence of sexual auto-erotism is basic to the sense of reality, and the pleasure principle is the regulatory principle of mental functioning. The typical defense of this phase occurs when the ego abandons its synthetic function and glosses over disparate aspects of reality—disavowal. Narcissistic personality disorders are found in this phase and the treatment is that of optimal disillusionment, preferably by psychoanalysis if the proper transference is formed.

Around six to eight years of age the Oedipus complex is resolved and the superego forms. This definitive step moves the person to obey the reality principle, and anxiety takes on a moral nature as self-regulating systems take over. Narcissism becomes infused into the ego ideal and the reality principle rules. At this point the setting-up of permanent counter-cathexes or repression is the typical defense, and we have the era of the infantile neuroses and neurotic character disorders. The treatment of such disorders is psychoanalysis with interpretation, if possible.

The final phase begins with the consolidation of the repression barrier and a definitive ego-id differentiation. This occurs through identifications that take place during the latency phase of libidinal development, or with a reworking during adolescence of the entire psychic structure. The result is the final consolidation of the repression barrier; the individual then enters into adult life. Realistic threats are the primary danger and signal anxiety is used by the ego. Narcissism eventually becomes transformed into wisdom, humor, creativity, and empathy, and the individual accepts the transience of life. Renunciation and the reality principle prevail and introspection is used to maintain good adult functioning.

Freud's tripartite model of the psyche is useful for understanding neuroses and the portrayal of behavior due to intrapsychic conflicts during these last two phases; the topographic model may still be used for the understanding of dream, errors, and neurotic symptoms during these last two phases. The regulatory principle of mental functioning may be thought of during this final phase as more than adaptation to reality, rising to a creative principle during which the individual attempts to further discover novel aspects of reality or even achieve transcendence (Chessick 1974, 1978*a*). Arlow and Brenner (1964) disagree sharply with Gedo and Goldberg's view, insisting that only the structural (tripartite) model should be used in understanding all phases and all clinical phenomena. The subject remains controversial and unresolved.

7

PSYCHOTHERAPY OF THE WOLF-MAN

In February 1910, a helpless young man of 23, unable even to dress himself, and accompanied by a private doctor and valet, appeared in Freud's consulting room. According to a letter from Freud to Ferenczi, quoted by Jones (1955), the patient initiated the first hour of treatment with an offer to have anal intercourse with Freud and then to defecate on his head.

The patient's extreme neurosis rendered him totally incapable of dealing with even the simplest matters of life. He had undergone various treatments involving hydrotherapy and electricity, and had visited numerous sanatoria as well as consulting the famous Professors Ziehen and Kraepelin. In spite of all this disappointing experience with psychiatry, the patient wrote later that as soon as he met Freud he knew "at once" that Freud was what he was looking for:

> Freud's appearance was such as to win my confidence immediately. He was then in his middle fifties and seemed to enjoy the best of health. He was of medium height and figure. In his rather long face, framed by a closely clipped, already greying beard, the most impressive feature was his intelligent dark eyes, which looked at me penetratingly but without causing me the slightest feeling of discomfort. His correct, conventional way of dressing, and his simple but self-assured manner, indicated his love of order and his inner serenity. Freud's whole attitude and the way in which he listened to me, differentiated him strikingly from his famous colleagues whom I had hitherto known and in whom I had found such a lack of deeper psychological understanding. At my first meeting with Freud I had the feeling of encountering a great personality (Gardiner 1971, p. 137).

One should never underestimate the remarkable impact of the first meeting with patients of this degree of pathology. Even as I quote these lines from the Wolf-Man I am reminded of a case that I saw today, the daughter of a physician, who has been to five psychiatrists. She had received electric shock treatment, insulin therapy, and practically all the drugs in the psychopharmocological armamentarium, but no one suggested intensive psychotherapy, apparently because she clearly suffers from schizophrenia. When I asked her if she was interested in working with me in intensive psychotherapy she remarked spontaneously that she thought it might be worthwhile because I was the first psychiatrist who did not intimidate her; when pressed to define intimidate, she mentioned the tendency to lecture and authoritatively instruct as some form of supportive authoritative psychotherapy which carried with it the secret message that she is "a hopeless case who must be ordered about like a child."

Freud's courage in taking on the Wolf-Man as a patient was remarkable; I believe this case is so instructive that it deserves a separate chapter for the consideration of every psychotherapist. The case history itself, which is among Freud's best works (Freud 1918B;17:3ff), is the most complex and difficult of his case histories. It was written at a time when Freud had separated from Adler and then Jung, and was an attempt to illustrate the profound difference between Freud's theories and those of his competitors. The case history illustrates the importance of childhood neuroses in the generation of adult neuroses, and the vital role of infantile sexual fantasies and experiences in the formation of neurotic symptoms. It is the most elaborate and important of all of Freud's case histories and presents his view of the central role of infantile sexuality in the formation of psychopathology.

Freud restricts his description of the treatment to that of the infantile neurosis itself, which had raged about fifteen years prior to the psychoanalysis. The treatment, as mentioned, began with the Wolf-Man's immediate feeling that here was what he was looking for, and with Freud's willingness to take him into a classical psychoanalysis. This was followed by four years of struggle in which, although nothing changed essentially, the patient seemed to gather considerable intellectual insight. Finally Freud, in exasperation, told the patient that the treatment had to come to an end at a fixed date; under this pressure a flood of material appeared and the patient regained his capacity to function in a self-sufficient manner.

The four-year treatment is only the beginning of the remarkable story of the vicissitudes of the Wolf-Man and psychoanalysis, but it is this treatment that is described in Freud's case history, and we will attend to it first. The patient came from a wealthy Russian family. In spite of the fact that his father apparently had a manic-depressive psychosis, and that the patient himself exhibited apathy, indifference, and inability to function, Freud recognized his patient's excellent intellectual capacity and social reaching-out. Thus, a curious contrast was presented between the archaic personality and behavior in the clinical setting, and what Freud recognized to be the Wolf-Man's potential. Freud, clearly interested in the infantile neurosis of this patient, was fascinated by his intelligence and personality in spite of the florid regressive symptoms.

At around the age of eighteen months the patient allegedly recognized the primal scene—or at least a reconstruction of this observation took place, but no actual memory. Freud explains that whether this primal scene was an unconscious memory of an actual event or a fantasy of the patient, the psychic reality is such that the effect is identical in both cases. The case also demonstrates that infantile traumas and fantasies really date from very early life and are not much-later fantasies that have been projected backwards into the past.

Freud did such a thorough job of analyzing the neurotic products of his patient's infantile conflict that some authors have argued that he removed the patient's protection against a psychosis. Indeed, my own patient, the physician's daughter quoted above, said, "I fear intensive psychotherapy because it would get to the heart of my problems and remove my defenses. Those defenses are not much but they are all that I have." Jones (1955) describes a cardinal feature of the Wolf-Man's case as consisting of "complicated defensive reactions against an unusually strong tendency to a homosexual solution of the Oedipus situation." The patient clearly was forced to use passive and erotized defenses against his powerful rage, but I suspect we would more inclined today to label this as narcissistic rage rather than an unresolved Oedipus complex (Gedo and Goldberg 1973, Kohut 1977). The pathology in this case is kaleidoscopic, and the chronology is difficult to follow. In a footnote, Freud (1918B;17:121) presents a brief chronological outline and with this as our base let us have a look at how the case of the Wolf-Man unfolds.

He was born on Christmas day 1886, in a caul, which meant, in the superstition of the time, special good luck (Freud was also born in a caul). This, and the date of his birth, fostered a later identification with Christ. Undoubtedly his narcissistic fantasies were enhanced by the fact that he was the younger child of wealthy landowners. Freud was well aware of the Wolf-Man's narcissistic fixation on the grandiose delusion of invulnerability: "He . . . looked upon himself as a special child of fortune whom no ill could befall" (p. 99). I will discuss this aspect in greater detail later.

His first neurotic symptom seems to have been a disturbance of appetite; he had been a feeding problem in his first years and had been warned repeatedly, "If you don't eat you will die." It is significant that his mother, with whom he was closely identified, had many bowel complaints and was often absent from home or preoccupied. He was raised from the beginning by an affectionate servant, a peasant who acted as a nurse. At around age 1½, the alleged primal scene occurred. At 2½, when he observed the maid Grusha scrubbing the floor on her hands and knees with buttocks projecting and her back horizontal, he was faced once again with the posture which his mother had assumed in the copulation scene. He was seized with sexual excitement and urinated on the floor at the time, an action which

Freud attributes to identification with his father and urethral eroticism.

At 3¼ the patient began to be seduced by his sister who played with his penis; this constituted a blow to his masculine self-esteem, which was also not helped by the fact that his sister was favored by his father. The defense against this situation of being helplessly used as a selfobject was the formation of aggressive fantasies and rage on the one hand, and active masturbation, seductively performed in the presence of the nurse, on the other. The nurse reacted by threatening castration, which disrupted the defense and threw the boy's sexual life back into regression, into an anal sadistic fixation.

In the summer of his fourth year, after his affectionate nurse was succeeded by a harsh governess, the patient developed rageful and unruly behavior. His active sexual interests were replaced by masochistic fantasies of being beaten on the penis and by castration fears. In fact, his bad behavior was an effort to force punishments and beatings out of father, so as to obtain from him masochistic sexual satisfactions.

At the age of four occurred the famous wolf-dream, which suddenly ushered in a remission of the behavior disorder but also the appearance of a wolf phobia. His last sexual aim, the passive attitude towards his father, was repressed and he identified with his castrated mother. The nightmare occurred just before his fourth birthday; the wolf phobia constituted his infantile neurosis.

His rather desperate mother began to instruct him in religion at the age of 4½. After being told the story of Christ's passion he became obsessed with the problem of Christ's relationship with God. Gradually the wolf phobia shifted into an obsessional neurosis with a complex routine and religious content. He became very pious but tortured by obsessional, blasphemous thoughts and compulsive rituals; during the latency period he suffered from attacks of the obsessional neurosis with a subsequent loss of intellectual and social interests.

It should be noted that at the age of five he hallucinated the loss of his finger which was traced by Freud to castration fears. Most important, the patient at ten developed a relationship with a male tutor who obtained a great influence over him. Under the German tutor's influence "there arose a new and better sublimation of the patient's sadism" involving, among other things, enthusiasm for military affairs.

He apparently functioned relatively well in early puberty. He made sexual overtures to his sister and upon being rebuffed turned to a series of servant girls, but at the age of seventeen developed gonorrhea. Secondary to the gonorrhea, a severe emotional breakdown took place, characterized by withdrawal, apathy, and a general inability to function. Freud argues that the gonorrhea revived his fear of castration and shattered his narcissism, compelling him to abandon his hope of being personally favored by destiny: "He fell ill, therefore, as a result of a *narcissistic* 'frustration'" (p. 118). It should be noted that the patient's sister, who was 2½ years older, became overtly schizophrenic and committed suicide about two years after the outbreak of his adult neurosis.

The acting-out involving his bowels is attributed by Freud to a form of hysterical conversion. At the time the patient reached Freud he could only have a bowel movement through an enema given by a man. Freud boldly promised the patient a complete recovery, through the analysis, of his intestinal activity. Gedo and Goldberg (1973) explain, "This parameter would be classified as the provision of a unifying relatedness to an omnipotent and therefore, idealized object." Clearly the patient's attachment to Freud and the setting of a termination date for treatment were the key to understanding the treatment.

The crucial primal-scene wolf-dream arose out of the terrifying discovery that castration was a necessary condition of intercourse with his father, a discovery which led him to repress his passive masochistic homosexual wish and replace it with the wolf phobia. The analysis of the wolf dream and the infantile neurosis (wolf phobia) is at the center of Freud's case study. It is not necessary for our purposes to present details of Freud's long analysis of the wolf dream, contained in section IV of the case history, except to note that the undertaking certainly indicates Freud's crucial reliance on dream analysis especially in psychotherapeutic situations where the sheer volume of material results in doubt and confusion.

The resolution of the third phase of the sickness, the obsessional neurosis, occurred through the transference to the strong masculine tutor, thus allowing the patient to sublimate and displace the passive impulses onto the tutor and also to identify with the tutor. The complex anal erotism had to do with the patient's identification with his mother's pains, complaining, and diarrhea, and was based on the fantasy that the mother was made ill by what the father did to her. By having a bowel movement the patient identified with the woman having a child; the man giving him the enema represents a substitution in which the patient identified with the castrated mother. Thus the wish to be substituted for the mother, coupled with the terror at the castration required, is the crucial conflict of the case, according to Freud.

Recapitulating the sexual development of this patient, we see that it begins with a disturbance of the appetite in the oral phase of life. This is followed by urethral erotism in the scene with Grusha in which the patient identifies with his father. The seduction by his sister and the threat of castration by the nurse then caused a regression to an anal sadistic position of the libido. The anal sadistic impulses became converted to masochism and passivity and his naughty behavior attempts to entice a beating from the father. This is a very common clinical picture.

In the crucial wolf-dream, an anxiety phobia replaces the anal sadistic fantasies "in a single blow" due to castration anxiety and the repression, because of it, of the wish for a passive role. The object toward which there was a dangerous sexual aim (passive-feminine-homosexual) is replaced by a dangerous wolf. Freud considers this as the stage of the totemistic father surrogate. Simultaneously, there was a conversion, of the passive-feminine-homosexual repressed complex, to the bowel.

Higher ego mechanisms of defense were adopted later in the development of the third phase, an obsessional neurosis. Freud mentions the crucial importance of religion in helping the patient to go from a lower to a higher organization: we often see this process reflected in the development of adolescents. The patient identified with Christ and could now love his father (God) and so drain off the unconscious passive-feminine-homosexual libido. This is also a way of draining off his sadistic impulses through identification with Christ's masochism. Furthermore, the sublimation from the sensual to the spiritual lessened the intensity of the struggle and permitted intellectual advance, although the patient still suffered from a struggle with the obsessional solution.

In puberty the patient was able to maintain masculine genital behavior, but suffered difficulty in his relationships with women until the final breakdown after he developed gonorrhea.

There is some debate in the literature (Frosch 1967, Blum 1974, and Meissner 1977) as to whether or not the Wolf-Man suffered from a childhood *psychosis*, but it should be noted that although the patient identified with Christ he did not really believe that he *was* Christ. His active masculine aims were discouraged by the fear of castration, which led him to develop a passive-feminine-homosexual aim leading to a desire to have intercourse with the father. Because castration would set things right, however, there is thus both a fear of castration and a desire for castration. The repression of this conflict with the famous wolf dream leads to the wolf phobia.

Why was the wolf phobia replaced by an obsessional neurosis a few years later? Freud believed that the knowledge of the story of Christ gave the patient a chance to sublimate the predominant masochistic attitude toward his father, but also, as the patient grew older and his ego became stronger, this gradual shift clearly indicated the development of a strong internal self-regulating system or superego. At this point the ego has to struggle between unconscious homoerotic or hostile temptations on the one hand, and the threat of castration punishment meted out by the superego, on the other.

What makes this case so important and fascinating for *psychotherapists* is the crucial question of what really led to the excellent therapeutic results of the first four-year analysis, and also the fascinating subsequent history of the Wolf-Man. After analysis the patient remained at the level of relatively good adult functioning from 1914 to 1919, at which time the Bolshevik revolution in Russia stripped him of all his possessions and left him (at first) a penniless, dispossessed refugee. He was clearly in a demoralized state which presented itself as an obstinate "hysterical" constipation. Freud cleared this up upon analyzing him a second time, for another four months in 1919. Also remarkably he took up a collection for the Wolf-Man and repeated this collection every spring for six years so that his patient could pay his wife's hospital bills and take some holidays himself. At this point he was clearly "Professor Freud's famous patient," and his sense of narcissistic entitlement led this previously scrupulously honest man to conceal the fact that during the years that Freud was subsidizing him he received some valuable family jewels from Russia, which he hid from everyone. For about three of these years the patient again functioned very well; however, for the second three years, from 1923 to 1926, he began to develop hypochondriacal symptoms heralding his incipient fragmentation, brought on by the news of Freud's operation for malignancy in 1923.

This news clearly destroyed the patient's fantasy that Freud was the omnipotent parent; that old barometer of confidence in Freud, the Wolf-Man's constipation, soon reappeared, followed by hypochondriacal preoccupations about his teeth and his nose. In 1923 the patient became preoccupied with observing himself for long periods in the mirror. By the time his mother arrived from Russia to stay with him in 1923, the year of Freud's first surgery, the Wolf-Man was decompensating; by 1926 the Wolf-Man had developed what can only be described as a full-blown paranoid psychosis. At this point Freud referred him for further analysis to Dr. Ruth Mack Brunswick, who herself was analyzed by Freud, and who later became overwhelmed by her own inner problems and addicted to drugs, leading to her premature death (Roazen 1975). Brunswick's report, as well as a number of descriptions both by and about the Wolf-Man, are all contained in a volume edited by Gardiner (1968).

Brunswick had a special interest in the psychoses, and although she presents a case history rich with ingenious dream interpretations, the essence of her treatment consisted of an attack on the Wolf-Man's megalomanic delusions that he was a favorite of Freud's. She forced the patient to confront his rage about having been abandoned by Freud, not only through Freud's referral of the Wolf-Man to Brunswick, but as a consequence of the destruction, by Freud's illness, of the illusion of omnipotence required of an idealized parental imago. The unanalyzed passive-homoerotic or idealizing transference towards Freud had been kept intact under repression by displacing rage, first toward tailors and then other doctors and dentists and finally by the formation of a paranoid thought-system. It must be pointed out that Freud fostered a certain dependency in this patient not only later on, when he supported him financially, but during the initial treatment during which he functioned as a teacher, authority, and father figure. This comes out in the Wolf-Man's recollection of Freud (Gardiner 1968) and it is consistent with Freud's general attitude, as a Viennese physician, toward his patients.

This third period of treatment lasted five months, from October 1926 to February 1927, after which the Wolf-Man became relatively productive as a minor bureaucrat. Two years later he returned to Brunswick, exhibiting no trace of the psychosis; however, potency disturbances presented themselves in the course of "a sudden, violent, and repetitive love relation," and a somewhat "irregular" analysis over a period of several years occurred, which Brunswick described as revealing "hitherto forgotten memories all relating to the complicated attachment of the pre-schizophrenic girl [the patient's sister] and her small brother."

Brunswick points out that the loss of equilibrium attained after the first analysis was due to Freud's illness:

> The threatened death of a beloved person mobilizes all one's love. But the love of this patient for his father—represented by Freud—forms the greatest menace to his masculinity: satisfying it involves castration. To this danger the narcissism of the patient reacts with tremendous force: the love is partly repressed, partly converted into hate. This hate in turn generates the death-wish against the father. Thus Freud's illness, heightening the dangerous passive love of the patient, with consequent increase in the temptation to submit to castration, brings the hostility to a point where some new mechanism is needed to provide an outlet; and this is found in projection (Gardiner 1968, p. 305–6).

Brunswick believed that the use of a female analyst avoided this problem and indeed in subsequent years the Wolf-Man was cared for by a succession of female housekeepers, lived with his mother, and was further seen by the female analyst Muriel Gardiner. At the same time, his narcissistic needs were assuaged by his remarkable position in the psychoanalytic movement, a position which he maintained throughout his entire long life. The relationship with Gardiner included her sending him food packages after World War II and having his memoirs published. As he grew older he suffered from periods of depression and despair, but it is hard to label these neurotic since they were related to the vicissitudes of his real life and the aging process, as well as to the death of his mother when he was 66. Clearly, the combination of Freud's analysis and Brunswick's reanalysis, as well as his privileged position in the psychoanalytic movement and his relationship with a remarkable number of analysts and doctors who saw him on an irregular basis, enabled the Wolf-Man to lead a long and tolerably healthy life, in spite of European wars and social upheavals.

Not much is said about other significant deaths in the Wolf-Man's life. He was 19 when his sister Anna committed suicide by poison. At that time he was already ill with his neurosis and did suffer from a subsequent depression after the suicide. When he was 22, his father died and was buried next to his sister. It should be noted that at that time he wished to marry —but Freud insisted on a delay until his psychoanalysis was over. It was only shortly after his father's death that he went into analysis with Freud; "I had found in the person of Professor Freud a new father with whom I had an excellent relationship." After his analysis he gave Freud a gift and visited Freud with Therese, his prospective bride. He felt that he had gained Freud's approval of the marriage.

When the Wolf-Man was 54, in 1938, Therese committed suicide by turning on the gas, at the very time the Nazis occupied Vienna. In my opinion, the Wolf-Man's reaction is typical of a narcissist: "The question kept hammering away in my mind: how could Therese do this to me? And as she was the only stable structure in my changeable life, how could I, suddenly deprived of her, live on?" (Gardiner 1968, p. 122). At this point, Dr. Gardiner was instrumental in getting the Wolf-Man to Brunswick for further help. She and the Wolf-Man lived five minutes' walk from each other; Gardiner met him by chance on the street. Gardiner, according to Anna Freud, "befriended the Wolf-Man for more than thirty years, supported him in his depressions, dealt patiently with his misgivings, doubts, and uncertainties, encouraged him in his self-expressions and autobiographical revelations, and finally compiled and edited the disconnected sequences which were produced" (Gardiner 1968, p. xi).

We can only speculate about the uncanny capacity of the Wolf-Man to encourage the continuing interest of a vital segment of the early psychoanalytic community. Such a capacity for stirring up the interest of others is usually absent in schizophrenic people, but it is not rare in a polished and intelligent narcissistic personality. It seems clear to me that we are dealing with a borderline personality disorder or at best a narcissistic personality disorder in a man who never was really capable of forming a mature, loving relationship with anybody, but whose survival throughout a long life rested on an uncanny capacity to keep more successful individuals interested in him.

We see, therefore, that Freud's history of an infantile neurosis is more than just the story of a psychoanalysis; it demonstrates the incredible vicissitudes of the psychotherapy of a borderline personality disorder as well as the remarkable capacity of such patients (in contrast to schizophrenics) to find what they need to keep going in a variety of ways, either because of or in spite of a sequence of therapists. It also illustrates the difficulty of pinpointing the specific therapeutic factors in psychotherapeutic interaction, especially with patients suffering from more severe psychopathology.

Gedo and Goldberg (1973) present an outstanding discussion of the Wolf-Man; they use this complicated case to illustrate the various modes of functioning that a given patient can exhibit at different times during his or her life. The various therapies the Wolf-Man received represent the appropriate application of the techniques of unification, optimal disillusionment, and interpretations in psychoanalytic psychotherapy to a long-lived, amazing individual.

Study of this case also tells us a great deal about the physicianly vocation of Freud and the kind of human being that he was; in his reports he clearly soft-pedals the protective atmosphere which he afforded his patients, working with them in his own home—in order to emphasize the technical and truly novel aspects of psychoanalytic method. But it cannot be concluded from this case report that Freud's technical method was more important than his own behavior and the ambience he provided for every patient. Freud's remarkable courage should also be noted; how many psychotherapists today would consider beginning intensive outpatient psychotherapy with a patient who launched the first session by offering to have anal intercourse with them and to defecate on their heads?

Freud's paper "On Transformations of Instinct as Exemplified in Anal Erotism" (1917C;17:126ff) is a footnote to the case of the Wolf-Man. It underlines the basic principle that in the unconscious the concepts of feces, money, gift, baby, and penis are easily interchangeable. Freud emphasizes the repressed wish of a woman to possess a penis and equates this wish with her wish for a baby. The equation penis=feces=gift is illustrated in the interpretations of section VII of the case of the Wolf-Man. Freud reminds us that in the development of the libido in man, the phase of genital primacy is preceded by a "pregenital organization" in which sadism and anal erotism play the leading parts.

Freud was much impressed with the special, pleasurable fantasy reported by patients diagnosed as having hysteria or obsessional neuroses, a fantasy that he labeled "A Child Is Being Beaten" and he devoted a rather long paper to describing the subject (1919E;17:177ff). In these days of child pornography the shame and guilt that accompanies such a fantasy is perhaps less than in Freud's day, but this fantasy is common and does occur with a certain vagueness, just as described by Freud.

From his experience Freud believed that this fantasy begins in boys who have a masochistic wish to be beaten by the father; as in the case of the Wolf-Man, this wish represents a defense against homoerotic wishes for the father. This may shift into the fantasy of a boy being beaten by a woman (mother). In girls, three phases are involved. The first and originally conscious desire is the girl's nonsexual wish that her father would beat another child of whom the girl was jealous. This is followed in the unconscious by a change to the masochistic pleasurable fantasy of being beaten by the father; finally, in the conscious fantasy that emerges, a child is being beaten by a stranger. Thus the beating affords punishment to absolve the guilt for the incestuous wish and also provides a regressive substitute for it.

The fantasy, sometimes accompanied by masturbation, begins to appear even before school age. It is clearly connected to the genesis of perversions. The therapist will remember from our discussion of the Wolf-Man that before the onset of the phobia he developed a behavior disorder; its primary aim was to provoke the father into beating him. This represented a masochistic form of gratification that rested on same premises as the "child is being beaten" fantasy.

The sadistic aspect is important: thus in the first phase of the girl's beating-fantasy, the real phrase should be "my father is beating the child whom I hate." This in the second phase switches to the masochistic "I am being beaten by my father." A third phase is simply the vague conscious derivative: "a child is being beaten," while the patient looks on. The first phase gratifies the child's jealousy and represents the assurance that father loves only her. The second phase represents the girl's sense of guilt over her incestuous love for her father and includes a regressive substitute for that love. Freud claims that in the third phase, the fact that the child being beaten is inevitably a boy indicates that in girls there is a wish to identify with the boy and to possess a penis.

In this paper Freud expresses the hope that the origins of all perversions in childhood can be found through study of the vicissitudes of the Oedipus complex. He writes, "In this way the beating-fantasy and other analogous perverse fixations would also only be precipitates of the Oedipus complex, scars, so to say, left behind after the process has ended, just as the notorious 'sense of inferiority' corresponds to a narcissistic scar of the same sort" (p. 193). In this passage and in a further paragraph Freud recognizes the narcissistic aspect of the perversions.

He describes how repression transforms sadism into masochism in three ways: "It renders the consequences of the genital organization unconscious, it compels that organization itself to regress to the earlier sadistic-anal stage, and it transforms the sadism of this stage into masochism, which is passive and again in a certain sense narcissistic" (p. 194).

It is interesting to compare this statement with Kohut's (1971) discussion of phase-inappropriate disappointment in the idealized parent imago during the late preoedipal stage of development. The narcissistic blow consequent to this phase-inappropriate disappointment in the idealized parent imago during that particular phase leads to a resexualization of pregenital drives and derivatives, leading to the formation of perversions in fantasy, or as acted out, or both. On this theory, which of course postulates a separate line of development for narcissism, the appearance of the "child is being beaten" fantasy in the preschool child would in some cases be a signal of narcissistic injury of a phase-inappropriate magnitude in the late preoedipal stage of development, rather than a vicissitude of a pathological resolution of the Oedipus complex itself.

Before the wolf dream, in addition to behavior designed to provoke beating by the father, the Wolf-Man had fantasies in which boys were beaten, especially on the penis. That the administrator of the beating was a woman is not mentioned by Freud in his case report; this substitution has been previously explained as a distortion so that the fantasy may attain acceptance into the conscious mind. Thus in the final conscious fantasy the boy changes the sex of the person *doing the beating* so that a woman is beating a boy; the girl changes the sex of the person *being beaten* so that a man is beating a boy.

Freud's comment on "A Childhood Recollection" from Goethe's *Dichtung und Wahrheit* (1917B;17:146ff) indicates, as in the "child is being beaten" fantasy, the bitterness children feel about the expected or actual appearance of a rival sibling. In this case Goethe's memory of having thrown all his dishes, pots, and pans out the window is interpreted by Freud as a violent expression of the wish to get rid of the hated rival sister or brother. This behavior has a similar motivation to that of the beating-fantasy in girls, in the first phase of which *another* child is being beaten. Many other acts of naughtiness or destructiveness in children can be interpreted in the same way: as reflecting the wish to be the undisputed darling of the mother and father. Freud adds "If a man has been his mother's undisputed darling he retains throughout life the triumphant feeling, the confidence in success, which not seldom brings actual success along with it" (p. 156); one wonders if he is talking about Goethe or Freud. At any rate it is clear that the Wolf-Man's rivalry with his sister was intense, and an additional explanation of his naughty behavior certainly lies in this rivalry. The privileged status of being Professor Freud's famous patient represented the Wolf-Man's ultimate triumph over his sister.

What about Freud's heroic technique of setting a termination date for obsessional patients who are bringing a great deal of material to light in their analysis but changing nothing in their life? Subsequent clinical experience has indicated that this not a very successful technique; it really represents the therapist's feeling that no further change will occur as a consequence of routine intensive psychotherapy. As Freud puts it, the treatment itself has become a compulsion and the therapist is faced with the clinical judgment of whether breaking up this new compulsion will do the patient more harm than good.

This question can only be decided on the merits of the individual case, but it is most important to recognize the serious danger involved, such as a disintegration into psychosis. Kohut (1977) warns that the insistence on cognitive penetration within a fixed time limit, as Freud exercised in the case of the Wolf-Man, "overtaxed the resilience of the Wolf Man's psyche and caused it to crack." That is to say, an "endopsychic cleavage" occurs under such pressure, in which the really crucial basic material "sinks into the darkness and remains out of sight." The purpose of such a cleavage is "the creation of a self-protective shield vis-à-vis the possibility of an attack by overly radical psychic surgery, which, by opening up the area of his deepest depression, of his most severe lethargy, and his most profound rage and mistrust, could, in a single-mindedly zealous attempt to establish complete mental health, endanger psychological survival" (p. 177). Thus one of the most important lessons intensive psychotherapists can learn from the case of the Wolf-Man is the great danger to the patient from the narcissistic psychotherapist who applies unempathic pressure to a patient to produce material, give up symptoms, or "get well."

8

PARANOIA

The full title of Freud's basic work on the subject of paranoia is entitled "Psychoanalytic Notes on an Autobiographical Account of a Case of Paranoia (Dementia Paranoides)" (1911C;12:3–84). This work consists of an essay about an autobiographical book written by a patient who had partially recovered from a severe attack of paranoia. The *Memoirs* of Dr. jur. Schreber was published in a censored form in 1903. Seven years later Freud came across this autobiography and discussed it at length with his friend and colleague, Ferenczi. This led to Freud's highly controversial essay on Schreber's *Memoirs*, an essay which is still the subject of considerable debate today.

The problem of paranoia and the closely related condition of paranoid schizophrenia remains extremely important from the clinical point of view, since a substantial number of current patients present some variety of these conditions. The psychotherapist must be prepared to approach these conditions from some kind of hypotheses; the approach which Freud offers in the case of Schreber is an admittedly narrow one in which Freud claims that he is astonished to discover that in all cases of paranoid disorder "a defense against a homosexual wish was clearly recognizable at the very center of the conflict which underlay the disease, and that it was in an attempt to master an unconsciously reinforced current of homosexuality that they had all of them come to grief" (p. 59). As discussed later, his approach has been criticized by a number of authors, but because the problem of paranoia and paranoid schizophrenia is so clinically important it is most advisable for the practicing psychotherapist to immerse himself in the complicated details of Schreber's case to formulate for himself some understanding of the transformation we call paranoid. It is of course not necessary that we agree in all details with what Freud had to say, but I would advise considerable caution in brushing aside the carefully worked out theory that Freud held to throughout the remainder of his professional life.

We are indebted to Niederland (1974) for considerable background which was not available to Freud. Niederland's careful research into Schreber's background as well as the views of certain other authors about Schreber is mandatory reading for every psychotherapist. Schreber's father was a physician who became famous for his introduction of so-called *Schreber-gartens* and the *Schreber Vereine*, an association devoted to methodical cultivation of activities in fresh air: gymnastics, gardening, calisthenics, and sports. He was also a dominating, obsessive, cruel, and sadistic man with homicidal tendencies that surfaced at the time of his own breakdown.

Baumeyer (1956) points out that Schreber's mother was quite nervous and was subject to quick changes of mood. One of his three sisters, two years older than the patient, was a hysterical lady who died at the age of 104; a second was four years younger and unmarried, and the third was six years younger. One brother, three years older, developed general paresis and committed suicide in 1877, the year before Schreber married. This marriage was unhappy. Two miscarriages occurred before 1884; the marriage remained childless.

His first admission for mental illness, in 1884 at age 42, was for a period of six months, and followed his defeat as a candidate to the Reichstag. The symptoms were severe hypochondriasis and a suicide attempt. At that time he was treated by the famous neurologist Flechsig, described dramatically in chapter 12 of Niederland's book as a psychiatrist famous as a neuropathologist and neuroanatomist. Flechsig produced many publications filled with anatomical illustrations and various kinds of sections of neuroanatomical structures; a remarkable photograph of Dr. Flechsig in his office shows the doctor dwarfed by a picture of a giant brain on the wall behind him.

Schreber's second hospitalization, at age 51, was for eight years, during which he was suicidal and maintained he was a young girl frightened of indecent assault. This occurred after his appointment as *Senatspräsident* and was preceded by an important dream, which recurred three times, that his old nervous disorder of hypochondriasis had come back—this was nightmarish. He also experienced the hypnogogic fantasy "after all it really must be very nice to be a woman submitting to the act of copulation," as well as multiple nocturnal emissions.

This second breakdown occurred when his wife, who had been spending several hours a day with him, went away for a few days; it is interesting that his wife kept Flechsig's portrait on her table for years. The illness went through an acute and probably catatonic phase and then crystallized into a paranoia which became increasingly encapsulated so that he could be released with his delusions in 1902. The *Memoirs*, written in 1900 and meant to be a religious treatise, was published in 1903. His family promptly attempted to buy up all the copies available, but a few escaped and Freud obtained one of them.

Schreber's third hospital admission, in a catatonic state, took place five years later, six months after his mother died and just after his wife had a cerebral-vascular accident. He remained in the hospital in a deteriorated state until he died at 68 in the spring of 1911, only a short time before the publication of Freud's paper.

It should be noted that Schreber's father died at the age of 53 from an intestinal obstruction and that Schreber broke down at the age of 51, which was the same age at which his father suffered an accident in his gymnasium—a ladder fell on his head. The father never recovered his "old self" after that.

Although Schreber recovered only partially from his second hospitalization, he was able to function in a limited way as a lawyer, but he continued to have the delusion that he was a woman with female breasts. Schreber was an intelligent man who at one point in his career attained a prestigious legal and political position.

Freud's interpretation stresses the feminine passive longing for Flechsig, which was indicated, by an outburst of homosexual libido accompanied by nocturnal emissions after the absence of his wife, and also the frustration of childlessness. The presence of his wife before the outbreak of his second illness protected him from the outbreak of homosexual libido, and Freud believed that the nocturnal emissions were accompanied by homosexual fantasies.

This was then followed by the acute psychotic breakdown and a paranoid crystallization. From then on appeared a "contact" with a supernatural power that became Flechsig, but also involved his brother, his father, the sun, and God. The crucial delusion of the case was that he was going to be transformed into a woman by God, an act which had to precede his admission by God as a redeemer. Schreber protested that he did not want this to happen but that it had to occur before mankind could be saved; in this process Schreber becomes God's woman. The crucial point of the systematized delusions in the paranoid patient is to reconstruct the world so that his anxieties make sense and are alleviated.

Freud attempted to show the relationship between the delusion of being a woman and the delusion of being favored by God. The precipitating cause of the final illness was the patient's election to a high post and the unhappiness with his wife over the childless marriage. Freud asks, "Why did the homosexual desires burst out at this time?" He attributes such desires to Schreber's frustration with his wife and to the male climacteric—a crucial time for Schreber and other men—at the age of 51. The initial outbreak of homosexual desire began in the treatment with Flechsig; this was impossible for the patient to accept, with the result that the desire gradually transferred to God; Freud believed that the primary homosexual love object was Schreber's father.

Freud's famous formulation of the psychodynamics of paranoia, with which every psychotherapist must be acquainted, are clearly presented in the third section of Freud's essay. Briefly, these are (1) I do not love him; I hate him, because he persecutes me; (2) I do not love him; I love her (erotomania) because she loves me; (3) I do not love him; she loves him (delusions of infidelity); and (4) I do not love him; I do not love at all, I do not love anyone, I love only myself (megalomania). In the case of Schreber, megalomania is a compensation for the ungratified passive longings; the delusion formation makes gratification of the feminine homosexual wishes justifiable and inevitable, as God's will.

Basically the patient had developed a passive dependent need orientation which seemed to accelerate as he was called upon to be masculine and aggressive by his successes in professional life. Alternate possibilities are: (a) that the male climacteric brought him more femininity or homosexuality and less masculinity; (b) that the wish to have a baby and frustration at not being able to continue his family name ushered in the homosexual longings; (c) that homosexual longings especially represented the wish to replace his lost father and brother. Baumeyer (1956) emphasizes the difficulties consequent to Schreber's professional success and the implied call as *Senatspräsident* to be masculine and aggressive. Macalpine and Hunter (1955) stress Schreber's wish to have a baby and his frustration at not continuing the family name.

Interestingly enough, it is never made clear whether Flechsig took a maternal or paternal role or both. We know that one kind of homosexuality can be understood as an intense identification with the mother very early in life. Macalpine and Hunter (1955) do stress the confusion in Schreber's sexual identification, but they see the homosexuality itself as a defense against the desire to have a baby, which they see as the central wish-fantasy in the case. Baumeyer (1956) and also Niederland (1974) stress Schreber's need to repress his aggression in a situation that calls for aggressive behavior in a highly professional position; thus the outbreak of homosexual libido and the longing for a new father figure is understood as the fear of replacing the father. Niederland (1974) writes, "We cannot fail to see that Schreber in his social relations with Flechsig, as well as his delusions (God-sun-father) during his illness, succumbed to passive feminine fantasies only after having been put in the unbearable situation, before each outbreak, of assuming an active masculine role in real life, either by facing the father as the rebellious son, or by becoming a father figure himself" (p. 41).

In his essay Freud discusses rather briefly the relationship of paranoia to schizophrenia. He points out that in paranoia the liberated libido becomes attached to the ego and "is used for the aggrandizement of the ego." This concept is taken up in more detail at one point in his paper *On Narcissism* (1914C;14:86). Freud rejects the term schizophrenia as unfortunate because of the literal meaning of the word and prefers the word paraphrenia (attributed to Kraeplin)—a term which has not come into common use. He distinguishes between paraphrenia and the transference neuroses in that in paraphrenia the important step is the withdrawal of libido from object relations to investment in the ego. The investment of the ego with this excess libido produces the state of megalomania; a failure of this defense or psychic function gives rise to the hypochondriacal symptoms. Thus just as anxiety precedes the formation of the various neuroses, hypochondriasis precedes paraphrenia. "Further psychical working-over" can reduce the symptoms of hypochondriasis in paraphrenia, and of anxiety in the transference neuroses—a matter of great clinical importance.

Since paraphrenia usually brings about only a partial detachment of the libido from objects, it contains three groups of phenomena: (1) those phenomena representing what remains of a normal or neurotic state—the remains of the more-or-less normal prepsychotic personality; (2) those representing the morbid process—successful megalomania, or hypochondriasis, which is a symptom of the incompleteness of the megalomanic process; and (3) a restoration process in which the libido is once more attached to objects, but under distorted conditions that reduce the discomfort. Thus the hallucinations and delusions are an attempt at recovery, an attempt to recapture a relationship to the world.

Freud's distinction between paranoia and paraphrenia remained somewhat fuzzy (see footnote in Freud 1911C;12:76). The difficulty in the clinical distinction of these conditions is just as great today. Critics point out that Schreber's deviation was trans-sexuality rather than homosexuality and that his mental illness was schizophrenia and not paranoia. Numerous publications and a few formal investigations indicate that cases of paranoia often fail to show evidence of homosexual motivation either in their conscious or their unconscious productions. For example, Klein and Horowitz (1949) searched for homosexual content in the case records of a large number of hospitalized paranoid patients of both sexes. Even using a very wide definition of homosexuality including, besides erotic homosexual needs, feelings, and conflicts—the fears of being considered homosexual, fears of being or becoming homosexual, and fears of homosexual attack—they found such content in only one-fifth of the total group. The authors conclude that in many patients, the appearance of the fear of being homosexual was essentially an expression of failure, blows to pride, or general distrust of being an acceptable person.

Ovesey (1969) attempts to distinguish between homosexuality and pseudohomosexuality. He argues that anxiety about homosexuality has three motivational components. These are sexual—truly homosexual, seeking homosexual gratification as a goal—and dependency and power motives, nonsexual goals expressed through the use of the genitals. Anxiety about dependency and power-striving when expressed sexually are defined by Ovesey as pseudohomosexual. The famous equations of Freud then can be applied to either homosexual or pseudohomosexual strivings, since as far as the patient is concerned, all are experienced in the same way.

The critical question that each psychotherapist must answer is, given a case of developing paranoia: Is this specific case based on an outburst of homosexual libido, or on power or dependency problems appearing in the patient's mind in a genitalized or sexualized homosexual form? There simply is no agreement on this subject at the present time. My clinical experience is that in cases of paranoia one can always trace this development to the longing for the love of a man, in the case of males—and less easily, in the case of females, to the longing for the love of a female. Although Ovesey argues that the pseudohomosexual conflict develops in men who fail to meet successfully society's standard of masculine performance because of an inhibition of assertion, I am inclined to agree with Freud, especially with respect to men, "that what lies at the core of the conflict in cases of paranoia among males is a homosexual wishful phantasy of loving a man" (p. 62).

I further agree with Freud that schizophrenia has an important organic component whereas some paranoia does not; the confusion arises in the nosology when we experience a mixture of schizophrenic disorganization and paranoia. In those cases where the important genetic diathesis of schizophrenia is missing—the borderline patients—one often sees a mixture of paranoia and a whole variety of neurotic formations, further indicating that all of these are capable of taking place in the absence of the basic schizophrenic process. The psychotherapist who claims that he has not found evidence of homosexual longings in a paranoid patient must be very careful that he is not manifesting some countertransference need in which he does not permit himself to be aware of these powerful longings which, in the case of therapist and patient of the same sex, would undoubtedly also be aimed at the person of the therapist. The kinds of difficulties that homosexual patients can produce in therapists' countertransference are illustrated, for example, in *Why Psychotherapists Fail* (Chessick 1971), in the cases of Mr. H. and Mr. I. (pp. 111–114) and in the case quoted from Greenson (1967) that follows these cases.

Freud was aware of the opposition to his generalization about the basis of paranoia. In "A Case of Paranoia Running Counter to the Psychoanalytic Theory of the Disease" (1915F;14:262ff) he presents the interesting case brought to his attention by a lawyer who was asked by a young woman to protect her from the alleged molestations of a man. Although on the surface she seemed to be paranoid about the man and to be defending herself against love for a man by transforming the lover into a persecutor, meticulous and careful investigation by Freud revealed her homosexual attachment to an elderly lady boss for whom she worked and whom she described as like her mother. The case offers a clever warning of the danger of basing a hasty opinion of the dynamics of a patient on a superficial knowledge of the descriptive facts of the case!

Ovesey's (1969) contrasting views have great clinical importance. He explains, "The desire for dependency through the paternal love of a father-substitute is the most superficial form of the dependency fantasy. The same fantasy on a deeper unconscious level is integrated in a more primitive fashion through the equation *breast = penis*. The patient who resorts to this equation attempts to gratify his dependency needs through the oral or anal incorporation of the stronger man's penis" (pp. 62–63). On the other hand, "The power-driven male tries to dissipate his weakness in a compensatory fashion through a show of strength, and to this end he is continuously engaged in competition with other men. There is no discrimination about this competition; it is about anything and everything. Unfortunately, his conviction of inadequacy is so strong that he concedes defeat in advance. The result is a chronic pseudohomosexual anxiety" (pp. 57–58). Ovesey's main contribution is to point out that the patient can misinterpret his frightening power (with secret lack of confidence) and dependency strivings as feminine, or dream or conceive of them in homosexual genital terms. This then leads to anxiety about being a homosexual (pseudohomosexual anxiety) which can then lead to paranoid defenses. However, *the question of why the patient chooses genital expression of his power and dependency strivings remains unanswered in Ovesey's formulation.*

It should be noted that in Schreber's delusional system the world would have to be destroyed before it could be redeemed and restored by Schreber as God's woman. This idea of the end of the world, according to Freud, is a projection of the patient's sense of inner catastrophic alteration. Niederland (1974) writes, "The destruction of the world is the projection of this uncanny feeling of a devastating and pathological change within, caused by detachment of the libido from the representation of the external world (decathexis). The libido thus liberated is withdrawn into the self and is used for its aggrandizement (megalomania). This development is made possible by the paranoid's early fixation at the stage of narcissism to which he tends to regress" (p. 25). It is almost impossible to disagree with Niederland's conclusion that the *Memoirs* of Schreber represents his complex struggle for identification with his father as well as his battle against it (which would entail the loss of his autonomous self), a struggle that accompanies and intensifies his homosexual conflict as elucidated by Freud.

It should be emphasized that although repressed homosexuality is very important in the development of paranoia, hostility is also a significant etiologic element, especially since it is very much involved in the mechanism of projection, which of course is the central mechanism of paranoia. It is this hostility, and not so much their repressed homosexuality, that makes paranoid patients so extremely difficult to treat. It is often difficult to discern whether such hostility represents primitive oral destructive impulses toward the mother figure, or is a defensive hostility converting the possibility of love into the certainty of hate—or both. Regardless of origin, hostility forms the great barrier to the treatment of paranoia and is a continual threat to the therapeutic alliance.

9

AGGRESSION AND DESTRUCTION

Schur (1972) points out the remarkable change that occurred in Freud's attitude between *The Future of an Illusion* (1927C;21:3ff) and *Civilization and Its Discontents* (1930A;21:59ff). In *The Future of an Illusion* there is a sense of optimism and a hope that reason and the ego can overcome illusions, human weakness, and stupidity. *Civilization and Its Discontents* is marked by an undercurrent of deep pessimism. Schur speculates that this change reflects the milieu of the Western world around Freud at the time he wrote the book in 1929 at the age of 73. In fact, the original title of the latter monograph was "Unhappiness in Civilization." In this work Freud finds religion noxious and philosophy useless; art does have a beneficial effect by allowing an indirect gratification of the pleasure principle. Human life rests on a never-ending conflict between the attempt to obtain the freedom for personal gratification and the opposing demands of society. It is this inevitable conflict, so Freud maintained, that leads to the discontents and widespread neuroses and suffering of civilized men.

Culture has to call up every possible reinforcement to erect barriers against the aggressive instincts of men; this powerful, instinctually aggressive tendency is the main obstacle to culture. The characteristic way of dealing with human aggression is to internalize it into the superego and to direct the harsh aggressions against the ego, resulting in internal tension and a sense of guilt. Thus, in *Civilization and Its Discontents*, the role of outwardly directed aggression, even though postulated to be based on the death instinct, gains a central and major empahsis parallel to Freud's earlier emphasis on the sexual drive in the etiology of the neuroses. Furthermore, renunciation of outwardly directed aggression gives rise to conscience of a harsh nature, which then demands further renunciation. For Freud, the sense of guilt is the key problem in the evolution of civilization; the price of progress in civilization is paid in the forfeit of happiness in exchange for a heightened sense of guilt. Schur speculates that Freud's physical suffering from his cancer was also depleting his capacity to enjoy life.

In his later years Freud became increasingly concerned with the problem of aggression. As his great contemporary Einstein recognized in 1946, "The real problem is in the minds and hearts of men. It is easier to denature plutonium than to denature the evil spirit of man." Almost in desperation, Einstein (Freud 1933B;22:199–202) wrote a letter to Freud that remains one of the clearest statements of the problem ever written. Composed in 1932, it is usually entitled "Why War?". It states: "Thus I am led to my first axiom: the quest of international security involves the unconditional surrender by every nation, in a certain measure, of its liberty of action, its sovereignty that is to say, and it is clear beyond all doubt that no other road can lead to such security." Einstein then lists the factors that have led to the failure of all efforts to reach this goal. First, all governments seem to show a "political power-hunger," which of course is hostile to any limitation of national sovereignty. Second, a group of people now called the military-industrial complex encourages this political power-hunger: ". . . that small but determined group, active in every nation, composed of individuals who, indifferent to social considerations and restraints, regard warfare, the manufacture and sale of arms, simply as an occasion to advance their personal interests and enlarge their personal authority." However, focus on the military-industrial complex leads to more basic considerations. How is it possible for this small group to bend the will of the majority, who stand to lose and suffer by war, to the service of its ambitions? We see this happening again and again, even in the supposedly most advanced and civilized of nations.

This significant question cannot be answered, argues Einstein, simply by explaining that the military-industrial complex has control of the schools, of the press and communications media, and of the usual alliance of the churches, in all reactionary and warlike causes. Although these small groups have had amazing success in arousing wild and unbounded enthusiasm of men for killing and destruction on an increasingly massive scale as our technology improves; and although historical and rational knowledge indicates that the masses of men who want to kill so much stand inevitably to lose the most by wars that settle absolutely nothing—the situation clearly indicates a third factor at work. "Man has within him a lust for hatred and destruction," writes Einstein. He asks Freud, "Is it possible to control man's mental evolution so as to make him proof against the psychoses of hate and destructiveness?"

Einstein must have been disappointed in Freud's rather unexciting answer to his letter. This answer, in addition to an earlier paper (1915B;14:274ff), contains Freud's views on war. In the 1915 paper Freud states flatly that human aggressiveness as a primary need inevitably entails war. In fact, "Our unconscious will murder even for trifles." War is the vicarious expression sanctioned by the state, of this unconscious wish to murder. In the 1932 answer to Einstein he revises the view that war is inevitable and suggests that the answer lies in a kind of social engineering, a diversion of human aggressive impulses "to such an extent that they need not find expression in war." As Roazen (1968) points out, the search for a "moral equivalent" of war was also William James's (1967) solution to what he called "pugnacity."

Freud (1933B;22:203–215) also suggests that anything that encourages the growth of emotional ties between men must operate against war. Thus, whatever leads men to share important interests produces a community of feeling, an identification with the whole of humanity. Above all, whatever fosters the growth of civilization works at the same time against war. The reason for this is that the two most important psychological characteristics fostered by civilization are "a strengthening of the intellect, which is beginning to govern instinctual life, and an internalization of the aggressive impulses, with all its consequent advantages and perils" (pp. 214–215). Freud expresses his profound hope that the evolution of civilization and the reasoned dread of the consequences of war may put an end to the waging of war before mankind is destroyed. The slow progress of this procedure greatly worries him, and he cannot help but wish that an upper stratum of men with independent minds could be educated—perhaps like Plato's philosopher-kings—to give direction to the dependent masses. Thus, he presents what he admits is a utopian expectation that a community of men could develop "who had subordinated their instinctual life to the dictatorship of reason" (p. 213).

The basic axiom is that man contains in his personality a powerful drive toward hatred and total destructiveness. The best thorough psychoanalytic discussion of the aggressive drive is by Hartmann et al. (1949). We must face squarely the fact that the aim of the aggressive drives is "total destruction of objects, animate or inanimate, and that all attempts to be satisfied with less, with battle with or domination of the object, or with its disappearance imply restrictions of the original aims" (p. 18). The aims of aggression are modified by a simultaneous cathexis of the object with libido, by displacement of the aggression to other objects—"the problem of man in search of a target"—by restriction of the aims of aggressive drives, and by sublimation of aggressive energy, for example in the building of civilization. The authors point out how de-aggressivized psychic energy is a necessity for ego development and function, and that the capacity to neutralize large quantities of aggression is an important sign of ego strength. Clearly, both the self and others are endangered by instinctual aggression, and the capacity to form lasting relationships with others rests on the capacity to neutralize aggression.

As an example, Barrett (1958) gives Dostoyevsky credit for a remarkable portrayal of "the center of man's nature: contradiction, ambivalence, irrationality." Perhaps man is not the rational but the demoniacal animal. A rationalist who loses sight of the demoniacal cannot understand human beings." The concept of the demoniacal in man as dramatically presented by Dostoyevsky, Nietzsche, and others represents a crucial issue that must be solved if there is to be peace. It represents what Barrett calls a shadow that surrounds all human enlightenment.

Is human aggression a product of social training? Does it arise from frustration of narcissistic needs in infancy (Kohut), or from other sources of frustration that society constantly provides at all stages of life (Marx)? Is it an inherited evolutionary drive (Hartmann) developing over millions of years, or does it represent a death drive, present in all protoplasm, turned outward (Freud)? There is no agreement on these questions. It is apparent that the entire subject is in its scientific infancy. The need for research is overwhelming, not only on the subject of man's evolution and ethological factors, but in finding alternatives to violence. A series of twenty-one essays (Ng1968) includes disagreements on many aspects of the alternatives to violence, but emphasizes over and over again the need for research; the authors propose an enormous variety of hypotheses and ideas that are fertile for scientific study. Shaw (1978) presents a fine review of current thinking on man's aggression.

This demoniacal aspect of man can be approached in at least five ways, and all of them are valuable and important to understand if we are to deal with our proclivity for hatred and aggression: (1) evolution and ethology, (2) group psychology, (3) psychoanalysis, (4) rational, conscious psychology, and (5) existentialism. Many of the disagreements among adherents of these points of view are analogous to the blind men each feeling a different part of an elephant and disagreeing about what an elephant is like. All the approaches have a valid contribution to make, and therefore all must be reviewed here, to place Freud in perspective.

Evolution and ethology. The evolutionary and ethological viewpoint states that the evolution of man's mind has not kept pace with the development of his technological capacity. The most important protagonist of this viewpoint is Konrad Lorenz, but there are many others. Lorenz (1952, 1966) defines ethology as the comparative study of behavior. He conceives of behavior in all species, including humans, as essentially having evolved as equipment for survival and constituting at base certain innate patterns which are released or triggered by various appropriate stimuli. Lorenz follows the hydraulic model (Nisbett 1976) in his belief that the energies of these behaviors accumulate, and if no triggers for release are found in the environment the innate patterns will appear eventually anyway.

The first prehuman primates (for example, *Ramapithecus*) appeared in Africa and Asia in the Miocene geologic epoch—between twelve and thirty million years ago—in a fertile and abundant time. Over the harsher and drought-ridden Pliocene epoch—between two and ten million years ago—a variety of prehuman forms evolved from the variety of prehuman primates. Under the harsh conditions of the 10-million-year Pliocene, the prehuman (hominid) form became a carnivore: this period saw the basic making of man as we know him. Since the fossil record of the period is extremely poor because the dry conditions did not provide enough water for lime to turn bone into stone, our knowledge of this critical period in man's evolution is deficient, and interpretations are controversial (Leakey 1978).

From this distant and unimaginably long evolutionary past, three possibly instinctual forms of behavior—besides the obvious instinctual species-preserving drives for survival, care of the young, and sexual gratification—may or may not have been installed within us. The least controversial of these forms is known as imprinting, in which during a six-week to six-month optimal period in human infants there takes place a permanent identification of the parent object as a refuge in time of anxiety. This is well reviewed by Vaughan (1966). Disturbances such as being overwhelmed by anxiety during the critical imprinting period, or lacking a consistent mother figure, would obviously lead to profound and lasting damage to the entire personality structure; even, from my psychiatric experience, damage to the perceptual apparatus of the ego itself.

Another possible instinctual form of behavior is what Ardrey (1966) superficially calls the "territorial imperative," i.e., man's imperative to hold and defend territory, a force as strong as the "almighty forces" of sex or the maternal instinct or the will to survive. His evidence is a hodgepodge of debatable observations, and leads him to conclusions about modern countries that are not even remotely supportable.

However, Ardrey forces us to remember the importance of the 10 million years of formative influence of the harsh Pliocene environment, and emphasizes the major changes in man during that period, from a vegetative prehuman primate to a carnivorous hominid form that banded together for survival. Thus, the "nation" psychology, the tendency to form what Erikson (Evans 1967) calls "pseudo-species," is deep within us.

Lorenz (1966) turns to the more general subject of intraspecies aggression, which he sees as species-preserving in evolution, assuring balanced distribution of animals of the same species over the available environment, selection of the strongest by rival fights, and defense of the young. Thus, because it has species-preserving functions, intraspecies aggression has not been eliminated even in species requiring close social aggregation for survival. In order to permit social aggregation in the face of intraspecies aggression, certain inhibitor mechanisms obviously have to evolve, such as ritual and symbolic aggression and submission behavior. (The classic example of this, incorporating both aggression and territoriality, is the American football game.)

Furthermore, in those species capable of vicious destruction, such as the wolf, these inhibitory rituals and symbolic gestures—which literally stop murder at the last minute—are reliable and well developed; while in man, who in his natural state is not so endowed with murderous ability, such inhibitors to intraspecies aggression did not have to evolve. Man resembles not the wolf but the rat, for rats, exceptionally among carnivores, do sometimes kill other rats.

The paradox, of course, is that man has now become capable of instant, vicious destruction, thanks to science, and he lacks the automatic inhibitor mechanisms to stop spontaneously carrying out such destruction. Lorenz's solution, again similar to that proposed by Freud and James, is for us to develop our own set of ritualistic nonlethal and symbolic forms of aggression, such as the football game, using Kant's categorical imperative to form the stopping point. This solution, to say the least, seems utopian and loses sight of the enormous difficulty involved in making people behave rationally in their own best interests.

Koestler (1969) reviewed carefully the possibility that man is actually one of evolution's mistakes. Evidence indicates this to be probably true, although the views of all the writers in the field of evolution and ethology are far from established and have been attacked from many sides (Montague 1968). For example, Berkowitz (1969), besides opposing the work of Ardrey, Lorenz, and others as oversimplified, points out that Lorenz's solution of providing aggression in symbolic forms could actually lead to an increase, rather than a decrease, in man's aggressive drives. The current debate about whether the obsessive portrayal of violence on television increases violent acting-out is surely relevant to this possibility.

On the other hand, there is no doubt in Clark's (1966) conclusion to his *History of the Primates*:

> If Man has gained his intellectual dominance over his fellow creatures by concentrating his evolutionary energies on the development of his brain, it remains to be seen whether he can now maintain his position by contriving a method of living in orderly relations with members of his own species. If he fails to do so, he may yet follow the example of many other groups of animals which have achieved a temporary ascendancy by an exaggerated development of some particular structural mechanism. He may become extinct (p. 121).

Freud On Groups. The second appraoch to the problem, the study of group psychology, begins with Freud's (1921C;18:67ff) important treatise *Group Psychology and the Analysis of the Ego.* This work was inspired by the collapse of the Austro-Hungarian Empire at the end of 1918 and by the panic and distress that followed. It proposes the rudiments of a sociology that rejects the concept of an autonomous social instinct and is based instead on Freud's libido theory and his emerging notion of the ego ideal. In the latter sense it is a transitional work to be more completely realized in *The Ego and the Id* (1923B;19:3ff).

Freud starts by accepting and recapitulating the theories of LeBon and McDougall on the group mind, so far as these theories go. The behavior of groups is like that of a primitive savage or child; emotions become extraordinarily labile and intensified, and intellect is reduced. Freud writes: "A group is impulsive, changeable and irritable. It is led almost exclusively by the unconscious. . . . Though it may desire things passionately, yet this is never so for long, for it is incapable of perseverance. It has a sense of omnipotence. . . . A group is extraordinarily credulous and open to influence. . . . It goes directly to extremes; if a suspicion is expressed, it is instantly changed into an incontrovertible certainty; a trace of antipathy is turned into furious hatred" (pp. 77–78).

As far as leadership is concerned, exaggeration and repetition affect the group far more than logic; it respects force and demands strength or even violence from its heroes. LeBon believed that a group wants to be ruled and oppressed and to fear its masters, and Freud seems to be in agreement. They also believe that the group seeks a strong-willed leader who has a fanatical belief in his ideas.

It is clear, then, that groups tend always and naturally to behave toward each other as children or primitive savages; there is a collective lowering of intellectual ability of the group just by virtue of its being a group. This *barbarizing tendency*, as I shall call it (Freud calls it a regressive tendency), is inherent in the psychological nature of all groups, and it calls out continuously for a particular type of leader.

Freud then raises the question of how to procure for the group precisely those features that were characteristic of the individual and that are extinguished in him by the formation of the group. That is, how can we develop a *civilizing tendency* for the group and work against its inherent barbarizing tendency?

Unfortunately, Freud has little to say on this problem either in this treatise or elsewhere. He points out the importance of a group leader, but he is most interested in delineating the psychodynamics of group formation rather than addressing himself to the question of how to civilize a group and keep it civilized. Kris (1943) explains that this work ". . . was not written as a treatise in social psychology . . . (but) to clarify further the structural model of the personality which he was developing at the time."

Freud is more interested in the "primary group," one in which there has not been very much civilization, or organization, as McDougall terms it. In the primary group, each member has put the leader in the place of his ego-ideal and has consequently identified himself with the group in his ego. This leads to one of Freud's favorite concepts, that man is an individual creature in a horde led by a chief. He continues with a discussion of the so-called primal horde, an anthropological theory not widely accepted (discussed in chapter 19).

Group formation, argues Freud, is always a regressive phenomenon in itself, because it takes place through identification and thus is based on a more primitive level of human functioning than individual object-choice. Similarly, there is a tendency to pick the leader of the group not through intellectual or mature object-choice but through what would now be called a consensus process, described by LeBon according to Freud as follows: The leader need often only possess the typical qualities of the individuals in the group in a particularly clearly marked and pure form, and need only give an impression of greater force and of more freedom of libido; and in that case the need for a strong chief will often meet him half-way and invest in him a predominance to which he would otherwise have had no claim.

The grave implications of this material for a group that is trying to establish and maintain itself as a democracy should be apparent. Freud was aware of the danger, but did not address himself to these implications. Certainly he had nothing but scorn for America, which he considered a "gigantic mistake." In the American struggle, from a historical point of view, we can most clearly see the interplay of factors in the group that tend to barbarize and to civilize; and in America's choice of leaders and more especially its candidates for leadership over the years, one sees the emergence at various historical junctures of demagogues, mediocrities, and idealists very much in accordance with Freud's descriptions. Those who wish a full exposition of Freud's political and social thought are referred to Roazen (1968).

The first profound discussion of what to do about the inherent barbarity of groups appears in Machiavelli (Chessick 1969*a*). Machiavelli's thought is pertinent and contemporary, whether or not we agree with his conclusions. Furthermore, his approach, developed in the early part of the sixteenth century, has some amazing similiarities to that of Freud. His basic conclusion is that *nothing* can be done directly to combat the barbarizing tendency of the group. If a leader, or prince, as Machiavelli calls him, attempts to go against this tendency, he will be put out. Therefore the leader should play at all times to the barbarizing tendency in order to remain in power. Any changes in the group must be imposed by force by the leader, but since remaining in power is always the principle task of the leader, such changes must be within the context of the need for rule and oppression characteristic of the barbaric group.

One might be hard-pressed to quarrel directly with the cynical precepts of Machiavelli; in many ways his pessimistic description of men resembles that of Freud. Yet in both of their descriptions it is clear that something vital concerning the nature of man has been left out.

In his description of the mind of the individual man, Freud saw the ego as substantially immersed in defensive operations dealing with its "three harsh masters"—the id, the super-ego, and external reality. Hartmann (1958) and his coworkers proposed that the ego was capable of more than simply defensive operations; that a creative and autonomous "conflict-free sphere of the ego" also existed to a greater or lesser extent, depending on the individual, and therefore made possible a less pessimistic view of what the individual could create and accomplish.

Similarly, men are often wicked as individuals and usually wicked in groups, but that is not the whole story. 'Cannot the group mind also have a "conflict-free sphere" that varies from group to group depending on (1) the inborn autonomous capacities of the individuals in the groups, and (2) the amount of internal and external stress that ties up the group's capacities?

If so, we should have to speak to two kinds of states or political groups. The first of these, adequately described by Machiavelli and Freud, is immersed in defensive operations due to internal or external stress and has little capacity for autonomous function or for displaying civilized behavior. Such a group would tend to cry out for a leader who would reflect its mediocrity at best and oppress it at worst; the leader would then simply perpetuate the existing state of affairs and be utterly unable to civilize the group even if he should want to. Unfortunately, this is the state of most nations in the world today.

On the other hand, a second type of group is possible, which contains considerable potential to be civilized. Perhaps the most common example of such a group is the thirteen original American colonies, which saw its leader voluntarily renounce being crowned a king, and the formation of the Constitution of the United States. Since a group that has temporarily overcome its inherent barbarizing tendencies is clearly possible, the crucial question is how such a group could come to be *and how it could maintain itself*.

A tyrannical, mediocre, or cynical leader also tends to barbarize the group, using the inherent barbarizing tendency for his own ends. The leader's approach to human nature seems to be a vital factor: as Freud recognized, he can temporarily bring out the best or the worst in the group; the more powerful he is, the more this is true. Shaw's play *Caesar and*

Cleopatra portrayed this with deadly accuracy even before World War I. Shaw's Caesar is in conflict with his mediocre advisors, who justify by sanctimonious arguments their wish to destroy those who stand in their way.

Galbraith (1967) speaks of the need for an "emancipation" from the "monolithic" goals of the new industrial state—the production of goods and incomes—to prevent our lives from being completely at the service of these barbaric goals. The vehicle of emancipation is to be the scientific and academic community, who are obligated to scrutinize continually these goals with "skepticism which insures that there will be systematic questioning of the beliefs impressed by the industrial system." Galbraith insists that such scrutiny of images or false goals impressed on us by the "technostructure" is the obligation of the scientific community, and, he declares, "nothing in our time is more important."

Recent Psychoanalytic Contributions. Alexander (1951) straddles the second and third approaches to the problem, group psychology and psychoanalysis, in his lengthy discussion of the psychological aspects of war and peace. He sees the giving up of nationalism as an "advance in the extension of unselfishness," a further step analogous to such past historical steps as in primitive times the brother's renunciation of violence against the father so that a clan could form. As the clan was the great obstacle to the formation of a nation, so the nation is the great obstacle to the formation of a world community. Such renunciation of selfish interest always involves a conflict.

Alexander's answer to Einstein is that one of the two superpowers will have to conquer by force most of the smaller countries and become the "point of crystallization" of a world community; the rest of the countries will then gravitate toward it. This is a rather disconcerting idea, since even small wars are becoming increasingly dangerous. What guarantee do we have that when one of the two superpowers sees its hegemony falling apart, it may not in desperation touch off the final war? We have no guarantee, but that does not invalidate Alexander's theory; for it is not inconceivable that world government will come about not by reasonable agreement but by world conquest by one power. Such an event is technologically much more feasible than it was in the days of Alexander the Great or Caesar. But what a horrible cost in human carnage this will take! If Alexander is correct, however, this is a stage in evolution, and nature traditionally has been indifferent to massive slaughter as evolution proceeds, as Russell (1962) points out.

McNeill (1964) comes independently as a historian to a similarly pessimistic view. It is quite instructive that his "apocalyptic fears" in the first edition of the book *Past and Future*, written in 1952, had to be revised for its second edition, published in 1954; the author of the encyclopedic *The Rise of the West* (1963) has to conclude that there is still hope for a peaceful solution of these problems. One statement of McNeill's remains impossible to challenge: "Human irrationality is as real and powerful as ever. We face our contemporary difficulties with a psychological nature little if at all different from that with which men have faced the world since the beginning of history" (1964, p. 68).

Turning more directly to the psychoanalytic approach, not much has been added since Freud's emphasis on the aggressive instinct in man, although many question whether such an "instinct" exists. An important step forward has come from our psychoanalytical understanding of the psychoses, especially paranoia (also see chapter 8). Just how murderous and brutal our aggressive proclivities are has been elucidated by clinical study and historical research. Paranoia is now understood as an attempt to deal with murderous rage by attributing the rage and hatred to others rather than oneself. A far deeper understanding of paranoid projection and its roots has been developed, but this is not of as great a significance to the present discussion as is the recognition that we all contain latent psychosis, and that the proclivity to brutality and paranoid projection is constantly present in the unconscious of everyone.

The psychoanalytic point of view is summed up by Storr (1968), beginning with a crucial quotation from the psychoanalyst Winnicott: "If society is in danger, it is not because of man's aggressiveness, but because of the repression of personal aggressiveness in individuals." Storr continues, "Control of the destructive aspects of hostility between human beings can be approached from two different, yet complementary angles. One is to consider in what way it is possible to reduce the paranoid element in hostility, that is, to prevent aggression from turning into hate. The other is to see how to encourage the expression of the more positive aspects of the aggressive drive" (p. 109).

A text edited by Bychowski (1969) contains psychoanalytic thinking on the "evil in man." Bychowski (as well as the present author) has been interested in borderline types of patients for many years, and concerned with what are technically known as "malevolent introjects." The point is that all hatred and aggression developed during infancy in man is not instinctual. Some arises from infantile deprivation and some from the introjection of the hatred of the parents. These aspects of the hatred and paranoia of man are amenable to medical treatment, and are therefore extremely important to understand. Cycles of projection and reintrojection of rage and hatred may lead to a progressive self-perpetuating buildup of aggression (Kernberg 1976).

The most recent contribution is from the work of Kohut (1972, 1977) emphasizing the phenomenon of narcissistic rage—the rage generated when narcissistic injuries, or blows to one's pride or self-esteem have been suffered. Whereas Freud thought that the untamed aggressive drive counteracts the rational attempt to achieve reasonable compromises, Kohut believes that it is not the drive-nature of man that is the major problem. In fact he believes the original drive in infancy is assertive in nature, and changes to hate and aggression only as a consequence of phase-inappropriate disappointments in empathic soothing. He prefers to focus on narcissistic aspirations and the subsequent fury at the thwarting of hidden grandiosity which produces a deadly, implacable rage that consumes the individual with a need for revenge, regardless of the personal cost. This is a relatively new approach and will surely be the subject of further investigation.

Durkin and Bowlby (1968) outline certain aspects of aggression peculiar to humans. The first of these is called *animism*, the human tendency to attribute all events to somebody or some god's will. Evil is often attributed to minority groups or neighbors—the bad guys—who should then be destroyed. Secondly, humans tend readily to displace and project their aggression, as a function of human defense mechanisms. This leads to otherwise apparently senseless destruction and war. Notice that generalizations from animal studies are not sufficient to explain these peculiarly human phenomena.

The rational approach of Bertrand Russell. The greatest hope for reducing man's proclivity to hatred and paranoia comes not only from medical treatment but from the amelioration of social conditions. This leads us to the fourth or rational, conscious approach to the problem, perhaps first emphasized by Marx and Engels.

Russell views the capacity to endure a more-or-less monotonous life as an important springboard to success, and a trait that must be developed in childhood. He sees the desire for superficial excitement, if tolerated by parents, as leading to a passive, drugged state of mind. Developing without too many distractions and dissipations—that is, a childhood with regularity and opportunity for true leisure—permits reflection on and adherence to distant achievement rather than preoccupation with immediate pleasure. Psychotherapists speak of this as "ego-span." As so-called free time increases, the "love of excitement" (Russell 1951, 1962) in our culture has become a serious problem, to the point where excitement-seeking occupations have become a cornerstone of our economy; it has become almost unpatriotic, for example, to admit that one is ignorant of the current TV shows and personalities in the excitement–entertainment world (see also Lasch 1978).

One factor Russell does not mention has impressed itself on me from psychiatric practice—the disillusionment process of middle age. Middle-aged men make wars for young men to fight. What is the meaning of this?

The tight, machine-like quality of modern society and modern communication makes it impossible for most people to stay effectively out of the ruts of middle age. They become swept up by the drive toward material acquisition, envy, and routine; and as middle age descends they become dimly aware that it has not all been worthwhile. This leads to frustration, anger, and the classic psychiatric syndrome of middle-age depression. The paunchy senator insisting on the production of more armaments is related to the depressed middle-aged man who wishes he were young and virile again and is in a rage because he has had his turn.

Russell believes that the causes of malevolence in men are "partly social, partly physiological." Because of the "haunting fear of ruin" that most people have, anything "that increases the general security is likely to diminish cruelty." Obviously general security cannot be achieved by making one portion of mankind secure at the expense of another, since this only increases the dominant group's fear that the oppressed will rebel.

Russell hopes to increase courage through education—courage in facing poverty, courage in facing decision, courage in facing the hostility of one's own herd and above all the courage to think calmly and rationally in the face of danger, and to control the impulse of panic fear or panic rage. Human malevolence will be reduced if we can improve the social, physical, and medical conditions of human life, essentially through applied science. Russell feels that this reduction in malevolence will eventually come about "when men have acquired the same domination over their own passions that they already have over the physical forces of the external world."

Existential anxiety. It is most important to be aware of the problem of "existential anxiety," a factor to consider both in explaining the propensity of middle-aged men to create wars and eagerness of the masses to go to war. I have discussed the technical aspects of existential anxiety in a book (Chessick 1969).

Barrett (1958) reminds us of the concept "resentment," which builds up as society becomes increasingly organized and bureaucratized; on the edge of such a society pile up the "underground" men of Dostoyevsky and the "pale criminals" of Nietzsche. This resentment, says Barrett, becomes a "powerful and sometimes unaccountable motive in man."

Our time has seen the "encounter with nothingness." This has been brought about by (1) the decline of religion and belief in God and in an eternal moral order; (2) the collectivization of the state backed by a brutal police and based on the creation of either artificial consumer needs or dogmatic mythologies with subsequent depersonalization of the individual; and (3) the advance of science, which has destroyed all sense of certitude in nature and reduced our conception of our role in the universe to an irrelevant minimum. Nietzsche has been recognized as the original spokesman for the dangerous consequences of the first of these factors, Jaspers (1957) for the second, and Kierkegaard (1946) for the third.

There is a variety of solutions to what Kaufmann (1957) calls the "existentialist motifs." These motifs are the quest for an authentic existence and scorn of the inauthentic, the problem of how to meet death, and the experience of time, which brings us nearer to death. Some religious existentialists have recommended a "leap" into traditional religious faith, for example. Others have stressed the return by each individual man to his freedom of choice to make his life authentic. For example, Jaspers (1957) writes: "In the world *man* alone is the reality which is accessible to me. Here is presence, nearness, fullness, life. Man is the place at which and through which everything that is real exists for us at all. To fail to be human would mean to slip into nothingness. What man is and can become is a fundamental question for man."

Jung (1933) recognized that a yearning for life to make sense and for a way to face our impending death is present in us all, especially as we become older. Erikson (1959) argues that one will have either "ego integrity" or "despair" in the mature years of life, depending on what has gone before. Maturity, or wisdom, as Erikson calls it, can be in a sense thought of as the capacity to face calmly our own death.

These subjects are obviously extremely important and of intense interest to us all. Kierkegaard (1954) points out that all men are in despair, and that three categories of solution have been found: the religious, the unsuccessful, and the demoniăcal. There is considerable psychological insight here, especially considering that he was writing in 1849. It is the "demoniacal" solution to existential anxiety—our anxiety over the irrelevance and brevity of our lives—that is of interest in the present context. Psychiatrists today speak of a counterphobic reaction as a common type of defense against anxiety. In such a defense the person wildly plunges into the extreme situation that he fears the most. For example, a teen-ager struggling with unresolved dependent feelings may quickly plunge into a premature marriage to "prove" his masculinity and independence, or may run away and join the armed services, which "makes a man" out of you.

There are of course other kinds of demoniacal solutions, some bordering on insanity, such as the wild personal inner turmoil of Nietzsche and of the poets Rilke and Hölderlin—but what interests us most for this discussion is the counterphobic solution to existential anxiety. This is the desire to place oneself in a situation where death is likely and to "cheat death."

There is a great need for cooperative exploration by psychologists, psychiatrists, and philosophers into the notion of a demoniacal and counterphobic solution to existential anxiety. Such solutions may represent an important factor in the propensity of middle-aged men to make wars and the enthusiasm of masses of people to follow them into war. Hitler's Germany certainly demonstrated how the demoniacal and the religious solutions could be cleverly combined to produce a pagan religion based on "racial purity" and the making of war. Nationalism is a regressive scourge, and our unwillingness to give it up represents an immaturity in us that must be studied and eradicated. Toynbee (1969) writes: "The quest for alternatives to violence ought to be given the first place on mankind's crowded current agenda. This item should come first because it is the most urgent of all and is also the most difficult."

> Clinging to Europe's farthest edge, the prisoners could see the fatal shores of Troy across the straits where the most famous, most foolish, most grievous war of myth or history, the archetype of human bellicosity, had been played out. Nothing mean nor great, sorrowful, heroic nor absurd had been missing from that ten years' catalogue of woe. Agamemnon had sacrificed a daughter for a wind to fill his sails, Cassandra had warned her city and was not believed, Helen regretted in bitterness her fatal elopement, Achilles, to vent rage for the death of his friend, seven times dragged dead Hector through the dust at his chariot wheels. When the combatants offered each other peace, the gods whispered lies and played tricks until they quarreled and fought again. Troy fell and flames consumed it, and from that prodigious ruin Agamemnon went home to be betrayed and murdered. Since then, through some 2,500 years, how much had changed?
>
> B. Tuchman, *A Distant Mirror: The Calamitous 14th Century*
> (Tuchman 1978, pp. 565–6)

10

SPECIAL CLINICAL PROBLEMS

Love. In 1918 Freud brought together three of his earlier papers under the title of "Contributions to the Psychology of Love" (Freud 1910H;11:164–176, 1912D;11:178–190, 1918A;11:192–208). The first of these is very well known and deals with a special type of object-choice made by men in which the love object must be a woman to whom another man can claim the right of possession, who is in some way or other of sexually questionable repute, and which leads to jealousy on the part of the lover. A long series of passionate attachments to women of this type is formed and pursued with compulsive intensity; such attachments especially involve the urge to rescue the woman loved. The psychodynamics of this syndrome are traced to the infantile sexual conflicts.

In current psychotherapeutic practice the type of problems described in the second and third papers—impotence and frigidity—are much more common and, in spite of the exaggerated claims of behavior therapists and sex therapists, such patients continue to present themselves in the hope of relief through intensive psychotherapy, often after having tried numerous simpler and briefer techniques to no avail. The second paper has not received sufficient attention from clinicians, which is unfortunate because Freud points out how aware the clinician must be in uncovering situations of *relative* impotence. Patients will freely complain if they have a serious problem with sexual impotence and in fact this is often a presenting complaint in the desire for psychotherapy. However, patients with a relative degree of impotence do not volunteer this information or may even be unaware that a problem exists—they push the issue into the twilight of the preconscious.

In the clinical paper (1912D;11:178–190), Freud points out that a completely normal attitude in love requires a combination of what he calls the *affectionate* and the *sensual* currents. The affectionate current, which always carries with it contributions from the sexual instincts, refers to the child's primary object choice; these affectionate fixations of the child are joined at the age of puberty by the powerful sensual current which has a clear and primary sexual aim. The task of puberty is to pass away from objects that are prohibited by the barrier of incest and which are therefore unsuitable in reality, and to find a way to other extraneous objects with which a real sexual life may be carried on. "These new objects will still be chosen on the model (imago) of the infantile ones, but in the course of time they will attract to themselves the affection that was tied to the earlier ones" (p. 181).

Obviously, in the case of infantile sexual conflicts or fixations, the fusion of the affectionate and sensual currents cannot take place. In the masturbation fantasies of the patient, part of the sensual current—or all of it—may be discharged in the state of fantasy and connected in the usual disguised fashion to the original infantile sexual objects. The genital sexual activity of such people is impaired and, as Freud writes, "shows the clearest signs, however, that it has not the whole psychical driving force of the instinct behind it. It is capricious, easily disturbed, often not properly carried out, and not accompanied by much pleasure" (p. 182). These unfortunate individuals are in the paradoxical position of not being able to desire where they love and not being able to love where they desire.

Freud thinks that the very process of civilization and education interferes with the fusing of the currents of affection and sensuality. Thus a man is "assured of complete sexual pleasure only when he can devote himself unreservedly to obtaining satisfaction, which with his well-brought-up wife, for instance, he does not dare to do" (p. 185). Thus the man can achieve only full gratification of sexual activity either in masturbation fantasies or with a debased sexual object toward which he feels free to allow "the entrance of perverse components into his sexual aims," which he does not venture to satisfy with a woman he respects.

Freud does *not* draw the conclusion from this that total sexual unrestricted freedom on the part of both sexes—the so-called sexual revolution—will solve the problem. He insists that an obstacle is required in order to heighten the libido; and he points out that "where natural resistances to satisfaction have not been sufficient men have at all times erected conventional ones so as to be able to enjoy love" (p. 187). He tries to explain this on the basis of the complex developmental vicissitudes and the many components of the sexual instincts. Rather than advocating sexual revolution Freud rather pessimistically concludes that the cost of civilization will inevitably have to be a certain dampening of sexual enjoyment.

For the clinician the important point is that a careful exploration of the details of the patient's sex life and fantasy life can serve as a map of his or her affectionate and sensual currents, and a guideline to conflictual and fixation points. This is true even in patients who do not present sexual complaints; the psychoanalytically informed psychotherapist always takes a very careful and detailed history of all aspects of sexuality *when the patient is comfortable enough to talk freely.* A preliminary phase of establishing a relationship may be necessary before this is possible, especially with those patients who deny any sort of sexual difficulty. If the initial phase of psychotherapy has been successful this material usually presents by itself at the opportune time, for somewhere in the patient's preconscious mind is the realization that not all is as successful as he or she would like to think.

The third paper (Freud 1918A;11:192–208) can be thought of as an appendage to Freud's *Totem and Taboo* (1912X;13:1ff). From the clinician's point of view its importance lies in Freud's emphasis on the hostile element that in many cases underlies frigidity. Freud tries to explain this hostility on the basis of the fact that the man who deflowers the woman is not the longed-for father, but a substitute. Often this leads to disappointment on the wedding night and the requirement of "quite a long time and frequent repetition of the sexual act before she too begins to find satisfaction in it" (p. 201).

Freud describes a spectrum or "unbroken series," from cases of mere initial frigidity which—sometimes with the help of sex therapy—can be overcome—"up to the cheerless phenomenon of permanent and obstinate frigidity which no tender efforts on the part of the husband can overcome" (p. 201). These latter cases are very important in the practice of intensive psychotherapy and often involve, in my experience, not only infantile sexual conflicts and fixations but also serious narcissistic difficulties. The importance of defloration has changed in our day, with its early and widespread sexual activity among teen-age girls, and cultural attitudes toward the whole subject are markedly different than in Freud's time. Still, Freud was right when he said, "We may sum up by saying that a woman's *immature sexuality* is discharged on to the man who first makes her acquainted with the sexual act" (p. 206). The vicissitudes of this immature sexuality can take many forms, from the repetitive adolescent sexual acting-out, to a woman shifting her psychological attitude toward her husband during the course of a long marriage when she "discovers" in middle age that the object for the discharge of her immature sexuality is not the same object that is suitable for mature sexual relations. I believe this to be an important factor in our time of a higher incidence of divorces among people who were apparently satisfactorily married.

Freud feels that in an uncommonly large number of cases the woman remains frigid and unhappy in the first marriage and after a divorce and remarriage she is able to become a tender wife to her second husband. "The archaic reaction has, so to speak, exhausted itself on the first object." I am not convinced from clinical experience that an uncommonly large number of second marriages work out better than the first. The notion of an archaic reaction exhausting itself in practice however, finally allowing the sensual and affectionate currents to come together, could form an important explanation in the success of the sex therapies. In cases seen for intensive psychotherapy however, the archaic reaction does not disappear in practice but must be worked through in the transference. The danger always persists that after this archaic reaction is worked through, the woman's choice of object will change and the marriage will dissolve. The compassionate psychotherapist keeps in mind the agonies and anxieties of the husband during such a psychotherapy; if the need arises, he often must feel called upon to send the husband for psychological help, and he should explore with the woman from time to time the reaction that she notices in her husband under the influence of her increasing maturity. Thus the maturation of his wife may represent a serious psychological blow and a profound loss for the husband, and this may lead to many complications.

Visual Disturbances. Freud's brief paper on psychogenic disturbance of vision (1910I;11:210–218) is an important clinical gem. He clearly delineates those cases of visual disturbances in which, so to speak, the ego throws away the baby with the bath, from other forms of disturbance of vision. In the former cases, which are a manifestation of hysteria and not very common today, looking becomes invested within intense erotic content and the prohibition not to look as well as the punishment for the wish to look results in a visual disturbance.

Freud carefully explains that "Psychoanalysts never forget that the mental is based on the organic, although their work can only carry them as far as this basis and not beyond it. Thus psychoanalysis is ready to admit, and indeed to postulate, that not all disturbances of vision need be psychogenic, like those that are evoked by the repression of erotic scoptophilia" (p. 217). I have illustrated elsewhere (Chessick 1972) the extreme complexity of psychosomatic disturbances of vision. I describe the psychotherapy of a borderline patient during which the patient developed angiospastic retinopathy and indicated how careful the therapist must be in dismissing any visual disturbance complaint as "hysterical blindness." The appearance of any visual disturbances in psychotherapy should call for immediate ophthalmologic examination, for serious and permanent damage to the organ may occur if these cases are denied proper medical treatment. This is true regardless of how clear the psychodynamics involved seem to be, for we must always remember that mental phenomena are ultimately based on physical ones. *All organic symptomatology arising in psychotherapy must be approached by a combination of vigorous medical investigation and treatment as well as psychotherapeutic process.*

Depression. Freud's final paper in the series on metapsychology,

"Mourning and Melancholia" (1917E;14:239ff), sets forth a number of ideas and implications that are still being followed and investigated by his followers. The two most important lines of investigation are in the field of depression and in the field of narcissism; the final paper may be considered an extension of Freud's paper "On Narcissism" (1914C;14:69ff). The paper begins with a caveat sometimes overlooked by critics of Freud—that depression or melancholia "whose definition fluctuates even in descriptive psychiatry, takes on various clinical forms the grouping together of which into a single unity does not seem to be established with certainty; and some of these forms suggest somatic rather than psychogenic affections" (p. 243). He thus drops all claim to general validity for his statements about melancholia and accepts the fact he may be speaking only of a small group within what might be called the group of melancholias.

Freud offers a general clinical distinction between mourning and melancholia based on the fact that the features are the same except for the profound disturbance of self-esteem which is characteristic of melancholia and absent in mourning. Since mourning is a reaction to the loss of a loved person, Freud suspects that a similar kind of influence may be at work in the production of melancholia if there is a pathological predisposition, and he sets out to investigate this pathological predisposition.

Beginning with Freud, Goldberg (1975) presents an excellent review of the history of psychoanalytic concepts of depression, and he points out that certain key concepts seem to occur over and over. These are (1) the persistent connection of depression with the mother–child unit in the oral phase of development; (2) narcissistic issues are always raised in the description of object relations of the depressed patient, centering around identification and the regulation of self-esteem; and (3) a regular association of depression with aggression or hostility, superego, and resultant guilt.

"Mourning and Melancholia" would get high marks as a philosophical paper and it represents in essence Freud reasoning out loud on the subject. The cornerstone of his reasoning is the clinical impression that the various self-accusations of the melancholic usually fit someone whom the patient loves, or has loved, or should love. Thus Freud considers the key to the clinical picture the perception that the self-reproaches are reproaches against a loved object which have been shifted away from the object onto the patient's own ego. He adds that in both obsessive compulsive disorders and melancholia such patients succeed by the circuitous path of self-punishment "in taking revenge on the original object and in tormenting their loved one through their illness, having resorted to it in order to avoid the need to express their hostility to him openly" (p. 251). He mentions that the person who precipitated the patient's emotional disorder is usually to be found in the patient's immediate environment—clinicians take note!

This reasoning led to many later psychoanalytic investigations of the psychodynamics of depression and also led Freud to the issue of narcissistic object choice and narcissism. Goldberg (1975) underlines the definition of narcissism as psychologic investment in the self and points out that

> The narcissistic object is one that either is like the self (looks like the self) or is an extension of the self (is experienced as a part of the self). Thus the narcissistic object can be separate from *or* a functional part of the self. The "regression of object cathexis to narcissism" indicates an increase of feeling or interest in the self: what we would call a heightened self-centeredness. This follows upon object loss and may result in the object being internalized. Therefore, the lost object can be replaced by another one or replaced through an identification. Depending on how such a loss is handled, one may experience depression or merely a shift in object interest (p. 127).

There is a fuzziness of the concepts of internalization, identification, and introjection, a confusion which tends to creep into the literature even today. I would suggest that we reserve the term "introjection" for a massive internalization of the object—setting up, so to speak, a massive representation of the object in the ego; "identification" could be used to represent an internalization of parts or selective aspects of the object and could represent a relatively later mechanism of defense typical in adolescence; "internalization" could be used to represent either of the above. Furthermore, Kohut's (1971) notion of transmuting microinternalizations, where aspects of the soothing function of the mother are internalized and form an important part of the ego structure and the self-regulating systems, is very important. Freud did not make these distinctions. He usually used the term "identification" for all of the above and occasionally used the term "introjection," by which he generally meant a massive internalization. Later authors gave to introjection the cannibalistic or incorporative aspect of the oral phase. Although Freud does mention in this paper a cannibalistic phase to libidinal development, more emphasis on this aspect of internalization is found in the work of his follower Karl Abraham (1954). The basic principle is that melancholia is a pathological state "involving narcissistic blows to the ego experienced as losses and involving more wholesale or traumatic internalization of the offending object" (Goldberg 1975, p. 128). As Freud points out, the predisposition to fall ill of melancholia then lies in the predominance of the narcissistic type of object choice in the patient's psychic functioning.

Jealousy. One of the most common clinical presenting complaints of patients is that of jealousy, discussed by Freud in "Some Neurotic Mechanisms in Jealousy, Paranoia, and Homosexuality" (1922;18:222ff), a paper which remains a basic classic on the subject. Freud described three layers or grades of jealousy: competitive, projected, and delusional. The practicing psychotherapist is often called upon to decide which layer or grade of jealousy he is dealing with and in addition, to determine—when several layers are present—which is closer to the patient's consciousness and what is repressed.

Normal jealousy is essentially *competitive* and occurs when a successful rival has inflicted a narcissistic wound and a loved object is lost. The jealousy of the second layer, *projected* jealousy, rests on the fact that it is so difficult in marriage to maintain fidelity in the face of continual temptations. A person attempting to deny these temptations in himself may feel the pressure so strongly that he makes use of an unconscious mechanism to alleviate the situation. The patient projects his own impulses to faithlessness onto the partner to whom he owes faith—thus the partner is seen as being unfaithful and the patient feels without guilt, or at least notes that the partner is not any better than he is. This jealousy may seem at times to have an almost delusional character, but it is primarily based on hidden fantasies of the patient's own infidelity or wishes to be unfaithful.

The more ominous layer of jealousy is the true *delusional* type. In these cases the unconscious repressed wishes are also toward unfaithfulness but the object is a member of the same sex. "Delusional jealousy is what is left of a homosexuality that has run its course, and it rightly takes its position among the classical forms of paranoia" (p. 225). Thus if the patient for example is a man, it is as if he is saying, I do not love a certain man—my wife loves him! This is described in detail in the case of Schreber (see chapter 8). Freud points out that in paranoia, delusions of persecution as well as delusions of jealousy serve as a defense against unconscious homosexuality. In delusions of persecution, the enmity which the persecuted paranoiac sees in others is the reflection of his own hostile impulses against them (see chapter 9). When there is a focus on one individual of the same sex as the persecutor, the ambivalence of the unconscious love as well as the nonfulfillment of the claim for love produces the rage, which is then projected onto the persecutor.

Finally, Freud reminds us of typical mechanisms in homosexual object choice. In one type of case there is fixation on the mother and an identification with her which enables the son to keep true to her at the price of becoming a homosexual. In a second type of case there is a withdrawal from women out of horror derived from the early discovery that women have no penis. Another motivation toward homosexual object choice can involve either regard for the father or fear of him. Freud then adds a fourth dynamic in which an exceedingly hostile and aggressive attitude toward rival siblings of the same sex is transformed under repression into the opposite, and a homosexual love object is chosen. In the first of these mechanisms notice that the man (for example) identifies with his mother and chooses a love object in whom he rediscovers himself, and whom he might love as his mother loved him. In this situation the love object is a narcissistic selfobject (Kohut 1971).

Masochism. The problem of masochism gained increasing importance to Freud in the final years of his life. His major paper, "The Economic Problem of Masochism" (1924C;19:157ff), presents his definitive statement on the subject, based on his notion of the death instinct. This paper ties together a number of theoretical and clinical loose ends and is therefore difficult to review adequately. In some ways it is an extension of his earlier major theoretical work, *Beyond the Pleasure Principle* (1920G;18:3ff). The paper begins by straightening out the distinction between three principles introduced and discussed in the earlier work. The *nirvana principle* is defined as the endeavor on the part of the mental apparatus to keep the quantity of excitation present in it as low as possible, or at least to keep it constant. The *pleasure principle* is defined as a regulating principle that causes mental events to take a direction such that the final outcome coincides with at least an avoidance of unpleasure or a production of pleasure. At first Freud assumed these two principles to be either correlated or identical, but he realized in "The Economic Problem of Masochism" that they are not, since there are unquestionably states of increasing tension, such as sexual excitement, which are pleasurable. In *Beyond the Pleasure Principle* he had already suggested that the rhythm or temporal characteristics of the changes and excitations might determine the pleasurable or unpleasurable quality of a state. He defines the nirvana principle as attributable to the death instinct and the pleasure principle to the influence of the life instinct. The *reality principle* represents in turn a modification of the pleasure principle under the influence of the external world.

Freud then turns to the clinical distinction of three kinds of masochism. One kind—*erotogenic masochism*, or pleasure in pain—lies at the bottom of the other two of these. *Moral masochism* refers to the profound unconscious sense of guilt discovered in neurotic patients by psychoanalytic clinical work. *Feminine masochism* has to do with the form of perversion in which secret fantasies place the subject in a feminine situation of being castrated, copulated with, or giving birth to a baby. Feminine masochism, which underlies masochistic perverted performances, represents pleasure in pain and as such is "entirely based on the primary, erotogenic masochism—which, of course, he believed to have its basis in the death instinct.

Thus "a very extensive fusion and amalgamation, in varying proportions, of the two classes of instincts take place" and "corresponding to a fusion of instincts of this kind, there may, as a result of certain influences, be a *de*fusion of them" (p. 164). This corresponds to the remarkable concept of the taming *(Bändigung)* of one instinct by another—the action by which the libido can make the death instinct innocuous. In a later paper (Freud 1937C;23:225) he defines this process thus: "The instinct is brought completely into the harmony of the ego, becomes accessible to all the influences of the other trends in the ego and no longer seeks to go its independent way to satisfaction. If we are asked by what methods and means this result is achieved, it is not easy to find an answer."

Translated into clinical experience, I believe that this description emphasizes one of the most serious problems in the intensive psychotherapy of the borderline patient (Chessick 1977). Dealing with the raw aggression pouring out of the patient—an aggression which seems to represent the consequence of a regressive defusion in the patient's instinctual life—and somehow, in Freud's sense, "taming" this aggressive output, seems to be a crucial task that determines whether the treatment will succeed or fail. In my clinical experience there is no doubt that this self-destructive aggression does carry with it *a form of gratification* which the patient is required to renounce in the interest of obtaining maturity and mental health. In some cases this gratification seems so intense that the patient is unable to make the renunciation and the treatment fails. It is not necessary to postulate a death instinct to explain this phenomenon. We know that the unbridled, massive discharge of sexual desire can be intensely pleasurable; the unbridled discharge of aggression can also have gratification attached to it. The self-destructive aspect could be understood here as a secondary phenomenon, part of the price the patient pays for the pleasure. This remains an unresolved clinical issue (see chapter 21).

In moral masochism (described above) the direct connection with sexuality has been loosened, as Freud points out. Here the pleasure is not in having physical pain inflicted, but in humiliation and mental torture. Freud designates a clinical sign of such patients in that they have a negative therapeutic reaction, and need to remain sick and to endure pain and suffering as a most powerful serious resistance. Recent work makes it clear that not all situations of negative therapeutic reaction are based on moral masochism; the narcissistic blow of discovering that the therapist knows something that the patient does not may contribute to a rage and even a departure from treatment that appears to be a negative therapeutic reaction (Chessick 1974).

Freud believed that moral masochism or the unconscious sense of guilt rests on a wish for punishment at the hands of the father. This is a regressive distortion of the wish to have a passive or feminine sexual relationship with the father. A case in point is the early behavior disturbance of the Wolf-Man (see chapter 7) in which the young boy's misbehavior clearly was designed to invoke a beating from the father, resting in turn on a passive feminine attitude toward the father.

In "Dostoyevsky and Parricide" (1928B;21:175ff) Freud gives an interesting clinical example of his notion of masochism. Dostoyevsky's very strong destructive instinct, especially his aggression toward his father—which might easily have made him a criminal—was instead directed mainly against his own person "and thus finds expression as masochism and a sense of guilt." Freud regards Dostoyevsky's epilepsy as hystero-epilepsy, not a true organic epilepsy.* This reaction is at the disposal of the neurosis and attempts by somatic means to get rid of amounts of excitation which it cannot deal with psychically. Dostoyevsky's affective epilepsy began with feelings of impending death, which Freud regards as punishment for his death wish to his father and identification with the hopefully dead father. This in turn is seen as a secondary to Dostoyevsky's fear of his feminine attitude toward his father. The seizures, which were punishment for the death wish, stopped in Siberia when the Czar administered the unconsciously needed punishment. This analysis also explains Dostoyevsky's masochistic identification with criminals and his need to ruin himself by compulsive gambling. The gambling further represents a manifestation of his urge to masturbate, an urge connected with his latent sexual wishes toward his father.

Feminine Psychology. I have already dealt at length with the unsolved problem of feminine psychology in chapter 14 of *Great Ideas in Psychotherapy* (1977*a*); therefore, my discussion of Freud's views on this subject will be brief. The interested reader is referred to my previous book and to a thorough review of the subject by Eissler (1977). The paper "Some Psychological Consequences of the Anatomical Distinction Between the Sexes" (1925J;19:243ff) contains Freud's reassessment of the entire subject, written when he was 69, and contains the germs of all his later work on the topic. (A complete review of his views with appropriate references is found in the editor's introduction to this paper.) In this work Freud clearly states that the woman's discovery that she has no penis is a wound to her narcissism, which leads to a certain sense of inferiority, jealousy, and the loosening of the girl's relationship to the mother as love-object. Thus "Whereas in boys the Oedipus complex is destroyed by the castration complex, in girls it is made possible and led up to by the castration complex" (p. 256). The little girl turns to the father for a baby instead. This leads

*Scholars today generally agree that the story of the "murder" of Dostoyevsky's father, on which Freud's argument for this diagnosis rests, is at best unproven; most scholars agree that the father died of apoplexy (Snow 1978).

Freud to the logical conclusion that the Oedipus complex in girls escapes the fate it meets with in boys—in girls it may be slowly abandoned or dealt with by repression. Here Freud is led to some disparaging remarks about women. I have discussed the fallacies in this approach previously, as mentioned above (Chessick 1977*a*).

A very important warning must be added here for the practice of intensive psychotherapy. *Freud's unfortunate, disparaging remarks about women must be separated from his depiction of the vicissitudes of the Oedipus complex in women.* Clearly his attitude about women is a reflection of his age and his culture. The practicing psychotherapist should not be misled by these prejudicial remarks into ignoring Freud's basic description of female sexuality. The little girl *is* disappointed by the narcissistic blow that she has no penis; she turns out of this disappointment to the father in order to obtain a baby from him, which in a way substitutes for the lost penis. As Freud explains, a wave of repression of this narcissistic wound (and the corresponding wish for a penis) occurs at puberty, an event which has the function of doing away "with a large amount of the girl's masculine sexuality in order to make room for the development of her femininity." Along with the blossoming of the feminine orientation, there is a shift in the narcissistic focus on the genitals from the clitoris to the vagina. The existence of this clitoral–vaginal transfer has not been refuted by experimental work on the physiology of the female orgasm, since the transfer is primarily a normal shift in narcissistic emphasis as a function of the development of femininity. If it has not occurred, a miscarriage of female adult sexuality has taken place. This is a matter of the greatest clinical significance and must be watched for in the assessment of the psychodynamic structure of female patients.

Freud's second important paper on the psychology of women (1931B; 21:223ff) further emphasizes the intensity and long duration of the little girl's preoedipal attachment to her mother. This paper is a restatement of the finding of the previous paper (discussed above) six years earlier and is continued a year later in Lecture 33 of the *New Introductory Lectures* (1933A;22:3ff). As pointed out in *Great Ideas in Psychotherapy* (Chessick 1977*a*), this paper represents Freud's final answer to Horney. Freud essentially saw the little girl beginning as a little man, whereas Horney argued that feminine Oedipal feeling develops spontaneously in the girl, who then temporarily takes flight in the phallic narcissistic position. Freud's writing on female sexuality contains an unusual phenomenon—some criticisms of a number of other authors' papers. Strachey writes, "It is a curious thing that he seems to treat them as though these papers had arisen spontaneously and not, as was clearly the case, as a reaction to his own somewhat revolutionary paper of 1925" (Freud 1931B;21:223). Freud points out that where a woman's attachment to her father was particularly intense, analysis showed the attachment to have been preceded by a phase of exclusive, equally intense and passionate attachment to her mother. This is an important clinical point. For example, Freud notes that certain women who seem to have chosen a husband on the model of their father repeat toward the husband in their married life their bad relationship with the mother. Thus the husband of such a woman was meant to inherit the relation to the father, but actually inherited the relation to the mother. Here we have the. important clinical point: "With many women we have the impression that their years of maturity are occupied by a struggle with their husband, just as their youth was spent in a struggle with their mother" (p. 231). Boys are more easily able to keep intact their attachment to their mother because they are able to deal with the ambivalent feelings for their mother by directing all their hostility onto their father.

In his review of the literature, Freud oddly makes no reference to his own previous major paper (1925J as discussed above). Against Horney and perhaps even Jones he approves the views of his three "pioneers in feminine psychology." This was Freud's phrase, according to Deutsch (1973), to depict the early female psychoanalysts Ruth Mack-Brunswick, Jeanne Lampl-de Groot, and Helene Deutsch. These views of Freud's "pioneers" have been discussed in *Great Ideas in Psychotherapy* (Chessick 1977*a*) and are falling increasingly into disrepute.

In Lecture 33 of the *New Introductory Lectures on Psychoanalysis* (1933A;22:112–135) Freud reviews this same material in a less technical way and ends with an unbelievably disparaging discussion of adult women. At the same time an important clinical point is made in Freud's opinion that a mother is only brought unlimited satisfaction by her relationship to a son; he considers it to be the most perfect and free from ambivalence of all human relationships. According to Freud, a mother can transfer to her son the ambition which she has been obliged to suppress in herself, and she can expect from him the satisfaction of all that has been left over in her of her masculinity complex. In the light of the disparaging comments about women that follow this paragraph, one wonders if Freud is talking about his own life history. Is Freud's narcissistic rage showing here? Was he stirred to achieving greatness by an attempt to live out his mother's ambitions?

Freud's attitude toward women continued to the end of his life. In the posthumous *Outline of Psychoanalysis* (1940A;23:141ff) he points out that it does little harm to a woman if she remains with her feminine Oedipus attitude unresolved: "She will in that case choose her husband for his paternal characteristics and be ready to recognize his authority" (p. 194).

Part III

TECHNIQUE AND PRACTICE

No one who, like me, conjures up the most evil of those half-tamed demons that inhabit the human breast, and seeks to wrestle with them can expect to come through the struggle unscathed. Might I perhaps have kept the girl under my treatment if I myself had acted a part, if I had exaggerated personal interest in her—a course which, even after allowing for my position as her physician, would have been tantamount to providing her with a substitute for the affection she longed for? I do not know. Since in every case a portion of the factors that are encountered under the form of resistance remains unknown, I have always avoided acting a part, and have contented myself with practising the humbler arts of psychology. In spite of every theoretical interest and of every endeavour to be of assistance as a physician, I keep the fact in mind that there must be some limits set to the extent to which psychological influence may be used, and I respect as one of these limits the patient's own will and understanding.

Sigmund Freud, *Fragment of an Analysis of A Case of Hysteria* (1905E;7:109)

11

TRANSFERENCE—THE CASE OF DORA

For three months in the autumn of 1900, Freud treated a hysterical eighteen-year-old girl named Dora. Immediately after she broke off therapy, he wrote the case up; the paper contained several mistakes about dates and times and also some contradictions. This case report (Freud 1905E;7:3–122) is a logical extension of *The Interpretation of Dreams*. It was written to demonstrate the use and importance of dream analysis in psychoanalytic work as well as to present his current views on the psychodynamics of hysteria, and is worthy of very careful study by the psychotherapist. The report presents the first detailed consideration of transference, and also illustrates Freud's meticulous attention to the slightest detail in the study of psychological data.

The therapy essentially breaks up due to the counter-transference flounderings of the therapist. For example, rather than trying to interpret the long second dream in the somewhat forced way that Freud does, it may be argued that this dream is probably a resistance dream characterized by the desire to dominate the therapy hour. Dora, a very vengeful girl, sought revenge on her father, on Herr K., and then on Freud; an erotic transference developed which Freud should have foreseen, as he later admitted. The sexual excitement accompanying this transference resulted in her leaving treatment (p. 74).

The eighteen-year-old Dora was the second of two children; her older brother was nineteen-and-a-half. She did not get along at all well with her mother who is described as having a "hausfrau psychosis," meaning that she spent most of her time cooking and cleaning, mainly as an effort to escape sexual or spontaneous libidinal relationships with her family. Dora's father is described as a rather well-to-do businessman in his late forties. His brother was a hypochondriacal bachelor; his sister had died of "marasmus"—apparrently some sort of melancholia.

When Dora was six, her father became ill with tuberculosis and at that time began an affair with a Frau K. who began nursing him at the sanitarium or resort area where he stayed. Frau K. was married to a gentleman called Herr K., and had two children. When Dora was eight she developed chronic dyspnea, although it is notable that she had been suffering from bed-wetting previous to the chronic dyspnea attacks; when the attacks of chronic dyspnea occurred the bed-wetting stopped. Some attention had been paid to the bed-wetting by her father, who hovered over her bed and made efforts to keep her clean. When the patient was ten, her father developed impairment of vision due to a retinal detachment. The etiology of this became apparent when the patient was twelve and her father had a confusional attack which was seen by Freud and diagnosed as a case of taboparesis. There was no question about the luetic origin of the father's symptoms.

At the time of her father's confusional attack, the patient developed two symptoms; migraine headaches which disappeared by the time she was sixteen, and attacks of nervous coughs which lasted from three to five weeks and which continued until the onset of her treatment with Freud. At age sixteen these nervous coughs had developed into an aphonia; at this point the patient was first seen by Freud. He proposed psychoanalytic treatment which she refused.

When the patient was seventeen, she developed a feverish disorder; by eighteen she had become steadily worse: she developed low spirits and wrote a letter about suicide; she was unable to concentrate; she suffered from fainting spells, amnesia episodes, and, along with the previous symptoms of aphonia and nervous cough, she developed a rather unsociable personality. At this point she was brought to Freud for treatment, for the second time.

Study of the case revolves mainly around the analysis of the major symptoms—the nervous cough and the associated aphonia. In the psychological history we find that the patient became quite friendly with the Frau K. who was carrying on an affair with her father. Quite an intimate relationship existed between the two women, which continued until the patient was sixteen, when she accused Herr K. of making a sexual advance. She slapped his face and ran off but did not tell anyone of the sexual advance for two days. Nine months after this accusation (whether the sexual advance actually occurred is not clear), she was put to bed with the feverish disorder.

Delving deeper into the psychological history, one finds that when Dora was fourteen Herr K. had passionately kissed her on the lips. She reacted to this with a sensation of disgust and a feeling of pressure on the thorax which was followed by formation of a phobia. She avoided walking past any man whom she thought to be in any state of sexual excitement or affectionate conversation. Freud writes,

> It is worth remarking that we have here three symptoms—the disgust, the sensation of pressure on the upper part of the body,

> and the avoidance of men engaged in affectionate conversation—all of them derived from a single experience. . . . The disgust is the symptom of repression in the erotogenic oral zone, which, as we shall hear, had been overindulged in Dora's infancy by the habit of sensual sucking. The pressure of the erect member probably led to an analogous change in the corresponding female organ, the clitoris; and the excitation of this second erotogenic zone was referred by a process of displacement to the simultaneous pressure against the thorax and became fixed there. Her avoidance of men who might possibly be in the state of sexual excitement follows the mechanism of a phobia, its purpose being to safeguard her against any revival of the repressed perception (Freud 1905E;7:30–31).

Thus all three of the symptoms served as defenses against sexual wishes.

Another aspect of the case is the so-called "homosexual" relationship between Dora and Frau K. Dora often spoke of Frau K.'s "adorable white body" and they spent much time talking intimately about sexual matters. Although Freud was not aware of it at the time, we might understand this intimacy as a defense against Dora's deeper infantile wishes to be soothed and to suck at the white breast of Frau K. Both the phobia and the "homosexual" relationship illustrate the oral (pre-Oedipal) aspects of the polymorphous perverse sexual wishes of the patient who develops hysteria.

The actual analysis of the case hinges around the interpretation of the dream, in the second part of Freud's paper. The psychodynamics were these: Dora was confronted with frank sexuality by Herr K. and she definitely responded with feelings of sexual excitement toward him. At the same time, Dora was very vengeful and angry at all men, considering them evil and undependable. Because of this, she could not give in to her sexual impulses toward Herr K. She had an incapacity for meeting real erotic demands which Freud explains as one of the most essential features of a neurosis, especially of hysteria. The confrontation with real erotic feelings therefore caused a conflict which led to a regression. The specific type of regression made sense in terms of the conflict, and it appeared in the dream, which represented an infantile appeal to father—to help her repress her erotic impulses—just as he had helped her as an infant to keep her from bed-wetting. Thus she appeals to father in her fantasies to save her from Herr K., who had aroused her sexual feelings directly.

We see therefore how a present conflict causes the patient (a) to regress to an earlier level of satisfaction where she had realized some pleasure from her relationship with her father; and (b) to call upon father to help her repress her sexual impulses toward Herr K. and thus solve the conflict. However, the price of this regression is the revival of oedipal love for the father, and incestuous guilt. So now the patient is forced to erect defenses against the oedipal love for her father.

Dora had many such defenses: for example, there is the compromise formation of identification with Frau K. The patient identifies with Frau K.'s intercourse with her father and gains a vicarious gratification of her love impulses toward her father—a gratification which lessens the energy cathexis on these impulses. One also sees projection in Dora's constant rumination that her father and all men are bad and that she hates them because of their sexual interest in her. The defensive meaning of this projection is, "It is not I who have sexual impulses toward father but it is father who is bad and all men are bad because they have sexual interest in women."

However, the major defense that Dora used against her infantile sexual longings toward her father is that of conversion. In order to understand this, we have to understand Dora's infantile sexual fantasy concerning the nature of intercourse, a fantasy characteristic of patients who develop hysteria. Some of these patients imagine intercourse as fellatio; the fantasy is that babies are born as a result of the mother sucking the father's penis. Here again we see the all-pervading oral aspect of the sexual polymorphous perverse fantasies of the patient who develops hysteria.

An analysis of the conversion shows the meaning of the symptoms. Dora's attacks of aphonia are traced to the absence of Herr K. These attacks turn out to be just the reverse of Frau K.'s behavior. Whenever Herr K. was home, Frau K. would be "sick" as a way of avoiding sexual relations with him. On the surface level, Dora's sickness or aphonia means, "If I were his wife I should love him in quite a different way; I should be ill from longing when he is away and well from joy when he was home again." The deeper meaning of the aphonia is connected to the attacks of nervous coughs, which began around the time the patient's father had his attack of lues: this meaning lies in the fantasy of fellatio with her father. Freud honestly explains (p. 48), "But the conclusion was inevitable that with her spasmodic cough, which, as is usual, was referred for its exciting stimulus to a tickling in her throat, she pictured to herself a scene of sexual gratification *per os* between the two people whose love affair occupied her mind so incessantly. A very short time after she had tacitly accepted this explanation her cough vanished—which fitted in very well with my view; but I do not wish to lay too much stress upon this development, since her cough had so often before disappeared spontaneously." Freud also notes the identification here with mother and Frau K. and that Dora is in the passive situation (sucking); whether this refers to deeper homosexual strivings or oral strivings or not is a matter of controversy.

To recapitulate, when Dora was confronted with actual sexuality by Herr K, she was unable to respond with erotic feelings because of her vengeful pride, her tendency to run from reality into fantasy, and other aspects of her personality. In order to avoid an erotic response, she summoned up help for the repression of her sexual impulses by fleeing from the conflict through a regression to infantile gratifications. Hence, she regressed to the infantile oedipal conflict, summoning up her love for her father to help her repress her love for a mature man; and she gained secondary gratification by developing an illness which required care and by touching her father's heart with her sickness and forcing him to separate from Frau K. (who really stood for Dora's mother).

At the same time Dora had to pay the price of her regression to earlier oedipal satisfaction by having to erect defenses against unacceptable oedipal longings. Her main defense was conversion. The conversion symptom, that of nervous cough and aphonia, represented first of all a substitute gratification through the tickling of the throat and through the gain of being taken care of due to an illness. It also represented a punishment—the unpleasant nature of cough and hoarseness is obvious. The conversion symptom was accompanied by the fantasy gratifications of having sexual intercourse through the mouth with father, identifying with mother on the oedipal level, and at a deeper level, homosexual gratification through identification with the mother (and perhaps at the deepest level through the fantasy of sucking on Frau K.'s breast). Through the conversion symptom the psychological conflict was converted into a physical conflict, thus lessening Dora's anxiety about the unacceptable oedipal wishes and giving, in a distorted, symbolized form, some gratification to these wishes. The physical conflict alleviated the guilt about the oedipal wishes by the punishment of the symptoms themselves.

A follow-up of Dora's case was published by Deutsch (1957), who describes her as one of the most repulsive hysterics he ever met:

> In the first interview where the patient was seen about twenty years after she had broken off treatment with Freud, she continued to complain of ear noises, dizziness, and attacks of migraine. She then started a tirade about her husband's indifference, about her sufferings, and how unfortunate her marital life had been. She felt her only son had begun to neglect her. He often stayed out late at night and she suspected he had become interested in girls. She always waited listening until he came home. She expressed a great amount of hostile feelings towards her husband especially her disgust with marital sex life. Dora's fate took the course that Freud had predicted twenty-four years earlier after the three months analysis with her. She clung to her son with the same reproachful demands she made on her husband and who had died tortured by her vengeful behavior (pp. 159–167).

A number of Freud's comments on this case deserve careful attention for their clinical value. For example, in his prefatory remarks he mentions the difficulties that are encountered when the physician has to conduct six or eight therapeutic treatments a day. He advises against making notes during a session "for fear of shaking the patient's confidence and of disturbing his own view of material under observation" (p. 9). Freud frankly admits that he had not at that point succeeded in solving the problem of how to report for publication the history of a treatment of long duration. In Dora's case he recorded the wording of the dreams immediately after the session and used these notes when he rewrote the case from his outstanding memory at the end of the three-month period. However, he mentions that it would be wrong to suppose from this case that dreams and their interpretation occupy such a prominent position in all psychoanalysis.

Freud's comments raise some important clinical issues. In my opinion Freud is correct in that taking detailed notes, and far worse, tape recordings during the actual psychotherapy sessions will shake the patient's confidence and disturb the material in a hopeless fashion, and is frankly a disservice to the patient—unless it is explained to the patient in advance that notes or tape recordings are for supervision or are part of a research project; even then, it must be realized that the therapy will be quite seriously distorted. Of course, during the few initial history-taking sessions, the therapist must put down for his case records important names, dates, etc., and most patients accept this in the first few interviews without protest, since it is expected from any responsible doctor.

Obviously the time to take notes to insure maximum value is immediately after a session—and this brings up the issue of "the decline and fall of the fifty-minute hour" (Greenson 1974). Greenson has presented an eloquent plea for retaining the fifty-minute hour, which nevertheless has become a rarity. Ideally, to follow Freud, who began in 1913 to divide his working day with patients into fifty-five-minute hours, such a schedule allows a ten-minute period at the end of each session for refreshment and note-taking. For economic reasons, most therapists shun the fifty-minute hour; one can squeeze more patients into the working day if there are no time gaps between patients. So one shortens the hour not for the altruistic purpose of treating more suffering humanity or accumulating more analytic experience; the matter almost always comes down to financial gain. Greenson impressively points out, "It is obvious that taking patient after patient on an assembly-line schedule is an act of hostility, subtle and unconscious though it may be."

If a psychotherapist cannot bring himself to retain the fifty-minute hour, he should at least schedule a fifteen-minute break between every two patients. It is not acceptable to demand of the patient—in addition to such other requirements as payment, punctuality (especially about leaving the session on time), and a certain amount of restraint of physical behavior in the office—that the patient also fit into an assembly-line schedule. All such demands are for the convenience of the therapist and the therapist alone, and at some level or other they take something away from the patient. Patients are willing to accept certain realistic arrangements made to meet the needs of the doctor, but they react poorly to manifestations of therapist greed and mechanical disinterest, or to lack of consideration in matters of privacy, as in the use of a tape recorder (especially in the aftermath of Watergate).

In a short footnote (pp. 16–17) Freud raises the clinical issue of an organic disorder masking or presenting itself as a psychiatric disorder. In this "footnote" case a patient who allegedly had hysteria turned out to have an early stage of tabes. When he suspected that the case was perhaps not primarily psychogenic, Freud immediately instituted a careful physical examination. Although there is a *great deal* to be said against doing physical examinations on our patients ourselves, it is strongly recommended that all patients at the beginning of psychotherapy be sent for a careful physical and neurological examination. Freud's continual vigilance in looking for organic causation in the so-called psychogenic disorders enabled him to maintain his primary identity as a physician.

Indeed, Freud at this point certainly practiced authoritatively. For example, when Dora met an explanation of his with an emphatic "no," he took it to signify "yes"—later, when she had an association which seemed consistent with his explanation, he used this as "a fact which I did not fail to use against her" (p. 59). In spite of that, Dora continued to deny his contention for some time, apparently up to the last therapy session at which point "Dora had listened to me without any of her usual contradictions" (pp. 108–9). Freud seems to evade the point that once a patient has, out of negative transference, decided to leave therapy the emotional investment in the process is gone and the patient simply waits out the last session.

The case of Dora illustrates the importance of paying close attention to symptomatic acts during the therapy session. For example Freud notes and interprets Dora's playing with "a small reticule of a shape which had just come into fashion; and, as she lay on the sofa and talked, she kept playing with it—opening it, putting a finger into it, shutting it again, and so on. I looked on for some time, and then explained to her the nature of a 'symptomatic act' " (p. 76). Such acts are discussed in *The Psychopathology of Everyday Life* (1901B;6:1ff). A typical example today is the constant removal and replacing of a wedding ring on the finger while the patient is talking. Notice that Freud "looked on for a while" rather than jumping on the patient immediately—a mark of mature technique.

Probably the most important reason for psychotherapists to study the case of Dora is that it represents a failure in psychotherapy. The primary reason for the failure, as Freud correctly notes, was missing the first warning sign of a transference reaction. Freud missed it, probably thinking he had ample time since no apparent further stages of transference had developed in the verbal material. Hence, the transference took Freud unawares, and Dora acted out an essential part of her recollections and fantasies instead of reproducing them in the treatment, by leaving therapy. Thus Freud makes it clear that meticulous attention to transference manifestations—especially negative transference manifestations—are the cornerstone of a successful treatment, and that neglect of such manifestations inevitably leads to often unexpected and surprising failure.

I have discussed this problem at length in *Why Psychotherapists Fail* (Chessick 1971). As a patient's defences are undermined in uncovering psychotherapy, the pressure of unconscious drives focuses increasingly on the therapist. To deal with this properly, a suitable therapeutic alliance must first be established, along with an understanding of the transference and an insight into the countertransference. In 1900, when Freud treated Dora, all this was barely recognized; in fact, as Jones (1955) remarks, the case is amazing in that anyone would "take the data of psychology so seriously." Freud himself recognized how the revenge aspects of the transference led to the breakup of the treatment: "Her breaking off so unexpectedly, just when my hopes of a successful termination of the treatment were at their highest, and her thus bringing these hopes to nothing—this was an unmistakable act of vengeance on her part" (p. 109). Indeed, it has been my clinical experience that whenever the therapist feels a certain jubilance about the progress of a case or a session, the patient often follows this reaction (no matter how the therapist tries to hide such feelings) with an upsurge of resistance which often manifests itself by plans to disrupt the treatment for one reason or another. As Freud noted, such resistance is a manifestation of negative transference and a reaction of narcissistic rage to the therapist's narcissistic gain in the success of the treatment, no matter how positive the transference and therapeutic alliance may appear to have been on the surface.

In more severe cases, such as borderline patients, this resistance is often accompanied by the patient's overt or covert suggestion that the therapist step out of the role of therapist and show concrete manifestations of love and interest in the patient. In the mildest form, the patient demands that the therapist do a lot of talking about his own personal life and activities and so become a real object (Tarachow 1963) of gratification; in the extreme form, the patient demands physical manifestations of affection.

If this is not forthcoming, a certain number of patients will indeed carry out the threat and leave treatment in spite of the therapist's best efforts. The answer to this "crucial dilemma," as I have described it previously (Chessick 1968), is nowhere better stated than by Freud in the case of Dora, in one of the most beautiful and poignant passages ever written by Freud (p. 109). It is reproduced on the title page of Part III of the present book. Please turn back to it and read it over.

The moving countertransference emotions produced by the erotic demands of attractive and apparently helpless young patients represent a great threat to the psychotherapy of the patient, and may challenge the personal psychotherapy of the therapist at every turn. At this early date in his career—and perhaps because of his narcissistic investment in using this case to illustrate the interpretation of dreams in psychotherapy—Freud's countertransference produced a blindness to the rage and demanding behavior of this patient, a selective scotomata to the negative aspects of her personality—which suddenly jumped into the foreground just at the moment he was feeling the most jubilant about the success of his therapeutic efforts.

When the same thing happens repeatedly to the insufficiently analyzed therapist, the unfortunate reaction is not to go back for further personal help but rather to react to the narcissistic blow with counter-rage. Not only does this facilitate a breakup of the individual treatment, but the anticipation of further such disappointments spills over into all the therapist's work and produces a vicious cycle of further failures. The typical reaction is a combination of depression and loss of confidence in the process of intensive psychotherapy itself, a displacement to avoid the blow to personal self-esteem. We are left with the phenomenon of therapist discouragement and the common switch to short-cut techniques that are more gratifying, from the primal scream to psychopharmacology. It is the story of Breuer all over again (see chapter 4).

Proponents of Kohut's psychology of the self have pointed out another aspect of Freud's countertransference in the crucial quotation given on pp. 138–9 of this chapter. They suggest that Freud's interpretation of this fourteen-year-old girl's disgust in the situation described as "hysterical" is unempathic, and they ascribe his failure of empathy to an intense countertransference commitment to his sexual theories. What do you think about it?

12

TRANSFERENCE AND COUNTERTRANSFERENCE

On October 1, 1907, a 29-year-old man, suffering from aggressive impulses and fantasies, began an 11-month treatment with Freud. He is described by Freud as a "youngish man of university education" suffering from (a) fears—that something may happen to his father and to a lady he admires (even though his father had been dead for nine years); (b) compulsions—such as impulses to cut his throat with a razor; and (c) prohibitions—some of which were against ridiculous or unimportant things, and which were often so connected as to make it impossible to comply with them all. Freud reported on the progress of the case to his Wednesday evening group a number of times. In April 1908, while the case was in progress, he delivered a four- or five-hour report to the First International Psychoanalytical Congress (Jones 1955, p. 42). The final write-up of the case along with some notes preserved from the original sessions (Freud 1909D;10:153ff), is entitled "Notes upon a Case of Obsessional Neurosis." The case has generally and unfortunately become known as the case of the Rat Man, but following Lipton (1977) we shall use Freud's pseudonym of "Paul Lorenz."

Although Freud reported that the eleven-month treatment was successful, he adds in a footnote that the patient was later killed in World War I. This case and the case of Dora (previously discussed in chapter 11) are the two most important case histories for psychotherapists; they demand extremely careful study. The eleven-month psychotherapy of Paul Lorenz is probably the best autobiographical sketch of Freud at work. In my judgment, the case represents what is generally known in psychotherapy as a transference cure; that is, it is the interaction in the transference and the countertransference between the patient and the therapist, rather than any brilliant symbolic interpretations, that brought about improvement in the patient's mental health. Freud, who did not conceive of the case in this way, spends much of the presentation in theoretical discussion and intellectual explanation, illustrating the great progress he had made in understanding the obsessional neuroses.

Section I, the essence of the case presentation, is unfolded in a more-or-less session-by-session manner thus making it rather difficult to read, but giving a realistic flavor to the impression the patient made on the therapist. I will review briefly some of the highlights of the case before discussing the therapy. The best way to familiarize oneself with the details of the case is to read Freud's presentation which, as usual, is brilliant in its literary impact.

Freud first saw the prospective patient sitting up in his study (a matter to be discussed later). The next day the patient, now on the couch, began by reporting his sudden rejection, when he was 14 or 15, by a 19-year-old student friend, an event which he considered to be the first great blow of his life. Without transition and without questions from Freud, he launched immediately into a description of his sexual life, a description which involved scenes of creeping under his governess's skirt, watching another governess express abscesses on her buttocks, and sexual play with governesses. Even in childhood he had dealt with this sexual experience in a neurotic way: he was tormented by the feeling that his parents knew his thoughts and that his father might die if he thought about such things as wishing to see girls naked.

In the second session Paul Lorenz presented the famous rat-torture story told to him by the cruel captain. Freud writes that while telling this story, "His face took on a very strange, composite expression. I could only interpret it as one of *horror at pleasure of his own of which he himself was unaware.* He proceeded with the greatest difficulty: 'At that moment the idea flashed through my mind *that this was happening to a person who was very dear to me*' " (1909D;10:166–167). The persons very dear to the patient were the lady he admired and his father. Then the idea occurred to him that unless he paid back the captain and the lieutenant, this thought would come true—he then presented a long, obscure, and detailed story about money that had to be paid. The third session was filled with a classical description of his ambivalent efforts at fulfilling his obsessional vow.

Freud reports how he opens a therapy session (if he says anything at all) by remarking that he asked at the fourth session "And how do you intend to proceed today?" (p. 174). The patient occupied this session by describing his father's death, nine years before, at which he was not present. When his aunt died, eighteen months after his father's death, the patient began to experience intense self-reproach, which Freud spent the sixth session trying to explain to the patient. In the seventh session the patient admitted his intense ambivalence about his father: he realized that his father's death and the inheritance he would receive might enable him to marry the lady that he admired. This seventh and final session, reported in detail, was taken up by fantasies and reports of aggression toward his younger brother.

Freud then launches into a discussion of some obsessional ideas and their explanation, including the famous classical example of how, on the day of the departure of his ambivalently loved lady he felt obliged to remove a stone from the road; the idea had struck him that her carriage would be driving on the same road in a few hours time and might come to grief against this stone. A few minutes later it occurred to him that this idea was absurd—and he was obliged to go back and replace the stone in its original position in the middle of the road, and so on.

The precipitating cause of the neurosis, according to Freud, was a challenge of real life in which he had to decide whether to make a wealthy marriage, following his father's wishes, or whether to pursue his own life and marry the lady he loved in spite of her poverty. The neurosis led to an incapacity for work which postponed both his education and the decision.

The patient's ambivalent feelings about his father, who had a passionate, violent and often uncontrolled temper, emerge repeatedly in the material. Even at age 27 (several years after his father's death), while having sexual intercourse he thought, "This is glorious—one might murder one's father for this!"—an echo from the childhood neurosis. At 21, after his father died, he developed a compulsion to masturbate. Later, in a complex ritual, he opened the door for his father in the middle of the night; then, coming back into the hall, he took out his penis and looked at it in the mirror. This act seemed to be related to his father's beating him for masturbation—during this beating his father had apparently been overcome by what Freud called "elemental fury." Although it was not repeated, the beating apparently made an important impression on the patient; from that time on the patient described himself as a coward out of fear of the violence of his own rage. (According to the patient's mother the beating was given between ages three and four and was administered because he had bitten someone rather than for such a sexual offense as masturbation.)

Freud presents a careful solution of the complex story of the rat torture and the need to pay back the money to prevent the torture from being inflicted upon his father or the lady he had admired; the solution is based on symbolic interpretations of the meaning of the word "rats," and so forth. This explanation led to an apparent disappearance of what Freud calls "the patient's rat delirium."

The rat punishment stirred up the patient's anal erotism. Rats are interpreted as representing money, syphilis, penis, and worms. A rat burrowing into the anus unconsciously became equated with the penis burrowing into the anus. Rats came to represent children who bite people in a rage; when the captain told the rat story the patient unconsciously felt the desire to bite his cruel father masked by a more-or-less conscious, derisive feeling toward the captain that the same torture should be applied to the captain. A day and a half later, when the captain (unconsciously, the father) requested him to run an errand repaying some money, he thought in a hostile way that he would pay back the money when his father and the lady he admired could have children (the patient's admired lady was unable to conceive). This in turn was based on two infantile sexual theories: that men can have children and that babies come from the anus. The lady he admired was condemned to childlessness because her ovaries had been removed; the patient, who was extraordinarily fond of children, hesitated to marry her for this reason. The reader must decide for himself whether he is convinced by Freud's solution to the rat problem presented in section G of part I.

The second part of the case history is theoretical and discusses various aspects of the psychodynamics of the obsessive compulsive neuroses. These aspects involve magical thinking and personal superstitions; the omnipotence of thought (a relic of the megalomania of infancy); obsessive ideas (formations of long-standing representing distortions, uncertainty, and doubt) which draw the patient away from reality to abstract subjects; ambivalence with much repressed sadism; displacement of affect and of ideas; isolation—temporal and spatial—of the idea from the affect and from the world to the isolated life of abstractions; and regression, wherein preparatory acts become the substitute for final decisions and thinking replaces acting. Thus an obsessive thought, according to Freud, is one whose function is to represent an act regressively (to be discussed later).

In the obsessional neuroses the complex is often retained in the consciousness but with a dissociation of its affect. The starting point of a neurosis may be mentioned by the patient in a tone of complete indifference since he is unaware of the significance of the material. The two cardinal symptoms of obsessional neuroses are the tendency to doubting and a recurring sense of compulsion. Fundamentally, a deep ambivalence dominates the patient's life—significant people in the patient's existence are both intensely loved and intensely hated. In the obsessional neuroses these emotional attitudes are sharply separated. Freud saw the doubting as a result of this ambivalence, and the sense of compulsion as an attempt to overcompensate for the doubt and uncertainty. In the obsessional neuroses, the omnipotence of a patient's thoughts, in which the patient is terrified of wishes coming true in the real world, and the belief in the power to make thoughts come true in some magical way, was applied by Freud to various primitive beliefs in magic and, of course, to religion. Just as he believed infantile sexuality to be the root of hysteria, Freud stressed infantile sexuality as leading to a nuclear complex in the obsessional neuroses. As in the cases of hysteria he believed that the unravelling of these nuclear complexes would automatically lead to a resolution of the neuroses.

From the point of view of the psychotherapist, however, the importance of this case hinges on the transference and the countertransference as well as on Freud's actual behavior, that might be attributed to acting out in the countertransference, at least in (debatable) part; and also to Freud's overall personality, to be discussed later. Patients with obsessive compulsive neuroses, which we now know to be often not far psychologically from schizophrenia, are very good at the intellectual game of interpreting symbols. They tend to disclose their symptoms in a teasing manner, a little bit at a time—a pattern related to their anal erotism and their aggressions. Paul Lorenz began the treatment by flattering Freud: although he claimed to have read Freud's work it appears that he read practically none of it. It is not hard to see this subterfuge as the patient's desire to "get in through the back door." The transference rapidly became very intense, with the patient in the second session repeatedly addressing Freud as "captain." Freud relates this salutation to his own statement at the beginning of the second session, in which he told the patient he was not fond of cruelty like the captain and had no intention of tormenting him unnecessarily. The patient at this point is saying "Oh, yes, you are the captain."

I will endeavor to establish that although Freud showed an intense desire to understand the patient and certainly did not display any fits of temper toward him—he was in some ways extremely benign to him—Freud's personality carried enough forcefulness (or countertransference) to bear a resemblance to both sides of the patient's father—the kind and gentle side and the harsh-tempered side—so that the patient could fasten upon Freud's personality and receive a corrective emotional experience. This case has led some therapists astray in that the exposition emphasizes symbolic and intellectual material; in my opinion, however, the key to the success of the treatment is Freud's personality as well as his interpretation of the patient's *feelings* in the transference. I cannot help but wonder if such a case—in which during the second session the dazed and bewildered patient calls the analyst "captain" and gets up from the sofa—would these days be considered a suitable case for formal psychoanalysis.

Perhaps the best place to mark the development of the transference is in the discussion of the fee. Freud in his characteristically keen way observed that the florin notes with which the patient paid his fee were invariably clean and smooth. Later on, when Freud had told the patient his hourly fee, the patient thought to himself "So many florins, so many rats" (p. 213), and related this thought to a whole complex of money interests which centered around his father's legacy to him. The cruel captain's request to the patient to pay back charges due upon a packet connects together father, son, captain, money, rats, and Freud. Later on, in an important transference dream, the patient dreamed that he saw Freud's daughter with two patches of dung in place of eyes; it is not difficult to see this as a punishment for Freud's fee (taking money from the patient).

During the dramatic session wherein the patient insists that Freud is the captain, Lorenz broke off when describing the rat torture and got up from the sofa, begging Freud to spare him the recital of the details. Freud is gentle but relentless at this point and even tries to say some of the repulsive phrases for the patient; he does not mention whether or not he ordered the patient back onto the sofa, but I doubt it. There is little doubt, however, that the patient experienced the second session as a beating or torment, but one must add that the patient set up this situation out of an intense need to act out the transference. Clearly, whether Freud liked it or not, the patient was determined to experience Freud as his father. As Freud writes, "Things soon reached a point at which, in his dreams, his waking phantasies, and his associations, he began heaping the grossest and filthiest abuse upon me and my family, though in his deliberate actions he never treated me with anything but the greatest respect" (p. 209). This behavior labels the treatment as truly psychoanalytic (whether or not one wishes to call it a formal psychoanalysis), and uncovering in the transference, regardless of the "irregularities" or parameters (Lipton 1977). While he talked in this way the patient would get up from the sofa and roam about the room, which apparently Freud permitted him to do; eventually the patient explained that he was avoiding physical nearness to Freud for fear of receiving a beating. Freud writes dramatically, "If he stayed on the sofa he behaved like some one in desperate terror trying to save himself from castigations of terrific violence; he would bury his head in his hands, cover his face with his arm, jump up suddenly and rush away, his features distorted with pain, and so on" (p. 209). Freud's general reaction to all this material seems to have been *the model of what we call the analyst's analyzing attitude*, in which he remains relatively calm and free of anxiety, while constantly attempting to understand and explain the material. Freud was able to do this because, although the patient was dramatizing his fears and had many destructive fantasies toward Freud and his family, in his deliberate actions and throughout the excellent therapeutic alliance he was consistently proper and polite, never attempting to act out any of his fantasies toward Freud or others (remember that the patient characterized himself as basically a coward). It was the *patient's ability to maintain the separation between his correct behavior and his irrational raging transference fantasies that permitted him to receive a successful uncovering psychotherapy*.

At the same time there is no question that Freud as usual was very forceful in his interpretations and in his authoritative conviction of the correctness of his explanations and interpretations. Based on the patient's material, Freud engages in an intellectual philosophical dialogue with the patient, replete with explanations and arguments; Freud was an active psychotherapist in the intellectual sphere. For example (p. 180), he presents to the patient a long explanation of ambivalence based on a quotation from Shakespeare's *Julius Caesar*. The patient admits that the explanation is plausible but, "he was naturally not in the very least convinced by it" (p. 210). Freud adds in a footnote that it is not the aim of such discussions to create conviction, and that a sense of conviction is attained only "after the patient has himself worked over the reclaimed material, and so long as he is not fully convinced the material must be considered as unexhausted." Clearly involved here is a dangerous circularity which does not leave much room for the possibility that the therapist's explanation or interpretation may be wrong. In fact, Freud is so sure of himself that in one place (p. 185–186), when the patient questions whether all his evil impulses originated from infancy, Freud promises to prove it to him in the course of the treatment. In this situation again Freud is certainly taking the position of the captain or the leader, consistent with the authoritative role of the Viennese physician at the turn of the century.

What I am trying to stress here is *not* a criticism of Freud as a therapist or a person, for I think that his intuitive handling of the patient was outstandingly brilliant. His basic approach was tolerant, reasonable, and consistent with what one expected from a reputable and ethical physician of his time; the patient took advantage of the unavoidably assertive aspects of Freud's behavior to re-enact for himself a dramatic transference in which he feared an extremely hot-tempered father, and to re-experience a relationship with a father of a different nature. In a sense the patient provided himself with a corrective emotional experience; Freud's brillance as an intuitive psychotherapist was that he allowed the patient to do this. Freud's gratification in the case seems to have come from unraveling the intricate intellectual mysteries of the patient's obsessional symptomatology. Freud's personality and intellectual curiosity were assertive enough to make a transference resemblance possible; at the same time, he provided instances of extremely kind behavior which fit the gentle side of the nature of the patient's father.

We note, for example, in the original transcript of the case, that Freud sent his patient a postcard—perhaps from one of his vacation trips. The postcard is signed "cordially" (p. 293). At another point one of the most dramatically cryptic statements ever written by Freud appears: "Dec. 28—He was hungry and was fed" (p. 303). As is characteristic in obsessional patients, these direct acts of kindness toward the patient stirred up the expected ambivalent response; they also give us a glimpse of Freud's basic and consistently humane attitude toward his patients—he was anything but disinterested and impersonal.

At one point (p. 260) he requests the patient to bring a photograph of the lady he admires, an act which stirs up what Freud described as "violent struggle, bad day." The patient is in conflict about leaving the treatment at this point. I think it is an excellent technical procedure during uncovering psychotherapy to request patients to bring photographs of the significant people in their lives; I often do this because a photograph fixes better in my mind the person being talked about and brings home to the patient the intensity and the seriousness of my inquiry (as well as providing a mirroring experience).

Freud saw his patients at home for almost fifty years; the setting in which he worked appears repeatedly in this case history. We are especially fortunate to have a recently published book of photographs of Freud's offices before he left Vienna (Engleman 1976); and at this point the serious student of psychotherapy should have a careful look at the book. Freud often illustrated his remarks about the conscious and the unconscious by pointing to the antiques standing about in his rooms. The photographs of his offices vividly portray the impact that these antiques must have had on the patient. In the present case, he speaks of the destruction of Pompeii, explaining how everything conscious is subject to a process of wearing away, while what is unconscious is relatively unchangeable. Thus the objects covered by lava in Pompeii remain preserved in their original state, but the destruction of these objects begins when they are dug up; Freud draws the analogy between these facts and the process of uncovering psychotherapy. Interestingly, in the intuitive way of a great teacher, he concludes the explanation by praising the pupil, which of course produces the optimum mental set for the reception of new ideas.

A careful study of the photographs and their captions describing Sigmund Freud's Vienna home and offices in 1938 brings us visually as close as possible to the atmosphere that Freud provided for his patients. Also worthwhile, to recapture the old-world ambience of Freud's work, is a visit to the Freud museum, which preserves three rooms of Freud's small offices at Bergasse 19, in Vienna.

I believe that for psychotherapists, Freud provides both a personal model and a model in his approach to patients that remains unsurpassed for the purpose of imitation and aspiration. This is not hero-worship: as I have pointed out from time to time in this book, Freud had his faults; but it has been my experience, upon returning repeatedly over my professional lifetime to his writings, that Freud as a symbol of honesty and integrity combined with a humane attitude toward his patients still remains a most refreshing source from which we may all take inspiration.

For example, Gay (Engleman 1976) writes, "Freud was a very busy man, but when he was needed he was there. This was hardly the style of the unshackled Bohemian or of the self-absorbed genius." He continues, "Freud was a supremely honest man." Gay indicates the same quiet decency behind Freud's scientific stance. He explains, "But he was more humane than he readily allowed. His case histories and his private correspondence disclosed his pleasure in a patient's progress, his delicacy in managing a patient's feelings." Freud's overriding life purpose—to know and to understand what goes on in the human mind—which tended to make him seem single-minded, one-sided, and imperious, produced a high level of concentration on his work that patients experienced as an intense form of caring about them, and as an insistence that the patient take a similarly scientific attitude toward his own psyche. I am certain that both of these aspects of Freud's approach to patients were essential to his therapeutic results; he wrote little about these aspects simply because he took them for granted as the obligation or calling of any physician who is dedicated to his patients' welfare. Besides his basic honesty, which Gay calls "the principle of his existence," Freud was a splendid listener and "he trained his sensitivity to the highest pitch of refinement, for he soon realized that the hysterics who came to him for relief had, literally, much to tell him."

Ransohoff, in her captions to the photographs, emphasizes the same thing. For example, she notes that comfort and well-being are the keynote motives of Freud's consulting room and that "Freud was not the silent, uncommunicative analyst portrayed in caricature. He could be enthusiastic in his responses to his patients. On occasion he would even announce a celebration: by getting up from his seat to select and light one of his favorite, forbidden cigars." She mentions the comment by Lou Andreas-Salomé on the evenness of Freud's mood, his serenity, his kindness; and after all, what kind of man could write on his eightieth birthday, "Life at my age is not easy, but spring is beautiful, and so is love."

Looking at the photographs and visiting the Freud museum one can come to understand why Freud at one point (1926E;20:253) wrote that his "self-knowledge" told him that he had never really been, properly speaking, a doctor. Indeed, although these photographs reveal the study and consulting room of a unique man and a remarkable collector of antiquities, they certainly do not reflect the atmosphere of a doctor's office. How remarkably eloquent the setting and atmosphere of the psychiatrist's consulting room speaks about his sense of identity! Behind Freud's chair are large, framed hanging fragments of Pompeiian-style wall paintings dominated by mythological figures. Below these fragments, on a pedestal, is a dignified Roman head—a symbol of a nation dedicated to the rule of law. Ransohoff suggests that "here in Freud's corner the mythological figures from Pompeii and the head of the Roman citizen illuminate contrasting aspects of man: his impulsive animal nature and the civilizing influence of conscience and law. Here is a suggestion of images of the Id and the Superego, two aspects of Freud's hypotheses of the structure of the mind." I cannot help remembering my visit to the chairman of a very prestigious department of psychiatry a couple of years ago: he sat behind an enormous, beautiful desk containing only a bevy of telephones; in back of him were several long shelves containing only one object: a stethescope.

Zetzel (1970) published a brief paper on "Freud's Rat Man," further investigating the dynamics of the case. She helps to revive for us the situation occurring at the death of his older sister, which took place when he was between three and four years of age—it was at this time that his father had given him the beating. The death of his sister at the height of his infantile neurosis set this patient on the path toward becoming a "decompensated obsessional neurotic" instead of a "well-integrated somewhat obsessional character." She explains that his positive identification with Freud as a father surrogate "may have been the central factor which impelled him towards greater mastery of unresolved intrapsychic conflict" (p. 228).

Gedo and Goldberg (1973) carried this investigation further by reminding us how Zetzel also pointed out that the patient was unable to grieve or accept the finality of his father's death. Zetzel quoted from Freud's notes: "I pointed out to him that this attempt to deny the reality of his father's death is the basis of his whole neurosis" (Freud 1909D;10:300). Gedo and Goldberg explain that this patient demonstrates Freud's concept of disavowal, what Kohut (1971) has called the "vertical split." According to Zetzel, this disavowal occurred in Paul Lorenz because he could not deal with the prior trauma of his sister's death, a presumed inability that resulted from his experiencing his sexual and hostile impulses as the causative agents of the tragedy. The disavowal produced "a chronic split in the self as the outcome of unmanageable stress" (Gedo and Goldberg 1973, p. 113) in which one aspect of the self remained at the level of magical thinking and grandiosity—outstanding regressive features in the case of Paul Lorenz, as in many obsessional neurotics.

Kanzer (1952) believes that Freud's reply to the Rat Man's begging the psychiatrist to spare him recital of the details of the punishment—that he had no taste whatever for cruelty and no desire to torment him—led the Rat Man to equate Freud with the captain; but Gill and Muslin (1976) argue that the Rat Man had already made this transference and it persisted *despite* Freud's remark. They feel that Freud's earlier interpretation of transference was both an explanation and an effort to avoid the repercussions of the transference—repercussions which could disrupt the treatment. This analysis is more congruent with Freud's general behavior toward the patient. Gill and Muslin see this case as a demonstration that early interpretation of the transference is sometimes necessary in order to avoid the development of an unmanageable transference situation.

Lipton (1977) presents a scholarly and impressive review of the entire matter, which has already produced a considerable literature. His approach underscores the natural behavior of Freud's physicianly personality on the treatment as producing a therapeutic alliance most beneficial to the uncovering, and warns us against ascribing to "technique" the deliberate assumption of a cold and even discourteous attitude. This kind of behavior produces what he calls "iatrogenic narcissistic disorders" by "establishing an ambience in which the patient has little opportunity to establish an object relationship." Reasonably humane physicianly behavior is *not* a matter of learned technique; it follows naturally from the maturity attained through the successful intensive psychotherapy of the psychotherapist, and in many ways is a measure of the success of the therapist's personal treatment. No treatment can succeed without it.

In his paper "The Dynamics of Transference" (Freud 1912B;12:98–108) Freud points out that transference in psychotherapy can be a powerful resistance if it is either negative transference or an erotized positive transference; these must be removed by interpretation aimed at making such transference conscious, while the other aspects of positive transference can be left to persist and become the vehicle of success in the treatment. *The recognition of various aspects of the transference and the proper interpretation of transference remain the most difficult skills in the technique of intensive psychotherapy.* This recognition and interpretation is actually much more complicated today than it was at the time of Freud, because we now recognize that certain types of narcissistic transferences which also occur in psychotherapy can be very subtle and tricky to recognize and interpret. Kohut (1966, 1968, 1971, 1972, 1977) has described these in three papers and two books, and his work represents a major step forward in our understanding and treatment of narcissistic and borderline personality disorders.

Freud's "Observations on Transference Love" (Freud 1915A;12:158–174) also opens up the issue of countertransference, which Freud does not discuss at any great length in any of his writings. An important point made in the paper on transference love is:

> The more plainly the analyst lets it be seen that he is proof against every temptation, the more readily will he be able to extract from the situation its analytic content. The patient, whose sexual repression is of course not yet removed but merely pushed into the background, will then feel safe enough to allow all her preconditions for loving, all the phantasies springing from her sexual desires, all the detailed characteristics of her state of being in love, to come

> to light; and from these she will herself open the way to the infantile roots of her love (p. 166).

It is obvious that the responsibility in this situation falls entirely on the psychotherapist. If the therapist has had a thorough intensive psychotherapy and does not manifest a disruptive countertransference, and as soon as the patient becomes convinced that he or she is really safe from an assault or a sexual seduction on the part of the therapist, he will be rewarded by a flood of important material regarding the infantile roots and fantasies of the patient's erotic drives. This is why it is almost invariably a mistake to engage in any form of physical contact whatsoever with any patient, since at some level this is inevitably interpreted on the part of the patient as a potentially repeatable gesture, regardless of the context in which the physical contact has occurred. Physical contact invariably shifts the focus of the patient's ego away from uncovering and reporting the material and toward the effort of attaining repeated gratification from the therapist.

Freud explains that for those therapists who are still young and not yet bound by strong ties it may be a very hard task indeed to deny the gratification of the patient's love and the sense of narcissistic conquest such love proposes. One crucial battle the analytic psychotherapist must wage in his own mind is against the forces which seek to drag him down from the analytic level; the therapist's major protection in this battle comes from his own psychotherapy. Thus in intensive psychotherapy we are dealing with highly explosive forces and, as Freud explains, we need to proceed "with as much caution and conscientiousness as a chemist"; if such caution and conscientiousness are not observed, the dangers to both patient and psychotherapist are similar to the dangers of handling explosive chemical substances. The permanent ethical obligation on the part of the psychotherapist is quite clear; any slipping from this obligation is a mandatory signal for further intensive psychotherapy of the psychotherapist.

A detailed discussion of the dynamics of the transference itself is presented in Freud's very difficult paper "Remembering, Repeating and Working Through" (Freud 1914G;12:146–156). In this extremely condensed paper Freud points out that the transference is actually a manifestation of the compulsion to repeat, a compulsion which is one of the conceptual cornerstones of our understanding of patients in psychotherapy. Freud explains that the compulsion to repeat, by the formation of the transference, replaces the impulsion to remember "not only in his personal attitude to his doctor but also in every other activity and relationship which may occupy his life at the time—if, for instance, he falls in love or undertakes a task or starts an enterprise during the treatment" (p. 151). For example, the patient does not say that he remembers that he used to be defiant and critical toward his parent's authority—instead he behaves that way to the doctor. "He does not remember how he came to a helpless and hopeless deadlock in his infantile sexual researches; but he produces a mass of confused dreams and associations, complains that he cannot succeed in anything and asserts that he is fated never to carry through what he undertakes" (p. 190).

Because of the compulsion to repeat, it is necessary to ask all patients not to make any important decisions affecting their life without discussing them at length in the therapy; Freud recommends not until finishing the treatment. Since intensive psychotherapy lasts a long time, Freud's request is usually impractical and can be unreasonable. On the other hand, the therapist must prevent if possible the sudden announcement of a major decision already made by the patient and carried through without prior discussion in the psychotherapy—an action which represents a serious form of acting out in the transference. To extract the patient's promise to discuss major decisions before taking action is a form of protection for the patient; but of course the main instrument for curbing this dangerous acting-out lies in the proper recognition and interpretation of the transference.

Another important stimulus to the countertransference of the psychotherapist is the arduous task of working through of resistances, which represents "a trial of patience" (Freud) for the therapist. The first step in overcoming resistance is made by uncovering the resistance and at least acquainting the patient with it intellectually. However, "One must allow the patient time to become more conversant with this resistance with which he has now become acquainted, to *work through* it, to overcome it, by continuing, in defiance of it, the analytic work according to the fundamental rule of analysis" (p. 155). In these situations, a sense of growing impatience in the therapist is an important manifestation of countertransference; and careful study of the therapist's impatience will often reveal new material about what sort of stimulus the patient is presenting. Most typically it reveals that we are dealing with one of the narcissistic transferences (Kohut 1968).

For example, if an idealizing transference has formed, the therapist may become impatient with what appears to be a lack of emotion in the patient each time an inevitable separation occurs through cancellations or vacations. The patient instead displays coldness and withdrawal into aloof irritation, sometimes accompanied by a feeling of fragmentation, hypochondria, and "deadness." The therapist may become astonished by the patient's absolute refusal to recognize any need on the part of the therapist for vacation, and by the cold, grandiose retreat that occurs when such interruptions are announced. Similarly when the mirroring transferences have formed, the apparent lack of object-relatedness with regard to the therapist may be mistaken for the outgrowth of widespread resistance against the establishment of a transference. It is actually characteristic of the mirroring transference that the obvious and typical manifestations of object-relationship in the transference appear to be entirely absent.

At this point, in a mistaken and unprofitable direction against diffuse, nonspecific, and chronic ego resistances of the patient, the therapist may engage in frenzied therapeutic activity, causing a short-circuiting of the uncovering psychotherapy in a countertransference attempt to force the patient to form an object-relationship! At this point, as Kohut (1968) explains, many analyses of narcissistic personality disorders may be short-circuited "leading to a brief analysis of subsidiary sectors of the personality in which ordinary transferences do occur while the principal disturbance, which is narcissistic, remains untouched" (p. 101). Really necessary, instead, is a careful working-through of the narcissistic transferences by a calm, well-trained craftsman with clear metapsychological understanding and an absence of suggestive pressure from the weight of the personality of the therapist. A lack of emotional involvement in the patient, the feeling of boredom, and the precarious maintenance of attention are described by Kohut as typical warning signs indicating the reaction of the therapist to a mirroring transference. The impatience felt by the therapist in these cases really represents anxiety and rage over being used as a self-object by the narcissistic individual.

The last lecture Freud personally delivered is Lecture 28 of the *Introductory Lectures on Psychoanalysis* (1916X;15:448–463). As a discussion of the theory of the therapeutic effects of psychoanalysis, it should be compared with one of his last papers, "Analysis Terminable and Interminable" (1937C;23:211–254), which differs in some important respects. Lecture 28, however, contains the best answer to a constantly repeated criticism of psychoanalytically oriented psychotherapy—that it works primarily by suggestion. Through its emphasis on an understanding of the phenomenon of transference and on clarifying the difference between the manipulation of a patient in a positive transference—which is a form of suggestion, not a form of uncovering psychotherapy—and its emphasis on the use of the transference and interpretations for the purpose of uncovering unconscious psychic processes, this lecture decisively refutes the argument that psychoanalysis is merely a form of suggestion. Every intensive psychotherapist should read this chapter for himself.

13

DREAMS

The work that Freud considered to be his greatest masterpiece, *The Interpretation of Dreams* (1900A;4 and 5), may be approached through an easily readable summary in chapters 9 and 10 of Robert (1966). To me, one of the most remarkable things about *The Interpretation of Dreams* is that although it has gone through nine editions (Freud amplified it several times), large sections of this work are just as pertinent today as they were at the time of the foundation of psychoanalysis. Because it is such a major work Freud was under pressure to develop a nontechnical account, which he did in 1901 in the short work entitled "On Dreams" (1901A;5:631ff). This work contains a basic summary of Freud's conception of dreams but it omits the innumerable examples (including many of Freud's own dreams) which illustrate dramatically the creative agonies that Freud experienced in attaining his understanding of dreams. Psychotherapists should study *The Interpretation of Dreams* directly, especially the sections I will indicate below. (Chapter VII is discussed separately in chapter 8 of the present book.)

To summarize briefly Freud's well-known theory, dreams have "a meaning." Thus he writes (1900A;4:96), "Interpreting a dream implies assigning a 'meaning' to it—that is, replacing it by something which fits into the chain of our mental acts as a link having a validity and importance equal to the rest." This procedure is just as valid today as it was in Freud's time, and forms an important activity during intensive psychotherapy. What the dreamer remembers on awakening is the manifest dream content; the analysis of the dream reveals the hidden, or latent, content which has been transformed into the manifest content by the dream work. Interpreting the dream consists of discovering this latent content.

Freud saw children's dreams as simply wish fulfilments; even when they are complicated he insisted it was always easy to reduce them to a satisfaction of a wish. In adult dreams the same infantile wish fulfilment remains as the basic meaning, but the dream work changes the content so we are dreaming with the goal of fantasy fulfilment of a disguised, hidden, or repressed infantile wish. This disguise occurs through a compression or a condensation of the primitive elements in the dream, and through displacement, including a reversal or an exchange of important emotional investments in the dream. Thus what was strong and important in the latent thought is transferred to something weak and insignificant, and trivial items may take on an intense and central place. This "deceitful" shift of emphasis contributes the most to the apparent absurdity of dreams. Freud also stressed symbolism of dreams, but I believe dream symbolism to be the most treacherous and least reliable element in dream interpretation during intensive psychotherapy; thus symbol-reading should be avoided.

A dream represents a process of regression that manifests itself simultaneously in three ways: as topical regression from the conscious to the unconscious; a temporal regression from the present time to childhood; and as formal regression, from the level of language to that of pictorial and symbolic representations (for details, see Arlow and Brenner 1964).

Freud's brief paper (1908C;9:207ff) on the sexual theories of children presents the well-known fantasies that children have of fertilization through the mouth, of birth through the anus, of parental intercourse as something sadistic, and of the possession of a penis by both sexes. These fantasies are extremely important in the practice of intensive psychotherapy as well as in understanding dreams; they come up again and again, so that every therapist should be familiar with them and be watching for them in the material of his patients. No better description of the sexual theories of children exists than Freud's original one in this paper.

One can follow the actual analysis of a dream in Freud's case history of Dora (1905E;7:3ff), already discussed in chapter 11. The case centers on two main dreams, which are analyzed at length. I would suggest that the student begin, however, with the famous Irma dream constituting much of chapter II of *The Interpretation of Dreams* and from which Freud concludes that "when the work of interpretation has been completed, we perceive that a dream is the fulfilment of a wish" (p. 121).

The student reader may begin with chapter II (and the brief chapter III) of *The Interpretation of Dreams*, in which Freud demonstrates that a dream fits consistently into the general mental content of an individual, and can be interpreted and given meaning. The procedure for doing this (see chapter II, p. 100) was developed during his therapeutic work with cases of hysteria and other neuroses; it represents essentially the method of free association.

Chapter IV launches into the concept of distortion in dreams and develops the key principles that follow logically if one accepts the basic premise that every dream fulfils a wish. Thus the concepts of the latent dream and manifest dream, the concept of things being represented by their opposites, and of multiple meanings are presented. The notion of defense and the idea that "dreams are given their shape in individual human beings by the operation of two psychical forces (or we may describe them as currents or systems); and that one of these forces constructs the wish which is expressed by the dream, while the other exercises a censorship upon this dream-wish and, by the use of that censorship, forcibly brings about a distortion in the expression of the wish" (p. 144). This leads us to conclusions regarding the structure of the mental apparatus, and forms the connecting link between the formation of a neurosis and the formation of a dream, thereby implying that the procedures involved in the formation of a neurosis also take place in normal people.

Chapter IV contains scattered clinical insights such as the discussion of dreams which are produced specifically to prove that the theory that dreams fulfil a wish is wrong, and so on. It provides a fascinating picture of Freud at work in the early days and concludes definitively with the statement that a dream is always the disguised fulfilment of a repressed wish.

The beginning student could skim over chapter V and continue with chapter VI, sections A. through C. Here Freud introduces the concepts of condensation, multiple meanings, over-determination, displacement (of both emphasis or through elements related by association), and plastic representation—the transposition of thoughts into imagery, as in the plastic arts.

In sections D. and E. of chapter VI, Freud covers the somewhat obsolete subject of symbolization and of secondary elaboration or revision to make an acceptable or intelligible whole out of the dream. This subject is deemphasized in Freud's later writings about dreams and these two sections could be omitted without great loss to the beginner. The whole purpose of chapter VI is to help the student to translate the manifest dream into the latent dream content, just as Freud attempts to translate neurotic symptoms into repressed infantile wishes. In both conditions, the methodology for investigation and the manner of disguise used by the "censor" are identical. A number of authors (Ricoeur 1970, for example) have emphasized the similarity of this "translation" to hermaneutics rather than to the natural sciences.

Wollheim (1971) summarizes the dream theory as follows: "There is a persisting repressed wish, which forms the motive behind the dream. In the course of the day, this wish comes into contact, or forms an association, with a thought or train of thought. This thought has some energy attached to it, independently of this contact, through not having as yet been "worked over": hence the phrase, the 'residues of the day.' The upshot is that the thought—or association to it—is revived in sleep, as the proxy of the wish" (pp. 70–71).

One question remains to be asked about this process: Why should it assert itself while we are asleep? The answer is not that sleep is peculiarly conducive to the repressed wish, but that it prefers the disguised expression of it to any more naked version of the same forces. If the wish did not express itself in the disguise of the dream, it would disturb sleep. And so we come to the overall function of dreams: they are *"the guardians of sleep."* We see that the function of the dream is to discharge the tensions of the repressed forbidden wish; if these are extreme the dream will be charged with anxiety and the sleeper may even wake up.

The theory of dreams as the guardians of sleep brings us into the realm of modern physiological research. A complete review of the implications of recent neurophysiological research on sleep and dreaming for the intensive psychotherapist is presented by Fischer (1965). Although the matter is presently of great intellectual interest, modern physiological research has contributed little to the day-by-day clinical work of intensive psychotherapy, which concentrates on the psychological meaning of dreams as defined by Freud in 1900.

The matter is even more complicated because, as Freud recognized, dreams have many meanings. As he explains (1900A;4:279), "I have already had occasion to point out that it is in fact never possible to be sure that a dream has been completely interpreted. Even if the solution seems satisfactory and without gaps, the possibility always remains that the dream may have yet another meaning. Strictly speaking, then, it is impossible to determine the amount of condensation." This is one of the dividing-points between formal psychoanalysis and intensive psychotherapy, because in the latter, with less time available, the therapist must be more active in making choices both of how much to emphasize interpretation of dreams and of what aspects of the dreams to concentrate on in the psychotherapy. The details of the actual clinical working with dreams in intensive psychotherapy have been presented in chapter 10 of the *Technique and Practice of Intensive Psychotherapy* (Chessick 1974) and will not be reviewed again here.

The existentialists (May 1958) distinguished three modes of experiencing the world, three simultaneous aspects of the world which characterize the existence of each one of us as being in the world. These are *Umwelt*—the world around us, the environment; *Mitwelt*—the world of beings of one's own kind; and *Eigenwelt*—the mode of relationship to one's self. Keep in mind these three modes of being in the world that every human experiences, for sometimes they appear dramatically in dreams. As an example, a patient with a chronic characterologic depression presented the following dreams during one session:

> In the first dream I was feeling pain in my chest and looked down at my nipples; I saw a plastic cap instead of the nipple. I opened the plastic cap where the left nipple would be and a lot of air pressure was released, after which I felt better. In the second dream I was

> driving over the Dakota badlands. It was a very desolate landscape and there were many cliffs and rocks that had to be negotiated; it did seem, however, that I was getting where I was trying to go. In the third dream, I was in lush country but all alone. In the distance I saw a gang of men crossing a river and heading in my direction. I loaded my gun and carefully took aim to be prepared for whatever might happen, for there were no sheriffs or police within a thousand miles. If these were bandits and marauders I was resolved to fight to the death; but I was not sure what they were.

One way of looking at this dream series in the course of a psychotherapy is that it indicated where the patient was at this given transitional point in his treatment with respect to his *Umwelt*, *Mitwelt*, and *Eigenwelt*. His relationship to himself indicated some feeling of a withdrawal of libido from the self-representation, in that a mechanical device replaced one of his nipples. The release of pressure had to do with the material of the previous sessions in which there was much discussion of his deep anger; of course, one could indicate the important symbolic aspect of this anger occurring at the nipples, with its oral aggressive implication. With respect to *Umwelt*, one gets a picture of how the patient experiences the environment around him—the desolation and rocky cliffs. At the same time there is hope, for the patient is very slowly progressing across this terrain. Finally, in the *Mitwelt*, we see clearly the patient's sense of personal isolation and danger. At the same time there is a similar ray of hope in that the advancing men may not *necessarily* be bandits or marauders; they may be friendly. Thus in this transition dream, as the patient is slowly moving away from a deep characterologic depression, there is a beautiful plastic representation of the patient's existential experience of the three modes of being in the world. This is an interesting example of how Freud's teachings may be supplemented and complemented by the findings of existential philosophy and psychotherapy. It is especially valuable in intensive psychotherapy to pay attention to the patient's experience of being in the world, since the time for thorough dream analysis is extremely limited.

In a short series of papers on the theory and practice of dream interpretation (1923C;19:108–121, 1925I;19:125–138) Freud presents some useful pointers on the psychotherapeutic approach to dreams. In approaching a dream one can proceed chronologically and get the dreamer to associate to the elements of the dream in the order in which those elements occurred in his account of the dream—this is Freud's original favorite classical method and is best, he advises, if one is analyzing one's own dreams. Other alternatives are to start from some particular element of the dream such as the most striking part of it, or the most intense aspect of it, and so forth; or to ask about the events of the previous day as associated with the dream just described; or to remain silent and let the patient decide where to begin.

A more important technical point is the question of the pressure of resistance—whether it is high or low at the point of approach to the dream. Thus if there is much resistance, the associations to the dream broaden instead of deepen, and it is unwise to spend too much time trying to make out the meaning of the dream. Freud specifically advises against an exaggerated respect for dreams since they are merely "a form of thinking," a definition often stressed by Freud. He also warns us to be on the lookout for obliging dreams or corroborative dreams that have the possible function of fooling the therapist.

He reminds us that the dreamer's ego can appear two or more times in the manifest dream, perhaps once as himself and also disguised behind the figures of other people. In contrast to the popular notion he writes, "Nor would it be of any avail for anyone to endeavor to interpret dreams outside analysis" (p. 128). Thus dream interpretation is not an isolated activity and can only be performed as part of the work of psychoanalysis or intensive psychotherapy. Freud's modesty with respect to dreams is quite thorough, and he repeatedly warns against pressing conjectures and interpretations of dreams on patients, especially interpretations toward which the dreamer has contributed little in the way of useful associations or memories. He reminds us that separation of the ego from the superego must be taken into account in the interpretation of dreams and that it sometimes accounts for multiple appearances of the ego in the same dream. As every good clinician knows, the success of dream interpretation depends primarily—as Freud points out—upon the level of resistance in the awakened ego at the time of the patient's examination of the dream. Thus the techniques for dealing with resistance are the most crucial to the eventual success of understanding the unconscious of the patient.

Freud's paper, "Wild Psychoanalysis" (1910K;11:220–230), should be required reading for all beginners in the field of mental illness; another title for the paper could be "Cocktail Party Psychoanalysis." In Freud's case vignette, a middle-aged lady has been told by her doctor that the cause of her anxiety is lack of sexual satisfaction and has been advised either to return to her husband (whom she had recently divorced), take a lover, or masturbate (I must admit with regret that even today this presents a popular misconception of the kind of advice psychoanalytically informed psychotherapists give their patients).

Of course Freud points out the obvious: he begins with the important clinical caution that one should not accept as true what patients report that their physicians have said or done to them. Physicians, especially psychiatrists, easily become the target of their patients' hostile feelings and often become, by projection, responsible in the patient's mind for the patient's own repressed wishes. In another publication (1910J;11:236–237) he gives an example of a patient who insisted that if she saw Freud he would ask her if she ever had the idea of having sexual intercourse with her father. Freud points out that it is not his practice to ask such questions, and warns us that much of what patients report of the words and actions of their physicians may be understood as revelations of their own pathogenic fantasies. Anyone in the practice of psychotherapy can attest to this; I have been amazed from time to time at what patients have reported to others that I have allegedly said or done to them. Conversely, I have received innumerable reports from patients of what other physicians have allegedly said or done to them; in the course of therapy it becomes apparent that these allegations are usually projections and fantasies.

In our present age of malpractice suits, such allegations may result in serious problems and Freud's warning must be carefully kept in mind when accusations are made that can damage the reputation of a psychotherapist or even lead to legal procedures. The contemporary tendency of the public, based on hostility to physicians and especially to psychiatrists, is to accept all these claims at face value; therefore, it is incumbent on any examining board to be extremely careful in evaluating such reports and to protect the isolated practitioner vigorously where such protection is justifiable and indicated.

Recent conferences on sexual acting-out between patients and therapists have tended to ignore Freud's warning and to concentrate instead on the clearly unethical aspects of such behavior when it actually does occur. This approach produces anxiety in the minds of even the most conscientious psychotherapists and tends to further isolate and estrange the clinician from his fellows; it is bad for the profession and it is bad for the mental health of the psychiatrist. In some hands this approach simply becomes more ammunition for a wide-scale attack on all intensive psychotherapy—indeed, the motivation behind the repetition and publication of unsubstantiated complaints can often be traced to a total rejection of the psychological method of healing employed in psychoanalytically informed psychotherapy.

Whether or not the doctor in Freud's case vignette actually gave his patient such poor advice, the scientific errors involved in misunderstanding the meaning of sexual life and in the notion that sexual abstinence produces mental disorders are obvious. More subtle are the technical errors which are worthwhile to call to our attention repeatedly. As Freud explains "If knowledge about the unconscious were as important for the patient as people inexperienced in psychoanalysis imagine, listening to lectures or reading books would be enough to cure him. Such measures, however, have as much influence on the symptoms of nervous illness as a distribution of menu-cards in a time of famine has upon hunger" (1910K;11:225). He continues: "First, the patient must, through preparation, himself have reached the neighborhood of what he has repressed, and secondly, he must have formed a sufficient attachment (transference) to the physician for his emotional relationship to him to make a fresh flight impossible. Only when these conditions have been fulfilled is it possible to recognize and to master resistances which have led to the repression and the ignorance. Psychoanalytic intervention, therefore, absolutely requires a fairly long period of contact with the patient" (p. 226).

Thus wild interpretations or attempts to rush the patient by brusquely telling him about his unconscious not only do not work; they usually inspire the patient's hearty enmity and may eliminate any further influence by the physician. Freud also points out that one may be *wrong* in such early surmises, and that one is never in a position to discover the whole truth. The technique of psychoanalytically informed psychotherapy, like other medical techniques, cannot be learned from books and must be accomplished with great sacrifice of time and labor.

This is one of the few places where I disagree with Saul's (1958) otherwise outstanding book *The Technique and Practice of Psychoanalysis*. Saul recommends an early discussion with the patient of the nuclear dynamics of the patient's problems. I think this can be very dangerous except in the most experienced hands. The best argument against such a procedure is presented in the previous quotation from Freud, who was certainly correct when he pointed out that wild or cocktail party psychoanalysis does more harm to the cause of psychoanalysis and psychotherapy than to individual patients, since it usually results in a stalemate, with the patient leaving therapy as an angry and vociferous opponent of the entire procedure.

14

BEGINNING THE TREATMENT

An important comment on beginning the treatment is made by Freud on the first page of his *Introductory Lectures on Lectures on Psychoanalysis* (1916X;15:15). He teaches that at the very beginning we point out the difficulties of the method to the patient, ". . . its long duration, the efforts and sacrifices it calls for; and as regards its success, we tell him we cannot promise it with certainty, that it depends on his own conduct, his understanding, his adaptability and his perseverance." I believe it is most important to confront the patient at the very beginning with the expense and the difficulty of what he is proposing to undertake in the process of intensive psychotherapy, and never in any way to minimize its length or hardships, or to try to "sell" the prospective patient on the procedure.

Continuing, Freud describes the role of the psychotherapist as follows: "The doctor listens, tries to direct the patient's processes of thought, exhorts, forces his attention in certain directions, gives him explanations and observes the reactions of understanding or rejection which he in this way provokes in him" (1916X;15:17). Although Freud later modified this position to a more neutral stance, and less and less frequently employed the word "doctor," it is still an excellent description of the challenges of intensive psychotherapy.

One of Freud's most famous statements on the first phase or beginning of psychotherapy comes from the paper "On Beginning the Treatment":

> Anyone who hopes to learn the noble game of chess from books will soon discover that only the openings and end-games admit of an exhaustive systematic presentation and that the infinite variety of moves which develop after the opening defy any such description. This gap in instruction can only be filled by a diligent study of games fought out by masters. The rules which can be laid down for the practice of psycho-analytic treatment are subject to similar limitations (Freud 1913C;12:123).

It should be noted that Freud follows this quotation with a warning that any such rules are only recommendations and may have to be modified as the case requires.

Following the chess analogy, we speak of strategy and tactics in psychotherapy. *One of the most common student mistakes in the conduct of psychotherapy occurs when the tactics are not consistent with the strategy. Strategy* refers to our ultimate goals and to decisions about our general approach in helping a given patient in the light of the patient's psychodynamics; while *tactics* refers to the day-by-day operation of the psychotherapeutic process. Thus, for example, if our strategy in the psychotherapy is decided to be one of general support and education and we find ourself employing the tactics of interpretation, something is going to go wrong with the treatment. In another example, Freud contrasts a strategy in which a case is used primarily for scientific research, with a strategy in which treatment is the primary goal. He notes, "Cases which are devoted from the first to scientific purposes and are treated accordingly suffer in their outcome; while the most successful cases are those in which one proceeds, as it were, without any purpose in view, allows oneself to be taken by surprise by any new turn in them, and always meets them with an open mind, free from any presupposition" (1912E;12:114).

This is not to suggest that the therapist should never change the strategy of the treatment in accord with the vicissitudes of the case; but on the whole the overall strategy and goal of the treatment should remain consistent and relatively permanent. The tactics, then, should be chosen on a day-to-day basis to match the strategy.

One must also be aware that *the strategy of the patient's unconscious is to resist uncovering*, and that the patient uses a number of tactics in the service of such resistance. For example, in the first of his six papers on technique Freud (1911E;12:86–96) points out how the patient may overwhelm the therapist with a mass of dreams far beyond what is possible to analyze in the given time. Worrying about the thorough understanding of any given dream or taking a "scientific" interest in dream material can interfere with the therapy, and one of Freud's therapeutic rules is to keep in touch all the time with the current thoughts and emotions occupying the patient's mind even though it means the inevitable loss of understanding of some dream material due to time limitations. However, the therapist may certainly be confident that any dream material "lost" by not completely interpreting an interesting dream will recur again in one form or another. Furthermore, a dream incompletely interpreted in one session should not be picked up in the next session unless the patient does so—thus in the subsequent session we deal with whatever the patient brings in at the beginning of the session, including new dreams, and we need not feel uneasy about neglecting the old dreams. These recommendations are even more important in intensive psychotherapy than in psychoanalysis, since in the former, a smaller frequency of sessions necessitates the loss of a certain amount of dream material.

Probably the most important and most difficult precept to learn in the practice of intensive psychotherapy is the achievement of evenly hovering or evenly suspended attention. Freud explains that the therapist

> . . . must turn his own unconscious like a receptive organ towards the transmitting unconscious of the patient. He must adjust himself to the patient as a telephone receiver is adjusted to the transmitting microphone. Just as the receiver converts back into sound waves the electric oscillations in the telephone line which were set up by sound waves, so the doctor's unconscious is able, from the derivatives of the unconscious which are communicated to him, to reconstruct that unconscious, which has determined the patient's free associations (1912E;12:115–116).

To use this procedure, which requires a certain innate talent, Freud points out that the therapist may not tolerate any resistances in himself which hold back from his consciousness what has been perceived by his unconscious—that is, every unresolved repression in the therapist constitutes a "blind spot" in his analytic perception.

This brings us back to the chess model of psychotherapy. In chess, the incapacity to see what is going on condemns one to permanent mediocrity. The disease of "chess blindness" *(amaurosis schacchistica)* was first delineated by the famous Dr. Tarrasch, and is briefly described in a fine book by Evans (1970). The famous championship game in which one grand master left his Queen *en prise* and his opponent was afraid to take it off and did not do so, fearing some clever trap, is also described by Evans.

"We must above all see what is more or less hidden," wrote Tarrasch (1959); but how does one learn how to do this? The problem is amazingly parallel to the problem of learning how to conduct the middle phase of psychotherapy. How often we hear the novice complaining that he does not "see" what the supervisor has picked up in the material, and therefore could not make the needed interpretation.

The more one studies the chess champions and their games, the more one becomes aware of the amazing complexity of mental functioning and the prodigious memory that is required to be a fine chess player. To isolate the factor of "seeing" the potentials on the board is almost impossibly difficult; perhaps the chess book that concentrates most on it is the only chess book I know of that presents programmed instruction, by Fischer (1966). The entire subject is badly in need of our attention, not only because of its intrinsic interest but because of the obvious parallel to psychotherapy.

Freud was the first to point out the chess parallel, since taken up many times by many authors. Perhaps the most thorough discussion of the "chess model" of psychoanalysis is that of Szasz (1957), in a very different and controversial paper; he points out the little-noted analogy that in chess, as in psychotherapy, "each player *influences the other continuously.*"

With the exception of a few remarks by Colby (1951) no author to my knowledge has pointed out in detail the parallel between teaching the middle phase of chess and the middle phase of psychotherapy. It is even difficult to admit that some psychotherapists have the analog of "chess blindness" when confronted with patient material; it seems incredible that the years of supervision have not uncovered this blindness and perhaps inclined the therapist to some other way of making a living. An additional benefit to the required study of chess in a psychotherapy training program, besides the usual virtues of developing patience, logical thought, and an understanding of the chess-model theory of psychotherapy, would be an improved awareness of the inherent difficulties in "seeing" what the patient is trying to communicate in the myriad of material. We need to focus much more on the problem.

This brings us again to my favorite subject, stressed in all my books and more than once in this one: the absolute necessity for a thorough intensive psychotherapy of the psychotherapist. Freud also again and again points out the importance of the analyst's own analysis and explains that if this is neglected not only will the psychotherapist be penalized by an incapacity to learn from his patients, but will also risk a more serious danger which may become a danger for others. As Freud explains, "He will easily fall into the temptation of projecting outwards some of the peculiarities of his own personality, which he has dimly perceived, into the field of science, as a theory having universal validity; he will bring the psycho-analytic method into discredit, and lead the inexperienced astray" (1912E;12:117).

There is a parallel between the overall strategy of uncovering in psychotherapy—the amount of evenly suspended attention that the psychotherapist demands from himself—and the amount of free association he hopes to understand from his patient. This is just another way of rephrasing what has already been said, in that the more we wish to learn about the patient's unconscious, the more we have to use the techniques of empathic identification with the patient by using our unconscious like a receptive organ aimed at the transmitter of the unconscious of the patient. Again, I stress that such procedures as taking copious notes or tape recording sessions will *invariably* represent serious interference with the procedure of uncovering psychotherapy, and no psychotherapist should fool himself into believing that the presence of a tape recorder in the room makes no difference to the patient or that the patient and the therapist "get used to it." *If* the strategy of the psychotherapy is to uncover the patient's unconscious, it may be generalized that *any* deviation from the procedure of the psychotherapist's evenly suspended attention—even answering the telephone during the session—will interfere with the pure transmission and reception of the unconscious. In psychotherapy it is at times unavoidable to step away from this strategy, but such steps should occur only when absolutely necessary and with a full understanding of the dangerous consequences and the possibility of countertransference.

This brings us to the famous and highly controversial and misunderstood notion introduced by Freud: "I cannot advise my colleagues too urgently to model themselves during psychoanalytic treatment on the surgeon, who puts aside all his feelings, even his human sympathy, and concentrates his mental forces on the single aim of performing the operation as skillfully as possible" (1912E;12:115). This quotation has been badly misunderstood because the remainder of the paragraph has not been studied. A full examination of paragraph "(e)" in this paper indicates that Freud is warning against two major disrupting factors in uncovering psychotherapy. First, he warns against the narcissism of the psychotherapist as manifested in the ambition to cure. Second, he warns against an overidentification with the patient, where sympathy replaces empathy and the patient begins to disrupt the personal life of the therapist. There is no reason to believe that Freud was ordering us to be cold and impassive toward our patients, although taken in context with a later statement: "The doctor should be opaque to his patients and like a mirror, should show them nothing but what is shown to him" (p. 118)—his comments have been used as an excuse by sadistic or schizoid psychoanalysts and psychotherapists to inflict suffering on their patients or to avoid any normal ordinary human or physicianly (Chessick 1974) involvement with their patients altogether. One glance at *Bergasse 19* (Engelman 1976) tells us that Freud was anything but opaque to his patients; looking at the office he occupied at once reveals the character of Freud the psychotherapist. There is not the slightest question that Freud was at all times a concerned physician, putting the basic welfare of his patient first and taking his obligation to his patients very seriously indeed.

Looking again at the pitfalls Freud was trying to avoid with his "surgeon" analogy, it is clear that the therapeutic ambitions of the therapist can be very destructive to the patient. The thorough analysis of the psychotherapist's reasons for becoming a psychotherapist is absolutely necessary before he attempts to undertake intensive psychotherapy. Those therapists who have an unresolved narcissistic problem in their need to be a magic healer are a public menace and are unfortunately all too common. This narcissistic ambition may be cleverly hidden behind ministerial humility, altruistic social work, psychological research, and medical treatment. The other equally lethal countertransference problem lies in overidentification with the patient and usually hides a wish to destroy the patient out of frustration with the case, either because the therapist does not understand what is going on in the case, or because the patient is not responding by fulfilling the therapist's neurotic need for dramatic cures, or providing other forms of gratification. This destructive wish also can be explained away by the insufficiently treated psychotherapist through a whole variety of rationalizations. Freud makes clear what he has in mind in the "surgeon" analogy by mentioning the quotation from the famous French surgeon Ambroise Paré, who wrote, "I dressed his wounds, God cured him."

Freud agrees that a psychotherapist may have to combine a certain amount of analysis with some suggestive influence, but he points out that this is not "true psycho-analysis." This is a correct statement but has led to a lot of unfortunate acrimony because of the irritating status problem involved, Freud was attempting to present a theoretical model of a "true psycho-analysis" in which the therapist listens with evenly suspended attention and by empathic identification receives the transmissions from the patient's unconscious, then transmitting these back to the patient via appropirate interpretation. In my judgment it is never possible to do *only* this in the years of an ongoing treatment relationship with a patient, since the treatment relationship is, of course, also an important human relationship—probably the most important human relationship the patient has ever had. The question therefore is not whether we should deviate from Freud's theoretical model but rather when and how often. There is a spectrum between the most pure possible psychoanalysis at the one end and essentially purely supportive psychotherapy at the other. Although the width of this spectrum remains a matter of controversy (Chessick 1969, 1977), any conscientious psychotherapist would agree that deviations from the theoretical model, when there is a strategy of uncovering intensive psychotherapy, must be performed deliberately, for good reason, and certainly not out of countertransference problems of the therapist.

The presence or absence of such deviations must be noted by the psychotherapist from the very beginning of the treatment. Thus Freud's recommendations on beginning the treatment are clearly aimed at minimizing any deviations from his theoretical model of true psychoanalysis. I have made my own recommendations on the beginning of the treatment in intensive psychotherapy (Chessick 1969, 1974); they are based essentially on Freud's recommendations, but with modifications for twentieth-century America and for the needs of intensive psychotherapy, dealing with cases other than classic neuroses.

For example, Freud's recommendation of taking on the patient provisionally for a period of one to two weeks means, in the context of psychotherapy, that we should not generally try to make recommendations to the patient in one interview, but rather, if possible, have three or four sessions with the patient over a period of one or two weeks before reaching any long-range plans or conclusions. His advice of mistrusting all prospective patients who want to make a delay before beginning their treatment, and his warning about the special difficulties that arise when the therapist and his new patient (or their families) are on terms of friendship or have social ties are just as appropriate today as they were in Freud's time. I can see no good reason to undertake the psychotherapy of a friend, or of members of families with whom one is on social terms, and I extend this to a refusal to undertake the psychotherapy of any neighbors within walking range of the psychotherapist's home. There is no shortage of psychotherapists in most major cities and it is more ethical to try to refer such patients to others.

As I have stated previously (Chessick 1977*b*), certain special difficulties arise, especially at the beginning treatment of any psychiatrist's family members. The fact that a person is a psychiatrist does not necessarily mean that he is free of major pathology, that he can make objective judgments about his family, or that he believes in the efficacy of psychotherapy at all. It also does not mean that he is so sufficiently free of narcissistic developmental pathology that he does not regard his family members as selfobjects and can empathize with their difficulties. When the chips are down, such parents and spouses sometimes may tend to put their professional reputations above their empathic considerations of the need for treatment of their wives and children.

For example, the experience of an adolescent child is an assault to the narcissism of any parent; the experience of a disturbed adolescent child is a many times more profound assault to the narcissism and idealized self-image of the parent who is also a psychiatrist. The parent with unresolved preoedipal problems will feel most assaulted. As Cohen and Balikov (1974) point out, "Many adults have made relatively stable developmental adaptations which provide compensation for many character problems which arise from poorly achieved separation-individuation from archaic objects. However, it is precisely in the parenting roles where these adaptations may break down. Derivatives of early developmental experience intrude and create transferences to the child which are once again internalized into the psychic structure." Of course, a similar danger point for the breakdown of such adaptations is in the marital relationship, especially after the late marriages commonly seen in physicians.

First, a *dangerous delay* can take place in referral for psychotherapy; in extreme examples, I have seen the most overt schizophrenic psychopathology blandly ignored by a highly respected psychiatrist father or husband. In two cases this happened *twice* with first an older and then a younger sibling; only when the patient began calling attention to himself in school by very bizarre behavior was treatment reluctantly employed.

Second, whether due to middle-age depression, too many years in the office, or to other factors, a peculiar loss of confidence in psychotherapy itself sometimes seems to occur in these psychiatrist fathers and husbands, a loss of confidence also communicated to their wives and children. Paradoxically, this may be true even though the psychiatrist is actively engaged in a busy psychotherapeutic practice. It produces a sense of despair in the prospective patient, and tends to delay self-referral for psychotherapy among the wives of psychiatrists.

Third, one should be very alert for the family "secret." I have observed this in several cases during treatment of both wives and children. Some important "secret" had to be kept from me in order to preserve the father's or husband's reputation. This often represents a factor in the delay of seeking psychotherapy, and is a great block to the beginning phase of the treatment. Interestingly, the most common "secret" is serious alcoholism, although I have encountered one case of drug addiction and several of perversion or impotence. These "secrets" of highly respected and successful professionals are known only to the immediate family.

Fourth, one may encounter a remarkable refusal of recommendations for treatment among the spouse or parent psychiatrists. Some of them (in my series, Chessick 1977*b*) already had clearly unsuccessful or limited treatments, and some of them had none at all. All admitted they were in need of treatment, but when the matter came up, every one refused to seek psychotherapy, even though it was made clear that their marital problems or their problems with their children made such therapy mandatory. My impression was that these people were primarily frightened; I was surprised at the profound fears and insecurity so prevalent in these apparently successful husband or father psychiatrists. One cannot react to this with anything but compassion for their intense suffering, which seems to be increased by the very act of sending a family member for intensive psychotherapy—and with a resolve to be as gentle and tactful as possible. Except in two cases where the adolescent was still living at home, I did not consider it my part to directly recommend psychotherapy for the father or husband; the recommendation often repeatedly and emphatically brought up to him by the family member involved, to no avail.

Fifth, there is no reason to believe that the pathology of the fathers and their "secrets" were the *cause* of the patient's disorders, any more than in the usual cases we treat. In general, after one sweeps aside these special considerations, the treatment of the spouses and children of psychiatrists must proceed exactly like that of any other psychotherapy; the fact that spouse or parent is a psychiatrist becomes more and more irrelevant.

However, certain other considerations, especially in the beginning phase of psychotherapy of professionals or their family members, are important, and I now turn briefly to these. The psychotherapist should be alert for what Loewenstein (1972) has called the "reinstinctualization" of certain normally autonomous ego functions. The most common of these, in a person who has grown up in an atmosphere of much verbal communication and psychiatric jargon, is the use of sophisticated psychoanalytic terminology to fool the therapist into thinking the patient is really observing, understanding, and commenting on himself, whereas the use of such terminology is just gibberish to serve as resistance and test the therapist. Conversely, because someone is a psychiatrist, it does not follow that he communicates at home with his wife and family. For example, one teenaged son of a psychiatrist was raised in an atmosphere where the television played constantly and there was almost no talk in the house.

In certain cases where great narcissistic problems are present in the psychiatrist husband or father, the psychotherapist must be prepared for problems regarding fee. The therapeutic contract and fee should be carefully spelled out at the beginning of treatment, and there should be no "favors," as this represents to the patient a tacit alliance between the psychotherapist and the husband or father of the patient. If there is a refusal to pay the bill, the psychotherapist must be prepared with strategies, for the psychiatrist husband or father here projects his narcissism onto the psychotherapist and assumes he is wounding the narcissism of the psychotherapist in revenge for the narcissistic wound inflicted on him by the psychotherapy of his wife or child. Problems of the fee and the challenge it presents to the narcissism of psychotherapists are reviewed in a masterful paper by Eissler (1974).

Similarly, the psychiatrist father and husband with especially narcissistic pathology is constantly on the lookout for "criticism" from his wife's or child's psychotherapist, and can be expected to frequently "pump" the patient for details about each session. At the first hint of criticism an explosion can be anticipated, including attempts to end the treatment or to force a change of therapists, or refusal to pay the fee or bring the patient to the sessions, and so forth. It is usually unwise to request a direct confrontation or consultation with the psychiatrist spouse or father at this point, since this prevents helping the patient recognize and work through a realistic appraisal of the psychiatrist spouse or father, and again sets up a tacit alliance against the patient between the two "authorities." Generally speaking, a crisis often occurs when the psychiatrist husband or father of this type realizes he is not going to be able to control the psychotherapy of his wife or child. At this point he may become outraged, severely criticize the psychotherapist, and try to stop the treatment.

The authority problem shows itself especially in the treatment of psychiatrists' wives, who often have great difficulty at the beginning in contradicting their husbands' gratuitous "interpretations" and pronouncements. Even some of the most bizarre pronouncements—for example, "It is normal for us not to have sexual relations since we are over thirty"—create conflict since they come from somebody who is supposed to be an expert. Such pronouncements carry a further danger of acting out on the part of the patient, who, by subtly bringing home selected tidbits from her psychotherapy, can set up an intense "lets you and him fight" interaction between the psychotherapist and psychiatrist husband or father. The alert psychotherapist, if his narcissism doesn't get involved, handles the problem by a careful investigation to determine what the patient has been carrying home. Evidence that such acting out has been worked through is present when the patient confronts the psychiatrist at home with an admission that for resistance purposes she has set up the situation. Such an investigation is far more therapeutic in dealing with acting out than setting up extratherapeutic conferences with the psychiatrist, as would again be the first tendency with a colleague, although in adolescent cases it may be necessary—preferably in the presence of the patient.

This brings us to the special countertransference problems encountered immediately on undertaking psychotherapy of the wives and children of psychiatrists. These problems clearly revolve around narcissistic use of the patient as a self-object to demonstrate to the colleague–husband or father that one is a fine psychotherapist indeed. "How will I do? What will he think of me?" become countertransference preoccupations especially if the husband or father (a) has a more lucrative practice with an overflow of patients that he refers to other psychiatrists or (b) is in an important political position in local psychiatry, with the power to influence others. As a general rule it is always unwise to accept referrals of other patients from the husband–father psychiatrist while his wife or child is in therapy with you, and also unwise to accept as a patient the wife or child of a psychiatrist who has real immediate power over the psychotherapist, such as the chairman of your department, and so on. Simply refer these to others.

Finally, special problems arise in the psychotherapy of the wives or children of residents in psychiatry. In my judgment it is frankly unethical to take on as a patient any resident or the wife or child or a resident over whose career one has great power. This situation obviously puts the resident in an awkward position and is certain to destroy the treatment. Such patients are easily referred to others. In general, the loyalty problems involving residents are even greater than those involving practicing psychiatrists. Since the future career of the resident is uncertain, "secrets" in these cases are especially troublesome and cannot possibly be brought out to someone who could literally destroy the career of the resident.

Another interesting phenomenon shows itself in phallic–narcissistic, competitive women married to psychiatrists-in-training. When the psychiatric resident is undergoing so-called training psychoanalysis and his wife is in psychotherapy, serious competitive problems may result. Some that I have encountered are: (a) distortion of the psychotherapy so that, for example, the wife insists on referring to her once-weekly psychotherapy as "my analysis"; (b) rage at the psychotherapist—why am I getting only "second rate" treatment?; (c) literal breakup of the psychotherapy with the wife getting herself accepted at the Psychoanalytic Institute on some basis or another, for example as a training case for a candidate, and so forth. These problems are more the usual derivatives of psychopathology rather than true special problems, but they certainly can be deleterious to the treatment.

Freud's principle of leasing a definite hour that the patient has to pay for, six days a week, is not applicable to intensive psychotherapy except in those cases where the therapist feels that the patient is acting out by skipping therapy sessions. With most patients, over a period of years, the matter of missed hours is a minor issue and the occasional hour missed for illness or for a scheduled vacation where the time of the vacation is set by the patient's employer or spouse or so on, calls for a reasonable and humane response by the psychotherapist. A few patients make missed sessions and the fee for the sessions central issues in the psychotherapy and these of course must be dealt with very strictly—even if it forces termination of the treatment—since they are essentially resistances to treatment and bring the patient's entire motivation for therapy into question. In this regard, it is helpful to remember Freud's comment that the treatment usually takes longer than the patient expects and that it is our duty to tell this to the patient before he finally decides upon the treatment.

In those cases where uncovering is the strategy of the psychotherapist I do not hesitate to explain the fundamental rule of free association to the patient at the beginning of treatment, even though certain authorities do not agree with this procedure. In uncovering psychotherapy I want the patient to free-associate as much as possible even if in a sitting up and face-to-face position. I realize that this position is much more limited in psychotherapy than in psychoanalysis, but the basic principle is a valuable concept for the patient to understand if possible, since it encourages the patient to say a number of things he would not ordinarily reveal in a social relationship, including many bizarre, offensive, or insulting remarks. It is important to encourage the patient to say whatever comes to his mind and to contrast the therapy situation with a social party.

Many patients find it is easier to say inappropriate, embarrassing, or uncomplimentary things when they do not have to face the therapist, and for that reason I am willing to use the couch in intensive uncovering psychotherapy when I think it is appropriate; but under no circumstances should the average psychotherapy patient be placed on the couch. This means that the psychotherapist will be stared at a number of hours each day, and like Freud, I am sure he will find this to be rather unpleasant but unavoidable. The facial expressions of the psychotherapist, as Freud pointed out, will influence the patient's material and distract the patient; but keep in mind that a whole variety of other manifestations of the psychotherapist, such as the ambience of his office, his tone of voice, and so on, give the patients similar material. It is *impossible* to remain opaque to a patient.

Finally, in answer to another debated issue, I firmly believe it is important to take a formal detailed history following the textbook form and directly from the patient (*not* as a written "homework" assignment) at the beginning of intensive psychotherapy. This history serves as legal protection for the psychotherapist, as a source of valuable clues to future exploration, and as vital data for review later on. If the patient is unable to give a history in the first few sessions, responsible members of the family should be called upon to provide what information they can, after requesting the patient's permission. This matter should not be neglected out of preoccupation with immediate psychodynamic material, and is best attended to at the beginning of the treatment.

15

TECHNICAL SUGGESTIONS

Freud classifies cases on the basis of three modes of development (Nunberg and Federn 1967). The severe but instructive cases show much difficulty at the beginning and later go smoothly. The insoluble cases begin splendidly and with high promise of success; later, severe difficulties appear. The typical cases show a moderate level of difficulty in the middle of the treatment. These classifications constitute both a warning about cases that seem to begin with great gains, and an encouragement in those cases that begin with severe problems. Yet Freud often stresses that one cannot determine at the beginning of a treatment whether a case is severe or mild.

Freud mentions certain tricks that patients use in the service of resistance, such as talking the treatment over every day with an intimate friend or, as he describes it in the case of women who in their past history were subjected to sexual aggression and of men with strong homosexuality in repression, the tendency to have nothing to say; these tricks are worth keeping in mind. In those patients who are able to talk freely in psychotherapy, Freud makes the most important recommendation that major interventions and interpretations be withheld until a proper rapport is formed with the patient. To insure this rapport, Freud explains, "Nothing need be done but to give him time. If one exhibits a serious interest in him, carefully clears away the resistances that crop up at the beginning and avoids making certain mistakes, he will of himself form such an attachment and link the doctor up with one of the images of the people by whom he was accustomed to be treated with affection." (1913C;12:139–140). This means that as long as the patient's communications run on without obstruction the transference is not interpreted; brilliant interpretations or solutions are not to be "flung in the patient's face," as Freud puts it. He continues by warning us to avoid the common beginner's mistake of taking "an intellectualistic view of the situation" (p. 141).

One of my favorite brief papers by Freud is "The Psychogenesis of a Case of Homosexuality in a Woman" (1920A;18:146–174). This paper is packed with important observations as well as some glimpses of Freud as a psychotherapist hard at work. The first clinical point he makes concerns the treatment of patients who are brought for cure by the order of somebody else, as for example, "My wife suffers from nerves, and for that reason gets on badly with me; please cure her, so that we may lead a happy married life again." As another example, "Parents expect one to cure their nervous unruly child. By a healthy child they mean one who never causes his parents trouble, and gives them nothing but pleasure. The physician may succeed in curing the child, but after that it goes its own way all the more decidedly, and the parents are far more dissatisfied than before" (p. 150).

Freud continues by noting that the treatment of homosexuality is never easy and succeeds only in those specially favorable circumstances where there is strong motivation for change. He points out that often a patient comes to be treated through social pressure and with a secret plan to obtain from the striking failure of the treatment a demonstration that everything possible has been done against the homosexuality, to which the patient can now resign himself with an easy conscience.

How, for example, does Freud approach the situation where the parents bring a child to be "cured"? He reports that he carefully avoided promising any prospect of cure and "I merely said I was prepared to study the girl carefully for a few weeks or months" (p. 152) for the purpose of deciding whether a long-term intensive psychotherapy or a psychoanalysis would be worthwhile. In fact, in this case, he realized that a treatment with himself (as a male) would be a mistake, so he broke the treatment off and recommended a woman therapist.

This paper also contains some pointers on family dynamics. For example, mothers with daughters of nearly marriageable age usually feel embarassed in regard to them, "while the daughters are apt to feel for their mothers a mixture of compassion, contempt and envy which does nothing to increase their tenderness for them" (p. 157).

Revenge on the father was an important motivation in the homosexual patient discussed here by Freud, and leads to a brief description of the psychodynamics of her suicide attempt. Freud points out that probably no one finds the mental energy required to kill himself unless, in the first place, "in doing so he is at the same time killing an object with whom he has identified himself, and, in the second place, is turning against himself a death-wish which has been directed against someone else" (p. 162). Freud continues by saying that it is typical in a case of suicide that several quite different motives, all of great strength, collaborate to make such a deed possible.

There follows an extremely useful vignette of Freud at work. The treatment goes forward without any signs of resistance and the patient participates intellectually but he notices that she is absolutely tranquil emotionally. "Once when I expounded to her a specially important part of the theory, one touching her nearly, she replied in an inimitable tone, 'How very interesting,' as though she were a *grande dame* being taken over a museum and glancing through her lorgnon at objects to which she was completely indifferent" (p. 163). Freud recognized how this remark concealed her attitude of defiance and revenge against her father and compared it to the typical intellectual isolation seen in obsessional neuroses where everything that has been accomplished is subject to mental reservations and doubt.

Here is Freud at work: "Then, when one comes to close quarters with the motives for this doubt, the fight with the resistances breaks out in earnest" (p. 164). We see Freud's dedication, tenacity, and willingness to actively participate in the battle against the patient's resistances, as well as his recognition in this case, that because he is a male, the need for defiance is so great that the treatment would stand a better chance of success if the therapist were a woman. *The mark of the professional psychotherapist, in contrast to the novice, is the capacity to recognize silent defenses and resistances at work in the therapy and the willingness to have it out with the patient in regard to these vital defensive systems, even at the risk of incurring great anger on the part of the patient and spoiling the pleasant atmosphere in which the patient, on the surface, seems to be intellectually cooperative.*

It is truly astonishing that one of the best summaries of the technical practice of psychoanalytic psychotherapy was written by Freud in his eighties. In fact, I can think of no better sequel to the reading of the present book than for the student to turn immediately to Freud's *An Outline of Psychoanalysis* (1940A;23:141ff), which contains the best succinct depiction of Freud's final views, written for readers who already have some familiarity with the subject. In chapter VI of this work, Freud briefly mentions all the curative factors in intensive psychotherapy—factors discussed at length in my previous books (1969, 1974, 1977*a*).

He identifies the after-education of the neurotic in which the therapist is put in place of the patient's super-ego and corrects mistakes for which the patient's parents were responsible. He warns us against the temptation to become a teacher, model, and ideal for other people and to create men in our own image, and explains that this behavior only repeats the mistake of the parents who crushed their child's independence by their influence. Only those severely ill patients who have remained infantile, explains Freud, should be treated as children with direct attempts to influence them: "In all his attempts at improving and educating the patient the analyst should respect his individuality. The amount of influence which he may legitimately allow himself will be determined by the degree of developmental inhibition present in the patient" (p. 175).

It is most important for the novice psychotherapist to understand that in choosing to influence or educate a patient directly, he is also making an implicit decision about the patient's potential for maturity. Assuming that the decision to influence the patient directly is not made on the basis of a countertransference problem of the therapist—which is usually the reason—the decision implies that the patient must be treated as a child with little potential for autonomous growth, and therefore, direct modification is the most we can hope for, switching the patient's dependency from the parents to us. This may be a legitimate technique providing we have a thorough metapsychological understanding of the patient and have given the patient every chance to realize his potential. Thus massive attempts to educate and influence a patient directly do not represent "kindness" but rather an expression of therapeutic despair. I hasten to add that this does not mean we never impart information to or educate patients; it is more a matter of the basic strategy of the psychotherapy itself—whether it will be primarily suggestion and influence, or primarily uncovering. Freud himself realizes this in the work cited, where he explains, "We serve the patient in various functions, as an authority and a substitute for his parents, as a teacher and educator; and we have done the best for him if, as analysts, we raise the mental processes in his ego to a normal level, transform what has become unconscious and repressed into preconscious material and thus return it once more to the possession of his ego" (p. 181).

Psychoanalytic psychotherapy is clearly directed to strengthening the weakened ego. Freud explains that the first part of the help we have to offer is intellectual work and encouragement to the patient to collaborate in the treatment. He reminds us to put off constructions and explanations to the patient until the patient has so nearly arrived at them that only a single step remains to be taken, though that step is in fact the decisive synthesis. Avoid overwhelming the patient with interpretations, which only increases resistance.

The second phase of our task is the removal of resistances, which is actually more important than strengthening the weakened ego. The overcoming of resistances "is the part of our work that requires the most time and the greatest trouble. It is worth while, however, for it brings about an advantageous alteration of the ego which will be maintained independently of the outcome of the transference and will hold good in life" (p. 179). In another work, written about the same time, (1937C;23:211–254) Freud was not so optimistic. In both works he reminds us that fighting against us are the negative transference; the ego's resistance due to repression—unpleasure at having to lay itself open to the hard work imposed on it; the sense of guilt and the need to be sick and suffer; "a certain psychical inertia, a sluggishness of the libido, which is unwilling to abandon its fixations" (1940A;23:181); the patient's capacity for sublimation; and the relative power of his intellectual functions. The limitations imposed by all these also mark the limitations of our success.

Freud concludes the important chapter VI on technique in *An Outline of Psychoanalysis* with a prescient suggestion about psychopharmocology. He points out that our work depends on *quantitative* relations, "on the quota of energy we are able to mobilize in the patient to our advantage as compared with the sum of energy of the powers working against us" (1940A; 23:182). He hopes in the future to exercise a direct influence by means of particular chemical substances on the amounts of energy and their distribution in the mental apparatus. One can see that the judicious use of effective psychopharmocological agents is completely compatible with the process of psychoanalytic psychotherapy even on a theoretical basis.

Freud's final suggestions on technique are found in a brief paper, "Constructions in Analysis" (1937D;23:256-270). He distinguishes between interpretation, which applies to something that one does to some single element of the material such as an association or parapraxis, and a "construction," in which the therapist lays before the patient a construct or reconstructed piece of the patient's early history as it appears from the material. Novices are especially warned to be very careful about such constructions; but even if the constructions are wrong Freud does not feel that any damage is done except for wasting the patient's time. Where the construction is wrong, nothing happens, and we have probably made a mistake. When new material comes to light we can make a better construction and correct our error.

Direct utterances of the patient after he has been offered a construction, such as "yes" or "no," "afford very little evidence upon the question whether we have been right or wrong" (p. 263). It is the indirect forms of confirmation which may be trusted, for example, a form of words that is used such as "I shouldn't have ever thought of that" or "I didn't ever think of that." Even better is when the patient answers the construction within an association that contains something similar or analogous to the content of the construction; I find this most confirming of all, along with the appearance of new memories as a response to the construction.

For example, a patient dreams that he is rescuing a number of people from a burning summer cottage—he is the hero and has saved their lives. After suitable associations it is reconstructed that the patient has presented a reaction formation against great hatred for his mother during this phase of his life, Next, the patient suddently remembers an incident that occurred at the actual site of the dream, in which his mother impulsively beat him severely for an incident that both he and she knew was not his fault.

Freud also notes that if the treatment is dominated by a negative therapeutic reaction, a proper construction will be followed by an unmistakable aggravation of the patient's symptoms and general condition. Obviously, only the further course of the treatment enables us to decide whether a construction is correct or useless, and Freud makes it clear that an individual construction is a conjecture which awaits examination, confirmation, or rejection. The use of the term "conjecture" at this point is extremely interesting as it leads directly to Popper's notion of science as proceeding by conjectures and refutations. I have discussed this process of hypothesis-formation in the way of interpretations and constructions and their subsequent refutation, at length in *Great Ideas in Psychotherapy* (1977) and in chapter 5 of the present book.

What we search for in uncovering psychotherapy resembles an archeologist's excavation in which we try to picture accurately the patient's forgotten years. Although we hope this picture will be followed by further associations and memories, sometimes we do not succeed and the best we can do is produce an assured conviction in the patient of the truth of the construction, which, as Freud explains, achieves the same therapeutic result as a recaptured memory. The purpose of his discussion is to answer the common objection to uncovering psychotherapy that the patient is in a "heads I win, tails you lose" situation. Clearly, in the proper therapeutic atmosphere the patient and therapist work together as partners in an effort to understand and accept or reject various constructions and interpretations as hypotheses. The patient must participate actively in this; therefore, when resistances arise these must be attended to first. Any therapist who creates a therapeutic atmosphere implying that cure somehow depends on the patient's accepting the therapist's constructions has an obvious narcissistic countertransference problem—quite common among unanalyzed or improperly trained "therapists."

I believe that Freud's exemplary personality is a good foundation for identification for the psychotherapist at work. He was a hard worker and remained so even when he was ill for many years with cancer of the jaw. His only sport was hiking during his summer vacations, but he was a substantial hiker. A man of tremendous energy with a boundless capacity for work, he was capable of intense concentration. Ellenberger (1970) feels that as time passes it will become more and more difficult to understand Freud, because he belonged to a group of men like Kraepelin, Forel, Bleuler, and others who "had gone through long training in intellectual and emotional discipline; they were men of high culture, puritanical mores, boundless energy, and strong convictions, which they vigorously asserted." Their ascetic and idealistic type is becoming "increasingly foreign to a hedonistic and utilitarian generation." (pp. 468–469).

Freud as a human being represents a worthwhile model. He was capable of physical courage and amazingly stoic endurance in the later years of his life, as a recent book by his physician Schur (1972) illustrates. He allied physical courage with moral courage, and "his conviction of the truth of his theories was so complete that he did not admit contradiction. This was called intolerance by his opponents and passion for truth by his followers" (Ellenberger 1970, p. 463).

Freud lived morally, socially, and professionally according to the highest standards of a man and of a physician of his time and status. He was a person of scrupulous honesty and professional dignity. He kept his appointments exactly, and set all his activities to a timetable, to the hour, the day, the week, and the year. Considerable dignity and decorum were expected of professional men of his day and Freud, who was punctilious about his appearance, lived up to these expectations. In many ways he may be said to have lived a life beyond reproach. In his genuine and human interest in patients, his boundless capacity for work, and his passion to discover the truth, Freud makes a very fine model indeed for any one attempting psychotherapy.

Balogh (1971, borrowing from Jones), gives a stirring picture of Freud at work:

> His time-table gives some idea of the fullness and orderliness of his life during the first fourteen years of this century. His first patient arrived at eight and so he had to be roused at seven, which was not always easy, since he seldom went to bed before one or two in the morning. He saw each patient for fifty-five minutes, taking five minutes off between each to refresh himself with a visit into the main part of the family apartment, which was adjacent to the separate office flat. If you go to Vienna now you will see a plaque at 19 Bergasse indicating that Freud lived and worked there. The family always lived on the first floor, but Freud's first office was at street level, his chair facing towards the garden at the back.
>
> The main meal of the day was family lunch; at this he talked little. If a child were absent, Freud would point silently to the empty place and direct an inquiring look at his wife. She would then explain the reason why the child had not appeared. A visitor present at the meal would find that the conversation with the family rested almost entirely with him, Freud being, no doubt, immersed in thoughts about the morning's work.
>
> After lunch he would take a walk in the city, stopping daily to replenish his stock of cigars at a special *Tabak Trafik*. At 3 P.M. there would be consultations, and then further patients until 9 or even 10 P.M. He allowed himself no break before suppertime until he was 65, when he had a 5 o'clock cup of coffee. After a late supper, at which he would be more communicative, he would retire to his

> study to write his many letters (always by hand), correct proofs and see to new editions (pp. 70–71).

Therapists interested in a thorough although controversial discussion of Freud's personality in the light of his culture and time are referred to the collection of essays by Gay (1978), and to an exciting collection of photographs and memorabilia edited by E. Freud et al. (1978).

Part IV

UNFINISHED DEBATES

Analysts, on the other hand, cannot repudiate their descent from exact science and their community with its representatives. Moved by an extreme distrust of the power of human wishes and of the temptations of the pleasure principle, they are ready, for the sake of attaining some fragment of objective certainty, to sacrifice everything—the dazzling brilliance of a flawless theory, the exalted consciousness of having achieved a comprehensive view of the universe, and the mental calm brought about by the possession of extensive grounds for expedient and ethical action. In place of all these, they are content with fragmentary pieces of knowledge and with basic hypotheses lacking preciseness and ever open to revision. Instead of waiting for the moment when they will be able to escape from the constraint of the familiar laws of physics and chemistry, they hope for the emergence of more extensive and deeper-reaching natural laws, to which they are ready to submit. Analysts are at bottom incorrigible mechanists and materialists, even though they seek to avoid robbing the mind and spirit of their still unrecognized characteristics.

Sigmund Freud (1941D;18:179) "*Psychoanalysis and Telepathy*"

16

CURATIVE FACTORS

A remarkable disquisition on curative factors in psychotherapy is presented in "Some Character Types Met With in Psychoanalytic Work" (1916D; 14:310ff). Freud points out that "under the doctor's guidance" the patient is asked to make the advance "from the pleasure principle to the reality principle by which the mature human being is distinguished from the child." This sounds remarkably like the description of psychotherapy as a learning process, presented in the various papers of Strupp (1969, 1972, 1973).

Like Strupp, Freud sees psychotherapy as an "educative process" in which the doctor "makes use of the influence which one human being exercises over another." Freud describes this as employing one of the components of love:

> In this work of after-education, he is probably doing no more than repeat the process which made education of any kind possible in the first instance. Side by side with the exigencies of life, love is the great educator; and it is by the love of those nearest him that the incomplete human being is induced to respect the decrees of necessity and to spare himself the punishment that follows any infringement of them (p. 312).

Running throughout Freud's writing is a certain ambiguity on the relative importance of the effect of interpretation of the transference in psychoanalytic cure and the effect of the physician's influence on the patient. For example, in a dramatic summary of the problem Friedman (1978) claims,

> At no time from his first psychoanalytic writings to his last did Freud ever lose sight of or minimize the importance of the affective relationship between patient and analyst. Throughout his work on the process of treatment a kind of running battle may be detected between the respective claims of understanding and attachment, although when one looks more closely one sees that it is not equal combat, but a struggle for survival on the part of understanding. To be sure, Freud was very much the champion of the voice of

> reason, but while he was cheering it on, he seemed to be advising his friends not to bet on it (p. 526).

The therapist is loved both in the transference and in the real relationship, on the basis of the therapist's physicianly vocation as it manifests itself to the patient over the months of long-term intensive psychotherapy. Concentration on the importance of this "love" as an influencing factor is what primarily seems to distinguish the so-called copper of suggestion from the "pure gold" of psychoanalysis, but Freud was not at all clear about such a distinction; his was a forceful personality and he was a natural and intuitive educator and physician. The contention that in long-term intensive psychotherapy the *combination* of properly timed interpretations as well as the therapeutic alliance and the experience of the caring personality of the therapist all work together as curative factors [described in my books (1969. 1971, 1974, 1977, 1977*a*)] is derived from the manifestations of this combination in the writing, clinical reports, and experiences as reported by others, of the therapeutic work of Sigmund Freud.

One of the thorniest contemporary issues is whether or not psychoanalytically informed psychotherapy should be considered primarily as a form of education for difficulties in living, or as a form of medical treatment for illness. This conflict is traceable to Freud's writing and reflects a conflict in Freud's personality. At one point, Freud writes, "You can, if you like, regard psychoanalytic treatment as no more than a prolongation of education for the purposes of overcoming the residues of childhood" (1910A;11:48). This "education" in Freud's view was seen as producing a replacement of repression—which he conceived of as a primitive defense—by conscious "*condemning judgment* carried out along the best lines" (ibid, p. 53). In addition he stressed the goal of the resumption of arrested development to permit sublimation of the energy of infantile wishful impulses and an increase in the direct satisfaction of libidinal impulses with the consequence of a happier life.

Yet, throughout innumerable passages in his writing, Freud speaks of psychoanalysis as a science, as a medical treatment analogous to surgery, and of the psychoanalyst as a doctor. He was steeped in the traditions of the science of his time and pursued a scientific ideal of strict truth; on the other hand, as Robert (1966) explains, "He felt a need to express himself esthetically, to give free reign to the imagination which his background, training and probably powerful inner inhibitions had led him to repress very early in his life." The mixture of the scientist and the artist in Freud is reflected by the two strains of pervasive, unresolved tension in his writings involving antithetical images of man—emphasized by Holt (1973) and reviewed in the introduction to this book.

"Analysis Terminable and Interminable" (1937C;23:211ff) was written in 1937 when Freud was 81 and is called by Jones "for the practicing psychoanalyst possibly the most valuable contribution Freud ever wrote." It is also probably his most pessimistic work as far as the hoped-for therapeutic outcome from psychoanalysis is concerned. This pessimism seems based primarily on a view of the potential for alterations of the ego expressed in this paper, a view somewhat different than that expressed in his other work. We may say that this is Freud's major paper on failures in psychotherapy [a topic to which I have devoted a book (1971)]. The alteration of the ego in intensive psychotherapy is viewed in Freud's paper as not having a prophylactic power over the occurrence of both fresh and different neuroses, or even the power to prevent a return of the neuroses that already have been treated. Thus here Freud views the ego as being helped to cope with the conflict that brings the patient to treatment, but this treatment does not assist the capacity of the ego to deal with another conflict that may arise later. In my clinical experience this is simply not true. All other views regard the ego alteration through intensive psychotherapy in a more general sense, as making it more capable of dealing with various problems as they arise later in life. About a year later, in *An Outline of Psychoanalysis* (1940A;23: see p. 179) Freud reverts back to regarding the alteration of the ego as advantageous in a more general sense, as holding good in life.

In "Analysis Terminable and Interminable" Freud also appears rather pessimistic about the personality of psychoanalysts who "have not invariably come up to the standard of psychical normality to which they wish to educate their patients" (p. 247). He explains, "It is therefore reasonable to expect of an analyst, as part of his qualifications, a considerable degree of mental normality and correctness. In addition, he must possess some kind of superiority, so that in certain analytic situations he can act as a model for his patient and in others as a teacher. And finally, we must not forget that the analytic relationship is based on a love of truth—that is, on a recognition of reality—and that it precludes any kind of sham or deceit" (p. 248). He states that a careful analysis of the therapist is required for such a standard, and warns us that the therapist's constant preoccupation with all the repressed material in his patients may stir up instinctual demands which he would otherwise be able to keep under control. Therefore, he recommends that "Every analyst should periodically—at intervals of five years or so—submit himself to analysis once more, without feeling ashamed of taking this step" (p. 249). This course of action makes the therapeutic analysis of patients and also the analysis of analysts an interminable task—and as far as I know, the recommendation is not generally followed. I have not been able to find, in the vast literature on Freud, a satisfactory explanation of his unusual pessimism in this particular paper.

For our purposes, the most important issue of this extremely important paper is its discussion of why psychotherapy fails. First of all, we know that if the strength of the ego diminishes, whether through illness or exhaustion, or if the strength of the instincts become altered or reinforced such as in puberty or the menopause, we are not surprised if previously defective repressions fail and symptoms have to form. We hope that psychotherapy enables the ego, which has attained greater maturity and strength, to demolish unnecessary repressions and construct more solid repressions in other areas, as well as encouraging sublimation. We agree, of course, that under conditions of a weakened ego or increased strength of instincts this arrangement may not always hold, but we think that its chances of holding are best if the patient's ego has been strengthened through psychotherapy.

It is important to understand, as Freud points out, that the difference between a person who has not had therapy and the behavior of a person after intensive psychotherapy "is not so thorough-going as we aim at making it and as we expect and maintain it to be" (p. 228). Certainly a more modest expectation for the results of psychotherapy would be useful; in my work I am more interested in the difference between the internal suffering that the patient has endured before therapy and afterwards, as well as in removing the external suffering that he brings on himself and his loved ones by his behavior. It is in these differences that the crucial value of intensive psychotherapy lies, and upon which the entire procedure must be judged. The objectives of intensive psychotherapy, in contrast to those of formal psychoanalysis, are a bit less extreme; we are not hoping for total rearrangement at all; we can rest content with Freud's statement that when we endeavor to replace repressions that are insecure by reliable ego-syntonic controls, we achieve only a partial transformation, and portions of both mechanisms remain untouched. Freud's point is that this holds true for psychoanalysis as well.

Clearly, in states of acute crisis, analysis or uncovering psychotherapy (as Freud points out) is to all intents and purposes unusable since the ego's entire interest is taken up by the painful reality. Putting these situations aside, for the purpose of therapeutic effort on the influence of traumatic etiology, the factors enumerated by Freud have decisive value: the relative strength of the instincts which have to be controlled, and the pathological alteration of the ego. The latter factor requires the most discussion since there are a great variety of kinds and degrees, either congenital or acquired, of alteration of the ego. When acquired, it is in the first few years of life during which the ego may be pathologically altered, for example, by being forced to the inappropriate use of the mechanisms of defense. Thus the mechanisms of defense may become dangerous themselves since the ego may have to pay too high a price for the services they render, in terms of restrictions of energy as well as when these mechanisms become regular modes of reaction, repeated throughout life, of the patient's character.

"This turns them into infantilisms, and they share the fate of so many institutions which attempt to keep themselves in existence after the time of their usefulness has passed" (pp. 237–8). Thus the adult's ego continues to defend itself against dangerous but no-longer-existing reality—and indeed the ego finds itself compelled to seek out those situations in reality which can serve as an approximate substitute for the original danger, thus justifying habitual modes of reaction. To say the least, this is an extremely important point to be kept in mind in understanding the behavior and situational exigencies which patients manifest.

Thus the patient makes a selection from the possible mechanisms of defense, choosing a few of them and usually the same ones, and seeks situations in adult life to justify their continued use. This is an alteration of the ego. The strength and depth of the root of these alterations is an important limiting factor in psychotherapeutic success or failure.

Freud also introduces a concept that I regard as dangerous, which he calls "adhesiveness of the libido"—a concept originally brought forward in the *Introductory Lectures on Psychoanalysis* (Freud 1916X;16:348) and which is not always differentiated from a general concept of "psychical inertia" discussed in "Analysis Terminable and Interminable." At any rate, the term refers to the need for detachment of libidinal cathexes from one object and the displacement to another. As Freud puts it, certain people are very slow in making up their mind to make this detachment, "although we can discover no special reason for this cathectic loyalty" (1937C;23:241). There is also the opposite type in whom the libido seems particularly mobile—in these latter cases the results of treatment are very impermanent since the new cathexes achieved by the treatment are soon given up once more.

In describing patients who suffer from a special adhesiveness of the libido or psychic inertia or from what Freud also calls a depletion of plasticity—sometimes attributed to old age where we deal with force of habit or exhaustion of receptivity—he is clearly introducing a limiting factor in therapeutic procedure. The reason I regard this concept as dangerous is that it is so difficult to demonstrate that a failure of the psychotherapy is due to such factors; thus an appeal to these factors can be used to excuse a poorly conducted psychotherapy or a therapist suffering from countertransference, which may result in no progress in the treatment.

On the other hand, there is no question that a certain percentage of patients literally do seem to suffer from what Freud has defined as adhesiveness of the libido, or, in other cases, a lack of receptivity and a certain rigidity. As soon as possible in beginning the treatment, it is important to try to identify such patients on the basis of their past history, age, and behavior in the treatment situation. With such patients, a well-conducted psychotherapy is a very long procedure, but when properly conducted small signs of progress should continually appear. Where progress is slow, the therapist's duty is to deal with the narcissistic countertransference problem that must inevitably arise in such treatments.

During his summer holiday in 1906, Freud composed a little book of a hundred pages, apparently to please his friend Jung. It represents Freud's literary abilities at their best and deals with a novel by Wilhelm Jensen entitled *Gradiva*. The bas-relief with which the hero of the story falls in love may be seen in the Vatican Museum. Jones (1955) reports that after Freud published this book "it became fashionable among analysts to have a copy of the relief on their walls. Freud had one himself in his consulting room." (A photograph of the relief is found in the frontispiece to volume 9 of the *Standard Edition.)*

Freud's monograph *Delusions and Dreams in Jensen's "Gradiva"* (1907A;9:3ff) is a charming introduction to Freud's explanation of dreams, neuroses, and of the therapeutic actions of psychoanalysis; it is useful from college seminars all the way to psychiatry residency programs. It represents Freud's first complete published analysis of a work of literature, thus beginning a new genre in literary criticism, one that has become quite popular—and much abused.

The book begins with a discussion of the question of dreaming as purely a physiological process in which dreams are comparable to twitching of the mind under the excitations which remain active in it as offshoots of waking life. This comparison immediately introduces the issue of modern physiological research on sleep and dreaming and the question of how such research fits Freud's theories of the dream (see also chapter 13). There seems to be considerable confusion on this matter; the best current review is Freedman et al. (1976). In the 1950s Aserinsky, Dement, Kleitman, and other researchers studied the rapid eye movement (REM) readily measurable beneath the closed lids of the sleeper in certain stages of sleep, a movement different than non-rapid eye movement (NREM) of other stages of sleep. In a young adult a typical night of sleep begins with NREM; about 70 to 100 minutes after sleep onset the period of REM sleep begins. A cycling occurs from the onset of REM sleep, constituting about twenty percent of the total sleep time, with each cycle lasting about 90 minutes, although during the last part of the night the REM periods lengthen.

Vivid dreams are recalled 74 percent of the time when subjects are awakened from REM sleep, but only 7 percent of the time from NREM awakenings, so that REM dreams closely resemble what persons ordinarily regard as a dream characterized by detail—vivid and visual dream recall. The inability to recall dreams may have a physiological as well as a psychological basis, whereas the forgetting of dreams is definitely related to psychological factors. Thus the state in which dreams can occur, REM sleep, is a universal and regularly occurring process, and the cyclical patterns of REM sleep represent a basic biological process on which the psychological process of dreaming is superimposed.

Freedman et al. (1976) explain that in REM sleep, motor expression of the dream content is definitely inhibited but not completely absent, thus supporting Freud's conclusion that during dreaming a motor paralysis permits the safe expression of generally unacceptable, unconscious impulses. In addition, the visual system is activated during REM sleep. This activation lends neurophysiological support to Freud's theory that during dreaming a regression from motor discharge to hallucinatory perception takes place. Thus the data from sleep and dream research seem to support Freud's theories. The mind makes use of these biological cycles to allow sleep to continue by the production of dreams during REM sleep. A complete discussion of the psychoanalytic implications of recent research in sleep and dreaming may be found in Fisher (1965).

Another important question raised by Freud's monograph on Jensen's *Gradiva* is whether a fantasy of this nature can be made the object of a psychiatric study. We know that Freud did this in a number of different ways, as in his work on the diary of Schreber (see chapter 8). Even though Freud recognized how easy it is to draw analogies and to read meanings into things, he insisted that the author of *Gradiva* "has presented us with a perfectly correct psychiatric study, on which we may measure our understanding of the workings of the mind—a case history and the history of a cure which might have been designed to emphasize certain fundamental theories of medical psychology" (p. 43). He argues that this feat is possible even though the author had no knowledge of psychoanalysis and the theories on which it is based.

A literary author proceeds differently from the psychoanalyst in that he directs his attention to the unconscious in his own mind and he listens to possible developments and lends them artistic expression. "Thus he experiences from himself what we learn from others—the laws which the activities of this unconscious must obey" (p. 92). This is true even though Freud admits in this work how easily our intellect is prepared to accept something absurd provided it satisfies intense emotional impulses.

Freud is such a powerful writer that it is difficult to resist his analysis of Jensen's *Gradiva* despite the fact that the analysis contains an obsolete theory of anxiety (p. 61). The monograph on *Gradiva* is especially useful because of Freud's emphasis on his sometimes overlooked conviction that the process of cure in analytic psychotherapy rests *primarily* on "the reawakened passion, whether it is love or hate" which "invariably chooses as its object the figure of the doctor" (p. 90). At the same time Freud cautions us that the case of *Gradiva* is ideal because Gradiva (Zoe) was able to return Harold's love but the doctor cannot: "The doctor has been a stranger and must endeavor to become a stranger once more after the cure; he is often at a loss what advice to give the patients he has cured as to how in real life they can use their recovered capacity to love" (p. 40). This reminds us again of an obvious error which continues to be made in descriptions of intensive psychotherapy. *The doctor is essentially a stranger, not a dear friend or a lover*; the patient must be induced to look elsewhere for the gratification of his or her needs for friendship or love. Otherwise psychotherapy becomes prostitution in which the patient is simply paying for temporary love or friendship that he or she is unable to obtain elsewhere.

In his controversial essay on Leonardo da Vinci (1910C;11:59–138) Freud discusses the art-science conflict in terms which some authors have felt to be autobiographical. The first section of this essay is worth special study. Freud is clearly fascinated by Leonardo's double nature as an artist and as a scientific investigator; the resemblance between the two men is obvious. The essay contains a remark about Faust, emphasizing his fundamental attempt to transform his drive to investigate back into an enjoyment of life; the process seems to have been the reverse in the case of Leonardo. Freud suggests that Leonardo's development "approaches Spinoza's mode of thinking" (p. 75). In Leonardo's case the need to investigate, which began as a servant of Leonardo's drive for accurate artistic expression, became the stronger need and overwhelmed his esthetic productivity. Thus his drive to investigate swept him away until the connection with the demands of his art was severed—leading into his innumerable investigations into almost every branch of natural and applied science.

The genius of Leonardo lies in the fact that he was a master in *both* art and science—despite the inhibition or impairment of his artistic productivity produced by his inexhaustible investigation of nature. Freud saw Leonardo's compulsive drive to investigate as a substitute for sexual activity, that is, as a successful sublimation allowing the sexual drive to operate freely in the service of intellectual interest. The power of this sexual drive produced an overwhelming sublimation in the case of Leonardo, who,

> ... had merely converted his passion into a thirst for knowledge; he then applied himself to investigation with a persistance, constancy and penetration which is derived from passion, and at the climax of intellectual labor, when knowledge had been won, he allowed the long restrained affect to break loose and to flow away freely, as a stream of water drawn from a river is allowed to flow away when its work is done. When, at the climax of a discovery, he could survey a large portion of the whole nexus, he was overcome by emotion, and in ecstatic language praised the splendor of the part

> of creation that he had studied, or—in religious phraseology—the greatness of his Creator (pp. 74–75).

At no point did Freud in his explanation—which sounds suspiciously autobiographical—allow for a legitimate autonomous sense of transcendence; for Freud *all* mental phenomena must be explained on the basis of the vicissitudes of the primitive instinctual drives. In this way Freud avoided his own speculative urges. Unfortunately, the tendency toward increasing mysticism that appeared in some of his followers has reached a bizarre peak in the so-called third-force psychologies of today, which have the net effect, at least in normal psychology, of denying the power of the unconscious. Whether there is room in Freud's theories for supraordinate concepts, with their own principles of development and source of motivation, such as the bipolar self (in Kohut's "broad" sense) and the autonomous striving toward transcendence—constitute unresolved debates to which we turn in the next three chapters.

17

NARCISSISM

As early as *The Interpretation of Dreams* Freud (1900A;4:157) discusses dreams based on the motivation of proving the psychotherapist or his theories to be wrong. He explains, "These dreams appear regularly in the course of my treatments when a patient is in a state of resistance to me; and I can count almost certainly on provoking one of them after I have explained to a patient for the first time my theory that dreams are fulfilments of wishes." Freud does not pursue this matter at length but it is the first hint that an explanation or an interpretation in psychotherapy—even though it is correct—may be experienced by the patient not as an elucidation or insight but as a narcissistic blow. In such cases the patient is not able to benefit from the explanation or interpretation, and rather responds to the feeling he gets of being "put down." This response may occur either overtly in cold and aloof withdrawal and silence, or covertly in dreams either pejorative to the psychotherapist or based on the wish that the psychotherapist will be proven wrong, shown to be incompetent or foolish, or even punished. The extreme example of this response is the well-known negative therapeutic reaction, discussed as a clinical phenomenon in chapter 12 of *The Technique and Practice of Intensive Psychotherapy* (Chessick 1974).

A frank discussion of types of fantasies is found in Freud as early as 1908 (1908E;9:142–156 and 1908A;9:157–166). He maintains (p. 146) that a happy person never fantasies; only an unsatisfied one does so, and that the motive forces of fantasies are unsatisfied wishes: each fantasy is a fulfilment of a wish and can be understood like a dream. Ignoring the comment that a happy person never fantasies—an extreme statement, in my opinion—let us continue by noting Freud's comment that fantasies are either ambitious wishes which serve to elevate the subject's personality or they are erotic ones. Thus Freud distinguishes primarily between narcissistic fantasies and sexual fantasies, but he quickly adds that these are often mixed together.

He insists that hysterical symptoms "are nothing other than unconscious fantasies brought into view through 'conversion' " (1908A;9:162). Furthermore, the contents of the hysteric's unconscious fantasies correspond completely to the situations in which perverts consciously obtain satisfaction. At this point Freud brings up the famous performances of the Roman emperors, ". . . the wild excesses of which were, of course, determined only by the enormous and unrestrained power posessed by the authors of the phantasies" (p. 162). He goes on to mention that the delusions of paranoiacs are fantasies of the same nature, but he goes off the track by not stressing the primarily narcissistic aspects of such fantasies, which revolve around power and control.

Clinically speaking, erotic and narcissistic fantasies usually appear in some combination. All such fantasies and daydreams, including masturbation fantasies, should be collected during intensive psychotherapy and carefully studied just like dream material. In each case an attempt must be made to determine whether the predominant aspects are erotic or narcissistic. The matter is really very complicated because *deprivation in one area can be tranquilized by satiation in another*. For example, a patient suffering from a narcissistic disorder may use intensive sexual activity, perverted or not, either through promiscuity or masturbation (a) as a way of tranquilizing narcissistic rage; (b) as a way of reassuring himself that he *is* a self and not fragmented; and (c) as compensation in the sexual realm for the weakness he may feel in other realms of human functioning. Conversely, a patient suffering from an unresolved Oedipus complex may immerse himself in highly competitive power struggles, behavior which appears on the surface to be part of a narcissistic disorder.

The year of 1913 was one of the low points in Freud's professional life. Coming just before World War I, this period marked the breakup, due to the defection of Jung and Adler, of the growing international psychoanalytic movement. The debates which led to this defection forced Freud's attention to the inexactitude of certain prior statements and definitions he had introduced, and motivated him to define them precisely and demarcate his psychoanalysis from that of Jung and Adler. Admittedly "fuming with rage," he wrote "On the History of the Psychoanalytic Movement" (1914D;14:3ff)—a frankly polemical paper—and "On Narcissism: An Introduction" (1914C;14:69ff). The latter work, which is condensed, very difficult, and one of the most famous of Freud's writings, had a revolutionary impact on his followers not only because it revised old ideas and introduced some new concepts, but because by this procedure it introduced some serious new confusions and difficulties. Aside from its theoretical interest, this paper has important ramifications for the clinical practice of intensive psychotherapy.

Freud's main point in this paper was his attempt to restrict the meaning of the term libido to sexual energy; Adler attempted to regard it as a force or striving for power and Jung widened it to mean the energy behind all life processes. In order to stick to his original conception of the libido, Freud had to make important theoretical revisions, the most fundamental of which was a change in his theory of instincts. Thus in this paper he made the first fundamental change in his instinct theory; the second change was made eight years after (to be discussed later).

Freud's famous U-tube analogy of the flow of libido is presented, beginning with the concept that all libido is first collected in the ego. We define its outward flow as the situation of object love—love for other objects than the self. However, it can flow back again or be withdrawn into the ego (not differentiated from self here) under various situations such as disease, an accident, or old age where this tendency into self-preoccupation and self-love is especially obvious. When the libido is attached to the ego, we have the situation defined as narcissism. In the early phase of life this situation is normal, according to Freud, and is called primary narcissism; in later stages of life when the libido is withdrawn again to the ego, the state is defined as secondary narcissism.

What Jones calls the "disagreeable" aspect of this theory is that Freud was hard-put to demonstrate non-narcissistic components of the ego! To say there is reason to suppose the ego is strongly invested with libido is not the same as saying it is composed of nothing else, writes Jones (1955, p. 303), but that "something else" is difficult to pin down and opens the theory to criticism of being a monistic libidinal conception of the mind. This theoretical aspect of narcissism is still not adequately resolved; considerable controversy rages about the subject. Clearly, at this point Freud conceived of two kinds of ego drives, the libidinal and non-libidinal. This theory was meant to be the prelude to a complete restructuring of psychoanalytic theory which was originally intended to be a book consisting of twelve essays and entitled "Introduction to Metapsychology" that Freud proposed in 1915. Only five of these essays were published; Freud destroyed the rest.

I will now proceed to look carefully at the paper on narcissism because it is so rich in clinical material, such as discussion of narcissistic and anaclitic object choices, and its introduction of the concept of "ego ideal." Furthermore, this paper is the agreed starting point for all psychodynamic studies of narcissistic personality disorders and borderline patients; it demands and repays prolonged study.

Freud begins by stating that narcissism is not a perversion, but rather "the libidinal complement to the egoism of the instinct of self-preservation, a measure of which may justifiably be attributed to every living creature" (pp. 73–74). The U-tube theory is then introduced. Another analogy offered by Freud is that of the body of an amoeba related to the pseudopodia which it puts out and withdraws. Thus as one observes the pseudopodia under the microscope, libido can either flow out to objects or flow back to the ego. This phenomenon of ego–libido spoils the neat dualistic early instinct theory that divides all drives into sexual or egoistic (self-preservative).

Freud immediately emphasizes the importance of the concept of narcissism in understanding schizophrenic phenomena; the megalomanic aspect of schizophrenic patients is explained as a consequence of secondary narcissism. Most of the libido is directed to the self, especially as seen in paranoid grandiosity. The converse phenomenon, where the most libido possible is directed to an object, if defined as the state of being in love.

A phase of auto-erotism is postulated as the very beginning phase of life, even before the nuclei of the ego have coalesced. Once the ego has begun to develop, the libido is invested in it; this is the phase of primary narcissism, according to Freud.

The second section of the paper begins with a discussion of hypochondria, in which the clinical phenomena of hypochondriasis are seen as the result of flooding of the ego with libido that has been withdrawn from objects. Thus the psychic mastery of the flooding of the ego with libido appears in megalomania and an overflooding (or damming up) is felt as the disagreeable sensations of hypochondriacal anxiety. No explanation is available as to *why* the libido-flooded ego should feel these disagreeable sensations, but an analogy is drawn to the so-called "actual neuroses" (see chapter 5), where dammed-up libido due to inadequate discharge leads to the disagreeable sensations of neurasthenia, and so on. In the case of hypochondriasis the libido flooding the ego comes from outside objects to which it has previously been cathected and is now being withdrawn; in the case of the actual neuroses the libido comes from inside the individual and has been inadequately discharged.

In concluding his subsequent discussion of schizophrenia, Freud distinguishes three groups of phenomena in the clinical picture: (1) Those representing what remains of the normal or neurotic state of the individual; (2) those representing detachment of libido from its objects, leading to megalomania, hypochondriasis, and regression; and (3) restitutive symptoms in which an effort is made once again to attach the libido to objects or at least to their verbal representations. These distinctions form the foundation of Freud's theory of schizophrenia.

Another clinical application of the concept of narcissism—the distinction between anaclitic and narcissistic choices of love objects—concludes the second section of this paper. The anaclitic object choice attempts to bring back the lost mother and precedes developmentally the narcissistic object choice. The latter is a form of *secondary* narcissism in which the person chosen to love resembles one's own self. For example, in certain forms of homosexuality, the object chosen is the child-self who is then treated the way the homosexual wishes his mother to treat him. To avoid confusion it is important to understand that in early development *primary* narcissism comes first; then, due to inevitable frustration, anaclitic object-choice occurs with the mother as the first object. Therefore, narcissistic object choice, when it appears, represents a form of *secondary* narcissism in which the person loves what he himself is or was, what he would like to be, or someone thought of as a part of himself.

In the first instinct theory the instincts were divided into the sexual instincts—easily modified and changed, relatively speaking—and the ego instincts, such as hunger and thirst, which are more fixed. In the second instinct theory certain ego instincts are thought of as non-libidinal or "ego interest," but some are thought of as ego–libido: that is, narcissism. In this theory the ego's integrity depends on how much ego–libido is available, and ego–libido represents the glue holding the ego together. Thus an anaclitic object relationship may be viewed in two ways: (a) the libido is directed toward the object that has been responsible for survival, the nutritive object, the mother; but (b) if all the libido goes toward this object, the ego becomes depleted and helpless and depends on the object. The concept of sexual energies flowing within the ego made it very difficult to separate sexual and ego instincts because the "alibidnous" part is not well defined—hunger and thirst do not quantitatively balance the libidinal instinct, and this theoretical revision is generally agreed to be unsatisfactory.

A tentative effort to improve this situation was made by postulating sexual instincts on the one hand, and aggressive instincts on the other—these latter would then represent the non-libidinal ego instincts. The notion of aggression as an ego instinct strengthened Freud's idea of dividing instincts between sexual instincts and non-libidinal ego instincts, and was determined through a discussion of sadism. The argument was that if self-preservative instincts include aggressive instincts along with hunger and thirst, they must become dominant over sexual instincts so that the reality principle could prevail. Since sadism permeates every level of living and can ally itself to all instincts as shown in the impulses to assert and control and aggress upon, the aggressive or sadistic instincts are seen as distinct from libidinal impulses. This is not a valid argument, since if sadism is found at every level of sexual development why should it not be considered a part of the sexual instincts? The attempt to find a place for the aggressive drives characterized all Freud's further attempts at instinct theory, including his final theory of the life and death instincts, and, as we shall see, still remains an important aspect especially of any consideration of narcissism and the borderline personality disorders.

The final section of the essay begins with an extremely important sentence: "The disturbances to which a child's original narcissism is exposed, the reactions with which he seeks to protect himself from them and the paths into which he is forced in doing so—these are themes which I propose to leave on one side, as an important field of work which still awaits exploration" (p. 92). Kohut's work may be understood as emanating from this statement.

At this point, the aggressive instincts in Freud's formulation should not be considered purely or basically as sadism, since he conceived of them here primarily as the will to power, control, and dominance, which only in certain cases involve a secondary need to inflict pain. Looking at it in this way we may say that when the ego instincts are flooded by a libidinal complement from the sexual instinct we have the clinical state of narcissism; when the sexual instincts are infused by an aggressive component from the ego instincts, we have the clinical situation of sexual sadism.

It is easy to see that what is missing in this third or temporary revision is the structural theory involving the id, ego, and superego; a step in this direction is present in the essay on narcissism, where in the third part Freud introduces the notion of the ego ideal, which in the course of development becomes infused with the subject's primary narcissism. Thus ". . . what he projects before him as his ideal is the substitute for the lost narcissism of his childhood in which he was his own ideal" (p. 94). This substitution is differentiated from sublimation, in which the aim of the instinct is changed, with an accent upon deflection from sexuality.

It follows from these considerations that the ego becomes impoverished by *either* object love *or* ego-ideal formation, and enriched by the gratification of object love or fulfilling its ideal. Self-esteem arises out of either of these enrichments and contains three components: (1) the leftover residue of primary infantile narcissism; (2) the sense of omnipotence corroborated by experiencing the fulfilment of the ego ideal; and (3) satisfaction of object-libido by an input of love from the love object. Thus loving, insofar as it involves longing and deprivation, lowers self-regard; ". . . whereas being loved, having one's love returned, and possessing the loved object, raises it once more" (p. 99).

Besides explaining the variety of easily observable everyday phenomena, these conceptions have an important bearing on the practice of intensive psychotherapy. It follows from them that if an individual is unable to love, that is to say, if there is a repression of the libidinal drive, only one source of self-regard is left—that of idealization, or that of "fulfilling the ego ideal." As Freud puts it, such persons tend to attach themselves to individuals who have achieved what the patient's ego ideal clamors for, who possess the excellences to which the patient cannot attain. This represents a cure by love and is the kind of expectation that often directs patients into psychotherapy. Thus an important unconscious motivation for seeking therapy is to develop an attachment to the successful person of the psychotherapist who has achieved the aims of the patient's ego ideal. This carries the temptation to form a crippling and permanent dependence upon the psychotherapist, and also contains the further danger that when some capacity to love is developed through the psychotherapy the patient will withdraw from the treatment and choose a love object still permeated by the patient's ego ideal, a phenomenon which Freud calls a cure by love. The disadvantage of this is that the crippling dependence is then transferred to this new love object, and we observe the clinical phenomena that Odier (1956) has called the neurosis of abandonment.

A final important hint leading to the work of Kohut is presented at the end of this essay, in which it is noted that an injury to self-esteem or self-regard—what today we would call a narcissistic wound—is often found as the precipitating cause of paranoia. The reason for this, from the above considerations, would be that any falling-short of the ego ideal, or any disappointment or depletion in the libidinal complement of the ego, would cause a withdrawal of libido from objects, with the subsequent clinical phenomena of hypochondriasis and megalomania.

An approach to depression based on similar considerations has been presented by Davis (1976). He sees the core of depression as a feeling of uneasy helplessness due to psychic emptiness, coupled with a pressure to accomplish. He writes, "When we observe the sequence of depressive phenomena, we see that depressive emptiness is brought on by an acute diminution in self-esteem, what Freud called 'a narcissistic wound.'" Chronically depressed persons are depressed because they suffer repeated narcissistic wounds due to psychodynamic factors, not due to biological or constitutional factors. On the view, the implications for therapy of depression are the need for alteration and modification of the self-esteem system of the patient.

In *Moses and Monotheism* (1939A;23:3ff), Freud has some interesting comments for the student of narcissistic disorders. He reminds us that the basic difficulties in the neuroses occur as the result of experiences in early childhood up to about the fifth year. These experiences are usually totally forgotten and are not accessible to conscious memory except for occasional screen memories. He points out that these memories relate to impressions of a sexual and aggressive nature, "and no doubt also to early injuries to the ego (narcissistic mortifications)" (p. 74). He explains that the "traumas" are either experiences involving the subject's own body, or sense perceptions, and that the young child makes no sharp distinction between sexual and aggressive acts. He clearly claims that the experiences of the person's first five years of life exercise a strong influence which nothing else later can withstand. Thus what children have experienced even at the age of two or three and have not understood will break into their lives later, govern their actions, decide their sympathies and antipathies, and even determine their choice of a love object. Sooner or later "the return of the repressed" establishes itself in the life of the individual. Such a phenomenon may remind us of the great Goethe, who, while a genius, looked down upon his pedantic unbending father and yet in his old age developed traits that were typical of his father's character.

After the first few years of life there is period of latency; then, at puberty or later, what Freud calls positive or negative effects of trauma begin to occur. The positive effects refer to the effort to re-experience and repeat the trauma and to revive it in an analogous relationship with someone else. This leads to unalterable character traits, the origins of which are forgotten. The negative effects are the defensive reactions leading to symptom formation. The crucial issue is that both the positive and the negative effects—restrictions on the ego and stable character changes—have a compulsive quality:

> . . . that is to say that they have a great psychical intensity and at the same time exhibit a far-reaching independence of the organization of the other mental processes, which are adjusted to the demands of the external world and obey the laws of logical thinking. They (the pathological phenomena) are insufficiently or not at all influenced by external reality, pay no attention to it or its psychical representatives, so that they may easily come into active opposition to both of them. They are, one might say, a State within a State, an inaccessible party, with which co-operation is impossible, but which may succeed in overcoming what is known as the normal party and forcing it into its service (p. 76).

The narcissistic and borderline disorders may be thought of as a waystation on the path to a complete domination by an internal psychical reality over the reality of the external world, and represent some kind of compromise by the use of a variety of defense mechanisms, such as disavowal of archaic psychic configurations and their manifestations, to enable the personality to function in at least a limited manner.

Freud speaks of what today some would call transformations of narcissism, occurring, he explains, as a consequence of the victory of intellectuality over sensuality. The advance in intellectuality, according to Freud, has as a consequence an increase in the individual's self-esteem. It also helps to check the brutality and the tendency to violence which are apt to appear where the development of muscular rather than intellectual strength is the popular ideal.

Freud says that the renunciation of instinct provides the ego a yield of pleasure, a substitutive satisfaction. The ego feels elevated and is proud of the instinctual renunciation as though it were a valuable achievement that deserves greater love from the superego, and the consciousness of deserving this love is felt by the ego as pride. The superego in this view is seen as bathing the ego with a sense of being lovable and worthwhile; the prototype of this is the preoedipal child who has lived up to parental expectations and receives their admiration and love.

Thus a pre-oedipal external regulating system has now become an internal regulating system and, depending on the harshness of the superego, can from within either bathe the ego in love or demand further and further renunciation. Here is an important differentiation between the psychoanalytic point of view and all others, a distinction that is extremely important for psychotherapists to understand. After the Oedipal phase of development the intrapsychic tensions between the ego on the one hand, and the id as well as the superego and the external world on the other, form the battleground out of which a compromise is hammered out, leading to the behavior of the individual. Thus the behavior output as a response to input from the external world is the vector result of an *enormously complex internal process* which can only be understood by examination of the whole life history of the individual, and an empathic identification with his internal processes.

Furthermore, because of the sharp connection between the id aggressions and the superego, the internal regulating system or the internalized parent is not simply a copy of the childhood parent but rather often a highly distorted version, usually much distorted in the direction of greater cruelty, severity, and harshness. This distortion enormously intensifies the kinds of problems with which the ego has to deal, and cripples it out of proportion to what seems to be its deserved fate in the light of what realistic knowledge we may have about the actual personalities of the patient's parents! In the projections which borderline and narcissistic patients make during psychotherapy we are frequently astonished by the cruelty and harshness attributed in the transference to parental figures, whereas our anamnesis has not revealed any such measure of ferocity in the real parents. Kernberg (1975, 1976) has attempted to explain this distortion by his controversial theory of early "splitting," resulting in unintegrated, repressed, primitive "all good" and "all bad" self and object representations, which are then projected in the transference.

In *An Outline of Psychoanalysis* (1940A;23:141ff), Freud notes that neuroses are acquired up to the age of six, even though their symptoms may not make their appearance until much later. He insists that in every case the later neurotic illness links up with the childhood neurosis. Since the neuroses are disorders of the ego, the etiological preference for the first period of childhood is obvious: "It is not to be wondered at if the ego, so long as it is feeble, immature and incapable of resistance, fails to deal with tasks which it could cope with later on with the utmost ease. In these circumstances instinctual demands from within, no less than excitations from the external world, operate as 'traumas', particularly if they are met half-way by certain innate dispositions" (pp. 184–5). We see that in this final work Freud had already clearly focused on neuroses (including what he calls severe neuroses) as disorders of the ego, opening the door along with Anna Freud to a whole new area of research and understanding in psychoanalytic psychology. A discussion of Anna Freud's extension of this is presented in *Great Ideas in Psychotherapy* (Chessick 1977*a*). A careful survey of numerous recent conflicting metapsychological viewpoints on the concept of narcissism is presented by Moore (1975), who is more inclined toward the views of Kernberg than those of Kohut.

The problem of narcissistic patients and borderline disorders has become a central one in our time. Freud's work on narcissism and the borderline disorders was very preliminary and sketchy, and this work has been considerably expanded by Kohut (1971, 1977). In two previous books (Chessick 1974, 1977) I have described at length the theoretical additions of Kernberg,* Kohut, and others to Freud, and I will just summarize some of Kohut's extraordinary and highly controversial contributions in the remainder of this chapter.†

Our self-assessment becomes closer to the assessment of others as our narcissism matures through a series of developmental pathways. In response to stimuli from the environment and due to an epigenetic preprogramming involving our heredity, these developmental pathways lead from autoerotism, to primary narcissism—in which the infant blissfully experiences the world as being itself—and then, due to inevitable disappointment in such narcissistic omnipotence, the formation of the grandiose self and the idealized parent imago. The grandiose self implies the conviction of being very powerful, if not omnipotent, with a demand for mirroring confirmation by the selfobject; the idealized parent imago attributes all omnipotence to a magical figure which is then viewed as a selfobject to be controlled and fused with this imago. By a series of microinternalizations in an appropriate environment, the grandiose self becomes incorporated into the ego or self as ambition, a drive or push which can be realistically sublimated and is itself drive-channeling and drive-controlling, resulting in motivated enthusiastic activity. The idealized parent imago becomes infused into the ego ideal (or, in the later theory, the other pole of the self) which attracts the individual toward certain goals and performs a drive-curbing function. The proper microinternalization of these formations leads ultimately by further transformations to a sense of humor, empathy, wisdom, acceptance of the transience of life, and even to creativity within the limitations of the individual.

If the grandiose self is not gradually integrated into the realistic purposes of the ego, it is disavowed (horizontal split) or repressed (vertical split) and per-

*Kernberg's views on the chronology of developmental stages have changed since publication of my (1977) book (see Kernberg 1976).

†What follows is based mainly on Kohut's (1971) "psychology of the self in the narrow sense," which represents an attempt to extend our understanding of narcissism within the framework of Freud's metapsychology. Discussion of Kohut's (1977) "psychology of the self in the broad sense" is beyond the scope of this book. Details of the clinical application of Kohut's theories to the treatment of patients are presented in a casebook edited by Goldberg (1978), of outstanding value to every psychotherapist.

sists unaltered in archaic form; the individual then oscillates between irrational overestimation of himself and feelings of inferiority with narcissistic mortification due to the thwarting of ambition. If the idealized parent imago is not integrated into the ego ideal, it is then repressed as an archaic structure, and the patient becomes unconsciously fixed on a yearning—out of the need to resume narcissistic peace—for an external idealized selfobject, forever searching for an omnipotent powerful person from whose support and approval he may gain strength and protection.

As a consequence of this developmental arrest and failure to properly integrate the archaic structures, characteristic "selfobject transferences" (Kohut 1977), previously called "narcissistic transferences" (Kohut 1971), occur. These "selfobject transferences" occur as the result of the amalgamation of the unconscious archaic narcissistic structures (grandiose self and idealized parent imago) with the psychic representation of the analyst, under the pressure of the need to relieve the unfulfilled narcissistic needs of childhood. It remains a matter of debate as to whether they are to be called transferences in the strict sense, because they are *not* motivated by the need to discharge instinctual tensions, nor are they produced by cathecting the analyst with object libido. One may wish to think of them as "transference-like" phenomena, but I will refer to them here as selfobject transferences, following Kohut's latest writing.

The goal of the idealizing selfobject transference is to share magically, via a merger, in the power and omnipotence of the therapist. Occuring as the result of therapeutic mobilization of the idealized parent imago are two basic types of such transferences, with a variety of gradations in between. The most obvious type is a later formation, apparently based on a failure of idealization of the father, which stresses the *search* for an idealized parent which the patient must attach himself to in order to feel approved and protected. A more archaic type of selfobject transference may appear, or be hidden under the other type; this transference is related to a failure with the mother, in which the stress is on ecstatic merger and mystical union with the godlike idealized parent.

Once such a transference has been formed, clinical signs of its disturbance are a cold, aloof, angry, raging withdrawal which represents a swing to the grandiose self; feelings of fragmentation and hypochondria due to the separation; and the creation of erotised replacement by often frantic activities and fantasies, especially those involving voyeurism, but with many variations.

The typical countertransference to the idealizing selfobject transferences occurs through the mobilization of the archaic grandiose self, in whatever unanalyzed residue is present, in the therapist; this leads to an embarassed and defensive "straight-arming" of the patient by denial of the patient's idealization, joking about it, or trying vigorously to interpret it away. Such countertransference produces in the patient the typical signs of disturbance mentioned above.

Three forms of mirror selfobject transferences are seen as a result of the therapeutic mobilization of the repressed and unintegrated archaic grandiose self. The purpose of these transferences is to share with the therapist the patient's exhibitionistic grandiosity, either by participating with the therapist in his or her imagined greatness or by having the therapist reflect and confirm the greatness of the patient. In the archaic-merger type of mirror transference, the patient experiences the therapist as part of himself, expects the therapist to know what is in his mind and what he wants, and demands total control of the type one demands from one's own arm or leg. In the alter-ego or twinship type of mirror transference, the patient insists that the therapist is like or similar to him psychologically or that the therapist and the patient look alike. In the third type, mirror transference proper, the patient recognizes that the therapist looks different, but insists on assigning to him the sole task of praising, echoing, and mirroring his performance and greatness. Kohut relates this to "the gleam in the mother's eye" as she watches her baby. It becomes very difficult at times to tell which type of selfobject transference has formed, especially in the less primitive transferences where it is hard to distinguish between the grandiose demand for mirroring and the demand for approval by the idealized parent.

Disturbance of mirror transferences leads to a sense of crumbling self, hypochondria, and hypercathexis of isolated parts of either the body, various mental functions, or activities. Compulsive sexuality, characterized by exhibitionism and other sexual varieties and perversions, often appears in order to combat the sense of deadness and an empty self; its purpose is to magically restitute the sense of self and of being psychologically "alive."

Typical countertransference reactions to mirror transferences are boredom, lack of involvement with the patient, inattention, annoyance, sarcasm, and a tendency to lecture the patient out of the therapist's counter-exhibitionism, or to obtain control by exhortation, persuasion, and so on.

It follows that in clinical work we can pick up certain early signs that selfobject transferences have formed. We note that the patient reacts to our empathic lapses, or to cancellations and vacations, or even to the gap of time between sessions, with (a) perverse or other sexual acting-out; (b) hypochondriasis; (c) irritable and arrogant behavior; (d) painfully depressive moods; and (e) a sense of emptiness and depletion. These signs may be understood as manifestations of partial fragmentation of the self due to the disruption of the selfobject transferences, and as attempts to restitute and discharge the painful tensions involved.

From this it is clear that the purpose of the selfobject transferences is to relieve the unfulfilled narcissistic needs of childhood for the selfobject to joyfully accept and confirm the child's grandiosity, and for "an omnipotent surrounding," which Kohut and Wolf (1978) regard as "healthy needs that had not been responded to in early life." When these responses are forthcoming, a sense of narcissistic peace and equilibrium results.

Thus the therapist must decide whether the transference is object-related or narcissistic in any given patient at any given time. Narcissistic injury produces narcissistic rage, and narcissistic injury can be defined as occurring when the environment does not react in an expected way—thus it may occur even on a realistic basis, as for example when no rewards are forthcoming for good work.

The patient may be embarrassed in reaction to his unconscious fantasy, presenting a clinical picture of timidity, shyness, and easy blushing with no apparent explanation. The exhibitionism is mobilized in the process of therapy with a sense of self-admiration and feeling invulnerable. The patient often hates himself and cuts off his own ideas and creativity out of a feared sense of narcissistic mortification. We hope in the therapy that he will microinternalize a new attitude from the therapist in which he finds that it is all right to do the best one can to get admiration. The therapist's benign view replaces the harsh critical view and detoxifies the patient's attitude toward himself.

Phase-inappropriate disappointment in the idealized parent imago that occurs very early in experiences with the mother leads to a need for optimal soothing from the idealized parent and a search for drugs, with a malfunctioning stimulus barrier. Such patients tend to become addicted to psychotherapy for just this reason. In the late pre-oedipal period, phase inappropriate disappointment causes a resexualization of pregenital drives and derivatives, with a high incidence of perversions in fantasy or acts. In early latency the severe disappointment in the idealized Oedipal object undoes the recently established and thus precarious idealized superego. This leads to the search for an external object of perfection, an intense search for and dependency on idealized selfobjects, which are conceived as missing segments of the psychic structure. For such patients each success can give only transient good feelings but does not add to the patient's self-esteem because the patient is fixed on finding an idealized parent imago outside of himself—he is at a developmental stage such that he must have an outside source of approval.

Idealizations can also appear in the transference neuroses. Idealization is the state of being in love in the transference. In the transference neurosis it does not lose touch entirely with the realistic features and limitations of the object. In other neurotic situations, idealization can represent a projection of the analysand's idealized superego onto the analyst and form a part of the positive transference, or defensive idealizations can form against transference hostility.

In the narcissistic disorders, however, the unconscious is fixated on an idealized selfobject for which it continues to yearn, and such persons are forever searching for external omnipotent powers from whose support and approval they attempt to derive strength. Thus in the narcissistic transferences there is a sense of an eerie vague idealization which becomes central to the material even to such an extreme delusion that the therapist is Jesus Himself. One does not get the feeling of relating as one human being to another, but rather of an eerie quality of unreasonable exultation to which the therapist reacts with embarrassment and negativism if he does not understand the material conceptually. The intensity of the distortion gives the therapist an idea of how desperate the patient is—and the greater the desperation, the greater the requirement for soothing from the therapist by presenting structure and explanations and focusing on the current reality.

The grandiose self and idealized parent imago are either split off or repressed if the development of narcissism is interfered with. If they are split off one gets Kohut's "vertical split" in which there is a barrier between two conscious parts of the self which are not integrated, and the patient acts as if one aspect of the self does "not know" about the other.

If these primitive narcissistic structures are repressed we get reaction formations or the sudden emergence of shame and self-consciousness, with many vague symptoms. Some of these are: (a) fear of the loss of the real self to ecstatic merger with the idealized parent, God, or the universe; (b) fear of loss of contact with reality due to intense unrealistic grandiosity; (c) shame and self-consciousness consequent to dealing with the intrusion of exhibitionistic libido; and (d) hypochondriasis—which represents an elaboration by the ego of the intrusion of archaic images of a fragmented body-self. In these disorders, acting out represents a partial breakthrough of the grandiose self and may be life-threatening.

In working with these developmental disorders, the therapist must participate by dealing especially with responses to separation and disappointments in the transferences, and staying nearer to everyday experiences rather than deep interpretations of the past. In fact, interpretations of the past may come as a narcissistic injury because the patient can't do much about it. The therapist takes a benign approach and fosters the development of the transference relationship by patient, craftsman-like work.

Narcissistic rage (Kohut 1972, 1977) is one of the most important and common clinical problems, and is characterized by the need for revenge or even preventive attack through sarcasm. It is aimed at the "enemy" who is experienced as a flaw in the patient's narcissistically perceived reality. The patient expects total and full control, so the independence or balky behavior of the selfobject is a personal offense. When the selfobject fails to live up to absolute obedience expectations, narcissistic rage appears and there is no empathy whatever for the offender. Such rage enslaves the ego and allows it to function only as its tool and rationalizer. Chronic narcissistic rage is even more dangerous, as secondary process thinking gets pulled more and more into the archaic aggression and the ego attributes failure to the malevolence of the uncooperative selfobject. Such rage may also be directed at the self as an object, which leads to depression, or at the body-self, leading to psychosomatic disorders.

The psychotherapist working with narcissistic and borderline disorders must have a thorough grasp of the process of working-through, in which minor disappointments in the narcissistic transferences, followed by characteristic reactions in the patient, must be calmly explained to the patient. Without this conceptual understanding, the temptation occurs to launch all kinds of extratherapeutic activities toward the patient. Some of these temptations are based directly on countertransference hostility and some are based on reaction formations to this hostility; but the principle remains that the therapist's temptation to step outside the role of the calm, benign craftsman is based on a misunderstanding of what is going on in the therapy and is motivated by countertransference. There is no end to the rationalizations which the unanalyzed psychotherapist may present to himself to justify his exploitation of and retaliation toward his patient.

In order to protect themselves against rejection and further narcissistic wounding, patients with an insufficient ego ideal tend to withdraw into grandiosity—which bothers and irritates people and produces further rejection leading to further withdrawal. In addition, the patient is much harsher on himself as he can fall back only on the harsh critical superego, for internalization of the love for the idealized parent imago has not occurred, as I will discuss below.

Clinically, narcissistic peace can be established with concomitant improved function when the idealizing transference occurs, but such transferences may also lead to a fear of loss of ego boundaries and fusion if the wish to merge with the idealized parent imago is so strong, and so may result in a negative therapeutic reaction. The patient must resist the threatened merging out of fear that if he submits he will end up more you than himself.

A gifted individual can actually realize some of the boundless expectations of his grandiose self but it is never enough, and the patient is plagued by an endless demand for superb performance. For example, we see the middle-age depression so common in successful people who have been on a treadmill and achieved money and power, for success brings no relief. Such patients always need acclaim and more success; they have the talent to make their wishes come true but they never get satisfaction since they are driven by a split-off grandiose self with its omnipotent bizarre demands. "Lying" and name-dropping in such patients can be understood as an attempt to live up to expectations of the grandiose self and thus must be removed from moral condemnation in the mind of the therapist.

For narcissistic patients, therefore, the handling of the transference becomes the essence of the treatment. These narcissistic "transferences" do not involve the investment of the therapist with object libido, as in the Oedipal neuroses, although they do involve a crossing of the repression barrier, of the mobilized grandiose self and idealized parent imago. It is therefore vital to have *a clear and precise understanding* of Kohut's notion of the development and vicissitudes of these concepts.

Between around eight months and three years of age Kohut postulates a normal intermediate phase of powerful narcissistic cathexis of "the grandiose self" (a grandiose exhibitionistic image of the self) and the idealized parent imago (the image of an omnipotent self-object with whom fusion is desired). These psychic formations are gradually internalized and integrated within the psychic structure. The grandiosity, as a result of appropriate minor disappointments, is internalized at around two to four years of age; it forms the *nuclear ambitions pole* of the self, driving the individual forward. It derives most from the relationship with the mother, and in the narrow theory is thought of as forming a part of the ego; in the broad theory, the "self" and ego are separated and thus the internalized grandiose self is conceived of as forming the nuclear ambitions pole of the self.

At around four to six years of age, at the height of the Oedipal phase, the idealized parent imago, which derives from both parents, is also internalized. In the narrow theory it was thought of as an infusion of both the superego and the ego with the love and admiration originally aimed at the idealized parent imago, which then serves as a vital internal source of self-esteem and the basis of the ego-ideal aspect of the super-ego. This basic ego-ideal forms a system toward which the person aspires; thus he is *driven from below*, so to speak, by his nuclear ambitions, and *pulled from above* by his ego-ideal. In the psychology of the self in the broad sense, the internalization of the idealized parent imago forms the other pole of the self, *the nuclear ideals pole*. In the broad sense, this notion of the bipolar self is the crucial concept of the psychology of the self.

When these two major internalizations have occured, a cohesive sense of self is formed, and the person is ready to go on and resolve the Oedipus complex. The super-ego can form, and moral anxiety (from within) replaces castration anxiety. The repression barrier is established and eventually consolidated in latency and adolescence, and anxiety becomes confined to function as signal anxiety (essentially Kernberg's "5th stage"). But for Kohut, even after adolescence still further transformations of narcissism occur, resulting eventually in mature wisdom, a sense of humor, an acceptance of the transience of life, empathy, and creativity. These transformations involve an increased firming of the sense of self, making mature love possible.

Thus in the narrow sense theory, the idealized parent imago, when internalized, performs in the pre-oedipal ego and superego a drive control and drive-channeling function, and in the Oedipal superego forms an idealized super-ego, which now leads the person. The infantile grandiose self forms the nuclear ambitions, and crude infantile exhibitionism is transformed into socially meaningful activities and accomplishments. Thus narcissism, when transformed, is both normal and absolutely vital to mature human personality functioning; it is no longer a pejorative term.

In the psychology of the self in the broad sense, these internalizations form into the sense of a cohesive self, and a complementary role in development is given to the Oedipal phase, besides that described by Freud. Here, it is the response of the parents to the child's libidinal and aggressive and exhibitionistic strivings—their pride and mirroring confirmation of his development—that permits these internalizations to occur smoothly. To clarify, in Freud's theory, for example, it is the boy's fear of castration by the father that causes him to identify with the aggressor and internalize the values of the father. For Kohut, it is *also*, at the same time, the father's pride in the boy's emerging assertiveness as it shows itself in the boy's Oedipal strivings and imitative efforts, that softens the disappointment of not possessing the mother and enables an internalization of the idealized parent imago as a nuclear pole of the self.

If, for example, the father or mother withdraws from the child as a response to their horror of his Oedipal strivings, this internalization cannot occur, and the child remains fixed in development on finding some individual *outside of himself* to which he attaches the idealized parent imago—a familiar clinical picture. His internal self-esteem in this case remains very low, and his self-esteem and sense of self require continual and unending bolstering from the external object who has been invested with the idealized parent imago. When such bolstering is not forthcoming, profound disappointment, narcissistic rage, and even a sense of impending fragmentation of the self occurs. Thus we have a complementary theory, in which new explanatory concepts *and* the structural theory of Freud are employed, in order to make sense of the common but puzzling aspects of the narcissistic personality.

Kohut stresses two key consequences of lack of integration of the grandiose self and idealized parent imago: adult functioning and personality are impoverished because the self is deprived of energy that is still invested in archaic structures, and adult activity is hampered by the breakthrough and intrusion of archaic structures with their archaic claims. These unintegrated structures are either repressed (Kohut's "horizontal split") or disavowed (Kohut's "vertical split"), and they quickly show themselves in the psychotherapy situation.

The patient wants us to respond as if we belong one hundred percent to him; a benign view of this desire, rather than an angry retort or harsh criticism, detoxifies the patient's attitude toward himself and prevents a withdrawal into arrogant grandiosity. As explained, outside success for such patients gives only transient good feelings but does not add to the idealization of the superego, for the patient is arrested developmentally on finding an idealized parent imago outside of himself—a stage where he still needs outside sources of approval. Narcissistic injury produces great rage, which also appears if the transference object does not live up to the expected idealization. Thus narcissistic and borderline patients present a psychic apparatus ready to ignite at any time, and with their poor ego ideal they cannot neutralize the explosions and disintegrations when they occur.

Kernberg (1976) warns that in working with borderline patients "The therapist tends to experience, rather soon in the treatment, intensive emotional reactions having more to do with the patient's premature, intense and chaotic transference and with the therapist's capacity to withstand psychological stress and anxiety, than with any specific problem of the therapist's past" (p. 179). In fact, intense and premature emotional reactions on the part of the therapist indicate the presence of severe regression in the patient.

The repressed or split-off grandiose self with its bizarre demands may drive the patient relentlessly and, as previously mentioned, even force him into "lying," bragging, and name-dropping in order to live up to expectations of the grandiose self. Certain types of dangerous acting-out may also occur as part of the effort to feel alive and to establish a conviction of omnipotence and grandiosity; one female patient of mine often rides a motorcycle at high speed down the highway when visibility has been obscured by fog. In working with such patients the therapist must deal with responses to separation and disappointment and stay near current experiences and strivings for omnipotence and grandiosity. Benign acceptance, conceptual explanation, and education of the patient have a major rolè in the treatment of narcissistic and borderline patients.

The vicissitudes of the transferences and the appearance of the rage provide the opportunity for the calm, nonanxious therapist, working as a careful craftsman, to help the patient understand and transform the archaic narcissism so that the aggression can be employed for realistic ambitions, goals, and ideals. The signs of successful resumption of the developmental process and the appropriate transformations of narcissism can be found in two major areas of the patient's life. First, an increase and expansion of object love will take place, due primarily to an increased firming of the sense of self. Thus the patient becomes more secure as to who he is and how acceptable he is; he thus becomes more able to offer love. The second area is in greater drive control and drive channeling and a better-idealized superego, as well as more realistic ambition and the change of crude infantile exhibitionism into socially meaningful activities. We hope to end up with a sense of empathy, creativity, humor, and perhaps ultimately, wisdom.

Kernberg (1975, 1976), working from modifications of the theories of Melanie Klein and other authors who utilize the so-called object relations theory, has presented quite a different metapsychological viewpoint of borderline and narcissistic personality disorders. It is important for the psychotherapist to be familiar with these theories (also summarized in Chessick 1977) and to make some choices. Detailed discussion is beyond the scope of this book, but in general my current view is that Kohut's work is more useful in the understanding of narcissistic phenomena, while Kernberg's work has better application in clinical work with borderline personality disorders. I agree with Kohut's distinction between narcissistic and borderline personalities; but he does not address himself to the treatment of the latter since they are not amenable to formal psychoanalysis. Unfortunately, their theories conflict sharply at certain points, and are not reconcilable.

18

METAPSYCHOLOGY

The Topographic and Structural Theories. As Freud progressed in his study of hysterical phenomena and dreams he constantly attempted to relate the clinical material to his development of a coherent theory of mental functioning. He first attempted to couch this theory in neurophysiological terms, as in his *Project for a Scientific Psychology* (1950A;1:283–397). However, he gave up attempting to base his theory on aspects of the functioning nervous system and, borrowing his basic concepts from the *Project for a Scientific Psychology*, restructured the theory using purely psychological conceptions totally free of neuroanatomical implications.

Chapter VII of *The Interpretation of Dreams* (1900A;5:509–622) is Freud's basic account of his theory of the mind; it has since served as the foundation for subsequent extensions and modifications of his views. Jones (1953, pp. 396–404) and Brenner et al. (1970) present brief and easily readable summaries of this extremely difficult chapter.

Chapter VII of *The Interpretation of Dreams* and Freud's paper, "The Unconscious" (1915E;14:161ff), written fifteen years later offer, in an almost overly condensed form, the basic concepts of depth psychology; these concepts constitute the *topographic theory* (Arlow and Brenner 1964), and may be described in its early form as follows:

(1) The system unconscious (*Ucs.*), or the infantile part of the mind; and the system preconscious (*Pcs.*), or the adult part of the mind,

(2) The system unconscious, containing mainly wishes and seeking to re-experience the sensations of previous gratifications.

(3) The unpleasure principle, later called the pleasure principle by Freud, which governs the system unconscious. According to the pleasure principle, accumulated mental energy must be discharged as quickly and fully as possible to bring the system back to the previous resting state. The system preconscious is guided by what Freud later called the reality principle.

(4) The system unconscious is oblivious to reality and operates essentially by condensation and displacement of mental energies; mutually contradictory tendencies can exist side by side.

(5) The dynamic notion that in the system unconscious, mental energies are freely mobile.

(6) The notion of a dynamic interplay between the unconscious and the preconscious, introducing the thorny metapsychological problem of repression as a major concept, discussed by Freud at length later in his paper on repression and Lecture XXXII of his *New Introductory Lectures.* I dwell on this subject in detail later in this chapter.

In chapter VII the rudiments of "repression proper" and "primal repression" are introduced. When the preconscious has *never* cathected a certain unconscious wish, Freud called this failure primal repression, and this store of infantile wishes, "which has from the first been held back from the *Pcs.*, becomes a *sine qua non* of repression" (p. 604).

If a preconscious wish or idea becomes associated with or cathected by an unacceptable unconscious wish, the preconscious cathexis will be withdrawn, in accordance with the unpleasure principle. This withdrawal of cathexis from a preconscious idea because of its association with an unconscious unacceptable wish, is called repression proper. As Freud conceived it at this point, if there is a strong instinctual drive associated with the repudiated idea, it may still try to force its way to the conscious, even if it has lost its cathexis from the *Pcs.* There then follows a defensive struggle, for the *Pcs.* in turn reinforces its opposition to the repressed thoughts, "i.e. produces an 'anticathexis' "; the result may be the appearance of a compromise formation in the conscious. Notice that primal repression leads to a pulling of associated ideas into the unconscious; repression proper is a pushing out of the system preconscious.

(7) The topographic theory is not to be thought of as a spatial theory but as a functional theory.

(8) The Kantian notion that consciousness is like a sense organ for the perception of psychic qualities. This will be discussed in chapters 20 and 21 when we evaluate the position of Freud in philosophy.

The famous diagrams in chapter VII of *The Interpretation of Dreams* are worthy of careful study. The notion of psychotherapy as a vehicle to bring the unconscious under the domination of the preconscious is presented first; the critical distinction between primary and secondary process is then established:

> The primary processes are present in the mental apparatus from the first, while it is only during the course of life that the secondary processes unfold, and come to inhibit and overlay the primary ones; it may even be that their complete domination is not attained until

> the prime of life. In consequence of the belated appearance of the secondary processes, the core of our being, consisting of unconscious wishful impulses, remains inaccessible to the understanding and inhibition of the preconscious; the part played by the latter is restricted once and for all to directing along the most expedient paths the wishful impulses that arise from the unconscious. These unconscious wishes exercise a compelling force upon all later mental trends, a force which those trends are obliged to fall in with or which they may perhaps endeavor to divert and direct to higher aims (pp. 603–604).

From this it appears that the *system unconscious* plays the same role for Freud as *noumena* did for Kant; Freud continues, "The unconscious is the true psychical reality; in its innermost nature it is as much unknown to us as the reality of the external world, and it is as incompletely presented by the date of consciousness as is the external world by the communications of our sense organs" (p. 613). Thus in this chapter of *The Interpretation of Dreams* the whole notion of dynamic psychiatry and its underlying philosophy is set down—the symptoms of mental illness are explained on a dynamic basis, as a result of the strengthening and weakening of the various components in the interplay of inner forces, so many of whose effects are hidden from view even while ordinary mental functions are apparently normal. It is the unique brilliance and creative genius of this book that led Freud to insist often that it was, of everything he wrote, his greatest work.

It should be noted that *all* the concepts of metapsychology have come under recent attack even from within the psychoanalytic community itself—thus the current controversy. In Freud's shift from the topographic theory to the later structural theory (id–ego–superego, as will be discussed later), certain aspects of clinical material were insufficiently reinterpreted at the time in the light of the newer metapsychology, leaving an inconsistency in the formulation of the theory of mental functioning. Arlow and Brenner (1964) give a complete review of the topographic and structural theories and attempt to resolve the inconsistencies. In current clinical practice Freud's structural theory, as he outlined it in the later stages of his life, still represents a useful set of functional concepts essential in organizing our thinking about the clinical data presented by our patients; but the theory contains serious shortcomings when applied to certain clinical data and to severe psychopathology (Gedo and Goldberg 1973).

Every practicing psychotherapist should be thoroughly familiar with *both* the topographical and the structural theories of Freud and be able to utilize them in discussing clinical phenomena; if he wishes to replace these metapsychological concepts he should do so with caution and only after prolonged study of the newer, equally complicated models such as those based on information systems (Peterfreund and Schwartz 1971). The basic theoretical paradigm of Freud is contained in the topographical and structural theories of psychoanalysis, and psychoanalytically oriented psychotherapy is at present based on this paradigm.

Pleasure Principle and Reality Principle. In many ways the subject of metapsychology is the most controversial and hotly disputed in the field of psychoanalysis. In the present book I try to deal only with those aspects of metapsychology that have immediate clinical application and attempt to avoid the highly complex intricacies of the subject, which has generated a literature that resembles medieval philosophy in its complexity and form.

"Formulations on the Two Principles of Mental Functioning" (Freud 1911B;122:215–226) has become one of the classics of psychoanalysis even though it is extremely difficult, condensed, and was badly received when first presented. It represents a turning point in Freud's interests and begins a series of papers on metapsychology which in turn were conceived as the first part of a book on the subject that was later abandoned (see chapter 17).

The basic point of the "Formulations on the Two Principles of Mental Functioning" is to introduce the distinction between the pleasure principle that dominates the primary processes of mental life and the reality principle which dominates secondary process thought. Primary processes are unconscious mental processes striving, under the domination of the pleasure principle, for the realization of wishes and a yield of pleasure as well as to avoid unpleasure; with the introduction of the reality principle, which occurs gradually, fantasy and daydream are split off and conscious thought guides the person to strive for what is useful and to guard against the imagination. Repression or flight is to some extent replaced by judgment and sublimation.

Freud begins, "We have long observed that every neurosis has as its result, and probably therefore as its purpose a forcing of the patient out of real life, an alienating of him from reality" (p. 218). "This sentence alone," writes Jones (1955, p. 313), "apart from very many other ones in Freud's writings, shows how unjustified is the reproach which has been levelled against him that he neglected the importance of the social environment in the genesis of the neuroses." This turning away from reality on the part of neurotics brings into focus the investigation of the development of the relation of neurotics and of mankind in general to reality. According to Freud, in the primary system such as operates in the young infant, in dreams, and in waking fantasies, no mental process has any other purpose than to elicit pleasure and avoid unpleasure. The failure of this system to obtain adequate satisfaction compels the further step of taking reality into account: "The psychical apparatus had to decide to form a conception of the real circumstances of the external world and to endeavor to make a real alteration in them" (Freud, p. 219).

This setting up of the reality principle leads to some basic changes in the psychic apparatus. The perceptual apparatus must be expanded in order to be aware of external as well as internal states, and the sense organs become more directed toward the external world. Consciousness becomes more interested in sensory qualities in addition to the qualities of pleasure and unpleasure "which hitherto had been alone of interest to it" (p. 220).

A special function is instituted to search the external world; the activity of this function meets the sense impressions halfway instead of awaiting their appearance. This searching function is defined as a "tension" by Freud. At the same time a system of "notation" is introduced to lay down the results of this periodical activity of consciousness, and this is a part of what Freud calls "memory." Ideas leading to pain and which therefore have previously been shut out by repression are now subjected to judgment. In this paper, drawing back from pain and shutting out reality is defined as repression, which may confuse the reader; some authors suggest the word "disavowal" as more suitable for this function; the reader must remember the paper was written before Freud's structural theory.

At any rate, motor discharge, which was initially under the pleasure principle for the purpose of unburdening the mental apparatus of accretions of stimuli, now shifts under the reality principle to action in changing the environment. Restraint upon action or motor discharge becomes necessary and is provided by means of the process of thinking, which is defined here as "an experimental kind of acting, accompanied by displacement of relatively small quantities of cathexis together with less expenditure (discharge) of them" (p. 221). Thus thought makes it possible for the mental apparatus to support an increase in tension with the delay of discharge, and thought becomes an experimental way of acting.

The ego permits small quanta of primary process energy to pass through; such quanta are then transformed by the ego into secondary process energy, using memory, and are more in tune with reality. This is Freud's conception of thought—the change of unbound primary process energy into secondary process energy—an experimental way of acting with comparison to memory and then modification and synthesis into secondary process.

The clinical point of this discussion is the explanation of pathological thought as presented in Freud's case of "Paul Lorenz," discussed in chapter 12 of the present book. Pathological thought occurs when the instinct itself is discharged in thought. Thus obsessional thought is a discharge, but a regressive one, and the instinct is not discharged through the motor apparatus as instincts should be, but rather in a substituted discharge of rumination or obsessional thinking.

The reality principle governs the process of thought, which contains judgment—in which there is a comparison of external reality with the conceivably successful memory traces, and finally a form of trial action as described above—an experimental way of acting using small amounts of energy. This process also makes the original impulse easier to deal with, since some of its energy has been borrowed and discharged in the thought process. Under this theory, such thinking as that employed in pure mathematics, which does not have action as its end result, would have to be defined as regressive! If a serious block of discharging energy in the operation of the motor apparatus is erected by the superego, then all the energy is dammed up, floods backwards, and hypercathects the thought systems, leading to a drainage through obsessive rumination—a situation beautifully dramatized in Shakespeare's *Hamlet*.

It is amazing how much is condensed into this little paper. The difficulty of passing from the pleasure principle to the reality principle is alleviated by preserving a special region where the pleasure principle reigns, such as in the fantasy life or play of children. A theory of education is presented in which the teacher's friendliness is seen as a bribe to replace the pleasure principle by the reality principle—here is an area where behavior therapy and psychoanalytic theory clearly overlap. Religion (see chapter 18) is seen as an extension of the same replacement, by demanding renunciation of pleasure in this life; even science, which is most attuned to the reality principle, offers intellectual pleasure during the work and promises practical gain in the end. Art is seen as a special way of reconciliation between two principles.

Finally, while the ego goes through this transformation "from a *pleasure-ego* into a *reality-ego*, the sexual instincts undergo the changes that lead them from their original auto-erotism through various intermediate phases to object-love in the service of procreation" (p. 224). This throws light on the choice of neuroses, since the particular phase of development of the ego and of the sexual instincts that is disturbed leads to characteristic neurotic formations. This idea is picked up in Freud's paper "On the Predisposition to Obsessional Neurosis" (Freud 1913I;12:313–326), in which he introduces the topic of the pregenital organization of the libido. Thus the obsessional neurosis is connected to either a fixation at, or a regression to, the anal–sadistic phase, a characteristic pregenital organization phase.

It should be clear to the reader that a whole philosophy is condensed into this brief paper. Of course, it is a controversial philosophy. One sometimes tends to forget that by this philosophy Freud is trying to explain some obvious clinical phenomena such as obsessive rumination, and in so doing presents us with some conceptual understanding that allows us to take an investigative stance to clinical phenomena patients present. As anyone who has sat for many sessions with a ruminating obsessive patient can attest, such phenomena can be very irritating. In addition, Freud's philosophy explains the great difficulty that patients have in distinguishing unconscious fantasies from memories, since in primary process thought, wishes are equated with their fulfillment and thoughts are given an actual reality. Freud himself was the first clinician to be badly misled by this fact when at first he accepted as factually true the innumerable stories of assault and sexual seduction in childhood presented by his hysterical patients. Such reports are not strictly lies and the patient is not to be condemned for them; they occur because it is not easy for a weakened ego to distinguish the fulfillment of a wish in fantasy from the memory of a happening. Clinically we often see patients who have spent their lives filled with guilt and atonement for wishes to which they react as if these wishes were actually accomplished in reality.

Repression. In this book I have tried to stay away from the technical and complicated issues of metapsychology as much as possible. However, in "On the History of the Psychoanalytic Movement" (1914D;14:3ff), Freud declared that the theory of repression is the cornerstone on which the whole structure of psychoanalysis rests, and his concept of repression goes back historically to the very beginning of psychoanalysis. Since Freud's notion of repression changed gradually, the reader sometimes becomes confused as to what he means by the term repression. Because of this confusion of meaning and because of the current clinical importance of this term, I will focus on the metapsychological paper "Repression" (1915D;14:14–158) and on an excellent review of the subject by Brenner (1957).

The distinction between repression and disavowal or denial (*Verleugnung*) was first made in Freud's much later paper, *Fetishism* (1927E;21:149ff). Disavowal as the ego's reaction to an intolerable external reality was further developed in some of Freud's last writing, especially chapter 8 of *An Outline of Psychoanalysis* (1940A;23:141ff). Recent studies of pre-oedipal pathology and narcissistic personality disorders have brought this distinction into focus, and are treated at length in chapter 17 of the present book.

Freud's brief paper on repression is one of his early works on metapsychology and begins by defining repression as an instinctual vicissitude, one of the resistances which seek to make an instinctual impulse inoperative. Repression is a preliminary stage of condemnation, "something between flight and condemnation" (p. 146). According to Freud, repression is not a defense mechanism present from the very beginning and cannot arise until a cleavage has occurred between conscious and unconscious mental activity; when the need to avoid pain is greater than the pleasure of gratification, repression occurs, and its essence "lies simply in turning something away, and keeping it at a distance, from the conscious" (p. 147). Notice that before the mental organization achieves the cleavage between conscious and unconscious mental activity, the task of fending off unacceptable instincts is dealt with by the other vicissitudes which instincts may undergo, e.g., reversal into the opposite or turning around upon the subject's own self.

Next, Freud introduces one of the most difficult of his concepts, that of primal repression, in which the ideational representative of the instinct is from the beginning denied entrance into the preconscious or conscious. At this point, astute psychiatric residents usually ask how there can be ideational content to an instinct if it never reaches the preconscious or consciousness. Primal repression is a hypothetical construct which seems to confuse the theory. One way to look at it is to realize that Freud is talking about unstructured rudimentary ideational material or pre-ego impulses which are simply *left behind* or outside of consciousness as the ego develops, and thus can never be subjected to secondary process. However, this answer is not very satisfactory.

At this point, even more astute residents may ask how such material can be kept in repression if there is no countercathexis. Here again we must say that this rudimentary unstructured material is simply left out as the ego forms its structure. Philosophers immediately argue that this is one of those concepts that cannot be proven and can never be known, since if it could be known, by definition it would not be in a state of primal repression. In Freud's notion of primal repression, we are dealing fundamentally with a metaphysical concept, a target for Ockham's razor.

Freud then defines repression proper, in which mental derivatives of repressed instincts or associated with repressed instincts are expelled into the unconscious. He insists that this material must be connected to primally repressed material, which has a magnetic attraction and draws its derivatives into the id: "Repression proper, therefore, is actually an after-pressure" (p. 148). Thus repression proper occurs not only due to a repulsion which operates from the direction of the conscious upon the unacceptable instinct; "quite as important is the attraction exercised by what was primally repressed upon everything with which it can establish a connection" (p. 148). Freud believes that repression would probably fail in its purpose if there were not something previously repressed ready to "receive" what is repelled by the preconscious!

Freud then proceeds to make one of his most important clinical observations. Repressed instinctual representatives proliferate in the dark, as he calls it, and take on extreme forms of expression which seem alien to the patient and actually frighten him by giving him the picture of an extraordinary and dangerous strength of instinctual forces. "This deceptive strength of instinct is the result of an uninhibited development in phantasy and of the damming-up consequent on frustrated satisfaction" (p. 149). In the neuroses there is great fear of various repressed instinctual derivatives; but when they have become exposed to the light in intensive psychotherapy they appear silly and relatively harmless. It is a serious failure of empathy on the part of the psychotherapist to assume that apparently minor wishes of an infantile nature should be as ridiculous to the patient as they obviously are to the therapist, and to ridicule such infantile desires. To the patient these are threats of the greatest magnitude coming from within himself, and much of his personality has been developed to protect him from what he considers to be explosive or catastrophically destructive ideation and wishes. It is only *after* a successful psychotherapy that a patient can look back on his unconscious ideation and regard it as a harmless set of infantile phenomena. In fact, when a patient begins to snicker at his own infantile wishes we know that he is making good progress in the psychotherapy.

Not everything that is related to what was primally repressed is withheld from the conscious; some derivatives get through but they are far enough disguised and removed. Repression can even receive a transitory lifting, as for example in jokes.

The entire notion of dynamic psychiatry rests on the concept of repression. Freud explains that the repressed (repression proper) exerts a continuous pressure in the direction of the conscious which must be balanced by an unceasing counterpressure: thus the maintenance of repression involves an uninterrupted expenditure of force, and its removal results in a saving of energy. Similarly, whenever an unacceptable idea acquires a certain degree of energy or strength, this activation leads to repression; thus a substitute for repression would be a weakening, by indirect discharge, of what is distasteful, and so on. Notice that both the energic charge of affect and the ideational presentation of the instinct undergo a fate—the former is transformed and the latter is repressed. At this point Freud thought that felt anxiety resulted from the transformation of these affects into anxiety. Two other possible fates for the affect are total suppression so that no trace of it is found or "it appears as an affect which is in some way or other qualitatively colored" (p. 153).

The implication of this theory seems to be that ordinary ideas always go first through the unconscious and then move into the higher integrated areas of conscious mental function. The lower systems of mentation must cathect the higher ones for the perception of an idea—or even of an external stimulus—to reach consciousness. The id thus retains or attracts certain perceptions where the cathexes are, and much elaboration has to occur before conscious perceptions take place. Freud explains, "The mechanism of a repression becomes accessible to us only by our deducing that mechanism from the *outcome* of the repression" (p. 154). In this theory, symptoms are substitutive formations that represent the return of the repressed, and thus the mechanism of forming symptoms is not the same as that of repression. The paper concludes with examples of symptom formation in the various psychoneuroses.

Brenner (1957) distinguishes four important stages at which Freud made important innovations in or significant additions to the concept of repression, In the first stage, (1894–1896) repression was thought of as a pathological mental process in which memories of a painful nature were suppressed in individuals who had a sexual experience in childhood—an experience which, "though pleasurable at the time it occurred, had been later considered bad or shameful and whose memory had consequently been repressed."

In the second stage (1900-1906) repression was thought of as occurring in normal as well as neurotic individuals, and infantile (primal) repression was a consequence of sequences in the maturation of the psychic apparatus and was the precondition of later repressions. Thus a store of infantile memories and wishes which never had been and never would be accessible to the preconscious constituted the infantile core of "the repressed." Brenner explains, "This formulation was in accord with Freud's experience that infantile memories and wishes were not recoverable or rememberable as such in later years and that their existence has to be *inferred* from their effects on mental life, notably in dreams and neurotic symptoms." As explained above in discussing Freud's paper, this store of inaccessible memories was thought to be the precondition of all later instances of repression; the conscious has to turn away from any derivatives of such infantile memories. A vague notion of an organic factor in repression was introduced at this time but was largely neglected in his later writings.

The theories of the third stage (1911–1915) were put forward in the paper on repression described above and in the famous paper, "The Unconscious" (1915E;14:161ff), to be discussed later in detail. Here, repression is still seen as an immature mechanism which is replaced in the process of psychotherapy or psychoanalysis by conscious judgment and condemnation of unacceptable impulses.

The final stage (1923–1939) was necessitated by the introduction of the structural theory of mind and the signal theory of anxiety described in detail in chapter 6. Anxiety is seen as the predecessor and motive for repression; the signal of anxiety arises as the anticipation of danger from intrapsychic conflict and of flooding due to the intensity of stimuli. Although Freud did not make a full final statement on the subject, upon shifting to the structural theory he seems to have concluded that of several defense mechanisms, repression is the basic one which the ego may employ against an instinctual drive which is the source of anxiety. The mechanism of repression is now seen as the establishment of a countercathexis by the ego, and therefore a substantial degree of ego development must take place before this can occur. The notion of primal repression shifts to represent early infantile repressions which occur by the same mechanism and are quite basic, since later repressions are by and large repetitions or consequences of the infantile ones; but the earlier basic conceptual distinction between primal repression and repression proper fades away.

In an excellent summary, Brenner mentions certain other aspects of the later theory of repression. Between the repressed drive and the counter-cathexis of the ego an equilibrium is established which may shift, for example, when (1) the defenses of the ego are weakened as by illness or sleep; (2) when drives are strengthened as in puberty or chronic frustration, and (3) when there is a correspondence "between the content of current experience and of the repressed drive." Repression is potentially pathogenic in that it produces a crippling of the instinctual life and a constriction of the sphere of influence of the ego, as well as causing a continuing drain on the ego's store of available psychic energy.

A common confusion tends to occur between Freud's notion of the pleasure principle and the principle of constancy, which Freud later labeled the nirvana principle, since at the beginning Freud himself assumed that these two principles were either closely correlated or identical. This is one of those subjects on which Freud changed his views several times; the appropriate references for his various viewpoints are given in "Instincts and their Vicissitudes" (1915C;14:121) in an excellent and useful footnote by Strachey.

Since conditions such as sexual excitement in which there is a state of increasing tension can be pleasurable, it seems clear that the principle of constancy and the pleasure principle cannot be identical. Freud's final conclusion rests on the suggestion that the pleasurable or unpleasurable quality of a state may be related to a rhythm of the changes in the quantity of excitation present. In *Beyond the Pleasure Principle* (1920G;18:3ff) he regards the pleasure principle as a modification of the principle of constancy or the nirvana principle. In this final speculation he maintains that the principle of constancy comes from the death instinct and its modification into the pleasure principle is due to the influence of the life instinct. The principle of constancy has been largely discredited by recent research on the physiology of the brain, the psychological functioning of infants, and sensory deprivation experiments.

Complemental Series. Out of this discussion Freud develops the clinically important notion of complemental series. He begins by asking whether neuroses are exogenous or endogenous illnesses—that is, are they the inevitable result of a particular constitution, or the product of certain detrimental or traumatic experiences in life? Freud maintains that a series of cases could be presented which vary in the amount of each of these factors, so that in some, constitutional factors seem overwhelmingly important, while in others the detrimental experiences seem to be the primary determinant of the formation of the neuroses. This notion was originally presented as the "etiological equation" in Freud's earliest works. However, in *Introductory Lectures on Psychoanalysis* (1916X;15:3ff) it is discussed at some length and several examples of complemental series are offered. In addition to the series formed by cases involving constitutional or biological factors on the one hand, and detrimental or traumatic experiences on the other, we have a series formed of those cases in which the intensity and pathogenic importance of infantile experiences are primary, and of those cases in which later adult experiences of an overwhelming destructive nature are clearly the major factor in the formation of the neurosis. Still another series is formed by those cases in which the destructive events in infancy such as parental seduction, etc., really happened, and by those cases based on the psychic fantasies during the early years that have no basis in fact.

The notion of complemental series is extremely useful in understanding the breadth of Freud's view. For example, even the thorny problem of the group of schizophrenias can be explained as a complementary series of cases: in some it seems clear that a major constitutional or biological factor is at work; in others there is ample evidence for profound detrimental and environmental factors in childhood. Freud's viewpoint leaves room for all types of cases and offers a neat integration of the psychological and the biological. Similarly, we know that any adult can be broken down and forced into neurotic symptomatology if sufficient psychic trauma are applied; this unfortunate empirical information fits into the second complemental series described above.

Perhaps the most interesting is the third complemental series, in which some neurotics allow the psychic reality of their infantile fantasies to influence their entire lives. Freud does not explain why this might be so, but it is perhaps related to his concept of the adhesiveness of the libido (see chapter 16), which he defined as the tenacity with which the libido adheres to particular trends and objects, an independent factor varying from individual to individual. The causes of such adhesiveness are unknown but probably represent a biological or constitutional factor. Not only is this adhesiveness of the libido of great significance in understanding the etiology of neuroses but it is a factor encountered in the intensive psychotherapy of all disorders, since there seems to be a remarkable variation in the timetable with which a patient can work through and free up from certain infantile positions. Awareness and an understanding of the individual patient's timetable is extremely important, for attempts to hurry psychotherapy increase resistance and interfere with the treatment (Chessick 1974).

Ego and Superego: The Structural Theory. Many aspects of Freud's *The Ego and the Id* (1923B;19:3ff) are important for the practice of intensive psychotherapy, besides the basic presentation in this work of the structural theory of the mind. [This theory is also summarized in Lecture 31 of *New Introductory Lectures on Psychoanalysis* (1933A;22:57–80).] For example, the notion of the relation of the ego to the id as analogous to a man on horseback is very important. The man has to hold in check the superior strength of the horse "with this difference, that the rider tries to do so with his own strength while the ego uses borrowed forces" (p. 25), and often a rider, "if he is not to be parted from his horse, is forced to guide it where it wants to go" —so sometimes the ego must transform the id's will into action as if it were the ego's own wish.

This analogy recurs in one of the even-more-obscure-than-usual passages in Kohut's *Analysis of the Self* (1971, p. 187). In Freud's view the ego rides the id like the rider rides on a horse. The goal of psychotherapy is to uncover the unconscious and help the ego to sublimate and control the power of the id. For example, if the patient is stuck with strong aggression or strong morality, there is a limitation on how much one can do; it depends on how much you can help the ego to sublimate, utilize, and control the id energy. Thus the ego has a drive-channelling function. The ego may also have what we could call a drive-curbing function—this represents the ego or rider off the horse. In an atmosphere of appropriate soothing, structures in the pre-Oedipal ego acquire form as a consequence of transmuting microinternalizations and the gradual integration of the archaic grandiose self—as described in the previous chapter. Separated from its instinctual origins, the ego maintains a certain dominance. This phenomenon is more or less an autonomous function of the self; an example is an autonomous professional skill such as that of a surgeon, which in adult life has become separated from its instinctual origin and allows the person to function autonomously in this area without being driven by the id.

Because there are so many confusing definitions and emerging concepts in this area, at this point I want to present a number of basic definitions and formulations for clarification, based on Freud's *The Ego and the Id* (1923B;19:3ff).

It is obviously important for therapeutic purposes to have a clear notion of the formation of the ego and the superego—the nature of this formation is still controversial. In the early phases of development Freud explains that "the character of the ego is a precipitate of abandoned object-cathexes and that it contains the history of those object-choices" (p. 29). The condition of identification is at least a major one under which the id can give up its object, according to Freud, and in the early years of life the separation from objects requires a precipitation of identifications with the lost objects in the ego. In an extremely important clinical passage Freud reminds us that if there are too many object identifications in the ego, "too numerous, unduly powerful and incompatible with one another" (p. 30), a pathological outcome will not be far off. As a consequence of the different identifications becoming cut off from one another by resistances, a disruption of the ego may occur; at least, conflicts between the various identifications can take place. Furthermore, as Freud points out, the effects of the first identifications made in earliest childhood will be most general and lasting. It follows that any psychotherapy aiming to produce major changes in the ego must struggle with these earliest identifications. Elsewhere (Chessick 1974, 1977), I have discussed at length the therapeutic techniques aimed at dealing with these early identifications.

The facts that the mechanisms of defense within the ego and the need for punishment are often not accessible to consciousness forced the revision in Freud's thinking from the topographic theory to the structural theory of the mind. In fact, the cruel, relentless, and even destructive attitude of the superego toward the individual of whose mind it is a part is in many cases very striking and may be entirely unconscious in the patient. Thus agressive energy is borrowed from the id by the superego and channeled into the superego's cruelty and destructiveness, all of which may go on outside the consciousness. In certain cases the superego may gain the position of a tyrannical power over the rest of the personality and proceed in the slow or even dramatic process of subjugating and destroying it. Kohut and Seitz (1963) explain: "Freud extended and deepened his study of the various components of endopsychic morality (the censoring and punitive forces, the standards of the ego-ideal, the approving and loving powers) and ultimately came to the conclusion that the essential cohesiveness of these variegated functions resulted from the fact that they have once been united, outside the personality, in the parental authority" (p. 135). This is all part of the increasingly significant position which aggression began to occupy in Freud's psychoanalytic theorizing after the World War I and which continues to the present day.

It is most important to understand that according to Freud's theory, the precursors of the superego are not very relevant; the superego is seen predominantly as the heir of the resolution of the Oedipus complex, and the firm consolidation of the mind into ego, id, and superego occurs at the point of the resolution of the Oedipus complex, followed by latency identifications and the consolidation process of puberty. The exact details of this consolidation remain somewhat in dispute, but the important clinical point is that before the age of four to six, when the Oedipus complex becomes central, one cannot speak of a significant superego or of an internalized behavior-regulating system unless, like the Kleinians, one introduces a major modification of Freud's thought.

Freud does not make a very sharp distinction between the superego and the ego-ideal. The ego-ideal is the result of identification in the resolution of the Oedipus complex; it is formed by a process seen as similar to the formation of the ego as a result of identification due to the loss of pre-Oedipal objects. Thus the superego is a special modification of the ego, formed by a process similar to the formation of the ego, but more specifically delineated in that process known as the resolution of the Oedipus complex, by identification with the parent of the same sex. It is under the strong pressure to resolve the Oedipus complex that this modification of the ego known as the superego comes into being.

In this theory the ego is that part of the id which has been modified by the direct influence of the external world—it is first and foremost a body ego, an extension of the surface-differentiation between the body and the rest of the world. It is ultimately derived from body sensations, especially those springing from the surface of the body; Freud liked to regard it as a mental projection of the surface of the body, akin to the famous cortical homunculus of the neuroanatomists in describing the projection of the pyramidal tract fibers on the cerebral cortex.

The ego comes into being by the rhythmical and phase-appropriate appearance of the mother administering to the infant's needs. This produces the beginning perception that a source outside the infant has the capacity to protect it from overstimulation and unpleasure; consequently, the initial anxiety of being overwhelmed from within by painful stimuli becomes replaced by anxiety regarding the appearance or disappearance of the mother. A phase-appropriate appearance and disappearance enables the ego to set up identification with the mother; drive channeling mechanisms develop so that gradually a delay in her appearance can be tolerated and eventually the process of separation-individuation can occur. However, until the time of the Oedipus complex subsequent to the formation of the cohesive sense of self, the ego remains quite primitive and limited in the variety of mechanisms at its disposal.

It is only after the formation of the superego and consolidation of the functioning units of the ego and superego that a solid repression barrier can be established. The final outcome of this is the adolescent process, a secondary separation-individuation resulting in an adult, healthy-functioning psyche. Thus the metapsychological description of the phenomena of the pregenital disorders must differ sharply from the description of the infantile neuroses or Oedipal disorders. One reason for the great confusion and different points of view on this subject in the literature and elsewhere is that very often pre-Oedipal dynamisms are described in terms of the structural theory as if they arise out of the functioning of a kind of rudimentary ego and superego precursors. This debatable use of the structural theory represents a fundamental parting of ways in psychoanalytic theorizing, with serious consequences for the type of psychotherapeutic approach chosen, as I have described in *The Intensive Psychotherapy of the Border-*

line Patient (1977). This debatable use of the structural theory also explains the confusion Arlow and Brenner (1964) pointed out between the use of the topographic theory and the structural theory in attempts to explain psychoses. Their effort has been to apply the structural theory to an explanation of psychoses in order to make the metapsychology of psychoses consistent with Freud's views. However, this approach still implies that it is possible to explain the pregenital phenomena of the psychoses by use of the structural theory.

The most important psychotherapeutic consequence of the structural theory which emerged out of the genius of Freud's old age is that the ego is now in the limelight of psychotherapy, especially as the site of anxiety. As Ellenberger (1970) points out, the main concern of psychotherapy is to relieve the ego's suffering under the pressures of three harsh masters—the id, the superego, and external reality—by reducing these pressures and helping the ego to acquire strength. "As a consequence of these new theories, the focus of Freudian therapy shifted from the analysis of the instinctual forces to that of the ego, from the repressed to the repressing. Analysis of defenses would necessarily uncover anxiety, and the task of the analyst was now to dispel the excess of anxiety and to strengthen the ego, so that it could face reality and control the pressure of drives and the superego" (p. 517). As explained in *Great Ideas in Psychotherapy* (Chessick 1977*a*), this approach, through the work of such pioneers as Anna Freud, Freida Fromm-Reichmann, and Franz Alexander, led to the entire field of psychoanalytic psychotherapy.

To review briefly Freud's conceptions of the superego and ego ideal we might begin with the paper "On Narcissism" (1914C;14:69ff), written *before* the structural theory was presented. In this paper Freud proposed two psychic agencies which function to preserve for the ego a sense of self-esteem. The first agent or ego ideal represents the series of achievements which, when reached, lead to a state of imagined infantile perfection and narcissistic bliss. He differentiated this agent from the agent which had the function of observing the real achievements and comparing them with the ideal standards. In *Introductory Lectures on Psychoanalysis* he considered this self-criticizing faculty to be the same as the dream censor (discussed in chapter 13), and as belonging to the ego, not the superego.

In *Group Psychology and the Analysis of the Ego* (1921;18:67ff) the separateness of the "conscience" and ego ideal from the ego began to appear in Freud's thinking. Here he conceives of the possibility of the ego-ideal-conscience as coming into conflict with the rest of the ego, and even raging with a critical cruelty against the ego. The extent of this cruelty, which can function unconsciously, was a major motivation for his development and presentation of the structural theory in *The Ego and the Id*.

It must be emphasized again that Freud considered the development of the superego primarily as a consequence of the resolution of the Oedipus complex. He increasingly emphasized the punitive and cruel aspects of the superego rather than its benign, loving aspect. In *Inhibitions, Symptoms and Anxiety* (1926D;20:77ff) he thought of the threat from the superego as an extension of the castration threat and finally, in *New Introductory Lectures on Psychoanalysis* (1933A;22:3ff), he viewed the superego as an internalized parental authority dominating the ego through punishment and threats of withdrawal of love. The apparent paradox of the clinically observed contrast between the harshness of the superego imitation of the parents and the gentleness of the parents in real life was explained through the borrowing by the superego of the child's own hostility to the prohibiting parent. Thus the superego is always thought of as having a direct connection to the id and as able to drain aggression from the id by turning it upon the ego.

Neuroses and Psychoses. Two brief papers present Freud's basic view on the difference between neuroses and psychoses (Freud 1924B;19:148–156, 1924E; 19:182–189). Because this difference is crucial, these papers are mandatory reading for the psychotherapist. Freud had already pointed out how a neurosis resulted from a conflict between the ego and the id; these two papers represent an extension of his monograph, *The Ego and the Id.* In the psychoses there is a disturbance in the relationship between the ego and the external world in which "the ego creates, autocratically, a new external and internal world; and there can be no doubt of two facts—that this new world is constructed in accordance with the id's wishful impulses, and that the motive of this dissociation from the external world is some very serious frustration by reality of a wish—a frustration which seems intolerable" (1924B;19:151). Thus frustration of infantile wishes remains as a common etiology in the onset of neuroses and psychoses; in a conflictual tension of this kind, if the ego remains true to the external world a neurosis develops; if it allows itself "to be overcome by the id and thus torn away from reality" (p. 151), a psychosis develops.

Freud points out the complicating factor whereby severe conflicts can occur between the ego and the superego and he attributes the narcissistic neuroses to this kind of conflict. Here, he implies a division of the conditions known as paranoia or paraphrenia away from other forms of schizophrenia such as hebephrenia, which end in a greater loss of participation in the external world.

He also opens the question of how the ego can deal with all the various demands made on it by the id, superego, and external world, which leads to his unfinished thoughts, continued later in papers on such aspects as "Splitting of the Ego in the Process of Defense" (1940E;23:273ff). He concludes, "One would like to know in what circumstances and by what means the ego can succeed in emerging from such conflicts, which are certainly always present, without falling ill. This is a new field of research, in which no doubt, the most varied factors will come up for examination" (p. 152). Thus he suggests that in its development it is possible for the ego to "avoid a rupture in any direction by deforming itself, by submitting to encroachments on its own unity and even perhaps by effecting a cleavage or division of itself" (p. 153).

In the second paper Freud (1924E;19:182ff) further studies the relationship of the ego to reality in neuroses and psychoses. At the beginning of the neuroses, the first step occurs in which the ego, in the service of reality, sets about repression of an instinctual impulse. The reaction against the repression and the failure of that repression is the second step, involving the formation of a neurosis which in turn signifies a flight from reality, since every neurosis in some way serves the patient as a means of withdrawing from painful immediate reality.

Psychoses also consist of two steps. The first of these directly drags the ego away from reality, while the second attempts to remodel reality in order to make good the loss. This remodeling produces the hallucinations and delusions of psychoses. At the same time these hallucinations and delusions are fraught with distress and anxiety because the remodeling is carried through against forces which violently oppose it—rejected reality constantly forces itself upon the mind and interferes with the remodeling process.

Furthermore, in both neuroses and psychoses the second step is partly unsuccessful. The repressed instinct in the neuroses cannot procure full gratification through the symptom formation. In psychoses the hallucinations and delusional systems that represent a remodeling of reality are not completely satisfying (see also chapter 21 of this book).

Freud emphasizes the blurring of the distinction between neuroses and psychoses because in both cases there are attempts to replace disagreeable reality by a "reality" which is more in keeping with the subject's wishes. Neuroses do not disavow reality, they only ignore it; psychoses disavow it and try to replace it.

In the paper *Fetishism* (1927E;21:149ff) Freud points out that disavowal necessarily implies a split in the subject's ego. Freud begins this paper with an important distinction, which he finishes in chapter 8 of *An Outline of Psychoanalysis* (1940A;23:141ff), between repression, which applies to the defense against internal instinctual demands, and disavowal, which applies to defense against the claims of external reality. Thus a third form of disorder is possible, in which a reality perception as well as a perception of reality based on a wish exist side by side—a split in the ego in which both faithfulness to reality testing and a remodeling of reality take place *simultaneously*. Freud suggests that this third form can occur more easily in children, who have a lesser degree of differentiation in their psychical apparatus.

The use of the term disavowal is not consistent in Freud. The term develops increasing significance at the outset of the paper "The Infantile Genital Organization of the Libido" (1923E;19:140ff). A footnote by Strachey in this paper (p. 143) traces the use of the term. In the two papers on psychoses, disavowal is used as a way of turning away from reality—a denial of reality. Usually Freud uses the term to represent denial of reality with respect to the discovery of castration. Thus two contrary ideas are held simultaneously in the conscious mind, an attitude which fits in both with the wish and with reality. In psychosis, in contrast to fetishism, the attitude which fits in with reality is absent. The splitting of the ego consequent on disavowal is hinted at in the paper "Neurosis and Psychosis" and is emphasized in the paper on fetishism. The unfinished sequel paper, entitled "Splitting of the Ego in the Process of Defense" (1940E;23:273ff), was published posthumously. Splitting represents a disturbance of the synthetic function of the ego. Freud's final statement on the subject is found in *An Outline of Psychoanalysis* (1940A;23:201–4). Here he contends that a splitting of the ego involving disavowal of perceptions of reality can be found in neuroses, psychoses, and perversions.

In the short note on "A Disturbance of Memory on the Acropolis" (1936A; 22:238ff) Freud describes his momentary feeling, standing on the Acropolis, "What I see here is not real"—a feeling of derealization. The phenomena of derealization primarily serve the purpose of defense; "They aim at keeping something away from the ego, at disavowing it" (p. 245). In this case standing on the Acropolis represented Freud's achievement of superiority to his father. The essence of success "was to have gotten further than one's father," but to excel one's father was forbidden. Thus to see Athens and the Acropolis represented the achievement of a forbidden wish and when it happened the ego had to disavow the experience by the momentary feeling "what I see here is not real."

From the psychotherapist's point of view, the important point is the distinction between repression and disavowal. Repression does not involve a splitting of the ego, but rather the setting up of countercathexes against unconscious energized mnemic residues pressing for expression. Disavowal, on the other hand, represents contrary sets of attitudes or perceptions present in the conscious mind at the same time and necessitates a splitting of the ego in order to maintain this condition. This is the starting point for understanding the important clinical aspects of the borderline and narcissistic personality disorders.

The best short description of Freud's metapsychological concepts is found in Lecture 31 of *New Introductory Lectures in Psychoanalysis* (1933A; 22:57–80). This extremely valuable summary is mandatory reading for every psychotherapist, even those nonpsychoanalysts who are described by Freud in the same work as "the many psychiatrists and psychotherapists who warm their pot of soup at our fire (incidentally without being very grateful for our hospitality)" (p. 8). This chapter is highly recommended for educated lay persons or nonpsychiatrists who are interested in a clear description of psychoanalytic theory. Because of Freud's marvelous prose style it is even good general reading for advanced college students.

Lecture 31 again emphasizes the capacity of the ego to split itself at least temporarily during a number of its functions; for example, "The ego can take itself as an object, can treat itself like other objects, can observe itself, criticize itself, and do Heaven knows what with itself" (p. 58).

Here again Freud differs from Kant, who couples the conscience within us with the starry heavens above. Freud writes, "The stars are indeed magnificent, but as regards conscience God has done an uneven and careless piece of work, for a large majority of men have brought along with them only a modest amount of it or scarcely enough worth mentioning" (p. 61). This lecture contains an error regarding Kant, when Freud states that in the id there is an exception to the philosophical theorem that space and time are "necessary forms of our mental acts." Kant, of course, stated that space and time are necessary forms of our *experience*; he said nothing about so-called mental acts in Freud's sense. (In *Beyond the Pleasure Principle* [1920G;18:3ff] Freud also misquotes Kant as stating time and space are "necessary forms of thought".) Freud speaks of unconscious mental *processes* as being timeless. The confusion here is due to Freud's shift from the topographical to the structural theory. According to Freud, "Instinctual cathexes seeking discharge—that, in our view, is all there is to id" (p. 72). Thus thoughts and experiences are *not* in the id. Thoughts, ideas, and experiences are in the ego: thoughts, impressions, and experiences which have sunk into the id by repression are no longer logical ideas and do not have to partake of the necessary forms of conscious ideation.

As a sort of clinical conclusion, Freud reminds us in Lecture 34 (of *New Introductory Lectures in Psychoanalysis*) that psychoanalytic activity is arduous and exacting; it cannot be handled like a pair of glasses that one puts on for reading and takes off when one goes for a walk. "As a rule psychoanalysis possesses a doctor either entirely or not at all" (p. 153). Freud enumerates a number of factors that limit the therapeutic effectiveness of psychoanalytic psychotherapy. For example, not everything can be brought to life again. "Some changes seem to be definitive and correspond to scars formed when a process has run its course" (p. 154). In the psychoses the instincts may be too powerful for the opposing forces that we try to mobilize. Thus a limitation upon psychoanalytic success is given by the form of an illness. Psychical changes take place slowly, and "if they occur rapidly, suddenly, that is a bad sign" (p. 156). The treatment must be adapted to characteristics of the illness. In "Analysis Terminable and Interminable" (1937C;23:211ff), Freud continues at length in an increasingly pessimistic vein about the therapeutic value of psychoanalysis.

19

TRANSCENDENCE

In Freud's first paper on religion (1907B;9:116ff) a weakness appears in his thinking which in later works led him to some very serious errors culminating in his book (with Bullitt) on Woodrow Wilson; this work can only be described as a disaster and is not even contained in the *Standard Edition*. The weakness, it seems to me, stems from a certain dogmatic arrogance in Freud's personality; others might call it stubbornness or a tendency to disregard opposing views. This character trait was extremely useful and important to Freud in the establishment of psychoanalysis; but in subjects such as religion, anthropology, and sociology—subjects removed from the clinical consulting room—he made the mistake of clinging to his convictions with the same tenacity he had shown in his experience-based convictions about the mental life of individuals. He apparently did not consider the fact that in his daily psychiatric practice he received continual confirmations of his formulations from his patients; no such confirmations are possible to support his sweeping generalizations about religion, God, the devil, Moses, and numerous other nonclinical subjects. I believe that Freud's attack on religion was both unfair and unfortunate, and was not characterized by a meticulous and dispassionate study of the values as well as the defects in religion. Such carelessness cannot be attributed simply to anti-Semitic experiences on Freud's part, since his views on the Jewish religion were the same as his views on religion in general.

Whatever, the real issue is whether or not Freud's statements about religion represent a total explanation of religion as he eventually insisted that they did. In the important early paper "Obsessive Acts and Religious Practices" (1907B; 9:116–128), Freud discusses the obvious resemblance between obsessively pietistic practices, and obsessive rituals and ceremonies in the obsessive compulsive neurotic. Although all religions recognize that excessive piety can be a spurious form of religion, this fact is obviously irrelevant to a general discussion of religion. It is even possible to accept Freud's statement that all believers are not aware of the motives which impel them to religious practices, but it does not follow from this that *all* the motives which impel believers to religious practices stem from unconscious infantile wishes! It is possible to argue that a religious motive, or, more generally, a motive toward transcendence or some kind of actualization exists in humans. St. Augustine insisted, in an even more extreme view (Nash 1969), that a force of Divine illumination may lead some people toward religious belief. All three of these viewpoints on the motivations behind religious belief are hypotheses which cannot be proven right or wrong at the present time, nor in any individual case is it possible to reduce religion positively to any one of these motivations.

Freud states that the formation of a religion "seems to be based on the suppression, the renunciation, of certain instinctual impulses. These impulses, however, are not, as in the neuroses, exclusively components of the sexual instinct; they are self-seeking, socially harmful instincts, though, even so, they are usually not without a sexual component" (p. 125). It is reasonable to conclude from this that "one might venture to regard obsessional neurosis as a pathological counterpart of the formation of a religion" (p. 126); but it is unclear how Freud evolves the second half of this sentence, wherein he calls religion "a universal obsessional neurosis," a statement which begins the tradition of pejorative, simplistic generalizations and name-calling that has marred psychoanalysis since the beginning.

Freud (1907C;9:130ff) argues that enlightenment about the specific facts of human sexuality should be given to each child before he is ten, and he couples this advice with an attack on the clergy. He correctly implies that clergy have in the past been a reactionary and suppressive force on the subject of sexuality, but he makes the strange argument that a priest will never admit that men and animals have the same nature. It is difficult to see how Freud himself could maintain that men and animals have the same nature, unless he is speaking strictly of biological functions, in which case he would be joined by Aristotle and Aquinas. This paper, "The Sexual Enlightenment of Children" (1907C: 9:130ff), is a call for revolution; indeed it may be thought of as the manifesto of the sexual revolution of our times. A similar manifestation of Freud's increasing conviction that he can explain all there is to know about religion is in the statement "The devil is certainly nothing else than the personification of the repressed unconscious instinctual life" (1908B;9:174). It is the phrase "certainly nothing else than" to which I object and which becomes increasingly common in Freud's writing on nonclinical matters.

Totem and Taboo (Freud 1912X;13:1—163) was one of Freud's favorites among his work, ranking in his mind with *The Interpretation of Dreams*, but it is primarily a controversial contribution to social anthropology and I will discuss only those aspects of interest to the clinician. Written when Freud was 57, in one of his great creative spurts, it begins by establishing the universal taboo on incest, with emphasis on the extraordinary precautions taken by primitive tribes to avoid any possibility of incest or even a relationship that might distantly resemble it. Freud explains that primitive tribes are much more sensitive to the issue of incest than civilized people, and any violation of this taboo is usually punished with death. The inference, of course, is that the temptation to incest is greater in primitive tribes.

A clinical digression is offered on the subject of the mother-in-law, as far as I know the only place that Freud discusses the subject, and it points to the value of asking patients about their relationships with their mothers-in-law! In Freud's opinion the mother-in-law is a common displacement object for the love of the patient's own mother and sisters, and the well-known "streak of irritability and malevolence" that is apt to be present in a man's feeling about his mother-in-law "leads us to suspect that she does in fact offer him a temptation to incest" (p. 16).

In this first section we are reminded that the totem, usually an animal, stands for the ancestor and protector of the clan. Members of a totem group are under a sacred obligation (a) not to destroy the totem, and (b) not to enter into sexual relations with each other. In the long second section, Freud reminds us that these two basic laws of totemism are the oldest and most important taboo prohibitions. He ranges over the enormous variety of taboos known and attempts to point out the similarity between the compulsions of neurotics and the compulsions underlying taboos in (1) the lack of obvious motivation for the commandments or compulsions; (2) their enforcement through an inner need; (3) their capacity for displacement and the danger of contagion from what is prohibited; and (4) ceremonial acts and commandments, like the compulsions of neurotics, emanate from the forbidden in an attempt to undo the dreaded harm. He stresses the emotional ambivalence underlying both neurotic compulsions and taboos.

In a much quoted sweeping generalization he compares the neuroses to distortions of art, religion, and philosophy: "It might be maintained that a case of hysteria is a caricature of a work of art, that an obsessional neurosis is a caricature of a religion and that a paranoic delusion is a caricature of a philosophical system" (p. 73), but he adds the less often quoted but very important differentiation that neuroses are primarily asocial and represent a taking flight from an unsatisfying reality into a more pleasurable world of fantasy. "To turn away from reality is at the same time to withdraw from the community of man" (p. 74). Here again Freud stresses the clinical point that neuroses are essentially precipitated by an unbearable reality.

Each section of this work may be read as an independent essay. The third section deals with the subject, "Animism, Magic and the Omnipotence of Thought." Freud's extremely important description of the development of our sense of reality testing is expanded in detail by Ferenczi (1950) in one of the most important classical clinical papers in psychoanalysis. Originally published in 1913, this paper was clearly under the influence of *Totem and Taboo* which was published in the same year. At the basis of magic is the belief in the great power of wishes, an attitude toward the world where thought is overestimated, compared to reality, and given an omnipotence. In man's conception of the universe an early animistic phase in which the world is infested by spirits is followed by a religious phase in which these magical powers are invested in God, who, although omnipotent, can be influenced; the development ends in a scientific phase which retains at least the omnipotent hope that knowledge can lead to power. This corresponds to stages in the childhood development of the individual of primary narcissism, object finding with dependency on the parents, and maturity.

Ferenczi's elaboration begins with (1) a period of unconditional omnipotence: the situation in the womb and shortly after birth which soon leads, because of inevitable disappointments in such unconditional omnipotence, to (2) a period of magical-hallucinatory omnipotence characterized by imagination and positive and negative hallucinations. This is followed by (3) a period of omnipotence by the help of magic gestures, such as evidenced in the residual adult phenomena of cursing, blessing, and praying. These three phases correspond to what Ferenczi calls the "introjection phase" of the psyche, by which he means there is no clear differentiation between the self and the outside world and all experiences are incorporated into the ego.

The next period, similar to Freud's description, endows every object with life, and is called (4) the animistic period. This is followed by (5), the period of magic thoughts and magic words, to which obsessive–compulsive neurotics regress. These five phases in the development of the sense of reality are characterized by the domination of the pleasure principle. The final phase, or stage of objectification, is marked by the ascendency of the reality principle. As Ferenczi explains, the essence of the development of the ego is the replacement, to which we are compelled by experience, of childhood narcissism or megalomania by the recognition of the power of natural forces and reality. Here, most important clinically is the sometimes-ignored phenomenon that regression in psychosexual development is accompanied by regression in the sense of reality; therefore, the regressed patient experiences reality differently than the mature psychotherapist. No amount of exhortation, demands, or punishment can change this situation, and if the therapist is not aware of how the patient is experiencing reality then he cannot understand some of the patient's behavior and consequently tends to become judgmental and often annoyed and retaliatory.

The final essay presents Freud's famous speculation about the beginning of totemism. To summarize, he begins with men in the state of primal hordes ruled by a father, as postulated by Darwin. The fear of and love of the father produce ambivalence; in infantile phobias this fear is also frequently displaced to animals. Freud postulates the killing and eating of the father by the brothers—the so-called totem feast. This procedure is displaced to a totem animal who then becomes a father to the group but is periodically killed and eaten in the holy mystery of identification on the "holiday," when the inhibition is suspended. Thus the two fundamental taboos arise out of the son's guilt over the wish to kill the father and possess the mother—the Oedipus complex, where Freud sees the beginnings of religion, ethics, society, and art. It is not hard to see why this book, with its sweeping generalizations, was badly received outside psychoanalytic circles as just "one more personal fantasy of Freud's" (Jones 1955).

The final section, however, contains an important warning to clinicians, since the two kinds of the most powerful longings to which human beings are subject are described. The wish to destroy the parent of the same sex and have sexual intercourse with the parent of the opposite sex is one of these; the other is the pregenital organization, which centers around ambivalence, the presence of two enormously powerful and opposite emotions toward the same individual at the same time. These days, in dealing with many pregenital disorders, we are constantly aware of the intensity of the ambivalence for the early parental objects, as the various aspects of these passions are projected onto the therapist in the vicissitudes of the transference. We tend to lose sight of the equally powerful emotions of the Oedipus complex, which revolve around primitive lust and the craving for power.

Near the end of *Totem and Taboo* Freud recognized that it is not so important whether primitive men actually carried out the murder of the father or simply were trying to deal with a wishful fantasy of killing and devouring him—either would have been enough to produce the moral reaction that created totemism and taboo. Freud repeatedly stressed that the acceptance or rejection of psychoanalysis rests on the understanding of the overwhelmingly powerful influence of this fantasy of destroying the parent of the same sex and sexually possessing the parent of the opposite sex. Innumerable opponents and deviants from psychoanalysis have attempted to ignore or water down this fundamental premise. I contend from twenty years of clinical experience with intensive psychotherapy that *Freud was correct*, and any psychotherapist who attempts to sidestep the important issues of the Oedipus complex, especially in the neuroses, does so to the great detriment of the patient. Despite the so-called sexual revolution of today I find this issue to be just as invested with taboos, prohibitions, and intensive defenses as Freud described them in his day. I also find student psychotherapists just as resistant to recognizing this material as were Freud's early contemporaries, even though they may pay intellectual lip service to it.

Totem and Taboo also reveals Freud's basic philosophy and contains a number of premises which, to say the least, are highly controversial. For example, he compares the old notion of the soul and the body as reminiscent of the unconscious and the conscious, especially in the way in which the soul remains concealed behind the manifest personality. He relegates the notion of the soul to the early phase of animistic thought as described above.

On the other hand, at the beginning of the fourth essay, he presents a very modest statement about religion, explaining that psychoanalysis does not trace the origin of anything so complicated as religion to a single source but only emphasizes one particular source. This does not mean, writes Freud, "it is claiming either that that source is the only one or that it occupies first place among the numerous contributory factors. Only when we can synthesize findings in the different fields of research will it become possible to arrive at a relative importance of the part played in the genesis of religion by the mechanism discussed in these pages. Such a task lies beyond the means as well as beyond the purposes of a psychoanalyst" (p. 100). It is well known that Freud's subsequent writings do not bear out his modesty in the area of religion.

There is a remarkable parallel between the philosophy of Freud and that of Thomas Hobbes (1588–1679), another long-lived genius. Just as Freud attempted to model his new science on classical physics, so Hobbes attempted to develop a new science of philosophy on the same model. Although Hobbes, like Freud, was accused of atheism, he actually conceived of God as "incomprehensible" and therefore outside the realm of philosophy; Freud went further and conceived of God as only a human creation born out of psychological needs, as described in *The Future of an Illusion* (Freud 1927; .21:3ff), to be discussed shortly.

Hobbes and Freud had a very similar view of the development of religion, beginning with Hobbes' premise that material competition, diffidence (fear), and seeking glory are the basic human drives. From this premise Hobbes concludes in the classic *Leviathan* that religion arises from animistic superstition, ignorance of causes, devotion toward what men fear and hate, and taking of things that are casual happenings for prognostics of the future, out of the wish to know the future. Religion for Hobbes is a completely human phenomenon that has nothing to do with God and is simply an inevitable and natural consequence of human nature. Therefore, for Hobbes, as for Freud, there is no such thing as a true or false religion—all are equally spurious creations of the human psyche.

Also like Freud, Hobbes was middle-aged when he turned his attention to philosophy, which he attempted to make a useful science by concerning it primarily with a mechanistic and materialistic account of the generative processes by which sensation and mental states come into being. He made the same basic generalization that Freud made regarding the individual man and a group of men; thus both Hobbes and Freud would agree that the natural principles of individual human psychology can be applied to mankind as a body, which Hobbes named the Leviathan. As Freud spoke of individual psychology and group psychology, Hobbes spoke of natural philosophy and civic philosophy. Like Freud, he believed that given certain premises about structures and energies in the human psyche, all human individual and group behavior could be naturally explained according to observable laws. Just as Freud's work represented a revolution in psychological thinking, Hobbes' philosophy was a revolutionary change from the medieval conceptions of man and universe.

Hobbes' famous theory of the study of causes that generate the artificial body known as the Leviathan or commonwealth is very similar to Freud's approach in *Totem and Taboo.* Hobbes explains that each man seeks self-preservation and security but is unable to attain these ends because his natural condition is war of all against all. In order to put an end to continuous civil war and the misery it brings for everybody, a transfer of some rights and liberties must take place by the covenant of every man to a sovereign body with absolute power, the commonwealth or Leviathan. This social contract or covenant is described in terms very similar to those in the final section of *Totem and Taboo* and is no more consistent with historical research than are the speculations of Freud in that section. Like Freud, Hobbes did not find it necessary to insist that a specific historical process took place through an explicit covenant any more than Freud insisted that the murder of the father had to be a historical happening. Like Freud, Hobbes attempts to explain from basic premises about primitive man how certain processes inevitably led to the formation of the social contract which constitutes the basis of the commonwealth. As Freud explains various totems and taboos, Hobbes deduces the variety of states and commonwealths as occurring in a natural fashion from the passions of man, without reference to metaphysical and transcendental considerations—a thoroughly naturalistic theory. Freud's deduction of the development of totems and taboos from the Oedipus complex is an identical revolutionary theory.

The same pessimism about the basic nature of man pervades both Hobbes' and Freud's writings; the same tension between rational and irrational man or, more generally, man as imminent and man as transcendent, remains unresolved. In the beginning of this book I described Freud's dualistic conception of man as outlined by Holt. Hobbes found himself in similar difficulty, for he requires this basically voracious and irrational creature to have the capacity to develop communal living as the result of an elaborate rational calculation of long-range interests. The same struggle between the domination of the pleasure principle and the domination of the reality principle at the dawn of the body politic is described in *Leviathan.* Professional philosophers attacked this description of the struggle as an inconsistency in Hobbes' philosophy; Freud would describe it as the very essence of the development of the individual and the collective human psyche. Notice again the common assumption that the phenomena of groups or the body politic (Leviathan) may be studied in the same manner as the phenomena of individual men.

From his "First Philosophy" Hobbes hoped to make generalizations that would lead to naturalistic explanations of the wide variety of known phenomena, and Freud expressed a similar desire. In a brief essay entitled "The Claims of Psychoanalysis to Scientific Interest" (Freud 1913J;13:164–192) he points out that psychoanalysis cannot be accused of having applied to normal cases findings derived from exclusively pathological material, for the evidence for psychoanalytic hypotheses to be found in normal phenomena such as parapraxes and dreams, he claims, was reached independently from the study of the neuroses. He continues by describing applications of psychoanalytic hypotheses to philology, philosophy, biology, child development, the history of civilization, esthetics, sociology, and education. This tendency toward the increasing generalization of the hypotheses of psychoanalysis to wider and wider fields involved Freud in numerous controversies and exposed him to a variety of counterarguments and conflicting evidence, much as happened in Hobbes' unsuccessful attempt to deduce all varieties of human and social phenomena from his "First Philosophy."

Such psychoanalytic generalizations have been carried on by a variety of authors to the present day and must be regarded by the clinician as peripheral to the major issues of psychotherapy; furthermore, the validity or invalidity of generalizations from psychoanalytic propositions to a variety of normal social phenomena is irrelevant to the validity of psychoanalytic propositions in our clinical work with patients. For example, Freud's (1914B;13:210ff) analysis of Michelangelo's statue of Moses, the proof or disproof of which remains so controversial, has no bearing on the use of his hypotheses in our day-to-day clinical work and merely illustrates the dangers of generalizations from insufficient evidence, and of greater and greater abstractions. It is far better to follow Freud's own dictum as he expressed it in "On the History of the Psychoanalytic Movement": "I learned to restrain speculative tendencies and to follow the unforgotten advice of my master, Charcot: to look at the same things again and again until they themselves begin to speak" (Freud 1914D;14:22). This dictum arose out of what Freud called his "splendid isolation" in which "I did not have to read any publications, nor listen to any ill-informed opponents; I was not subject to influence from any quarter; there was nothing to hustle me" (ibid).

In this same frankly polemical essay (1914D;14:3ff), Freud again illustrates to what extent psychologists will go to avoid facing the central role of sexual desire in childhood development, a role equalled in importance only by the vicissitudes of narcissism and narcissistic rage. At the time of this writing Freud was 58; the psychoanalytic movement was in a shambles, due to the secession of Adler and Jung. Although both these pioneers made historically important contributions, both retreated from the clinical experience that manifests itself again and again in the transference—that the vicissitudes of the Oedipus complex and the child's experiences of hatred and lust involving the parents are at the root of neurotic disorders. Jones (1955) believes that the essay on the statue of Moses, "The Moses of Michelangelo" (1914B; 13:210ff) represents Freud's identification with Moses confronting his back-sliding supporters and struggling inwards to control his passion and bitterness. Jones insists, "Every analysis conducted in a proper manner, and in particular every analysis of a child, strengthens the conviction upon which the theory of psychoanalysis is founded, and rebuts the reinterpretations made by both Jung's and Adler's systems" (1955, p. 65).

The subject of religion increasingly interested Freud in his later years. It seems to me that his hostility to organized religion was not far from that of Voltaire. As a simple example he discusses a reported case of demoniacal possession as "A Seventeenth Century Demonological Neurosis" (1923D; 19:69ff). For Freud the demonological possessions correspond to the neuroses in that demons represent bad and unacceptable derivatives of infantile wishes that have been repudiated and repressed. "We merely eliminate the projection of these mental entities into the external world which the middle ages carried out; instead, we regard them as having arisen in the patient's internal life, where they have their abode" (p. 72).

Although the concept of Satan evolved gradually in the Old Testament, the personification of Satan came only after the conquest and dispersion of the Jews by the Babylonians in the sixth century B.C. For the Jews, Satan is not an independent power of evil, but rather an avenging angel who produces destruction at the command of God. Only later, after the writing of the Torah (450 B.C.) and before the writing of the New Testament, the domination of the Persians over the Jews with the influence of Zoroastrianism led to the development of Satan as falling from God and becoming His adversary. By the time of the second and first centuries B.C., Jewish writing clearly borrows the Syrian and Babylonian notion that demons can invade the body.

For Freud it is obvious that God and the Devil were originally identical, a single figure split into two figures with opposite attributes. He regards these figures as projections of the fundamentally ambivalent attitude of the child toward the father. The implication of this notion is quite clear: Freud considered both the concept of God and that of the Devil as illusory projections from the human unconscious and as having no basis for existence in fact.

It is indeed remarkable that Kant also speaks of transcendental ideas as being the parents of "irresistable illusion." One of these transcendental ideas, which for Kant represents absolute perfection and the single basic condition of all objects of thought in general, is called God. Thus to think of God as a substance existing in experience is for both Kant and Freud an illusion. For Freud that settles the matter; for Kant it is only the beginning, for in his philosophy the notion of God becomes necessary as a basis for what he considers to be universal moral laws within us.

In 1927 at the age of seventy-one Freud wrote *The Future of an Illusion*

(1927C;21:3ff), beginning a series of studies that became his major concern for the remainder of his life. In 1907 he had discussed the matter of religion in a paper on obsessive acts and religious practices (discussed above). In that early paper, he drew the obvious parallel between obsessional rituals and religious rituals. He reminds us that the worshipper, like the obsessive patient, usually does not know the meaning of religious rituals and that the ceremonial in both cases is a protective measure. The ritualistic ceremonial defends against the temptations of sexuality and aggression, and magically protects against breakdown of the whole repressive process; the ceremonial represents a compromise formation in which displacement is crucial. Thus even at an early date, Freud states that the obsessional neurosis is a private religious system and that religion is a universal obsessional neurosis. He distinguishes between the temptations of the obsessional neuroses which are mainly sexual, and the repressed wishes defended against by religion—wishes which at that point he calls ego-instincts, and which are more concerned with aggression than sexuality. Thus, "Vengeance is mine, sayeth the Lord."

Although in this early work Freud is extremely scornful of philosophy, the work itself contains a philosophical viewpoint: a materialistic, atheistic ideology. He considers religion dangerous and all metaphysics superfluous and irrelevant. He defines religion as an illusion inspired by the infantile belief in the omnipotence of thought, as essentially a neurosis and a narcotic that hampers intelligence; religion is something man will have to grow out of and give up like an infantile neurosis. It is this parallel of religion to neurosis that convinced Freud that psychoanalysis can unmask and explain the so-called universal neuroses of mankind.

His psychoanalytic explanation of God appeared in 1910 in his study of Leonardo da Vinci (1910C;11:59ff). Here he maintains that the personal God is psychologically none other than a magnified father, and thus the root of religious need lies in the child's ambivalent attitude toward the father. In the *Future of an Illusion* (1927C;21:3ff) he adds a second major factor in the genesis of religion: the helplessness of mankind in the face of the many dangers with which he must cope—from the outer world, from within, and from his relationships to his fellow men.

It is interesting that the *Future of an Illusion* discusses the future of *two* illusions. The first illusion is that of religion (as already explained); the second is Freud's own hope that mankind can some day find it possible to endure the hardships of life without having recourse to the consolations of religion. Freud himself admits that he is indulging in an illusion:

> The voice of the intellect is a soft one, but it does not rest till it has gained a hearing. Finally, after a countless succession of rebuffs, it succeeds. This is one of the few points on which one may be optimistic about the future of mankind, but it is in itself a point of no small im-

> portance. And from it one can derive yet other hopes. The primacy of the intellect lies, it is true, in a distant, distant future, but probably not in an *infinitely* distant one. It will presumably set itself the same aims as those whose realization you expect from your God (of course within human limits—so far as external reality, 'Ανάγκη, allows it), namely the love of man and the decrease of suffering (1927C;21:53).

Freud continues by saying that the major first step in man's defense against the overwhelming power of nature is the humanization of nature, for impersonal forces and destinies cannot be approached; they remain eternally remote. This humanization relates man to the infantile prototype of the helplessness of a small child in relation to its parents. This helplessness, along with the longing for the father, is transferred to religion. "The gods retain their threefold task: they must exorcize the terrors of nature, they must reconcile men to the cruelty of Fate, particularly as it is shown in death, and they must compensate them for the sufferings and privations which a civilized life in common has imposed on them" (p. 18). Clearly these ideas protect man against the dangers of nature (Fate) and against injuries that threaten him from human society itself.

According to Freud, the function of the finished body of religious ideas as it is transmitted by civilization to the individual now becomes clear. He maintains that in taming the instincts, religion has performed great services for human civilization, but that this is not enough; although religion has ruled human society for many thousands of years, it has not succeeded in reconciling the majority of people to life and making them into vehicles of civilization.

Freud does not maintain that religious ideas are false; he maintains that they are illusions, beliefs derived from human wishes. Illusions need not necessarily be false, defining "false" as unrealizable or in contradiction to reality; it is more accurate to say that they represent beliefs which are highly unlikely in their realization, but are maintained fiercely because of the power of the wishes that underlie them. In this essay Freud disregards the philosopher's idea of God as reached through various philosophical systems or arguments, and addresses himself essentially to the God of organized western religion, an anthropomorphized Divine Providence, benevolent and interested in managing the affairs of men. He regards the philosopher's concept of God, reached through various metaphysical systems such as those of Aristotle or Kant, as essentially dishonest because these systems are so remote from the God of organized religion, and as representing a stretching of the meaning of words.

Freud addresses himself to the same issue as Kant: whether a transcendental idea can be discussed and dissected by the method of science. Using different terminology, he agrees with Kant that synthetic *a priori* judgments in metaphysics are impossible. This is why Freud considers metaphysics and transcendental ideas as essentially useless illusions, a stance that places him in exact opposition to the moral philosophy of Kant. Freud would maintain that the concept of transcendence as I have discussed it in previous works (Chessick 1974, 1977*a*) is an illusion, and that men must learn to endure the hardness of life with resignation and without the help of such mirages.

In *Civilization and Its Discontents* (1930A;21:59ff) Freud again reminds us that suffering comes from the superior power of nature, the feebleness of our own bodies, and the inadequacy of the regulations which adjust the mutual relationships of human beings in the family, the state, and society. Man attempts to cope with this unhappiness through chemical intoxication; permissible displacements of libido; the satisfaction obtained from such illusions as religion; withdrawal from reality and human relationships; and the enjoyment of beauty. The man who is predominantly erotic will give first preference to his emotional relationships to other people; the narcissistic man, who inclines to be self-sufficient, will seek his main satisfactions in his internal mental processes; the man of action will never give up the external world on which he can try out his strength. I have discussed this at length in the section on happiness in *Great Ideas in Psychotherapy* (1977*a*).

The deflections that Freud discusses help us make light of our misery; substitutive satisfactions diminish it, and intoxicating substances make us insensitive to it. Thus the substitute satisfactions, as, for example, those offered by art, are effective thanks to the role of fantasy. Freud sees *no place* for religion in this series, and indeed for Freud the purpose of life "is simply the program of the pleasure principle." Thus happiness, according to Freud, comes from the—preferably sudden—satisfaction of needs which have been dammed up to a high degree, an episodic phenomenon obviously modeled on the sexual orgasm.

The beautifully written *Civilization and Its Discontents* begins with the famous quotation, "It is impossible to escape the impression that people commonly use false standards of measurement—that they seek power, success and wealth for themselves and admire them in others, and that they underestimate what is of true value in life" (p. 64).

Thus Freud does assume a hierarchy of activities and values. For example, he considers "working with all for the good of all" to be a better path than withdrawal from humanity. From his own philosophy, however, no reason is given to choose one escape from misery over the other. On his grounds, even chemical intoxication is no more or less justifiable than creative work or scientific endeavor. Yet,

> One gains the most if one can sufficiently heighten the yield of pleasure from the sources of psychical and intellectual work. When that is so, fate can do little against one. A satisfaction of this kind, such

> as an artist's joy in creating, in giving his phantasies body, or a scientist's in solving problems or discovering truths, has a special quality which we shall certainly one day be able to characterize in metapsychological terms. At present we can only say figuratively that such satisfactions seem 'finer and higher' (p. 79).

It is curious that Freud nowhere considers the source of his obviously humanistic hierarchy of human endeavor, which collides head-on with his objectifying man as a physical-chemical entity with a mental "apparatus." This is an excellent example of the unresolved tension that runs throughout Freud's work, as discussed in the introduction to the present book, between the language of the scientific understanding and the language of the humanistic imagination (see also Chessick 1971). For Freud, happiness in the extreme is clearly the satiation of a crude and primary impulsive instinct in a wild periodic orgy that convulses one's whole physical being. This is not an exaggeration—I am using Freud's literal words from *Civilization and Its Discontents.* In spite of its distasteful impact on our finer cultural and esthetic sentiments, Freud's contention about extreme happiness is supported by considerable evidence.

Civilization and Its Discontents enumerates some of the ways in which civilized men find happiness and advises us not to look for the whole of our satisfaction in a single aspiration. Religion is viewed negatively, as restricting the sway of choices and adaptation, and depressing the value of life.

From this basic view of happiness it is clear why Freud sees civilization in fundamental opposition to gratification of man's instinctual needs and therefore as a basic obstacle to the achievement of sublime satisfaction and happiness. Clearly, civilization is built upon a renunciation of the discharge of powerful instincts, parallel to the training and development of a child into a civilized adult. Not only is the sexual drive restricted by civilization, but the fundamental aggressive drive is also sharply curbed. Thus if civilization imposes great sacrifices on man's sexuality and on his aggressiveness, it is clear why it is so hard for him to be happy in civilization.

Man's basic aggression becomes internalized into a harsh superego which produces a chronic sense of guilt. Freud feels that the sense of guilt produced by civilization remains to a large extent unconscious "or appears as a sort of *malaise*, a dissatisfaction, for which people seek other motivations" (p. 135–6). He notes that religions claim to redeem mankind from this sense of guilt, and considers those who believe in this claim to be under the influence of a delusion.

One aspect of transcendence is the well known oceanic feeling of something limitless, of being one with the external world as a whole. Freud explains this feeling as a residue of the time before the infant was able to differentiate between the self and the external world; therefore, although this oceanic feeling exists for some people, Freud rejects the notion that it has to do with the religious attitude. His entire attitude toward religious experience is summed up in a brief paper (1928A;21:168ff) which should not be missed, in which he analyzes the conversion experience on the basis of the convert's Oedipus complex.

Freud seems to reach a final decision on religion in Lecture 35 of the *New Introductory Lectures on Psychoanalysis* (1933A;22:158–182). He insists that religion is a serious enemy of science. Interestingly, philosophy in Freud's view is rather like a foolish cousin; it clings "to the illusion of being able to present a picture of the universe which is without gaps and is coherent, though one which is bound to collapse with every fresh advance in our knowledge. It goes astray in its method by over-estimating the epistemological value of our logical operations and by accepting other sources of knowledge such as intuition" (p. 161). Freud goes on to declare that philosophy has essentially a trivial influence on mankind (a statement proved false by recent Russian and Chinese history), whereas religion is an immense power and is all the more dangerous because it is so grandiose. It informs people of the origin of the universe, assures them of protection and happiness, and lays down laws to direct their actions.

Freud maintains that science and finally psychoanalysis simply set religion aside as an obsolete phenomenon of the infantile life of man. "Its consolations deserve no trust. Experience teaches us that the world is no nursery" (p. 168). Similarly, although Marxism has cleared away religious illusions, Freud believes it has also developed its own illusions by assuming that a change in the social structure will alter human nature.

Even in the last work he lived to see published, *Moses and Monotheism* (1939A;23:3ff), Freud is such an effective writer that it is difficult to avoid discussing at great length such a provocative and interesting work. As an example of the kind of arguments and discussions that Freud's views on Moses can provoke, the reader is referred to the highly controversial and lengthy arguments in books such as those of Robert (1976) and Bakan (1965). These works, along with innumerable other references on the subject of Freud, Moses, and Judaism, present endless controversies which would take another volume to discuss at length. Ellenberger (1970) describes *Moses and Monotheism* (which appeared serially in *Imago* in 1937 and as a book in 1938) as "Neither a pathography, nor a scholarly work, nor a novel." He reports that it bewildered many of Freud's disciples and provoked indignant protest from Jewish circles. Historians of religion pointed out its errors and impossibilities. Jones (1957) makes the crushing criticism that its major thesis rests on a belief in the inheritance of acquired characteristics, an erroneous doctrine which Jones reports that Freud stubbornly and dogmatically held all his life.

This work was written when Freud was over eighty and under the intense pressure of the Nazi movement threatening to overwhelm Catholic Austria. It discusses what Freud purports to be the origin of the Jewish religion as well as to some extent the origin and development of Christian religion, with a few asides about Moslem religion. In this sense it is a continuation of *Totem and Taboo* and *The Future of an Illusion.* Perhaps Freud again identified himself with Moses and viewed his departure from Vienna as the flight of Moses from Egypt, with the hope that psychoanalysis would arise again in the world after the demise of the Nazi movement; surely he saw psychoanalysis as being diluted and distorted by various defectors from the movement such as Adler and Jung. Above all, he was influenced by the unparalleled persecution of the Jews in Nazi Germany, a phenomenon which Freud regarded correctly as a regression to prehistoric barbarism.

The book begins by insisting that Moses was not a Hebrew, but an Egyptian of high rank and status. Freud reminds us that although the Egyptian king Akhenaton tried to force a monotheistic religion on his people, after his death the old religions were restored. He speculates that Moses refused to lay aside Monotheism and, having been rejected by the Egyptians, he chose the Hebrews as his people and with the help of his followers he imparted monotheism to the Jews and led them out of Egypt. Afterwards, a rebellion arose against Moses, who was killed by his people. About sixty years later a new chief, also named Moses, formed a compromise of monotheism and the Yahweh worship of the people in the Sinai peninsula. (The first Moses had led the Jews to the Sinai and united them with the Midianite tribe which worshipped a petty local god, Yahweh.) According to Freud, the tradition of the murder of the first Moses led to a lasting, unconscious sense of guilt among the Jewish people, and the memory of the first Moses was revived in the teachings of the Prophets. The wish for the return of the murdered Moses resulted in the belief forecasting the coming of the Messiah. Thus the story of Jesus Christ was a re-enactment of the story of the first Moses. Paul, who created Christian theology by accepting Jesus as the Messiah, called the prevailing sense of guilt "original sin." Thus the unmentionable crime was replaced by a shadowy conception of "original sin" and expiation was welcomed in the form of the Gospel of Salvation contending that Christ sacrificed Himself and thereby took over the guilt of the world.

Such a summary does not do justice to the brilliance of Freud's literary style and his vast erudition. Even though he at first considered this work a kind of speculative historical novel, the more he reflected about it the more he became convinced that it was correct, i.e., historically true. Clearly Freud's theory of the inherited unconscious transmission of historical events is the weakest link in his theory. Another controversial link is Freud's basic assumption that developmental steps in the life of individuals can be generalized to developmental steps in the various subgroups of the human species or in the human species in toto. This basic philosophical generalization pervades *Totem and Taboo*, *The Future of an Illusion*, and *Moses and Monotheism*.

For example, certain developmental steps are outlined as constituting the evolution of religion, which according to Freud began with totemism "with its worship of a father-substitute, with its ambivalence as shown by the totem meal, with its institution of memorial festivals and of prohibitions whose infringement was punished by death" (1939A;23:83). The next step was the humanizing of the being who was worshipped, so that in place of animals human gods appeared, whose derivation from the Totem was not concealed. This was followed by the return of the single father–god of unlimited dominion. The content of the old totem meal, claims Freud, is repeated in the rite of the Christian communion, in which the believer incorporates the body and blood of his god in symbolic form.

All religions are regarded essentially as illusions based on infantile wishes to be analyzed by Freud. At the same time there is a remarkable discussion of transcendence which finds Freud quite puzzled. He feels certain that the step that represents a decision against sensuousness and direct sense perception, and in favor of the higher intellectual processes, is a step forward deserving of pride. He notes that later in history intellectuality itself is "overpowered by the very puzzling emotional phenomenon of faith. Here we have the celebrated *credo quia absurdum*, and, once more, anyone who has succeeded in this regards it as a supreme achievement" (ibid, p. 118). His only explanation for regarding faith as a supreme achievement by those who have it is that perhaps men pronounced that which is more difficult to achieve to be higher. He never gives serious consideration to the possibility that the achievement of some form of transcendence might actually *be* higher, since for Freud reason and science are as far as man can go. And that, for Freud, is an article of faith!

The dangers and weaknesses in Freud's scientific world-view were quickly pointed out by his contemporaries, friend and foe alike. An eloquent summary of the problem is found in Zweig's (1962) portrait of Freud and his work. Zweig points out that the power of psychoanalysis ends "where the realm of inward faith, of creative confidence, begins." To be happy and creative "man must always be strengthened by faith in the meaning of his own existence," and "the human mind will continue to devote its plastic energy to the endeavour to find a meaning in life"—a statement which Freud regarded as absurd, infantile, and unhealthy. Recent work on the psychology of the self (Kohut 1971, 1977) has suggested a revision in this psychoanalytic attitude, emphasizing that a firm sense of self is manifested by such mental attributes as creative confidence and a sense of personal purpose and meaning. However, such a viewpoint cannot refute Zweig's contention that "truth unalloyed has always a sub-flavour of bitterness and scepticism . . . a purely intellectual analysis, cannot but be shadowed to some extent with gloom" (pp. 357–8). There *is* a kind of gloomy ambience in Freud's later writings, reaching an apogee perhaps in *Beyond the Pleasure Principle*, in his notion of the death instinct as *the* primordial force, a view he later modified.

A remarkable correspondence on this subject took place between Freud and his friend, the Swiss Protestant clergyman Oskar Pfister, the first "pastoral counsellor" to make use of Freud's findings. This most interesting correspondence (Meng and Freud 1963) is unfortunately out of print. We find Freud writing that most humans are trash and insisting that his pessimism and gloom are rational conclusions, not preconvictions, whereas the optimism of Pfister and others he regards as *a priori* assumptions. It is perhaps worthwhile to put this unsettled debate into outline form:

1. Freud claims most humans are trash, whereas Pfister insists that we must love mankind or we get an ugly distorted picture of what he labels "the calculating machine man."

2. Freud categorically rejects the notion of "psychosynthesis" in the psychoanalytic process, whereas both Pfister and Zweig ask for it, and Pfister claims that successful analysis leads to the will to be moral.

3. Freud claims to stand on pure empirical science only; Pfister writes, "on philosophy, music and religion, we differ."

4. For Freud science must be called upon to solve everything, whereas for Pfister human happiness and aspiration cannot be adequately approached through science. He reminds us of Nietzsche's observation that the belief in science is itself a metaphysical belief.

5. Freud stresses the icy isolation of man in the universe, whereas Pfister claims that man needs inner spirituality and philosophy.

6. Freud sees morals as due to the exigencies of communal living, whereas Pfister postulates a moral world order that exists outside man.

7. Freud relegates God and religion to infantilism whereas Pfister does not entirely do so; similarly, Freud sees the ego ideal as simply an internalization of the parents, whereas Pfister adds something more to human aspiration than "a mere apeing of the parents."

8. Freud is by his own admission a pessimistic, less pleasant person than Pfister, who is more pleasant, tolerant, and better able to put up with life, especially with its unfairness.

9. For Freud the mind is an insignificant step in nature, whereas for Pfister the appearance of mind is a most significant step.

10. Freud sees civilization going nowhere and finds no innate human aspiration, whereas Pfister sees a higher and better evolution of civilization (this is before World War II) and postulates that humans—in contrast to animals—aspire to climb higher and higher "over the dead and the images of our parents."

The crucial query is raised by Freud: "The question is not what belief is more pleasing or more comfortable or more advantageous to life, but of what may approximate more closely to the puzzling reality that lies outside us" (p. 133). The important and unresolved debates in psychology, philosophy, and religion begin here, even to the present day.

20

FREUD'S EARLY METAPHYSICS AND EPISTEMOLOGY

Freud's work constitutes a philosophical system and, as he himself stated, psychoanalysis brought him to philosophical knowledge. Jones (1953) points out that Freud never wavered in his attitude of belief in a regular chain of mental events, including the thoroughgoing meaningfulness and determinism of even the apparently most obscure and arbitrary mental phenomenon. This in turn was based on the simple theory of causality held in the nineteenth century before the age of quantum physics. His view on the subject of free will was that apparently free choices are actually decided by our unconscious mind but we claim conscious credit for the outcome; therefore, when unconscious motivation is taken into account, the rule of determinism still holds.

In his early book *On Aphasia* (1891) Freud declared himself an adherent of the doctrine of psychophysical parallelism. Throughout his career, he insisted that no evidence existed of psychical processes occurring apart from physiological ones, and that physiological or physical processes must underlie psychical ones. In all of this he followed the standard philosophy of science of the late nineteenth century. It is wise to remember that these viewpoints are by no means so generally accepted today as they were during Freud's time, and that numerous alternatives exist—the subject is still a matter of great controversy. At this time, therefore, *any* theory of mental functioning and of psychotherapy must rest on shaky premises regarding the relationship of the mind and the brain, and on the unresolved issue of free will vs. determinism. These problems are inherent in any science; they are only more apparent in the science of mental phenomena. However *a serious study of the foundations of every science runs into the bedrock of these impenetrable questions.* Such questions are examined in detail by Bertrand Russell in *Human Knowledge: Its Scope and Limits* (1948). The whole notion of what constitutes a theory of the mind is controversial and is discussed by Friedman (1976).

In Freud's view, in *The Interpretation of Dreams*,

> In consequence of the belated appearance of the secondary processes, the core of our being, consisting of unconscious wishful impulses,

> remains inaccessible to the understanding and inhibition of the preconscious; the part played by the latter is restricted once and for all to directing along the most expedient paths the wishful impulses that arise from the unconscious. These unconscious wishes exercise a compelling force upon all later mental trends, a force which those trends are obliged to fall in with or which they may perhaps endeavor to divert and direct to higher aims. (1900A; 5:603–604).

Many of the so-called modifications and new schools of psychoanalysis and psychotherapy are based on the attempt to avoid this profoundly deterministic view of the role of unconscious infantile life on adult behavior, a role which is very difficult for us to accept since we like to think about ourselves as free, mature, rational beings.

The essence of the Freudian system is that the psychical mechanism employed by neuroses is not created by the impact of pathological disturbance on the mind but is already present in the normal structure of the mental apparatus. Thus the following, written at the beginning of Freud's discoveries:

> The two psychical systems, the censorship upon the passage from one of them to the other, the inhibition and overlaying of one activity by the other, the relations of both of them to consciousness—or whatever more correct interpretations of the observed facts may take their place—all of these form part of the normal structure of our mental instrument, and dreams show us one of the paths leading to an understanding of its structure. If we restrict ourselves to the minimum of new knowledge which has been established with certainty, we can say this of dreams: they have proved that *what is suppressed continues to exist in normal people as well as abnormal, and remains capable of psychical functioning* (1900A;5:607–608).

Freud's entire system stands or falls on this premise, which underlies his belief that the interpretation of dreams is the royal road to a knowledge of the unconscious activities of the mind.

Thus the functional mental illnesses do not presuppose any disintegration or degeneration of the mental apparatus itself, but are to be explained on what Freud called a dynamic basis—"by the strengthening and weakening of the various components in the interplay of forces, so many of whose effects are hidden from view while functions are normal" (ibid., p. 608). This statement implies the essential dividing point between organic psychiatry and psychodynamic psychiatry. In the area of the neuroses and the personality disorders we assume biological factors to be relatively minor, whereas in the area of certain psychoses such as manic depressive illness they are clearly of a major importance.

A crucial link between Freud and philosophy is presented to us by Section F. of Chapter VII of his first great work, *The Interpretation of Dreams*, entitled "The Unconscious and Consciousness—Reality" (1900A; 5:610–621). Here Freud makes the basic statement that the unconscious is the true psychical reality. He contends that "*in its innermost nature it is as much unknown to us as the reality of the external world, and is as incompletely presented by the data of consciousness as the external world by the communications of our sense organs*" (p. 613). This is a profoundly philosophical statement which skirts the edge of Schopenhauer's notion of Will on the one hand, and of Kant's notion of the thing-in-itself, on the other. The conscious mind in this view is a kind of sense organ perceiving derivatives from the basically unknowable unconscious mind, just as the ordinary sense organs perceive data from the basically unknowable external reality "out there." This viewpoint further delimits the scope of man since not only can he know nothing for certain about the reality "out there"; he can know nothing for certain about the core of his own being.

Freud's attitude toward philosophy was quite clear and scornful. Thus in a letter to Eitington: "Probably you cannot imagine how alien all these philosophical convolutions seem to me. The only feeling of satisfaction they give me is that I take no part in this pitiable waste of intellectual powers. Philosophers no doubt believe that in such studies they are contributing to the development of human thought, but every time there is a psychological or even a psychopathological problem behind them" (Jones 1957, p. 140). I suspect that here he was exhibiting a fairly typical turn-of-the-century intellectual reaction to the writings of Hegel and other German idealist philosophers.

Early Views: Instincts Probably no other concept has caused as much confusion and difficulty for new readers of Freud than his notion of instinct (*Trieb*). Freud himself described the instincts as "at once the most important and the most obscure element of psychological research" (1920G;18:34). The main reason for this obscurity is that instinct deals with the unresolved issue of the borderline between the mind and the body; thus, Freud at the start defined instinct as "the psychical representative of an endosomatic, continuously floating source of stimulation," a concept "lying on the frontier between the mental and the physical" (1905D; 7:168). In this early definition (from *Three Essays on the Theory of Sexuality*) he did not distinguish between an instinct and its "psychical representative," but in later work he drew a sharp distinction between them. Thus in his later views an instinct can never become an object of consciousness; only the idea (*Vorstellung*) that represents the instinct can so become; furthermore, even in the unconscious an instinct cannot be represented by other than an idea. Thus, "When we nevertheless speak of an unconscious instinctual impulse or of a repressed instinctual impulse . . . we can only mean an instinctual impulse the ideational representative of which is unconscious" (1915E;14:177).

The differentiation between an instinct (in Freud's sense of the word) and its ideational representative in the psyche contains within it the unresolved problem of the relationship between brain and mind. The most helpful suggestion to the reader is to remember that Freud conceives of instinct in a looser and less precise manner than is denoted by the English term, which implies an inherited behavioral trait or pattern, especially of animals. Jones (1955) explains that other words such as "urge," "impulsion," or the American expression "drive," have been suggested as translations, but he regards none of them as entirely satisfactory.

This vagueness in one of the fundamental concepts of Freud's psychodynamics has been unfairly used to criticize the whole scientific foundation of the psychoanalytic approach; but Freud himself anticipated an answer to this criticism in the opening paragraph of "Instincts and their Vicissitudes." This paragraph contains one of Freud's basic statements on the philosophy of science and reminds us that no science, not even the most exact, begins with entirely clear and sharply defined basic concepts:

> The true beginning of scientific activity consists rather in describing phenomena and then in proceeding to group, classify and correlate them. Even at the stage of description it is not possible to avoid applying certain abstract ideas to the material in hand, ideas derived from somewhere or other, but certainly not from the new observations alone. Such ideas—which will later become the basic concepts of the science—are still more indispensable as the material is further worked over (1915C;14:117).

Freud maintains that these ideas must necessarily possess some degree of indefiniteness, and that strictly speaking they are in the nature of conventions, "although everything depends on their not being arbitrarily chosen but determined by having significant relations to the empirical material, relations that we seem to sense before we can clearly recognize and demonstrate them" (ibid.). After the most thorough investigation and observation in the field we formulate these basic scientific concepts with increased precision and progressively modify them, but they still remain rock-bottom, basic postulates.

Such a postulate, which Freud calls "indispensible to us in psychology," is that of an instinct. He goes on in the same essay to delineate the concept more clearly, first separating it from a stimulus which represents a single impact that can be disposed of by a single expedient action, for example, motor-flight from the source of stimulation. Thus instinct does not arise from the external world but from within the organism itself and it operates as a constant force rather than as a momentary impact. "Moreover, since it impinges not from without but from within the organism, no flight can avail against it" (p. 118).

Instincts, therefore, have their origin in sources of stimulation within the organism and appear as a constant force from which no action of flight will avail. We cannot actually tell what an instinct is—we can only define it operationally. This definition in turn rests on the principle of constancy, which Freud calls a biological postulate and defines thus: "The nervous system is an apparatus which has the function of getting rid of the stimuli that reach it, or of reducing them to the lowest possible level; or which, if it were feasible, would maintain itself in an altogether unstimulated condition" (p. 102). It is most interesting that this postulate as a mode of mental functioning is quite contrary to the findings of Piaget and many other investigators, which imply that the mental functions even in the most primitive state seek out stimulation and thrive on mastery, if the stimulation is not too overwhelming. It is clear that the notion of instinct as an explanatory causal hypothesis is highly controversial and fraught with philosophical difficulties; perhaps it is easier now to understand why Freud revised his instinct theory four times.

Although in most opinions Freud's final version of the theory of instincts is unsatisfactory, it is important to have a working knowledge of his notion of instinct and his four instinct theories in order to avoid becoming confused in reading his works.

One of the earliest ways in which the organism distinguishes between the inner and outer world is through the discovery that muscular action can avoid certain noxious stimuli; one can take flight from the outer world but not from the inner world. The formation of the ego and the mechanisms of defense is given its primary impetus by the need to develop protection against the constant instinctual forces from the inner world that cannot be avoided by the muscular action of flight. Freud sees an instinct as the "psychical representative of the stimuli originating from within the organism and reaching the mind, as a measure of the demand made upon the mind for work in consequence of its connection with the body" (1915C;14:122). Each instinct is characterized by a pressure (*Drang*) which is a measure of force or the demand for work and represents the "very essence" of an instinct. The aim (*Ziel*) of an instinct is "in every instance satisfaction, which can only be obtained by removing the state of stimulation at the source of the instinct" (p. 122). The object *(Objekt)* of an instinct is the thing in regard to which or through which the instinct is able to achieve its aim; the source (*Quelle*) of an instinct lies in the somatic-chemical or mechanical aspects of the body. Freud claims that the study of the sources of instincts lies outside the scope of psychology; "In mental life we know them only by their aim" (p. 123).

The difficulties multiply with Freud's question, "What instincts should we suppose that there are, and how many?" It is well known that Freud had a compelling need to keep the instincts divided into two homogenous groups. The original grouping was between the sexual instincts and the ego-preservative instincts, with very little attention paid to the latter since Freud at the time was so busy dipping into the id and uncovering the infantile sexual wishes. In 1905, in *Three Essays on the Theory of Sexuality*, the libido was first explicitly established as an expression of the sexual instinct; in a short paper on psychogenic disturbances of vision (1910I;11:210ff) Freud introduced the term ego-instincts, which he considered self-preserving.

In his paper "On Narcissism" (1914C;14:69ff) this duality broke down when the notion of ego-libido was introduced as a natural stage of development called primary narcissism. It then became necessary to distinguish between originally nonlibidinal ego instincts, and libidinal ego instincts. Sexual energies flowing within the ego made it impossible to separate sexual and ego instincts, and the "alibidinous" part remained poorly defined and did not balance the libidinal ego instincts. The great danger at this point was to fall into Jung's solution of using libido to represent *all* instincts, a monistic theory that rendered the whole concept of instincts and libido meaningless.

A third and transitional theory of the instincts was suggested indirectly in the paper "Instincts and their Vicissitudes" (1915C;14:105ff). Although the division between ego instincts and sexual instincts is preserved, a consideration of the relations between love and hate in this paper led Freud to the conclusion that hate was to be regarded as a nonlibidinal reaction of the ego. This implies that the important aspect of the nonlibidinal ego instincts is the aggressive or sadistic aspect. Freud suggests two kinds of sadism: (1) moral sadism, the drive for power or the control of the environment for self-preservation; and (2) sexual sadism, which appears in certain perversions and frustrations of the sexual instinct. Freud maintains that the impluses to assert, control, and aggress upon can be separated from libidinal impulses, but the argument is not convincing since if sadism is found at every level of sexual development, why can it not be considered a part of the libidinal instincts? In this theory sadism is considered partly sexual and partly nonsexual aggressiveness—with the nonsexual aggressive strivings for power and so on representing the nonlibidinal part of the instincts.

In the final theory of the instincts described in *Beyond the Pleasure Principle* (1920G;18:3ff), Freud elevates aggressiveness to an independent status of its own and abandons the notion of ego instincts entirely. Aggression in this final theory becomes a vicissitude of primary masochism.

The instincts are finally divided into *Eros*, the libidinal or sexual instinct, and *Thanatos*, the death instinct—representing a tendency to disorganization and an expression of the inertia of living matter, of the organic to become inorganic, dead, inanimate. As libido represents the energy of the sexual instincts, "destrudo" or "mortido" represents the energy of the death instincts (terms added by Freud's followers). This postulation of a primary death instinct is not generally accepted today, but it must be pointed out that *no better formulation has been offered.*

To claim that outwardly directed aggression is the primary instinct parallel or polar opposite to the sexual instincts forces one to postulate that man has an innate powerful, destructive, aggressive drive. Such a postulate leads, as explained, to the confusing question of why, since aggression is a component of all sexual stages of development, a separate aggressive instinct at a polar opposite to the sexual instincts should be postulated. Either the libidinal and aggressive instinctual phenomena start from something that is common to both and only become differentiated in the course of development, or each has a different origin and follows separate though at times intersecting lines of development. The first of these views is a monistic one like that of Jung; Freud tried to sidestep this view by separating out the aggressive aspect of the ego-preservative functions from the problem of erotic sadism. The final step was to remove aggressiveness from the ego instincts and give it an independent status as an instinctual group with an aim of its own. The ego is now thought of as being obliged to struggle with aggressiveness exactly as it is obliged to struggle with libido; it could give way to it, sublimate, repress, develop reaction formations, neutralize it by adding libidinal elements, or direct the aggression onto itself.

Unfortunately, the logic of the hypothesis seemed to force Freud to postulate the death instinct. Thus if the libido is the energy of the sexual instincts and is primarily and originally directed upon the self, we must similarly postulate that the energy of the aggressive instincts was originally directed upon the self—the stage of primary masochism. Therefore, the wish to destroy oneself is primary and a polar opposite to the wish to "love" oneself, using love here in a primitive undifferentiated sense. A further consideration of the final instinct theory will be deferred until detailed discussion of one of Freud's most important late philosophical books, *Beyond the Pleasure Principle* (1920G;18:3ff).

In Freud's view, the vicissitudes of an instinct have a defensive connotation. These vicissitudes are: (1) reversal into its opposite, which can involve either a change from active to passive aim, or a reversal of the content of the instinct; (2) a turning around upon the subject; (3) repression; and (4) sublimation, which Freud later says is not a vicissitude but a way of healthy discharge. These tendencies are all opposed to the instinctual pressure for explosive, straightforward discharge, regardless of reality.

In a turning around upon the subject, the first and second vicissitudes coincide in that both the aim and the object of the instinct sometimes change. For example, the wish to exercise violence or inflict pain on another person proceeds to a change of object to the self; this may also change the aim of the instinct from active to passive, and so the self is substituted as an object to take over the role of the other person. This is the situation of masochism; thus, sadism always precedes masochism in the third instinct theory (see above). In reversal into the opposite, the active aim to look at or torture, for example, is changed into the passive aim to be looked at and to be tortured, and this usually involves a turning around on the subject.

Freud's discussion of love and hate prepares the way for the final instinct theory. There is no polarity between love and hate for love is not an instinct; according to Freud it is an elaboration of the sexual instinct, whereas hate is an instinct and a primal emotion. Thus for Freud love is a higher-order reaction resulting from sexual satisfaction; and thus, speaking of a reversal from love into hate is not a description of the vicissitude of an instinct. Freud explains, "The case of love and hate requires a special interest from the circumstance that love refuses to be fitted into our scheme of the instincts" (1915C;14:133). He insists that love and hate "sprang from different sources, and had each its own development before the influence of the pleasure–unpleasure relation made them into opposite" (ibid., p. 138). Hate at this point is conceived as springing from the aggressive component of the nonlibidinal ego instincts. Thus sadism is the aggression of the ego instincts with vicissitudes of its own, although there is also a sexual sadism. The sadism of the ego instincts is a will to power or dominance. According to Freud, when the will to cruelty or torture is added we have the infusion of the sadism of the ego instincts with sexual sadism.

This distinction between sexual sadism as a part of the libidinal instincts, and hate or moral sadism as a vital component of the ego instincts, is clearly unsatisfactory and demanded revision, as Freud obviously understood. It is fascinating to see how Freud reached his final revision of the instinct theory and to study the various aspects of his personal and intellectual life that were at play when he created the polarity of the life and death instincts.

The vital question still remains, however, as to what *other revision* could be made of instinct theory, that would preserve the duality and not end with the extremely speculative notion of primary masochism or a death instinct. One can see Freud wrestling with this problem and trying to remain as close to his clinical material as possible for, as he explained at the beginning of "Instincts and Their Vicissitudes", everything depends on these basic concepts having significant relations to the empirical material; only by careful clinical observation can we formulate our basic scientific concepts with increased precision and render them serviceable and consistent. The notion of a death instinct is both unserviceable in the sense that it has no clinical utility, and runs against our common sense, so we are hard put to believe it. It is certainly possible to explain the phenomena of the repetition compulsion as part of a self-preservative urge to master rather than a manifestation of the primary need to inflict pain on oneself, and the former explanation is more consistent with the data of experimental psychology.

Why can we not postulate the two primary groups of instincts as libidinal and aggressive? The answer, as we have seen, is because we also postulate that the primary state of the organism involves these instincts infusing the self. So, in primary narcissism, the original investment of the libido is on the self. To be consistent we would have to similarly postulate a primary masochism in which the original investment of the aggression was also on the self. One cannot logically avoid the consequences of Freud's final revision of instinct theory—like Freud, we are forced to accept this revision by the logic of our theoretical formulations. The only way to avoid this situation is to throw out his theory of instincts entirely.

As a matter of fact, certain revisionists in the field of psychoanalysis have attempted to replace these theoretical preconceptions by the use, for example, of systems theory and in so doing discard the structural concepts such as id, ego, and superego as well as energy concepts such as force and energy, as discussed in chapter 22. This is a perfectly legitimate scientific enterprise and does not affect the practice of intensive psychotherapy or psychoanalysis in its clinical aspects. Personally, I prefer to stay as much as possible with Freud's basic concepts, since in the actual practice of intensive psychotherapy they have exceptional utility in helping to arrive at conceptual understanding of what is happening in the treatment. The introduction of systems theory coupled with the total abandonment of Freud's metapsychological concepts does not, in my judgment, lead to increased clinical effectiveness, although of course I recognize this issue as highly debatable, with strong arguments on both sides—an issue that is beyond the scope of this book. As one becomes older it becomes perhaps easier to understand and to empathize with Freud's concept of a death instinct; one cannot consider his postulation of such an instinct so outrageous as to *force* a radical revision of our theoretical concepts.

Instincts and the Mind–Body Problem Descartes asked, "Granted that a human mind and body are substances of different kinds, how can events in the one produce or modify events in the other?" It was difficult for Descartes to explain how an unextended mental substance which has no fundamental property except cogitation, and an unthinking material substance which has no fundamental property but extension, could ever come to grips with each other. According to Descartes, interaction between mind and body takes place only in human beings and only in the pineal gland; even there, mind somehow produces only a change in the direction of preexisting motion without changing its total quantity.

This unsatisfactory thesis was modified by Spinoza, who argued that there is one and only one substance, which he called God. This monist substance is both mental and material, but is neither a mind nor a body; each individual person represents a mode of the one substance. Each mode has bodily and mental attributes exactly correlated with each other; thus for any bodily fact about the mode John Jones there is a corresponding mental fact about him, and vice versa. Broad (1975) explains, "It becomes nonsensical to talk of interaction here, for interaction implies two terms; and here there is only a single term, considered under two different, but precisely correlated, abstract headings." Thus at a certain moment an individual A has a mental experience denoted by E_{ψ} ; the bodily correlate of this is an event in his brain denoted by E_{ϕ} . Then E_{ψ} and E_{ϕ} are just one and the same psychical–physical event $E_{\psi\phi}$ considered respectively in its purely mental and its purely bodily aspects.

Because Leibniz could not accept the monism of Spinoza he offered a different solution, presenting the rather bizarre theory of monads. Leibniz claimed that the ruling monad is one substance, and the monads which together constitute its organism are different substances of the same general character as itself, though at a lower order of clearness and intelligence. Furthermore, these changes are determined and reflected in all the monads in the universe, so that our perceptions of the ruling monad or mind causing the body to change is an illusion. It should be noted, by the way, that Leibniz was probably the first philosopher to assert that there are "unconscious perceptions" and to use this information as an important part of his philosophical discussions.

The occasionalists, both in a crude form and in a more sophisticated form proposed by Malebranche, revised Descartes by holding the view of psycho-physical parallelism. They argued that there is no interaction whatever between mind and body, and postulated the continued intervention of God to maintain the illusion that volition in the mind leads to bodily change. Thus for example, if at a certain moment a person decides to move a finger, God notices this and deliberately causes the finger to move in accordance with this volition.

Which of these views can best be ascribed to Freud's theory of the instincts? It seems that Freud vacillates on the question; at times he seems to maintain the view of Descartes when he speaks of instincts or energies of the body causing direct changes in the mind; whereas, in a more sophisticated vein, when he speaks of the mental representations of the instincts, he seems to lean toward the theory of Spinoza.

For Freud's purposes the Spinozistic viewpoint, considering man as one mode who can be studied under the attributes of mind or body (brain), seems best; the psychodynamic therapist limits himself to the attribute of mind and recognizes that for various reasons, changes in the body will have concurrent or concomitant mental representations and corresponding interferences with the dynamic balance of the forces of mentation. This theory is more sophisticated than that of Descartes because it avoids the impossible question of *where* mind and brain interact.

Another possible approach is that of Ryle or Skinner, who view mind as a ghost concept which is purely illusory, and which may be discarded; this approach is untenable for a variety of reasons (Chessick 1977*a*).

Freud's Views on the Mind-Brain Problem "Project for a Scientific Psychology" (1950A;1:283-387), a famous early work, was dashed off in two or three weeks, left unfinished, and was scheduled for destruction by Freud. It has recently received great attention in psychoanalytic circles because in spite of being ostensibly a neurological document, it contains the nucleus of the great part of Freud's later psychological theory. Strachey, in his introduction (pp. 283-293) to this work in the *Standard Edition*, writes that "The *Project*, or rather its invisible ghost, haunts the whole series of Freud's theoretical writings to the very end" (p.290). It is essentially a neurological theory which implies a strict psycho-physical parallelism; there is a coincidence between the characteristics of consciousness and processes in the Omega neurons which vary in parallel with them. Yet this work contains a curious mixture—which is probably why Freud abandoned it—between neurological descriptions of the various systems of neurons and quantities of excitations on the one hand, and the language of mental processes such as tension, wishes, and dreams, on the other. Emphasis is upon the environment's impact upon the organism and the organism's reaction to it, much in keeping with standard neurological theory of Freud's day. Internal forces at this point are considered essentially secondary reactions to external ones.

It was the subject of psycho-physical parallelism on which Freud—like Descartes—foundered, and which caused him to abandon the "Project." For example, he explains that the starting point of the investigation into the psyche "is provided by a fact without parallel, which defies all explanation or description—the fact of consciousness" (1940A;23:157), which Freud's early neurological theory had absolutely no means of explaining.

Thus, rather than tackle the essential philosophical problem of the relationship between brain and mind, Freud at an early date chose to give up his investigations of brain—although he was already an established neurologist—and to concentrate exclusively on the phenomena of mind. He left the investigation of the relationship of mind and brain for later research. One might expect that this unresolved issue committed him to some form of idealism, but he never doubted that there was a physical reality "out there," even though he never tried to prove it any more than Kant tried to establish the existence of *Dang-in-sich* (things-in-themselves). Furthermore, like Kant, he simply assumed that physical reality "out there" was in some way the *cause* of our perceptions of the external world, even though Kant's own philosophy demonstrated that the notion of causation could not be applied to the noumenal world.

Freud could have chosen to stay with the neurological machinery of his "Project" and become instead a modern behaviorist or empirical psychologist. He could have adopted a view similar to that of Ryle (1949) and insisted that the mind was a "ghost" in his neurological machine; or he could have anticipated the philosophy of Susanne Langer (1967, 1972) and viewed the phenomena of mind as a mirror phase of brain function, anticipating general systems theory—but he did not. The recognition of the immediate data of consciousness was for Freud so mysterious and so important that he could not allow himself to try to explain it away by any philosophy or to ignore it and concentrate only on neurological machinery.

It was by focusing on the data of our consciousness and therefore on what his patients had to say regarding the data of their consciousness, that Freud established the grounds of psychoanalysis. Thus he regarded the reported data of the patient about his own consciousness and mentation as legitimate material for the investigation of a natural science called psychoanalysis, much as our collected observations of the motions and positions of the stars and planets form the data of the natural science of astronomy. Once the "Project" was abandoned, these essentially metaphysical preconceptions never vary throughout Freud's work and can even be found in his very last description of psychoanalysis, published posthumously. He writes:

> We know two kinds of things about what we call our psyche (or mental life): firstly, its bodily organ and scene of action, the brain (or nervous system) and, on the other hand, our acts of consciousness, which are immediate data and cannot be further explained by any sort of description. Everything that lies between is unknown to us, and the data do not include any direct relation between these two terminal points of our knowledge (1940A;23:144).

Thus we shall hear no more about the brain from the neurologist Freud. Even so, some of the postulates from the "Project" survive and are applied as metapsychology to the data of consciousness in his later period. Detailed studies of the "Project" such as that of Pribram and Gill (1976) are very interesting historically, but cannot be said to throw any new light on the metaphysical and epistemological foundations of Freud's thought as manifested in his writings on psychoanalysis.

Freud's "Project for a Scientific Psychology," continues to be assessed and reassessed (see Brenner 1977 and the discussions following his book review). Freud initially formulated the mechanisms of mental function on the basis of his biological and neurological knowledge but then chose to leave these foundations implicit and even occasionally to deny their existence. These mechanisms became isolated from contemporary developments in psychology and neurophysiology and were elaborated into "a speculative tangle of concepts and casuistry" in the hands of post-Freudian psychoanalysts, so claim Pribram and Gill (1976, p. 10). They also believe that although Freud's metapsychological model has often been alleged to be a hydrodynamic one, it is actually an energic model based on electrical concomitants of neural activity. Even these two authors disagree in their book as to whether psychoanalysis should be rejoined to its biochemical and neurological origins, or should go its own way (which Gill feels to mean purging it of its natural science metapsychology.

There is still considerable argument about the "Project." For example, the authors just cited quote Kanzer as claiming the work to be an essentially psychological document, whereas they describe it as a neuropsychological document. Kanzer (1973) insists that not only was the work a psychological document, but that Freud kept right on with it after he was supposed to have disavowed it! However, most authors agree with Jones (1953) that Freud regarded the "Project" as an "oppressive burden," a judgment which perhaps marked the transition from Freud the dogged worker to Freud the imaginative thinker. Its relative sterility is explained by its divorce from clinical data; Jones points out that the work is more like the deductive reasoning of a rationalist philosopher than the work of a clinician, which Jones sees as a dangerous tendency that "might end in empty speculation, an arid intellectualizing of the underground urges." Jones reminds us that despite the philosopher–psychologist Herbart's conviction that in psychology deduction has equal rights with induction, Freud had been drilled in the sacred nineteenth-century medical doctrine that all conclusions were to be founded on experience and experience alone. For him the writing of the "Project" could be thought of as a metaphysical heresy, running against his fundamental epistemological and his own only dimly recognized metaphysical beliefs.

Freud's Epistemology Freud's paper "The Unconscious (1915E;14:161ff) is the most important of all his papers on metapsychology; he considered it one of this best works (Jones 1955). It is difficult to characterize this paper because it is probably the most important meeting point for Freud's clinical work, his psychological theories, and the philosophy-of-science issues implicit in the whole foundation of psychodynamic psychiatry. In a way this paper may be considered as part of the philosophical tradition of the West, fitting into a sequence with Locke's and Hume's treatises on human reason and understanding, as well as the work of Kant, Schopenhauer, and Herbart. The present author discussed this sequence in another book (1977*a*).

Freud wrote "The Unconscious" in three weeks in April 1915. The essay is neatly divided into seven sections, beginning with what is basically a philosophical argument for the justification of the concept of the unconscious, an argument with which even medical students should be familiar. Freud himself makes the connection between his notion of the unconscious and the philosophy of Kant: "Just as Kant warned us not to overlook the fact that our perceptions are subjectively conditioned and must not be regarded as identical with what is perceived though unknowable, so psychoanalysis warns us not to equate perception by means of consciousness with the unconscious mental processes which are their object" (p. 171).

As early as chapter VII of *The Interpretation of Dreams* (see above), Freud develops the notion that our perception of mental processes which are unconscious is, by means of consciousness, analogous to our perception of the external world by means of the sense organs. Although Freud does not mention it, this notion is quite similar to Kant's notion of "coming in to consciousness" in the Transcendental Aesthetic section of *Critique of Pure Reason* (1965). The parallel is all the more remarkable in that Kant explains how, as a representation comes in to consciousness it is placed in the manifold of time by an activity of the mind; Freud, as we shall see, associates the coming from the unconscious to the preconscious with an activity of the mind that places the idea in a time manifold and links it with words. The second section of "The Unconscious" reviews this point and also Freud's well-known "topographical" point of view (described in the next paragraph), and again reminds us that all psychical acts begin in the unconscious; given certain conditions, these can become "an object of consciousness." This statement connotes an active sense to the word conscious, a sense which is present in the German word used by Freud, *Bewusstsein.* (When Freud wishes to speak of a mental state's consciousness in the passive sense he uses the word *Bewusstheit*—the attribute of being conscious.)

A further confusion is resolved by Freud in distinguishing between the topographical *systems* conscious and unconscious, abbreviated Cs. and Ucs. respectively, so as to distinguish these systems from the use of the words conscious and unconscious in a descriptive sense. In addition, he postulates the system preconscious (Pcs.) which "shares the characteristics of the system Cs." and that "the rigorous censorship exercises its office at the point of transition from the Ucs. to the Pcs. (or Cs.)" (p. 173).

The crucial question, as to what happens when an idea passes from the unconscious to the conscious, is left unresolved. Jones (1957) asks, "Does a new imprint of the idea in question get made in the second locality, so that there would be two of them, or does some change take place in the original impression and its original place? Freud seemed for the moment to favor the latter view."

The third section of the "Unconscious" deals with the concept of unconscious feelings or emotions. This is an extremely difficult and unresolved subject. It begins by explaining (as we have seen) that an instinct can never become an object of consciousness—only the idea that represents the instinct can do so. Furthermore, even in the unconscious "an instinct cannot be represented otherwise than by an idea" (p. 177). Thus if the instinct did not attach itself to an idea we would know nothing about it. When we speak of an "unconscious instinctual impulse" we mean an instinctual impulse, the ideational representative of which is unconscious. Then Freud asks what we mean by such phrases as unconscious love, unconscious hate, unconscious anger, and so on. The affect—the feeling or emotion—is never unconscious:

> All that had happened was that its *idea* had undergone repression . . . affects or emotions correspond to processes of discharge, the final manifestations of which are perceived as feelings (p. 178).
>
> The affect belongs to the impulse and action. When ideas from the unconscious come up to the conscious, they stimulate an affect just as they may stimulate action or fantasies (p. 178).

This entire matter is discussed later in greater and clearer detail in *The Ego and the Id* (1923B;19:section 2). There, the transition between unconscious and preconscious is described as taking place through the unconscious ideation becoming connected with the word-presentations corresponding to it. Affects do not have to undergo this transition, but Freud still remains ambiguous on this point. At times he speaks of affects as in some way being unconscious; at other times he implies that the affects experienced when ideation becomes conscious are added by the higher integrative processes in the ego. Thus it is the ego, or in the earlier terminology the system conscious [Cs. (Pcs.)] that takes the energy associated with the idea and discharges it as a conscious or felt affect. In so doing it may transform this feeling in a number of ways or even express it as anxiety. The point is that affect belongs basically to a higher integrative system than the system Ucs.(1915E;14:179).

The fourth section of "The Unconscious" reviews the concept of repression and refines it, as well as introducing some important terminology. A metapsychological presentation is here defined as describing a psychical process in its "dynamic, topographical, and economic aspects." The economic aspects endeavor to follow out the vicissitudes of amounts of excitation or "psychic energy" and to arrive at some relative estimate of their magnitude. The topographical aspects refer to the systems already described, while the dynamic aspects have to do with the conflicting forces of energy known as cathexis, and anticathexis or countercathexis. What is not taken up in this section is a defense of the value of these metapsychological conceptions, which remain a matter of controversy even today.

The special characteristics of the unconscious are described in section five of the essay, as follows:

(1) The unconscious is made up of the ideational representatives of the instincts, which are exempt from mutual contradiction—thus there is no negation in the unconscious.

(2) Thought processes in the unconscious behave according to primary process. One idea may surrender to another all its cathexis (the motility of cathexis), a process known as displacement; one idea may appropriate the whole cathexis of several ideas, a process known as condensation; (symbolism and secondary elaboration are also listed as part of this primary process in the *Interpretation of Dreams*, but are not emphasized at this point).

(3) The unconscious has no conception of time. Ideas and impulses from different chronological ages are telescoped together, and only the present exists.

(4) The unconscious has no sense of outer-world reality. A sense of psychical reality replaces our sense of external reality so that a wish for something is equated with the actual happening. Thus unconscious processes are subject merely to the pleasure principle and operate according to displacement and condensation, which are the laws of primary process thought.

This primary process adds further impetus to the distinction between the system unconscious and the system preconscious or conscious, since the latter systems operate according to secondary process along the reality principle and thus are fundamentally different.

Jones (1957) calls the sixth section, on the intercommunication between the two systems, "the most valuable part of this essay." The relationship between the unconscious and the preconscious is *not* confined only to repression. Much preconscious material *originates* in the unconscious so that the preconscious may be said to have instinctual derivatives "imbedded" within it such as fantasy; attached to these derivatives is what Freud later calls tonically bound id energy. Thus in order for their derivatives to become stored in the preconscious, unconscious instinctual impulses must pass a censorship barrier between the unconscious (Ucs.) and the preconscious (Pcs.), and so "A very great part of this preconscious originates in the unconscious, has the character of its derivatives and is subjected to a censorship before it can become conscious" (p. 191). This implies a *second* censorship barrier between the preconscious and the conscious, a fact which curiously has been overlooked in many studies of Freud. The first of these censorships is exercised against the unconscious itself by the preconscious, and the second against the preconscious derivatives of the unconscious by the conscious.

The important clinical and philosophical point here is that, although in intensive psychotherapy we deal with the instinctual derivatives appearing from the preconscious to the conscious, it is not possible to actually reach into the unconscious itself. Furthermore, as psychotherapy lifts the barrier between the conscious and the preconscious and as tonically bound id energy in the preconscious is released through expression in the treatment, less energy is available for anticathexis of the unconscious by the preconscious, permitting more derivatives of unconscious material to emerge into the preconscious. Notice, however, that all unconscious material comes out as derivatives subject to the laws of secondary process—in this sense one never reaches the unconscious itself.

The unconscious contains inherited mental formations and what has been discarded in childhood in the process of ego formation; the basic repression barrier is between the preconscious and the unconscious, while the barrier between the conscious and the preconscious is experienced in clinical practice as resistance to free association or communication.

The situation is made even more complicated by the clinical fact, which Freud calls "a very remarkable thing," that the unconscious of one human being can react on that of another without passing through the conscious. No metapsychological explanation of this is offered by Freud; however, one of the lost papers on metapsychology (destroyed by Freud) apparently deals with this issue.

An example of such communciation is given by Freud (1913I;12:313ff). In this case report a previously satisfied wife develops neurotic symptoms when she discovers that her husband is unable to have children. Although she never mentioned the intense frustration that this discovery engendered in her—indeed, she did all she could to prevent her husband from guessing the cause of the trouble—her husband understood "without any admission or explanation on her part" what his wife's anxiety meant. He in turn felt hurt but did not show it; instead he reacted by failing, for the first time, in sexual intercourse with her and "immediately afterwards" he went off on a journey. In my clinical experience this unspoken communication of information from one individual to another is especially prominent in the relationship between husband and wife. It also appears frequently in the psychotherapy of schizophrenics, who seem to have an uncanny capacity both to communicate directly to the unconscious of the therapist and to read the therapist's unconscious in turn.

The last sentence of this difficult section of Freud's essay reminds us that a sharp and final division between the unconscious and preconscious systems does not take place until puberty. As Gedo and Goldberg (1973) pointed out, this means that different models of the mind may be necessary to understand psychological phenomena before puberty.

The final section of "The Unconscious" presents Freud's theory of schizophrenia. This well-known theory postulates that schizophrenics have given up the cathexis of objects with libido; they return this libido on the soma in the formation of hypochondriasis, and on the self in the formation of megalomania. Freud makes the crucial point that in schizophrenia *words* are subjected to the same process as that which makes dream images out of latent dream thoughts—thus words undergo condensation and displacement and indeed, a single word may take over the representation of a whole train of thought. However, there is an essential difference between dream work and schizophrenia: in schizophrenia the words themselves, in which the preconscious thought was expressed, become subject to modification; in dreams, it is not the preconscious thoughts or words which are modified, but what Freud calls the "thing-presentations" in the unconscious.

This crucial distinction between word-presentations and thing-presentations is a very early notion of Freud's first appearing in his early monograph *On Aphasia* (1891), and is sharply contradicted by the research of Piaget. Thing-presentations for Freud exist in the unconscious more or less as memory (mnemic) images, or at least as remote memory traces derived from memory images. The phrase "mnemic images of things" is used interchangeably by Freud with the phrase "thing-presentation."

In the preconscious, according to Freud, word-presentations become linked with thing-presentations; this linkage brings about a higher psychical organization and makes it possible for primary process to be succeeded by secondary process thought. In the clinical transference phenomena, repression denies the linkage of words to what is presented. In this situation, what the patient cannot put into words he communicates by attitudes and behavior. In a clearly Kantian statement, then, Freud insists that we can become conscious of the unconscious only *indirectly* and *after* the thing-presentations in the unconscious have become linked with word-presentations, a linkage which occurs in the preconscious.

Freud characterizes this discussion as "philosophizing." He sees the distortion of the word-presentations in schizophrenia as representing an attempt at recovery from the illness. The schizophrenic, according to Freud, is forced to be content with words instead of external things (because of withdrawal of libido from the outside world); the hypercathexis of word-presentations is an effort to regain the lost thing-presentations from both the external and internal world. The schizophrenic confuses these two worlds and ends up embedded in the word-presentations of each.

Freud's study *On Aphasia* (1891) is of considerable historical interest since it illustrates the fact that his neurological and psychological concepts were linked in a continuum of development in his thought. The great neurologist Hughlings Jackson made a deep impression on Freud. One of Freud's basic principles, that of regression, is based on the Jacksonian notion that the functions of the "speech apparatus" under pathological conditions represent instances of "functional retrogression (disinvolution) of a highly organized apparatus," and therefore correspond to previous states of its functional development. Notice the use of the phrase "speech apparatus," which antedates the notion of mental apparatus, as well as the basic concept that arrangements of associations acquired later and belonging to a higher level of functioning are lost while an earlier, simpler arrangement is preserved.* Here is the essence of Freud's explanation of aphasia: "Our considerations have led us to attribute a certain clinical type of speech disorder to a change in the functional state of the speech apparatus rather than a localized interruption of a pathway" (1891, p. 29).

For the most part, Freud's monograph on aphasia is only of historical interest, except for certain crucial passages which have been translated as Appendix B and Appendix C to his paper "The Unconscious" (Freud 1915E; 14:206–215), and which lie essentially within the field of pure epistemological philosophy. Reality in the human brain, according to Freud, is represented by (1) a thing-presentation which essentially constitutes a passive image, and (2) a human way of presenting things to ourselves, especially words. These words are linked to the thing-presentations; thus in the various aphasias, according to Freud, visual, auditory, or kinesthetic representations of the word are cut off from the thing-presentations. Learning for Freud occurs by connecting images with the words. In transference and neurotic phenomena patients are presenting images not connected with words and suffer from "nameless fears," showing that the linkage has been broken. The purpose of psychotherapy in the neuroses is to rejoin the words with the images or thing-presentations, as provided, for example, by the therapist's interpretations.

Thus an organic severing of the linkage between word-presentations and thing-presentations results in the phenomena of aphasia; the functional severing of this linkage is the process of repression fundamental in the neuroses. Within the unconscious, thing-presentations are cathected by the energy of the instincts and then strive for expression; but the process of repression forbids the linkage of thing-presentations with word-presentations, and therefore, such thing-presentations become incapable of expression in the

*This is dramatically illustrated in the film "2001" when a highly sophisticated computer is taken apart.

conscious. The linkage with words is a higher development, according to Freud, and has the eventual function of imposing a barrier between instinctual drives and impulse behavior. This barrier works through words in which a person thinks it over, talks it over, and thereby tames, neutralizes, or binds instinctual energy.

Notice, then, that a representation in the conscious mind is made up of a linkage between a thing-presentation and a word-presentation. For Freud there are four components of the word presentations: the sound-image, the visual letter-image, the motor speech-image, and the motor writing-image. A word acquires its *meaning* by being linked to a thing-presentation. As mentioned, Piaget's genetic epistemology is directly antagonistic to this theory, since, according to Piaget, the developing child *first* acquires conscious concepts and *then*, after the sensory-motor stage, learns to attach words to these concepts.

We are forced to conclude that the basic philosophical postulates of Freud's metapsychology—(a) psycho-physical parallelism, and (b) the notion that conscious representations are made up of thing-presentations which have become linked to word-presentations—are philosophically and experimentally debatable.

Freud's "A Metapsychological Supplement to the Theory of Dreams" (1917D;14;219ff) may be considered a rather turgid continuation of the subject. It contains some obscure statements which refer to a lost (destroyed by Freud) paper on the Conscious. The thesis of the paper is that the completion of the dream process consists of a regressive transformation in the mental apparatus, in which thought content, worded over into a wishful fantasy, becomes conscious as a sense perception, an hallucinated dream wish. Secondary revision occurs at the same time. Because this is a hallucination, it meets with belief in the reality of its fulfillment. This is essentially a restatement of the basic principles already quoted from chapter VII of *The Interpretation of Dreams*, propounded seventeen years earlier but here rounded off into a more polished form.

The dream wish, based on unconscious instinctual excitations, cannot find expression along motor paths during sleep. Therefore, it regresses through the unconscious "backwards" to the perceptual system itself; this regression makes dreams akin to hallucinations. In distinction to temporal regression in the psychoneuroses and the personality disorders, this is a topographical regression in which there is also a postulated return to earlier stages of psychosexual development. The word-presentations of the preconscious thoughts that are disturbing the dreamer are reduced backwards to the primitive thing-presentations which then undergo displacements and condensations under the laws of primary process. After secondary elaboration, all this appears in the perceptual system as a hallucination. Thus the dream itself is a wish-fulfilling fantasy.

One of the important premises underlying this thesis is the assumption that a wishful impulse may be dealt with along three different paths: "It may follow the path that would be normal in waking life, by pressing from the Pcs. to consciousness; or it may bypass the Cs. and find direct motor discharge; or it may take the unexpected path which observation enables us in fact to trace" (p. 226). In the first instance it would become a delusion, having as content the fulfillment of a wish. The second instance is that of direct motor discharge which, of course, cannot happen in the state of sleep. The "unexpected" path is that of dream formation, as has already been described in the foregoing discussion of topographical regression. Notice that in dream formation, in contrast to the psychoneuroses, both topographical and temporal regression occur, since the wish-fulfilling fantasy also represents a return to the early stage of hallucinatory wish fulfillment; in the psychoneuroses topographical regression does not occur. Neither is there a topographical regression in schizophrenia, since this condition is represented by primary process changes only in the word-presentations.

Again we see the fundamental distinction that runs throughout Freud's metapsychology and goes back to his early neurological work, between thing-presentations [(*Sachvorstellung*, replaced by the synonymous *Dingvorstellung* by Freud in "Mourning and Melancholia" (1917)] and word-presentations (*Wortvorstellung*). Here, the difficult German word to translate is *Vorstellung*, which covers the English terms "idea," "image," and "presentation"; the same problem arises in translation of Schopenhauer's philosophy.

A further philosophical assumption is Freud's comment, "It seems justifiable to assume that belief in reality is bound up with perception through the senses" (p. 230). Our reality-testing function is here placed by Freud in the perceptual apparatus so that "when once a thought has followed the path to regression as far back as to the unconscious memory-traces of objects and thence to perception, we accept the perception of it as real" (ibid).

In the same work, Freud places the perceptual system as coinciding with the system conscious. Thus he speaks of "the system Cs. (Pcpt.)". Reality-testing is based on the capacity of this system to orient itself in the world by means of its perceptions, distinguishing external and internal according to their relations to the muscular action of the system. "A perception which is made to disappear by an action is recognized as external, as reality; where such an action makes no difference, the perception originates within the subject's own body—it is not real" (p. 232). Cathexis of the system Cs.(Pcpt.) is required for reality-testing to occur efficiently. In dreams there is a voluntary withdrawal of this cathexis in the interest of maintaining the state of sleep; this withdrawal permits the wish-fulfillment fantasies to be temporarily accepted as undisputed reality.

In the hallucinations of schizophrenia a disintegration of the reality-testing function is postulated so that it no longer stands in the way of belief in reality, and Freud considers this to be such a disintegration that hallucination "cannot be among the initial symptoms of the affection" (p. 234). The reader is referred to Arlow and Brenner (1964) for further discussion of Freud's views of schizophrenia and problems with these views entailed by his important theoretical revisions, to which we now turn.

Freud, age sixty-six, in 1922. MARY EVANS / SIGMUND FREUD COPYRIGHTS.

21

FREUD'S FINAL METAPHYSICS AND EPISTEMOLOGY

Beyond the Pleasure Principle (1920G;18:3ff) introduces the final phase of Freud's metaphysical, epistemologic, and metapsychological views. The essence of this work is suggested in a paragraph of his earlier paper, "The Uncanny" (1919H;17:218ff), which was published in the autumn of 1919 but did not contain an allusion to the death instinct; Freud withheld *Beyond the Pleasure Principle* for another year. It is not always recognized what a deeply pessimistic work this monograph is; Freud himself modified the pessimism somewhat in later writings.

Written in his sixty-third year, this remarkable work is primarily a philosophical treatise. Balogh (1971) explains, "Perhaps more than in any other of his books one can see in *Beyond the Pleasure Principle* Freud's cool, clear, relaxed and supremely scientific mode of thought. One is shown how he conducted arguments, first with himself and then with colleagues. One gets a glimpse of the width of his reading in biology as well as among poets, philosophers and collectors of myths" (p. 97). Robert (1966) remarks on the echo of Nietzsche in the title and on how this monograph begins with a few remarks of limited clinical interest, "then soars almost immediately into a realm of pure speculation."

As against the death instinct, Freud places Plato's *Eros*, which he describes as exactly the same in its origin, function, and connection with sexuality as the erotic energy or "libido" of psychoanalysis. In what Robert calls "the dominant theme of this [Freud's] grandiose vision," *Eros* and the death instinct wage a confused struggle against one another and, at least as long as life persists, without any decisive outcome. Freud's followers quickly named the death instinct *Thanatos* and referred to the energy of the death instinct as *destrudo* or *mortido*, in contrast to *Eros* and its energy, libido. Freud's view at this point is clearly that *Thanatos*, with its sole aim of leading all living matter back to the inorganic state, is the most primordial instinct, and that *Eros* fights an inevitably losing holding action. Even the earlier essay, "The Uncanny" (1919H;17:218ff), contains an echo from *Also Sprach Zarathustra* where Freud discusses the uncanny aspect of the well-known psychological theme of "the double," which includes the uncanny apparent and constant recurrence of the same thing (a phrase borrowed from Nietzsche); in Freud's discussion of the fate neuroses in *Beyond the Pleasure Principle* a similar phrase—"perpetual recurrence of the same thing"—appears.

All commentators agree that the speculative hypotheses in *Beyond the Pleasure Principle* were put forward many years earlier in "Project for a Scientific Psychology," and here Freud returns, as in the "Project," to Fechner. Fechner distinguished three forms of stability: (1) absolute, which implies permanent immobility; (2) full stability, in which the parts of the whole are moved in such a way that each returns to the same place at regular intervals; and (3) approximate stability, in which each part returns to more or less the same place at regular intervals. Ellenberger (1970) contends that Fechner's system inspired the framework of Freud's ideas: "To the pleasure-unpleasure principle he added the death instinct (a return to Fechner's full stability) and the repetition compulsion, as intermediate between approximate and absolute stability".

Furthermore, the notion of the death instinct, as a destructive or self-destructive instinct, follows a nineteenth-century tradition often attributed to Hobbes and also propounded by Nietzsche. The classical pairs of opposites have been *Eros–Neikos* (love–strife) and *Bios–Thanatos* (life–death); Freud brought forth his philosophical concept of *Eros–Thanatos*, which became more and more fixed in his mind as a firm factual belief as is clear from his later writings. Even early critics pointed out that there was no biological support for the notion of death instinct, and much of Freud's argument for it confuses *Finis* (termination) and *Telos* (final aim) of life.

This confusion is even apparent in Freud's statement that Schopenhauer presented a similar philosophy: "For him death is the 'true result and to that extent the purpose of life' while the sexual instinct is the embodiment of the will to live" (p. 50). When Schopenhauer calls death the "true result and to that extent the purpose of life," he makes clear the differentiation between the termination of life and a definition of the purpose of life. Freud assumes that the termination of life is the same as the purpose of life. As explained in *Great Ideas in Psychotherapy* (Chessick 1977*a*), Schopenhauer did postulate that sexuality was a manifestation of the will to live, but he did *not* set against this some force in the opposite direction; in a much more empirical fashion he saw sexuality and procreation as an effort by man to immortalize himself in spite of what he frequently called man's inevitable doom—termination. He did *not*, as Freud postulated, see any secret purpose or force driving man constantly toward death. Therefore, the similarity between these two philosophies is extremely superficial.

It is worthwhile to examine *Beyond the Pleasure Principle* in detail. The year after its publication the diagnosis of cancer was made on Freud and he endured his first surgery; by this time some obvious physical deterioration had taken place. The first section of the work begins as a metapsychological treatise. The next two sections present some clinical observations; the rest of the work is openly admitted to be philosophical speculation.

The closeness of the earlier sections to Freud's "Project for a Scientific Psychology," drafted by Freud twenty-five years earlier in 1895, is immediately apparent in the first section. According to Freud, the lowering of the quantity of excitation is perceived as pleasurable by the organism, so the organism tries to keep this level low or constant. Freud begins with Fechner's Principle of Constancy, which he considers another way of stating the pleasure principle—the work of the mental apparatus is directed toward keeping the quantity of excitation low, and anything that increases that quantity is felt as unpleasurable. This is a special case of Fechner's principle of the tendency towards stability. The tendency of the organism to seek pleasure conflicts with countertendencies under the dominance of the reality principle which arise from the need for self-preservation. This tendency was described by Freud in an earlier work, "Two Principles of Mental Functioning" (1911B; 12:215ff).

In the second section Freud raises the problem posed by the dreams of patients suffering from traumatic neuroses, which have the characteristic of repeatedly bringing the patient back into the situation of the trauma, resulting in nightmares. In such conditions either the wish-fulfilling function of the dream is disturbed or "we may be driven to reflect on the mysterious masochistic trends of the ego" (p. 14). He deliberately leaves this unresolved and goes on to describe the famous example of his one-and-a-half-year-old grandson playing a game of disappearance-and-return with a toy tied to a piece of string. The child threw the toy over the edge of his cot and then pulled it back in by the string, hailing its reappearance with a joyful exclamation. Thus the second section introduces clinical data of the dreams of patients with traumatic neuroses, and child's play, both of which seem to contain elements that militate superficially against the pleasure principle. These clinical phenomena as well as the compulsion to repeat (described in section III) can be explained in two ways.

The first of these ways, which was Freud's original idea, represents these phenomena as part of the urge toward mastery. In this view the impulsion to relive and experience is for the purpose of mastery of the unpleasure, and the greater integration of the experience and the anxiety it involves is clearly a manifestation of the life force. For example, by the game in which he acts out the omnipotent fantasy that instead of being passive and helpless he can make mother return, the child is trying to overcome the sense of helplessness he experiences when mother goes away. Throwing away the object satisfies the child's revenge impulse toward the mother for going away.

Alternatively, the repetitive dreams of patients with traumatic neuroses, certain aspects of children's play, and the compulsion to repeat could be explained by "a mysterious masochistic force of the ego." Although the compulsion to repeat often leads to unpleasure, it is an innate tendency of the human psyche.

In the third section Freud points out the great clinical importance of the compulsion to repeat, both as manifested in the transference and as found in numerous clinical instances of self-defeating repetitive acting-out, as, for example, the criminal returning to the scene of the crime and other such repetitive self-defeating behaviors. He states that the greater part of what we re-experience under the compulsion to repeat must cause the ego unpleasure and recalls from the past experiences which include no possibility of pleasure either now or even long ago.

In discussing the so-called fate neuroses, Freud cleverly carries the argument one step further by describing the compulsion to repeat as a "daemonic power" which, of course, sets the stage for his attributing an enormous and overwhelming importance to this clinical material. The question is whether the compulsion to repeat indicates an intrinsic quality in the psyche toward pain, later to be defined as a death instinct; or a desire to avoid greater pain—for example, helplessness—by active mastery behavior. Although Freud originally held the latter position, in the present work he shifts to the former.

The fourth section, a monumental genesis of Freud's system of ego psychology, is also a crucial presentation of his metaphysical and epistemological beliefs. He begins, "What follows is speculation, often far-fetched speculation, which the reader will consider or dismiss according to his individual predilection" (p. 24). The opening of the discussion postulates that the system Pcpt.-Cs. lies on the borderline between the outside world and the inside of the psyche, and is turned toward the external world. This system, or the eye of the conscious, is responsible for our awareness or consciousness of mental phenomena, but no memory traces can be found in this system; thus experience is separate from the storage of it.

This notion, which began in the "Project" of 1895 (1950A; Part 1, Section III), is enlarged in a later paper on the "Mystic Writing-pad" (1925A;19:226ff). Clearly, if memory traces were stored in the system Pcpt.-Cs., no room would be left for anything else, so the elsewhere-stored stimuli only become conscious in the system Pcpt.-Cs., and energy can be discharged in this way. When it is a memory trace, psychic energy is bound; when discharged, it is unbound.

Besides the reception of stimuli from within and without, system Pcpt.-Cs. has another extremely important function: to serve as a protective shield against stimuli which are disruptively overwhelming. Freud thinks of the protective shield as supplied with its own store of energy and endeavoring to protect against overwhelming external stimuli by taking in these stimuli in small selected doses, which he defines as "samples" of the external world. He flatly continues that there can be no such shield against the inside or internal stimuli, a notion which also comes from the "Project" and which he later modified.

At this point Freud places himself in the tradition of Kantian theory: that time and space are necessary forms of experience. He explains that although unconscious mental processes are in themselves timeless, "Our abstract idea of time seems to be wholly derived from the method of working of the system Pcpt.-Cs. and to correspond to a perception on its own part of that method of working. This mode of functioning may perhaps constitute another way of providing a shield against stimuli" (p. 28).

When internal stimuli are very intense and too great, unpleasure is felt; the internal excitations can be treated as though they were acting not from the inside but from the outside, so that the shield against external stimuli can be brought into operation as a means of defense against them. This is the origin of the notion of projection; it is an excellent definition of this term, since it applies to a time before a repression barrier has been consolidated. Repression is ineffective against overwhelming internal stimuli, and the defense discussed by Freud is essentially an extrusion of these stimuli, which are then treated as if they originate from the outside; the price of this defense is a breakdown of the boundary between the self and the outside world.

Freud next turns to the question of what happens when intense *external* stimuli break through the shield so that the ego is flooded. The success of the ego binding the external stimuli is determined by (a), the degree of energy of the external stimuli, and (b), how much bound energy is available in the ego systems to form a bond for the energy from the external stimuli. Freud believes that the ego uses ego-libido to do this; it forms an anticathexis "on a grand scale," borrowing energy from all sides. This borrowing leaves less energy for binding fresh and new external stimuli. Thus a healthy person has a lot of ego-libido, with plenty of libido left over both for further attachment to objects and for binding the inevitable traumata of life. It should be noted that in this complex discussion of energies Freud moves very far away from the notion of energy as it is used in physics. His notion reminds one more of the early explanation of heat in terms of a fluid called "caloric."

In the traumatic neuroses, Freud postulates that trauma is so great and so swift that the extra energy is not brought up in time. Thus the ego is unable to feel anxious—here, anxiety is thought of as extra energy which heightens ego-integration—and is essentially unprepared. Thus under ordinary circumstances the ego first generates anxiety—a condition that Freud calls a state of hypercathexis—and with this greater energy, integration and defenses take place in the normal situation. In the traumatic neurosis the preparedness is lacking and the ego-integrative system cannot bind the external stimuli. Thus the ego's function and direction is to feel anxious and painful in order to mobilize sufficient energy to bind the trauma.

Freud maintains that this process is beyond the pleasure principle. Thus the first aim of the organism is to achieve anxiety. In traumatic neuroses the aim of the organism is to once again achieve anxiety that was not present when the trauma occurred. Once this anxiety has been created it is utilized for defense and integration. Freud's point is that the original need to achieve the unpleasant sensation of anxiety contradicts the pleasure principle and is prior to and beyond it. The need to develop anxiety "seems to be more primitive than the purpose of gaining pleasure and avoiding unpleasure" (p. 32). Thus there was once a time *before* the purpose of dreams was the fulfillment of wishes, a time before the whole of mental life had accepted the domination of the pleasure principle. The implication is that the need to endure pain and self-destruction is prior in time to and more fundamental than the need to seek pleasure and avoid unpleasure.

This argument rests on making the generation of anxiety an end in itself. The obvious alternative argument is to view the generation of anxiety as a means to an end, as part of a continuum based on the pleasure principle and leading to mastery of the trauma. This argument implies nothing beyond the pleasure principle.

In section five Freud brings his arguments together in the fashion of a true philosophical treatise. Thus the manifestations of the compulsion to repeat, now described as exhibiting to a high degree an instinctual character, are thought of as giving the appearance of a demonic force at work. Children repeat unpleasurable experiences as a manifestation of the need for repetition, which Freud now wishes to connect to the predicate of being "instinctual." A sharp definition of instinct is now presented: "*It seems, then, that an instinct is an urge apparent in organic life to restore an earlier state of things*" (p. 36). "An earlier state of things" implies the expression of inertia inherent in organic life. This is quite different than Freud's previous notion of instincts as impelling toward change and development. It follows from this that since inanimate things existed first, the aim of all organic life is to return to the earlier inanimate state; thus the aim of all life is death.

In this view, only conflict keeps us from achieving death, and there is no instinct toward development or perfection of the individual or the species. Freud's pessimistic theory may be thought of as the polar opposite of the rational optimism of the Greeks—as in contrast, for example, to Aristotle's viewpoint. For Freud in this monograph the sexual or life instincts oppose death by simply prolonging the journey toward death. Thus the instinctual force toward death becomes paramount and,

> Seen in this light, the theoretical importance of the instincts of self-preservation, of self-assertion, and of mastery greatly diminishes. They are component instincts whose function it is to assure that the organism shall follow its own path to death, and to ward off any possible ways of returning to inorganic existence other than those which are immanent organism itself (p. 39).

What we are left with, continues Freud, is the fact that "the organism wishes to die only in its own fashion" (ibid). Freud recognized that his view was extreme. Notice that even the life instincts are conservative in that they function mainly to bring the organism to death in its own way. Freud quotes Plato's famous myth in the *Symposium* to show how the sexual instincts drive toward an earlier state—even though prolongation of life is a basic function.

In section seven it is apparent that for Freud death is simply the termination of individual development, and is the end purpose of life. Death is not the result of some sort of decay or downtrend in the organism. Some complex biological arguments are presented to demonstrate that there is no biological evidence against the death instinct.

Freud is aware that at this point he is clearly in the area of philosophy, and he reminds us of what he calls "ancient Greek natural philosophies with their four elements—earth, air, fire, and water." He recognizes his affinity to the pre-Socratic philosophers, and his insistence on a dualistic instinct theory has the same evidence behind it as that presented by pre-Socratic philosophers in their various theories of the hidden structure of the world. The objection may be raised that Freud is talking here about forces, whereas the pre-Socratic philosophers were talking about substance; but even a brief acquaintance with the history of philosophy reminds us that Leibniz, in his famous windowless monads, was able to substitute the notion of force or energy for the notion of substance. In his metaphysics—which is primarily what Freud's theory at this point becomes—Freud is in the tradition of the pre-Socratic philosophers and the continental rationalists, especially Leibniz. In a later work he remarks on the similarity of his life-death dualism with that of the theory of Empedocles of Acragas—as discussed in detail in *Great Ideas in Psychotherapy* (Chessick, 1977*a*).

By introducing a mysterious masochistic trend or a primary death instinct, Freud moved away significantly from empirical clinical data on which previous instinct theories rested. This departure from tradition stimulated endless and tedious debate of the same nature that took place among the continental rationalists, and led to a despair that by reason alone one could arrive at an understanding of the secret or mysterious substance that made up the world. Although Freud insisted repeatedly on his aversion to professional philosophy, he certainly became a philosopher at this point; at the end of this work he claims he is not convinced of the truth of his own theories, and in *Beyond the Pleasure Principle* (1920G;18:59) he writes: "I do not know how far I believe in them." Later, however, he came to regard his speculations as proven facts. As he admits, "Unfortunately, however, people are seldom impartial where ultimate things, the great problems of science and life, are concerned. Each of us is governed in such cases by deep-rooted internal prejudices, into whose hands our speculation unwittingly plays" (p. 59).

In the final section Freud makes the curious point that "The pleasure principle seems actually to serve the death instincts" (p. 63), and he leaves the remainder of the discussion as "unfinished." What Freud calls the nirvana principle is represented by the fact that the dominating tendency in mental life is the effort to reduce, keep constant, or remove internal tension due to stimuli. This tendency finds expression in the pleasure principle, and Freud uses the principle as an argument for the existence of the death instinct. Modern psychological and neurophysiological research has clearly indicated that this fundamental principle is wrong (see the next chapter).

Attempts to attach these arguments to physics or biology, such as comparing the death instinct with the second law of thermodynamics, have been easily refuted by pointing out that such a comparison rests on a misconception of the kind of system to which the laws of thermodynamics apply. No support has been obtained from the realm of biology, either, and most thinkers have simply ignored or given up Freud's notion of a death instinct. Jones (1957) lists Melanie Klein, Karl Menninger, and Herman Nunberg as famous psychoanalysts who did employ this concept.

It must be recognized that Freud at this point was becoming increasingly preoccupied with the problem of human aggression and human destructiveness. From this stage of his life to the end, undoubtedly stimulated by the political and social events around him, Freud became increasingly pessimistic. Certainly the self-destructive behavior of our species cannot be denied; the all-pervasive aggression and destructiveness in man is now beyond question. The terms "life instinct" and "sexual instinct" on the one hand, and "death instinct" and "destructive instinct" on the other, are used thereafter by Freud synonomously and without any distinction.

In his later *New Introductory Lectures on Psychoanalysis* (1933A; 22:3ff) he arbitrarily and without significant further argument gives these two sets of instincts equal power and force. The attractiveness of this metaphysical system is that it produces two parallel forces of equivalent importance in human life. Similarly, a parallel series can be arranged for the energies of these instincts. For example, we begin with libido, the energy of the sexual instincts directed at the self in primary narcissism. This can be aimed outward, forming object relations, and taken back, forming secondary narcissism. The energy of the death instinct or destrudo is originally aimed at the self in the mysterious primary masochistic trend of the ego. It is turned out in aggressiveness against others and can be brought back as secondary destructiveness in suicidal behavior. The death instinct can, by definition, never be directly demonstrated, but it is clear that this theory offers a unified view of self-destructive and aggressive manifestations and therefore has heuristic value.

Perhaps the best way to see how Freud moved from science to philosophy is to recognize that his final theory of life and death instincts is founded on an essentially changed concept of instincts. In the earlier view, instinct was a tension of energy which impinged upon the mental sphere, a tension which arose from an organic force—the biochemical state of the body—and which aimed at removing the state of excitation in the organ in which it originated. In the new theory, instinct becomes a mysterious directive which guides life processes in a certain direction. The emphasis is no longer on the production of energy but only upon a mysterious function determining a direction, quite reminiscent of the monadology of Leibniz.

Criticism of "Beyond the Pleasure Principle" Schur (1972) attacks the very argument of *Beyond the Pleasure Principle*. He insists that the nirvana principle and repetition compulsion are taken as proof of the death-instinct concept, which in turn is used as an explanation for these same principles—"a classical example of circular reasoning." Thus Freud had already arrived at his hypothesis of the death instinct and was using various aspects of unpleasurable repetitiveness to confirm it, while at the same time using this hypothesis to explain the observed phenomena. Schur argues strongly on the side of interpreting these phenomena as part of the urge for mastery of trauma based on the pleasure principle, not beyond it. He characterizes the ambience in which Freud accepted the death instinct as follows: "Post-war Vienna was utterly gloomy, accentuated for Freud by worry about his sons and by the painful necessity of seeing his young patient-friend 'shrink' to death, followed only a few days later by the loss of his daughter Sophie." Jones (1957) claims, to the contrary, that the work was written before the death of Sophie and the onset of Freud's cancer.

The best formal refutation of *Beyond the Pleasure Principle* is found in an earlier monograph by Schur (1966). The essence of his refutation is that the phenomena Freud designated as beyond the pleasure principle can be explained within the framework of the unpleasure–pleasure principles, and that it is not necessary to postulate a nirvana principle at all. The attribute *daemonic* is not appropriate to the characteristic of repetitiveness that pervades human behavior, since it begs the question in the meaning of the term, which is derived from *daemon*, which postulates a malevolent motivating force. Schur (1966, p. 169) explains: "The tragic fact that such patterns, instead of serving survival, end in the destruction of the phenotype, does not denote the presence of an instinct whose aim it would be to achieve this fatal goal."

Ethologists such as Lorenz view species-specific repetitive behavior patterns as the result of evolution, with eminent survival value for the species. Even the repetitive dreams of patients with traumatic neuroses can be understood as representing the ego's wish to undo the traumatic situation and to master it, a process which has survival value based on the pleasure principle. No daemonic force needs to be postulated. In fact, Schur, basing his arguments on the work of the ethologists, prefers to substitute the term "compulsive (stereotyped) repetitiveness" for the term "repetition compulsion."

Bibring (1936) arrives at a complete impasse when he attempts to justify the theory of the death instinct. A vast and unsatisfactory literature has grown up on this topic, but it has been engendered by the error of moving instinct theory far from clinical data and into the realm of pre-Socratic speculation.

Dropping the notion of *Eros* and *Thanatos* as causal explanatory hypotheses involving mysterious forces, it is generally agreed, in no way vitiates the daily work of psychoanalytic psychotherapy. Dropping this notion simply leaves the theoretical aspects involving instincts and psychic energies in a state of disarray, which offends our natural tendency to neatness and order. The entire history of science has shown that for the progress of science to continue, it is not necessary to postulate mysterious entities as causal explanatory hypotheses. Thus the *origins* of human destructiveness and of human narcissism remain highly debated, but clinically speaking the energies of narcissism, sex, and destructiveness can be observed undergoing various transformations and combinations in the life of any person, and we can delineate developmental stages from more primitive to more mature transformations of such energies. From the point of view of scientific and therapeutic work that is sufficient. An identical attitude is maintained in physics, where transformations of energy are commonly studied even in classical mechanics; the metaphysical question "What is energy?" is not asked. Some philosophers—notably Wittgenstein—would characterize the very question as an improper use of language, akin to the question "What is substance?" which preoccupied philosophers of the eighteenth century and before. The abstraction of an operationally defined term into an entity seems to be a common human tendency which leads us into serious metaphysical difficulties.

Freud's Later Epistemology Freud's final major theoretical work, written in his sixties, and described as a "further development" of his thoughts in *Beyond the Pleasure Principle* is *The Ego and the Id* (1923B;19:3ff). Parts of this work have a curious although unintended resemblance to Kant's *Critique of Pure Reason.*

The term *id* was chosen to translate the German *es* (it), an impersonal term Freud used to designate the nonpersonal part of the mind as distinct from the ego or self. A clear distinction between ego and self is never made by Freud. The term *es* was used extensively by Nietzsche, but Freud's choice of the term was influenced by the work of the internist Groddeck.*

The concept of *it* fits more naturally within the German language, where it is grammatically correct to say, for example, "It dreamed to me," usually translated into English as "I dreamed". (The presence of this grammatical "middle voice" partly underlies Heidegger's repeated arguments in favor of German and Greek as the only appropriate languages for philosophy.)

The Ego and the Id presents what is now known as the structural theory of the human mind. This new theory became necessary for two major reasons (discussed later in greater detail). Freud realized that the unconscious contains more than repressed infantile sexual wishes, and that a large section of psychic functioning, especially involving defenses and resistances, goes on in the unconscious mind. In addition, the clinical discovery of patients with an unconscious need for punishment and failure required the postulation of a moral and punitive agency, at least a part of which is also unconscious.

The parallel between Freud's notion of this moral agent, or superego, and Nietzsche's discussion of "bad conscience" is emphasized by Jones (1957). He quotes at length from Nietzsche's *Genealogy of Morals* to demonstrate the parallel.

The ego, when defined as an entity through which the individual becomes conscious of his own existence and the existence of the external world, is also a historic philosophical concept; Ellenberger (1970) reminds us that this definition of the ego is almost identical to that postulated by Fichte. Freud's definition of the ego as "the coordinated organization of mental processes in a person" is strikingly reminiscent of Kant's understanding of the mind as an active ordering process. Thus for Kant the mind is not a "thing" at all—it is the ordering process itself (Jones 1969).

In the opening paragraphs of this work Freud writes, "To most people who have been educated in philosophy the idea of anything psychical which is not also conscious is so inconceivable that it seems to them absurd and refutable simply by logic" (p. 13). As Kohut and Seitz (1963) point out, he cleverly overcame an ingrained prejudice about the mind "in order to define consciousness as merely a sensory organ and to recognize not only that

*This remarkably intuitive physician achieved excellent results in psychosomatic disorders and published his approach in *The Book of the It* (1961). He correctly considered himself a wild analyst and there is a curious mysticism to his notion of the "it" that is more reminiscent of Schopenhauer than of Freud. Grossman (1965) reviews his life and work.

mental processes may occur outside of consciousness but that consciousness is not, at any time, an essential quality of mental activities" (p. 117).

At several points in his writings Freud makes derogatory comments about philosophy, and claims that he deliberately cut himself off from conscious study of philosophy, fearing to be influenced by philosophical speculation. For example, philosophers are supposed by Freud to propose that the Pcs. and the Ucs. should be described as two species or stages of "psychoid," here again implying that the philosophers can recognize perhaps a gradient of access to the consciousness but not the notion of unconscious mental phenomena.

In the first section the ego is defined as a coherent organization of mental processes and it is pointed out that the unconscious does not coincide with the repressed: "It is still true that all that is repressed is Ucs., but not all that is Ucs. is repressed. A part of the ego, too—and Heaven knows how important a part—may be Ucs., undoubtedly is Ucs" (p. 18).

Moving from what are essentially definitions in the first section, we come in the second section to a discussion remarkably reminiscent of Kant. Freud begins by asking "What does it mean when we say 'making something conscious'? How can that come about?" (p. 19). He then refers us to a discussion (already summarized) in his paper "The Unconscious," where it has been explained that mnemic residues emerge from the unconscious to the preconscious by becoming connected with word-presentations. Once this connection has taken place, the eye of the conscious can focus upon these word-presentations, at which point they become conscious. (This concept has earlier been discussed at length.)

In a turgid paragraph Freud turns to the old philosophical question of distinguishing between a vivid memory and an external perception on the one hand, and a hallucination on the other. His description of mental functioning at this point must be regarded as pure philosophy, in the tradition of the *Critique of Pure Reason.* Arlow and Brenner (1964) point out, in addition, a clinical root to Freud's painstaking distinction between nonverbal memory traces in the system Ucs. and their connection with word-presentations in the system Pcs. Freud believed that the infantile wishes remain unchanged in the system Ucs. and give rise to symptom formation when they press too hard on the repression barrier. These infantile wishes could gain access to the consciousness when they could be verbalized in the analytic situation, at which point the symptom disappears. "It was in correspondence with these clinical findings that he was led to assume that memory traces of the system Ucs. are nonverbal, while those of the Pcs. are verbal" (p. 17). In this way we see that Freud's hypotheses are *different* than those of speculative metaphysics, for they are formed out of that combination of creativity and experimental results that characterizes hypothesis formation in science. It is possible to argue that Kant's theory of mental functioning could be characterized as arising from a similar combination of his creative genius and his own introspective study of his own mental functioning.

In the psychotic patient there is not simply the barring of certain mnemic images from gaining access to a connection with word-presentations in the system Pcs. In neurotic repression these mnemic images still retain their libidinal excitation and indeed may be strongly cathected with libido and may bring about a failure of repression by the force of this libido, with the consequent formation of a neurotic symptom. However, in psychoses there is an actual decathexis of the repressed nonverbal mnemic images—a withdrawal of the libidinal excitation which was formally attached to them. Arlow and Brenner (1964) explain: "They are without libidinal charge and, as a consequence, the objects of the environment to which they correspond are deprived of their former importance and meaning to the individual. They have lost all emotional significance. They no longer exist for him" (p. 153). In the psychoses, on Freud's theory, if this detached libido is directed toward the patient's self, hypochondriasis develops; if it is directed toward the patient's ego, psychotic grandiosity and megalomanic symptoms follow.

Freud explains delusions and hallucinations as attempts to recathect object representations, and thus characteristic of a second or restitutive phase of the psychotic patient's illness. However, as previously explained, this recathexis is postulated by Freud as limited to word-presentations in the system Pcs. and not possible of being attached once again to the mnemic images in the system Ucs. Thus because delusions and hallucinations are derived entirely from a hypercathexis of auditory and visual components of word-presentations in the system Pcs., they have a distinctly different quality from vivid memories and external perceptions. Freud later modified this approach by introducing the concept of "reality testing" as an important ego function, as we shall see in discussion of a later paper, but he apparently retained his original thesis that the initial phase of psychoses is one of decathexis of the mnemic images in the system Ucs.

The Hegelian implication here is that thinking in pictures stands nearer to unconscious processes than does thinking in words, and as Freud writes, "It is unquestionably older than the latter both ontogenetically and philogenetically" (p. 21). Recent research with infants and young children does not support this Hegelian hypothesis.

An additional complication is introduced on the question of feelings or affects. No satisfactory psychoanalytic theory of affects has been developed as of this date; for example, the entire Jerusalem Congress of International Psychoanalytic Association of 1977 was devoted to this subject, as reviewed in the *International Journal of Psychoanalysis* (vol. 58). Freud's position, as described in the last chapter, is that whereas with unconscious mnemic images, connecting links with verbal presentations must be created before they can become conscious, feelings from the unconscious are transmitted directly and there is no distinction between Cs. and Pcs. where feelings are concerned. Thus here the Pcs. drops out, and feelings are either conscious or unconscious. "Even when they are attached to word-presentations, their becoming conscious is not due to that circumstance, but they become so directly" (p. 23).

In a remarkably philosophical conclusion Freud explains that the role of word-presentations is to bring unconscious mnemic images into conscious perceptions. "It is like a demonstration of the theorem that all knowledge has its origin in external perception." Although this statement seems to place Freud in the empirical tradition, he immediately continues: "When a hypercathexis of the process of thinking takes place, thoughts are *actually* perceived—as if they came from without—and are consequently held to be true" (ibid). This depiction of the end products of an experiential world is clearly in the tradition of Kant, rather than pure empiricism.

In the next section of *The Ego and the Id* Freud somewhat casually presents a moral philosophy. For example, he postulates that religion, morality, and a social sense, as well as science and art, are "the chief elements in the higher side of man," and that the first three of these were originally one and the same thing. Religion and moral restraints come about through the process of mastering the Oedipus complex, with the subsequent formation of the superego; social feeling comes about through the necessity of overcoming the rivalry that remains between the members of the younger generation. The superego is the heir of the Oedipus complex, and the formation of the ego ideal demonstrates that the ego has mastered the Oedipus complex. The ego ideal

> answers to everything that is expected of the higher nature of man. As a substitute for a longing for the father, it contains the germ from which all religions have evolved. The self-judgment which declares that the ego falls short of its ideal produces the religious sense of humility to which the believer appeals in his longing. As a child grows up, the role of father is carried on by teachers and others in authority; their injunctions and prohibitions remain powerful in the ego ideal and continue, in the form of conscience, to exercise the moral censorship. The tension between the demands of the conscience and the actual performances of the ego is experienced as a sense of guilt. Social feelings rest on identifications with other people on the basis of having the same ego ideal (p. 37).

This is Freud's answer to Kant's wonder about the moral law within!

As Freud continues in the remaining sections of *The Ego and the Id* he moves away from a Kantian discussion to the language of the humanistic imagination (Chessick 1971, 1974). A curious Aristotelian teleology and anthropomorphization creeps, perhaps unconsciously, into his discussion of the ego; for example, he compares the ego to the well-known homunculus of the cerebral cortex, known to neuroanatomists as the projection of motor neurons from the body. The homunculus is usually shown in neuroanantomy textbooks as a distorted picture of a little human being and indeed, Freud describes the ego as a little human being inside the head. This "poor creature" (p. 56), the little man within the man—the ego—is placed in the limelight of psychoanalysis.

In addition to a further discussion of the life and death instincts, already presented in *Beyond the Pleasure Principle*, *The Ego and the Id* bears an important relationship to the existentialist question of the fear of death. According to Freud's formulation, the more a man controls his aggressiveness, the more intense becomes his ego ideal's inclination to aggressiveness against his own ego. Thus the superego has a direct link to the id and can borrow destructiveness and turn it against the ego. Even ordinary normal morality, Freud points out, has a harshly restraining, cooly prohibiting quality. "It is from this, indeed, that the conception arises of a higher being who deals out punishment inexorably" (p. 54).

The fear of death, described by existentialists as an important aspect of man's being-in-the-world, is attributed by Freud to an intrapsychic interaction between the ego and the superego. This interaction has to do with the fear of loss of love, of the withdrawal of love by the superego, which is given the function of protecting and saving in the role of a father, Providence, or God. Underlying the fear of death is the infantile anxiety and longing due to the separation from the protecting mother. This linkage between existential dread and the longing for the mother is discussed at length in a previous work (Chessick 1969).

Freud's *The Ego and the Id* represents in a condensed form a philosophical position remarkably analogous to that of Kant. It begins with the topographic theory of the processes of mental functioning and shifts to the structural theory, partly in order to explain problems of morality and religion. A great similarity is found in the philosophy of Kant, who begins in the *Critique of Pure Reason* to delimit man as a phenomenal creature bound by the laws of chemistry and physics and hemmed in to restrictions in his knowledge by the nature of his mental functioning itself, and then moves to man as a noumenal creature—to the language of the humanistic imagination—in order to make room for faith, morality, and religion. It is true that Freud and Kant end up with different explanations for man as a noumenal creature as they attempt to account for his sense of free will and his need for morality and religion—but these explanations are consistent since any statements about man as a noumenal creature are "regulative." Since such explanations cannot be developed from direct experience it is necessary to appeal to homunculi, teleological explanations, and metaphysical causal explanatory hypotheses. Thus in this final period of his life (he was sixty-seven when this book was published), Freud has moved into the realm of philosophy. (In a later work, *New Introductory Lectures on Psychoanalysis* [1933A;22:3ff] he summarizes the first three sections of *The Ego and the Id.*)

In "The Economic Problem of Masochism" (1924C;19:157) Freud states flatly, "Kant's categorical imperative is thus the direct heir of the Oedipus complex." In Freud's view, moral laws within us can be explained by personality development rather than by Kant's regulative concepts of God and the self. Freud maintains that the Oedipus complex is the source of our individual ethical sense and our morality.

Perhaps this is why Freud reluctantly concludes:

> So it comes about that psychoanalysis derives nothing but disadvantages from its middle position between medicine and philosophy. Doctors regard it as a speculative system and refuse to believe that, like any other natural science, it is based on a patient and tireless elaboration of facts from the world of perception; philosophers, measuring it by the standard of their own artificially constructed systems, find that it starts from impossible premises and reproach it because its most general concepts (which are only now in process of evolution) lack clarity and precision (1925E;19:217).

Rapaport (1951) reminds us that philosophical psychology, the predecessor of scientific psychology, was a subsidiary of epistemology in that its major question was: How do we acquire our knowledge of the world of reality? The famous works in this area, such as Bacon's *Novum Organum*, Descartes' *Meditations on First Philosophy*, Locke's *An Essay Concerning Human Understanding*, Hume's *An Enquiry Concerning Human Understanding*, as well as many others, deal primarily with this important question.

Freud repeatedly postulates that attention is the function of the system Cs. Thus to obtain attention-cathexis and to become conscious are synonymous. In "A Note Upon the Mystic Writing Pad" (1925A;19:226ff) he follows a tradition established by Plato in the *Theatetus*, in which the mind is considered as containing a block of wax on which perceptions and thoughts are imprinted as a real block of wax receives the impression from the seal of a ring.

The well-known mystic writing pad contains a slab of wax over which is laid a thin transparent sheet, the top of which is firmly secured to the wax slab. The transparent sheet is made up of two layers which are detachable: the top layer is a transparent piece of celluloid, while the bottom layer is translucent waxed paper. Using a pointed stylus, one writes on the celluloid.

To destroy what has been written the double covering sheet is peeled back from the wax slab. Although such a pad provides a surface that can be used over and over again, the wax slab retains permanent traces of what has been written.

The celluloid portion of the covering sheet represents the protective shield against external stimuli mentioned by Freud in *Beyond the Pleasure Principle.* It is the task of this aspect of the perceptual apparatus of the mind to diminish the strength of the incoming excitations. Writing on the celluloid sheet leaves no trace on the celluloid if it is raised from the wax slab.

The bottom layer of the covering sheet, the surface receiving the pressure of the stylus through the celluloid, is the system Pcpt.-Cs. Here, too, no permanent trace of the writing remains when the two-layer covering sheet is lifted from the wax. Thus the system Pcpt.-Cs. receives perceptions but retains no permanent trace of them; hence, it can act as a clean sheet to every new perception. The permanent traces of the excitations are preserved in the unconscious series of mnemic systems lying behind the perceptual system—the wax slab of the mystic pad.

Cathected innervations are sent out and withdrawn in rapid periodic impulses from within into the system Pcpt.-Cs. This cathexis is necessary from within in order for that system Pcpt.-Cs. to function and receive perceptions which attain consciousness. Thus the system Ucs. periodically extends toward the system Pcpt.-Cs. by periodically cathecting it, making it possible for the latter to receive impressions from the outside world. This periodic recathexis of the system Pcpt.-Cs. enables it to have energy to function. Those periods during which the system Pcpt.-Cs. is not cathected from within are compared to the breaking of contact in the mystic writing pad, when the top sheets are separated from the wax.

According to Freud, this periodic non-excitability of the perceptual system, leading to a discontinuous method of functioning of this system Pcpt.-Cs., forms the basis of our concept of time. Furthermore, the system Pcpt.-Cs., can use the energy available to it either for forming a countercathexis or for a periodic hypercathexis toward the environment—which results in a focusing of attention on the environment. This periodic flickering-up due to fluctuation in the distribution of attention cathexis is called "the notational function of attention" by Freud. Thus the system Pcpt.-Cs. sends out periodic focus on the environment in a way analogous to the periodic cathexis of the system Pcpt.-Cs. sent out from the system Ucs.

We see how close Freud's view at times is to Kant's view, in which time is the a priori formal condition of all appearances whatsoever; all representations, whether or not they have external things as their objects, must be subject to the formal condition of our inner sense of intuition: namely, time (Copleston 1964).

Freud therefore presents a definitive epistemological viewpoint on conscious mentation. The eye of consciousness is a sense organ for the perception of psychic qualities. This sense organ is excitable by psychic qualities but devoid of memory. Conscious mentation is the effect of the attention-cathexis, and this attention-cathexis represents energy at its disposal. Early in development this energy is distributed according to the pleasure principle, and later by the reality principle. The energy may be utilized either as counter-cathexis to establish and maintain repression or as hypercathexis to produce consciousness.

Having discussed the nature of consciousness and our sense of time, Freud, in the tradition of a true epistemologist, turns in the brief paper "Negation" (1925H;19:234ff), to the nature of judgment. For Freud, judgment either affirms or disaffirms "the possession by a thing of a particular attribute" or "it asserts or disputes that a presentation has an existence in reality" (p. 236). The most primitive form of judgment attempts to decide by motor activity what is "me" and what is "not me", or what is internal and what is external. The next but still primitive form of judgment attempts to accept only the pleasurable and to reject painful excitations both from the internal and external world. Furthermore, at the beginning of mental development "what is bad, what is alien to the ego and what is external are, to begin with, identical" (p. 237).

Negation is a way of making conscious what is repressed. The content of a repressed mnemic trace makes its way up into consciousness on the condition that it is negated. Thus after an interpretation the patient may deny the existence of a repressed idea which he has just admitted into consciousness. A negative judgment is the intellectual substitute for a repression and this leads Freud to the whole issue of the function of judgment.

When the ego has come under the sway of the reality principle, the major function of judgment shifts to the question of the real existence of a presentation, a situation that we call reality-testing. This represents a step forward.

All presentations originate from perception. Thinking possesses the capacity to bring before the mind once more something that has once been perceived, by reproducing it as a presentation without the external object having still to be there. Freud writes, "What is unreal, merely a presentation and subjective, is only internal; what is real is also there *outside*" (p. 237). Thus the function of judgment is to discern whether a perception is *merely* internal or whether there is in reality a counterpart to the perception. Reality-testing, therefore, consists of convincing oneself that the object which is being perceived is still really out there. Furthermore, it must decide whether a given perception is faithful or whether it has been modified and distorted. Thus, consistent with modern cybernetics, reality-testing or judgment seems to be a scanning procedure in which a given perception is compared with previous perceptions in an effort to form a sense of conviction that the perception is actually coming from outside oneself.

Freud continues by defining judging as an intellectual act which decides the choice of motor action; it "puts an end to the postponement due to thought and which leads over from thinking to acting" (p. 238). This description of judgment comes from the "Project for a Scientific Psychology" which, as has been explained, rests primarily on psychophysical parallelism. At this point Freud clearly is not worrying about the philosophical inconsistencies in his position but is trying to establish how the function of judgment develops from the primitive functions of distinguishing between the internal and the external world, as well as from the incorporation of the pleasurable and extrusion of the unpleasurable.

A final sudden change is also introduced in theory. In this paper Freud conceives of the *ego* as periodically sending out cathexes to the system Pcpt-Cs., in contrast to his earlier notion, discussed above, of these cathexes coming from the system Ucs. This view is more consistent with his later structural theory of the mental apparatus.

Freud's work was clearly in the Kantian tradition of investigating epistemology through a focus on our thought processes. The task of integrating psychoanalytic metapsychology with Kantian epistemology was attempted by Rapaport in four major books (1951, 1960, 1961, 1967). Copleston (1964) points out that for Kant the metaphysics of the future should be a transcendental critique of human experience and knowledge; this critique represents what might be called a scientific metaphysics. For Kant the human mind's reflective awareness of its own spontaneous formative activity is the science of metaphysics or at least approximates a scientific procedure. Kant's concept provides a modest idea of the scope and power of metaphysics, especially if one compares it, for example, to the fantastic inflation of the same concept into a metaphysics of "reality" by such Absolute Idealists as Fichte, Schelling, and Hegel.

On the whole, Freud followed a similar procedure. Of course he reached different conclusions; for example, in a fragment published posthumously he writes: "Space may be the projection of the extension of the psychical apparatus. No other derivation is probable. Instead of Kant's *ápriori* determinants of our physical apparatus. Psyche is extended; knows nothing about it" (1941F;23:300).

It is not fair to criticize this quotation since it is only a brief note and was never developed by Freud. Although unsupported by arguments, it serves to illustrate that Kant's approach was on Freud's mind to the end.

Certain other discussions in Freud's last published works indicate that toward the end of his life he was beginning to grapple with direct epistemological problems. For example, he begins *An Outline of Psychoanalysis*

(1940A;23:141ff) with what he calls a basic assumption "reserved to philosophical thought." This assumption is that we know two kinds of things about our mental life: its bodily organ, the brain, and our acts of consciousness "which are immediate data and cannot be further explained by any sort of description." Everything that lies between, according to Freud, is unknown to us, "and the data do not include any direct relation between these two terminal points of our knowledge." He further assumes that mental life is the functioning of an apparatus "to which we ascribe the characteristics of being extended in space and of being made up of several portions," but nothing is known of the localization of this psychical apparatus in the organ of mind (brain). According to Freud, the extension of the mental apparatus in space, when projected, gives us our notion of space. Thus whereas Kant extracts our notion of space from experiential data, Freud attributes this notion to a projection of the extension of our mental apparatus in space.

A philosophical discussion is briefly continued in the same work on pages 196–7. Freud compares psychoanalytic psychology to that of other sciences such as physics, and he proclaims that in all sciences the problem is the same: behind the phenomena or qualities of the object under examination presented directly by perception,

> We have to discover something else which is more independent of the particular receptive capacity of our sense organs and which approximates more closely to what may be supposed to be the real state of affairs. We have no hope of being able to reach the latter itself, since it is evident that everything new that we have inferred must nevertheless be translated back into the language of our perceptions, from which it is simply impossible for us to free ourselves. But herein lies the very nature and limitation of our science (p. 196).

Thus for Freud, "reality" remains unknowable, and the yield from scientific work on our sense perceptions consists of an insight into connections and dependent relationships as they manifest themselves in the phenomenal world. He believes that this approach gives us an insight into connection and dependent relationships present in the world of "reality"—that which he calls the external world. In order to reach this understanding we have to infer a number of processes which are in themselves "unknowable" and interpolate them in the phenomena of our conscious perception.

Here Freud falls into the same error made by Kant. Kant also assumed that the "real" world, the noumenal world, was unknowable, and yet he spoke of it as being causally efficacious. By Kant's own philosophy the notion of causality cannot be applied to the noumenal world because "causality" is an a priori condition of our experience of the phenomenal world, and outside of this it has no meaning. Freud's use of the unconscious is more like

Kant's use of the regulative principles to which we are forced in order to explain certain phenomena, but which can never be proven by the method of science. Thus going back to the original example, one could never "prove" that our notion of space stems from the projection of our mental apparatus that exists in space. Because Kant at least attempts to extract our notion of space from phenomenal experience, he appears to be closer to a scientific procedure than Freud in his contention about space.

Freud picks this problem up again in an unfinished fragment "Some Elementary Lessons in Psychoanalysis" (1940B;23:280ff), where he discusses the nature of the "psychical." He brings us back to the same problem that Kant was trying to solve, by explaining that equating what is mental with what is conscious has the unwelcome result of separating psychical processes from the general context of events and the universe and setting them in complete contrast to all others—in other words, the Cartesian dualism. He makes the classic criticism against Cartesian dualism: we know that psychical phenomena are dependent to a high degree upon somatic processes and we cannot, in the Cartesian system, account for interaction between the psychic and the physical. He reminds us that psychophysical parallelism, as a result of this criticism, foundered on the impossibility of explaining the intermediaries in the reciprocal relationship of body and mind.

Freud offers his solution of the Cartesian dualism by redefining what is psychical. Consciousness is not the essence of what is psychical for Freud; it is only an inconstant quality of what is psychical, far more often absent than present: "The psychical, whatever its nature may be, is in itself unconscious and probably similar in kind to all the other natural processes of which we have obtained knowledge" (p. 283). Although Freud does not acknowledge explicitly the fact, these views lead him to a monistic materialist ontology most resembling that of Hobbes. "The core of our being," Freud writes in *An Outline of Psychoanalysis* (1940A;23:197), "is formed by the obscure *id*, which has no direct communication with the external world and is accessible even to our own knowledge only through the medium of another agency." For Freud, the id plays the role that the noumenal world plays for Kant. Freud then proceeds to tell us about this obscure, unknowable id in his discussion of the primal organic instincts, as he calls them, that operate within it (Eros and Destructiveness). In "Analysis Terminable and Interminable" (1937C;23:211ff), he compares his view to that of the pre-Socratic philosopher Empedocles, who postulated two powers, similar to Freud's, that operate on the four primal elements. One strives to agglomerate the primal particles of the four elements into a single unity; while the other, on the contrary, seeks to undo those fusions and to separate primal particles of the elements from one another. Freud insists that the philosopher's theory is a cosmic fantasy, while he claims biological validity for his theory.

Freud was not a professional philosopher. He seems unaware that by redefining the mental as psychical events which may or may not—usually not—possess the quality of consciousness, he is not eliminating the mind-brain problem. By insisting that mental events at their base have an organic or materialist nature, he runs into the same problem faced by Hobbes: how one moves from this obscure material base to the conscious phenomena of perception. In order to explain this problem, Hobbes was forced to introduce his doctrine of phantasms, which was completely inconsistent with his own philosophy.

Freud deals with the problem by ignoring it. From the obscure material base in the id ruled by the two primal organic instincts, to the psychic mnemic representations in the id or the unconscious, there is a crucial conceptual leap. Nothing is said in all Freud's writings about how this leap takes place. His work begins not with the organic "reality" in the id, which is unknowable, but with the primitive mnemic representations in the unconscious. He extends our conception of the mental, but it remains mental rather than organic. After making this extension of our concept of the mental, which is justifiable on the basis of the clinical data, he studies mental functioning in a manner very similar to Kant's approach in *Critique of Pure Reason*, and from it he draws certain principles of mental functioning which are at times similar to Kant's a priori principles of the understanding.

The argument about the therapeutic validity of psychoanalysis does not rest on Freud's failure to solve the mind-body problem, as it is perfectly possible to drop the organic aspect of the id as well as Freud's famous life and death instincts and carry on an effective clinical science of psychoanalytic psychotherapy.

The great debate in science regarding psychoanalysis concerns the issue of Freud's inference of unconscious mental processes filling in the gaps of our conscious perception of events. Allowing Freud to fill in the gaps in our conscious mental phenomena with his notion of unconscious processes permits psychoanalysis to study the data of mental processes in a manner akin to any natural science. It also permits Freud to make higher-level abstractions such as the pleasure principle or reality principle, and even higher abstractions such as the ego and superego, which are epistemological premises determined by a method similar to that of Kant when he established his a priori principles of the understanding.

Although in his approach Freud follows a time-honored procedure in classical science, he does not escape—any more than any other field of scientific investigation—the philosophical problems underlying the scientific method. What weakens psychoanalysis with respect to the other natural sciences is that some of the data investigated cannot be directly perceived or measured except by their effects, and must be inferred. It is Freud's correct point that granting this inference, psychoanalysis may proceed in the manner of a natural science.

It is only when he attempts to discuss the obscure nature of the id and the primitive life and death instincts that Freud falls into the error of Kant who, after eliminating the noumenal world from our understanding, proceeds to discuss it as if it were a world of presentational objects or "things." The same tension exists in the philosophy of Freud as exists in the philosophy of Kant. So that he could establish his preconceived pietistic moral viewpoints, Kant attempted to limit the sphere of reason in order to make room for faith. Somewhat similarly, Freud constantly finds himself involved in the language of the humanistic imagination with its anthropomorphizing concepts such as the ego or the life and death instincts, concepts which run counter to his philosophy of psychic determinism of the most rigid nature.

Many authors, as we shall see in the next chapter, have pointed out two fundamental weaknesses of psychoanalysis, first in the metaphysical area and second in its epistemological foundations. In the realm of the metaphysical, the notion of the id and life and death instincts belongs to the noumenal world. In the realm of the epistemological, as mentioned above, an inference—from consciously perceived data to the "data" of unconscious mental events—makes psychoanalysis different fundamentally from the other natural sciences, both in the nature of the data studied and in the difficulties of verification. This is why Popper, for example, rejects psychoanalysis as a science, since there is no crucial experiment upon which the basic hypotheses stand or fall—inferred data can always be invoked to maintain the validity of almost any hypotheses. For the same reason Wittgenstein (1967) also condemned psychoanalysis as "a mythological system." Fortunately, these theoretical weaknesses do not affect the clinical day-to-day practice of psychoanalysis and intensive psychotherapy, which are highly efficacious and related methods of treatment.

In a way, Aristotle is more sympathetic to the psychoanalytic approach than are modern philosophers. For example, Copleston (1962) reminds us of the beginning of *De Anima* where Aristotle explains that the problem of investigating the soul is very difficult because it is not easy to ascertain the right method to be employed—the speculative philosopher and the naturalist have different standpoints and so frame their definitions differently. Copleston explains, "It is not every thinker that has recognized that different sciences have their different methods, and that because the particular science cannot employ the method of the chemist or natural scientist, it does not follow that all its conclusions must necessarily be vitiated" (p. 69).

22

CRITICISM

Metapsychology for Freud is a causal explanatory system, substituting causal psychological explanations for our missing causal organic explanations of mental processes. He insists that his construction of a mental apparatus is justified by his clinical observations, but Basch (1973) makes it clear that philosophers of science have agreed that *no* hypothetical theory can be abstracted directly from observation. He quotes Einstein's statement that there is no logical bridge between phenomena and their theoretical principles. Thus for Basch, the mental apparatus is a bogus or pseudo-entity, one whose potential existence can never be proven or disproven. Basch explains:

> The experimental evidence has shown that sensory qualities, images, and words are not the building blocks of thought processes. Thinking is a biochemical and electromagnetic process which periodically and in small part may be translated into the form of subjective awareness. Becoming conscious is an activity of the brain signifying a brain state which occurs when a particular, as yet unknown, relationship obtains within that organ (p. 50).

Thus our division of the phenomena of consciousness into sensory qualities, images, words, etc., is not informative about the process of thinking. Nothing can be learned about the nature of thought through the psychoanalytic method. Freud himself stated (1933A;22:90): "First, I must admit that I have tried to translate into the language of our normal thinking what must in fact be a process that is neither conscious nor preconscious, taking place between quotas of energy in some unimaginable substratum."

It is clear that Freud had a great deal to say about the nature of thought. On the premise of psycho–physical parallelism, he attempted to construct a mental apparatus of a psychological nature only, totally extricating himself from the problem of what simultaneously goes on in the brain. Thought, for Freud, consists of two components. The first of these is judgment in which the system Pcpt.-Cs. compares an emerging word-presentation linked to a thing-presentation with successive memory traces to determine correspondence to reality. Second comes trial action, which for Freud represents an experimental way of acting, using small bits of energy cathexis without involving the motor apparatus; we commonly refer to this as thinking about the subject. Thus in the obsessive-compulsive neuroses, where the superego blocks in a massive fashion the infusion of energy into the motor apparatus, energy dams up, floods backwards, and hypercathects the thought system. The result is obsessive thinking which drains the energy in a substitute way.

Basch (1975, 1975*a*) points out many difficulties. For example, a basic epistemological premise maintained throughout Freud's writings is the assumption that perceptions are endowed with sensory quality and are therefore primarily conscious, while instinctual drives are not of a sensory nature and can become conscious only by becoming united with perceptual residues. Klein (1959) reviews the impressive body of evidence validating the fact that the brain registers and utilizes stimuli from the external world, stimuli which would never exist in subjective awareness; this contradicts Freud's fundamental postulate equating perception with consciousness in the system Pcpt.-Cs. In later publications Klein (1976) calls for the elimination of many aspects of metapsychology from psychoanalysis, and presents some alternative, more experience-near concepts.

Basch considers Freud's "Project for a Scientific Psychology" as the author's most comprehensive metapsychological effort, containing many of his basic ideas on the subject. Basch concludes: "Freud would have been more accurate had he said, in the language of the 'topographic theory', that sensory percepts are 'preconscious' from the very first" (1975, p. 16). Thus the manner in which a percept attains the state of subjective awareness remains unknown.

Since metapsychological concepts cannot be said to have been directly inferred from clinical work, they are subject to revision, without affecting the clinical findings and clinical practice of psychoanalytic psychotherapy. Metapsychological constructs are for the purpose of explaining clinical findings, and insofar as these formulations fail to achieve this explanation and are directly contradictory to independent evidence gathered by other valid methods of scientific investigation, Basch argues that they should be replaced. Thus although Freud's hypothetical-deductive theory of mentation is a brilliant model of epistemologic elegance, it must be replaced, insists Basch, by a twentieth-century counterpart (1973, 1976).

The basic official presentation of Freud's metapsychology is generally agreed to be found in chapter VII of *The Interpretation of Dreams*. Basch (1976*a*) subjects this chapter to a careful epistemologic analysis, pointing out that it is replete with undefined terms such as "mental process" or "psychical acts." For Freud, even terms such as "mind" or "mental apparatus" were self-evident. In his eagerness to get away from neurophysiology and problems of brain function, he seems to have ignored the fact that philosophers have been arguing about these concepts for thousands of years. In his psycho-physical parallelism, Freud equates the mental apparatus with the brain and in so doing he presents a study of thought formation in general psychology. In this study the concept of brain as a physical entity is replaced by the concept of "mental apparatus," essentially a brain without anatomical properties, carrying out mental functions. This conflicts with Ryle's (1949) criticism of the mind (or mental apparatus) as a ghost concept and resting on a category mistake. Basch would substitute the systems theory, known as the systems effect of ongoing relationships: "A system has an existence that is dependent on a lower order substrate, but generates effects that both transcend that substrate's capacity and could not have been predicted from examining the substrate alone" (1976*a*, p. 72).

Thus Freud kept trying to create a psychologic substrate for psychological effects working within the paradigm of Newtonian physics; but there is only one substrate, the brain, which is a matter for neurology to investigate. Psychotherapy investigates the laws of behavior for thoughts, ideas, and memories, but this approach neither necessitates nor implies establishing causal explanations for the behavioral process itself, according to Toulmin (1953).

In Freud, the Cartesian dualism reasserts itself in the implication that thought, mind, and mental apparatus are somehow something different and beyond the physical. The term "mental apparatus" cannot be defended as a way of categorizing psychologic phenomena in the manner that biologists make classifications, because "mental apparatus" has been given a generative capacity with causal substantive explanatory value. For Freud, the clinical observation that some mentation is conscious, some preconscious, and some unconscious became expanded into reified systems: the generative entities Ucs., Pcs., and Pcpt.-Cs. of the topographical theory.

Freud's concept of perception was simplistic, assuming the sequence "stimulus–perception–memory." We know however, that perception does not antedate conception, "but that, to the contrary, conception creates a 'perceptual set', which determines how stimuli are perceived" (Basch 1976*a*, p. 78). The whole notion that dream formation is based on a regression to hallucinatory wish-fulfillment assumes that perceptions, or sensory images, are the simple beginning of mentation in infancy; yet Piaget has demonstrated experimentally that evocative recall through imaging does not occur in mentation until about eighteen months of age. Similarly, "The progression from perception to hypothetical–deductive thinking and then to a muscular action described by Freud does not correspond with what is known today of mentation" (Basch 1976*a*, pp. 82–3).

Freud's application of Fechner's principle of constancy to stimulation and discharge in the mental apparatus was in error, since Fechner's principle does not apply to biological or living systems. There is considerable experimental evidence to support the contention that the brain is a stimulus-seeking rather than a stimulus-avoiding system. Similarly, Freud's use of a concept of "psychic energy" is untenable because it substitutes an obscure metaphorical force for a mathematical abstraction in the field of physics. The use of energy in physics has a precise mathematical and measurable meaning which it does not have in Freud's application of it to the mental apparatus.

Basch (1975*a*) gives us an example of how he would substitute systems theory for Freud's causal explanatory concepts. This approach has the advantage of being *au fait* with current experimental research and twentieth-century theoretical paradigms. For Basch, mind and brain form a hierarchy in the general systems sense, not a unity; the brain supplies the fuel and the molecular substrate in which message-processing takes place, and "mind" is "a word encompassing vicissitudes of encoded patterns whose relationship form [*sic*] a nonmaterial structure based on, but not equated with, brain" (p. 491). The paradigm used by Freud lacks the understanding that living systems are open systems which temporarily defy the laws of thermodynamics, move toward greater complexity, and resist disintegration. Living systems do not respond just passively but influence their environment by selective interaction and actively participate in shaping their own future—which explains why the traditional behaviorist models that naively equate behavior with what is public and overt, and eliminate private experience from consideration, are totally unsatisfactory. Instead of seeking a low-level equilibrium on Fechner's principle, the brain is continuously active in its need for optimal stimulation. As sensory-deprivation experiments have shown, the brain, instead of welcoming a peaceful state, engages in a veritable frenzy of activity in its search for stimuli and ends up by artificially providing them through fantasies, hallucinations, and so forth.

It should be noted that in general systems theory, *reality* is conceived in terms of "patterns of neural activity that reflect what signals have been received, the manner in which they have been connected with other signals past and present, and the reactions and interactions that have taken place as a result of the ordering activity" (Basch, pp. 495–6). Thus sense data represent information that the brain derives from stimuli. Such stimuli are replaced by a preconscious percept formation or, more accurately, a "not-conscious process." Our use of the term *reality* has been mistakenly reified and externalized, leading to the Cartesian dualism.

It seems to me, however, that even the general systems theory avoids the question of where the stimuli that constitute sense data originate. The theory leaves us with the Kantian dualism between the unknowable *things-in-themselves* and our knowledge of the phenomenal world. In fact, as Basch writes, "The world of so-called material objects is a part of the symbolic world; it belongs to the world of ideas as much as do our dreams. . . . This is not to deny that there is a reality apart from our reflections to which we react to perceptions, but this reality is one we never know directly" (p. 509). Thus the proposed new paradigm offers us nothing new on the old metaphysical question of our relationship to the external world; instead, it proposes a better modern explanation, more in keeping with experimental evidence, of the relationship of mind and brain.

Debates and Compromises Some of the difficulties of replacing Freud's metapsychology with a systems approach to the mind have been presented by Friedman (1972). He points out that Peterfreund's more formal theory (1971) of information and systems has only a superficial resemblance to the theories of Piaget. Actually, Piaget's theory is only one of many theories and models of mental life, and there is no one theory of Piaget, since he has repeatedly changed his conceptions. Friedman argues that the information-systems alternative is a high abstraction of potential causes and potential effects and he regards it as doubtful that "so abstract and formal a theory can make a bridge between physics and behavior" (p. 554).

The argument remains unsettled. One of the values of Peterfreund's book (1971) lies in his criticism of Freud's fundamental metapsychology, regardless of whether or not we wish to accept Peterfreund's alternative. For example, he argues convincingly that the psychoanalytic concept of psychic energy is "quite alien to the rest of the scientific world." Psychic energy appears in the psychoanalytic literature "as though it were an imponderable fluid with identity, a fluid with directional properties, a fluid whose identity can be changed, a fluid that can be dammed up, discharged, transferred, and so on. In general, current psychoanalytic theory appears to be based on a simple hydrodynamic model" (p. 53). Peterfreund pejoratively compares this "fluid" to other famous "imponderable fluids" in the history of science—phlogiston, caloric, aether, electric fluids, magnetic fluids, spirits, and essences.

Peterfreund presents a similar argument against Freud's crucial concept of the ego, a concept which is vitalistic and especially anthropomorphic. It is generally agreed that Freud in his later writings presented an increasingly anthropomorphic concept of the ego as a "ghost in the machine" (Ryle 1949) or "homunculus" (Skinner 1971) that recognizes, knows, fears, judges, and becomes the "master" of the id. Peterfreund sees Freud's ego theory as "a typically nineteenth-century vitalistic anthropomorphic concept to explain the nature of control, adaptation, regulation, integration, and organization."

Hartmann, Kris, and Loewenstein (1946) attempt to resolve the ego problem within the framework of general psychoanalytic theory. A basic anthropomorphization still remains in their work because, regardless of modifications in the language used, the mind is still viewed as an interplay of highly anthropomorphic entities such as ego and superego. Conflict is explained in terms of conflict among these various entities; the ego, furthermore, is spoken of as though it is an intelligent mind within the mind. The reason for this way of speaking is that psychoanalysts are attempting to present causal explanatory hypotheses rather than systems descriptions. Theories such as those of Peterfreund or Skinner make such fundamentally human concepts of conation, purpose, or striving seem to be illusory and to basically represent, as Friedman points out, an effort to eliminate intentionality. There are serious arguments against this (Chessick 1977*a*).

Two arguments remain current. The most radical of these, as presented by Peterfreund, would eliminate the metapsychology of Freud along with his concepts of psychic energy, id, ego, and superego. A less radical argument, based on considerable scientific evidence, challenges Freud's fundamental notion that thing-presentations exist in the unconscious and enter the preconscious by becoming associated with word-presentations, implying also, as Freud proclaims, that the earliest mode of infantile thinking occurs in hallucinatory plastic representations or mnemic images of thing-presentations.

This latter argument is very important and accounts for some of the extreme notions of the Kleinian school of psychoanalysis, in which highly complex and unbelievably sophisticated mental processes are attributed to the mind of the infant. Piaget's research established that during the earliest period of development, the so called Sensory-motor period, lasting at least until one-and-a-half years of age, coordination of action occurs in the absence of representation—without evocative memory—and during this time, adaptation is based on the recognition in action of familiar sensory-motor schemata being experienced at the moment. Thus evocative recall or imaging only develops around eighteen months of age, rather than at birth as assumed by Freud. Wish-fulfilling hallucination cannot occur in infancy, and the only "memory" present in infancy is based on the recognition of certain schemata in the presence of experience; there is no symbolic function or evocative recall of images. Thus Freud's early notion of retrogression of function assumes a primitive function that is not present.

A middle position is presented by Gedo and Goldberg (1973). These authors point out that in metapsychology we are dealing with various models of the mind, and at the present time it is not possible to devise one model which adequately portrays all of the crucial aspects of psychic life. They present five such models which are useful as conveniences: "a different model may be most useful and theoretically valid for the study of each of the various phases of an individual's life history." Although these models have been devised to explain mental conflicts, none of them represent autonomous functions such as perception or cognition—therefore, metapsychology becomes narrowed down and is no longer used to establish a basic general psychology. In a later work, Gedo (1979) also seeks to abandon metapsychology entirely, and offers a theory of his own.

It is the unwarranted extension of Freud's metapsychological explanations or working models into a general psychology that has created much of the difficulty and controversy as well as a collision with twentieth-century science. The use of these models as conveniences for organizing the clinical data of psychoanalysis, rather than their use as theoretical explanations of how the mind works, permits us to employ these extremely valuable models in the practice of intensive psychotherapy without committing ourselves to any notion that we have "explained" the working of the mind. Thus the primary purpose of each theory with its corresponding model is to facilitate the reduction and ordering of clinical data, a function which is extremely important to the psychotherapist in his continuous effort to conceptualize what is happening in the mind of his patient.

In the everyday practice of intensive psychotherapy I agree with Gedo and Goldberg that the use of models is much more practical and appropriate than attempting to restructure everything on the basis of behavioristic psychology or general systems theory. Although these models are organized in a hierarchy and appropriately so, their use avoids the issue of what "really" goes on in the minds of infants and reminds us that models are only conveniences or heuristic fictions (Chessick 1961) rather than representative of a general psychology or an attempt to describe the evolution of the mind and the brain.

Freud and Kant Among the innumerable studies of various aspects of Freud's thought, no overall studies exist from the point of view of metaphysics and epistemology. Important current studies of Freud's philosophy of science are those by Peterfreund (1971) and Basch, in a series of major papers (1973, 1975, 1975*a*, 1976, 1976*a*, 1977). These authors severely criticize Freud from two points of view. In the first place they attack Freud's philosophy of science—which is essentially Newtonian—and, as we have seen, his use of such concepts as psychic energy, which they vigorously claim is a meaningless concept produced by Freud as an effort to make psychoanalysis sound like Newtonian physics. This criticism has been addressed by Galatzer-Levy (1976) who does not see it as reason to completely revise the philosophical premises of psychoanalysis.

Piaget (1971) presents what is perhaps an extreme view about the postulation of any epistemologic premises in science or philosophy. He demands a "genetic epistemology" in which scientific study of the development of reality-testing in the child replaces philosophical reflection on how we get our knowledge and eliminates entirely the use of speculation and intuition in philosophy. Although he is polite about it, Piaget leaves little for philosophers to do except to seek what he vaguely calls "wisdom." This is an extreme illustration of Blanshard's (1969) contention: "Between the account of ideas and inference supplied by the psychologists, eager to construe their study as a natural science, and that of the epistemologists and logicians, there has gradually appeared a chasm that is now all but impassable."

A view less extreme than that of Piaget is found in the pronouncements of the scientist Lorenz (1977), who insists that all human knowledge derives from "a process of interaction between man as a physical entity, an active, perceiving subject, and the realities of an equally physical external world." He proposes to study human understanding "in the same way as any other phylogenetically evolved function which serves the purposes of survival, that is, a function of a natural physical system interacting with a physical external world."

Some post-Kantian commentators have insisted that Kant's philosophy *requires* the postulation of a real external physical world (e.g., Wilkerson 1976). Many of these authors insist that Kant's major philosophical advances were made in epistemology and the philosophy of mind; they disregard his ethics. I have reviewed the contributions of Kant to epistemology and the philosophy of mind here in a previous publication (1977*a*), where I placed Freud in the evolutionary development of general philosophical thought from Kant, Schopenhauer, and Nietzsche. The most important point, as Grene explains (1974), is that Kant has shown irrevocably that the mind as an agent shapes experience. Thus the entire empiricist image of experience as purely passive is mistaken and the existence of mind as an agent is presupposed in the very analysis of experience itself.

Freud essentially subscribed to this theory. As mentioned previously, the parallels between Freud and Kant have been explored most meticulously by Rapaport (1951, 1960, 1961, 1967), who unfortunately died before his work could be finished. Rapaport, who obtained his doctorate in epistemology, emphasized the relatedness of Kant's epistemology to the assumptions of Freud. He mentions that Piaget's studies have reached specific epistemological conclusions similar to those of Kant. Gedo (1973) presents an overall view of Rapaport's contribution.

Rapaport (see chapter 21) explains that philosophical psychology was concerned with how we acquire our knowledge of the world of reality. Freud, on the other hand, was concerned with the evaluation by the psychic apparatus of internal stimuli rather than external stimuli. Rapaport mentions the parallel to Leibniz, who formulated the problem of epistemology as, "How is it possible that reasoning arrives at conclusions which coincide with the outcome of processes occurring in reality?" He suggests that this query is parallel to Freud's question, "How can a mental apparatus regulated by the pleasure principle internally be adapted to external reality?" Although Rapaport concedes that Freud's finding—that the "psychological" appears as the determining cause of behavior (and even of some physiological processes)—points to idealism, he claims that Freud himself never made any concession to philosophical idealism—an opinion which is certainly questionable.

Basically, Freud would have agreed with Rapaport that a study of cognitive development would establish the validity of the Kantian categories, at least in general; and it is fair to say that it has been established in the previous literature—although not without notable dissent, even today—that Freud's basic epistemology is Kantian. One might argue that in the anthropomorphizations previously mentioned, Freud fell into the same error made by Kant when the latter discussed the noumenal world and the noumenal self. It is interesting that Kant, and probably Freud, would reply to this criticism by insisting that these concepts are regulative and therefore necessary in our explanations of human freedom and human behavior. Furthermore, it is remarkable that although few philosophers would still agree with Kant on this matter, many psychotherapists—including the author—still agree with Freud. A complete review of various contemporary theories of the nature of thought in psychology and philosophy is presented by Blanshard (1969). Freud's name does not appear in the index of this two-volume work, which is generally considered one of the finest overviews of the subject.

Natural Science or Hermeneutics? The empirical roots of psychoanalytic practice have been debated at great length by philosophers. Psychoanalysts have been prone to err in attempting to claim too much for their discipline and by insisting on comparing it with advanced empirical sciences such as physics. When psychoanalysis is thought of as analogous to physics it becomes vulnerable to criticisms such as those of Popper (1965), who maintained that science occurs only when there exists a community which agrees on certain empirical criteria by which statements can be falsified. Thus the theories of physics may be thought of as context-free and stand or fall by the classical methods of science. The theories of psychoanalysis are context-dependent, that is to say, psychoanalytic theory has grown out of the clinical treatment of neurotics and in that context it functions to provide suggestions for the interpretation of particular cases. In addition, it is associated with certain techniques such as the analysis of dreams, free associations, and the transference, for ferreting out repressed material in particular cases. Thus rather than explaining and generating testable hypotheses about conditions in general, psychoanalytic theory provide leads for the practicing psychotherapist. This function is discussed at length by Alston (1967).

One is reminded of such continental rationalists as Spinoza, who saw metaphysics as the queen of the sciences and was convinced that by applying scientific procedure and especially mathematics to metaphysical problems, demonstrations about reality could be provided. Kermode (1976) explains that the relevant difference between the physical and the hermeneutic sciences is that the former base their explanations on context-free laws while the latter are context-dependent: their explanations and interpretations are part of the process of context. He bases his explanation on the work of Schafer (1968), who sees interpretation as a process of giving meaning to what had lacked meaning; thus interpretation has more affinity for the humanities than for natural science—it is, in short, a hermeneutic activity. "It is simply a different kind of science and belongs to what discriminating Germans call the *Geisteswissenschaften.*"

Fischer and Greenberg (1977) review the psychoanalytic field and argue that although suggestion and the personality of the therapist are important matters in any form of psychotherapy, Freud did put forward a vast number of fruitful and challenging hypotheses concerning the nature of the human mind, and that many of these are far more testable than has been supposed. If this opinion is correct, psychotherapy tends more toward the natural sciences than that of hermeneutics. The debate remains undecided today.

The whole question of whether clinical medicine deserves scientific autonomy has been discussed by Forstrom (1977). He argues that clinical medicine should be regarded as a relatively autonomous science and not just an application of laboratory and basic sciences:

> Its contributions to medical knowledge are made within the context of patient care (the term "clinical medicine" is used here to emphasize this matter). It is distinct from other sciences in its domain of inquiry and its approach to this domain, studying relationships between events and processes of many kinds and levels as they occur in the human organism. . . . The practical justification of its approach, and of clinical medicine itself, rests in its accomplishments (p. 18).

The debate about whether psychoanalysis is primarily in the category of observational science or in the field of hermeneutics is discussed at length by Ricoeur (1970). He clearly believes that psychoanalysis is not a science of observation; rather, a psychoanalytic interpretation is "more comparable to history than to psychology." He regards the scientific status of psychoanalysis as having been subjected to devastating criticism by epistemologists, logicians, semanticists, and philosophers of language, who have generally "come to the conclusion that psychoanalysis does not satisfy the most elementary requirements of scientific theory." On reviewing the development of Freud's thought, Ricoeur insists that the development of Freudian theory can be understood as the gradual reduction or conversion of the notion of physical apparatus—in the sense of a machine which would run by itself—"to a topography in which space is no longer a place within the world, but a scene of action where roles and masks enter into debate; this space will become a place of ciphering and deciphering" (p. 70). From this it is clear why Ricoeur can write "There is no doubt that psychoanalysis is hermeneutics"—a discipline, according to Ricoeur, in which there is a correlation between energetics and hermeneutics, between connections of forces and relations of meanings. Psychoanalysis, like hermeneutics, concerns itself with coding and decoding rather than with a natural science.

Sawyer (1973) agrees with me that much of Freud's thinking is Kantian and sharply criticizes Ricoeur's work because it is based on the condition that Freud "not damage or destroy a world which Ricoeur thinks of as deeper, more meaningful. This is the world of mysticism, spirituality, art, and religion. Such a limitation on his encounter with Freud has distorted several of Ricoeur's interpretations."

On the other hand Jahoda (1977), claims that psychoanalysis *is* hermeneutics, and that Freud belongs to the *Geisteswissenschaften*, "for which the term humanistic sciences is the only available translation, even though not quite catching the connotation of the German term." She argues, however, that there is nothing in the psychoanalytic method which disqualifies psychoanalysis from the scientific task. Thomä and Kächele (1975), after an exhaustive review of the controversy over psychoanalysis as science or hermaneutics, conclude by a limited agreement with Jahoda. They distinguish steps in psychoanalytic theory: communicated observational data, clinical generalizations, clinical theory, metapsychology, and Freud's personal philosophy. Objectification and falsification, of course, apply chiefly to clinical theory and this fact confirms the scientific aspect of psychoanalysis.

Many books have been dedicated to discussion of the scientific and philosophical status of psychoanalysis. For example, an excellent book of reprints of various classical articles on the subject is offered by Mujeeb-ur-Rahman (1977). A thorough discussion of the position of psychoanalysis in scientific and philosophical thought would require a complete book of its own and is beyond the scope of the present work. For a similar collection of major critical essays on the subject of psychoanalysis in philosophy, see Wollheim (1974).

Perhaps the best conclusion to this debate was offered by Einstein (1967), who explains,

> It has often been maintained that Galileo became the father of modern science by replacing the speculative, deductive method with the empirical, experimental method. I believe, however, that this interpre-

> tation would not stand close scrutiny. There is no empirical method without speculative concepts and systems; and there is no speculative thinking whose concepts do not reveal, on closer investigation, the empirical material from which they stem (p. xvii).

Freud and Langer Langer (1942, 1967) presents a philosophical viewpoint which is absolutely essential to examining the basic assumptions of Freud. She begins by defining the "sign" as something that stands in a one-to-one relationship or correlation to something else. The sign signifies that something else, and the interpretation of signs is the basis of animal intelligence. There exist both natural signs—for example, a patter on the roof is a sign that it is raining; and artificial signs—for example, crepe on the door signifies that someone has died. Artificial signs are easier to interpret.

A "symbol," on the other hand, is a vehicle for the conception of objects. It is not like signs which are proxy for their objects. Thus signs announce their objects; symbols lead one to conceive their objects—for example, a personal name. Language or words can be both; human language is symbol-using whereas animal expression is not.

Discursive symbolism or language assumes the usual notion of thought and ideas in the intellectual sense. The old theory was that language is the only means of our articulating thought, and everything that is not speakable thought is feeling. Langer points out that mental life is greater than discursive reason. She emphasizes an aspect usually called "irrational," "artistic truth," "intuition," and so on. Conceptualizing the flux of sensations via the ear, eye, and so forth, for example, gives us concrete "things" which are nondiscursive symbols.

Presentational symbols, constituting nonverbal representations, connotations, inflections, voice emphasis, and so forth, are a prevalent vehicle of meaning and widen our conception of rationality. Langer reminds us to consider the most familiar sort of nondiscursive symbol—a picture: "Given all at once to the intelligent eye, an incredible wealth and detail of information is conveyed by the portrait, where we do not have to stop to construe verbal meanings. . . . Clearly, a symbolism with so many elements, such myriad relationships, cannot be broken up into basic units" (1942, p. 77). Thus a picture *has no vocabulary.* A picture is first and foremost a direct presentation of an individual object. Langer labels this "presentational symbolism" to distinguish it from language proper (discursive symbolism). The basis of symbolization, according to Langer, is the order of perceptual forms—a concept quite close to Freud's notion of mnemic residues in the unconscious.

Thus ideas first generated in fantastic form become intellectual property only when discursive language rises to their expression. Langer speaks of the doctrine of Cassirer: that linguistic thinking cannot be sharply divided into mythical and scientific, but rather there is a fusion of both. This doctrine is similar to Freud's discussion of the combination of word-presentations with thing-presentations as material rises into the preconscious mind and is given linguistic expression.

Similarly, Langer's (1942) theory of artistic emotion connects to the comprehension of an unspoken idea—"aesthetic emotion" springs from "overcoming barriers of word-bound thought and achieving insight into literally 'unspeakable' realities" (p. 211). This theory leads in her later work to a complete elaboration of the role of human feelings and nondiscursive images as the evolutionary basis of scientific and abstract knowledge. For Langer, "Rationality is the essence of mind, and symbolic transformation is elementary process"; therefore, feelings have definite forms which become progressively articulated.

Basch (1973) points out that Freud contributed a method of "exploring, understanding, and transforming presentational symbols." Langer (1942) points out that so long as we admit only discursive symbolism, or language proper, as a bearer of ideas, thought must be regarded as our only intellectual activity. It begins and ends with language, and of course, Langer believes that there are matters which require to be conceived through some symbolistic schema other than discursive language. Langer's mature philosophy outlines a process beginning with signs in animal life, and proceeding to feeling, symbol formation, and higher and higher transformations of symbols to the peak of discursive thought. This process clearly parallels Freud's notion of the movement from unconscious through preconscious to conscious ideation. Freud's error was in the naive nineteenth-century view that unconscious mentation consisted of mnemic images.

It is the separation of mind and brain that Langer (1967) tries to break down, defining mind as a "phase" of brain activity. *The transformation of presentational symbols as they present themselves in the patient's dreams, gestures, and rituals, into discursive symbols is a vital work of the psychoanalytic process and yields an intellectual power equivalent to the development of discursive thought.* As Langer (1942) points out:

> Every major advance in thinking, every epoch-making new insight, springs from a new type of symbolic transformation. A higher level of thought is primarily a new activity; its course is opened up by a new departure in semantic. . . . Ideas first adumbrated in fantastic form become real intellectual property only when discursive language rises to their expression (pp. 163–4).

In *Mind: An Essay on Human Feeling* (1967, 1972) Langer points out how all the dynamic activities of neurophysiology, when reaching a certain intensity, enter into the "psychical phase." This is the phase of being felt:

> It is this transiency and general lability of the psychical phase that accounts for the importance of preconscious processes in the construction of such elaborate phenomena as ideas, intentions, images and fantasies, and makes it not only reasonable but obvious that they are rooted in the fabric of totally unfelt activities which Freud reified with the substantive term "the Unconscious" (1967, p. 22).

As soon as feeling is regarded as a *phase* of a physiological process instead of a product or a byproduct of it, Langer (and Basch) hope that the paradox of the physical versus the psychical will disappear. Langer hopes to demonstrate that the entire psychological field is a vast and branching evolutionary development of feeling. The development of the phase of feeling stands as the turning point in the rise of the mind; furthermore, "simpler forms of feeling which become so specialized that they are no longer called by that word compose the mentality of man, the mind, the material of psychology" (1967, p. 55).

It is clear that the metapsychology of Freud is fraught with a number of philosophical and neurophysiological mistakes and confusions. One of the unanswered questions is whether, working from such philosophers as Langer and such recent scientific advances such as general systems theory, the whole field of metapsychology should be rewritten and reintegrated into modern science—or whether it would be better to maintain metapsychology as a set of heuristic fictions useful in the clinical practice of intensive psychotherapy. These experience-distant conceptions would then be maintained as "as-if" hypotheses (Chessick 1961) having either a clinically heuristic value, or as applicable to a hermeneutics—depending on one's view of psychoanalysis as a natural science or as a subdiscipline of hermeneutics. Modell (1978) points out in a recent review of the subject that the entire matter of the nature of psychoanalytic knowledge remains unsolved; but the "enigma of the epistemology of psychoanalysis" poses a challenging and exciting interdisciplinary opportunity for philosophers and psychotherapists.

Perhaps the most extreme rewriting of Freud's metaphysics and metapsychology is to be found in the two (recently published in English) incredibly obscure books by Lacan (1977, 1978). By returning to Freud's original language, in a study of the nuances of his German in a manner reminiscent of Heidegger's approach in *Being and Time*, Lacan ignores the structural theory, ego psychology, and the whole of organized psychoanalysis, and tries to place the unconscious at the center of psychoanalysis. The unconscious for Lacan, based on his reading of Freud, takes on the characteristics of a reflection of the speech of significant others around the person; even transference becomes "the enactment of the reality of the unconscious," based on desires, signs, and symbols. Thus for Lacan the transference is a reflection of the desires not of the patient but of the analyst: "Your desire is the desire of the Other." The whole ego-psychological theory of the transference then becomes "merely a defence of the analyst" (Lacan 1978, p.158), a misconstruction or *méconnaissance*, to use Lacan's term. Since for Lacan the unconscious is structured like a language, and all speech is a demand, an appeal to the Other, and what comes from the Other is "treated not so much as a particular satisfaction of a need, but rather as a response to an appeal, a gift, a token of love" (1978, p. 278)—it follows that "*only the integrity of the analyst and of the analytic situation can safeguard from extinction the unique dialogue between analysand and analyst*" (1978, p.132). Turkle (1978) presents an excellent view of this "French revolution" that somehow combines psychoanalysis and politics.

We have come to the end of a long road, investigating the thought of Freud from his earliest conceptions and struggle for identity to the metaphysical speculations of his old age. During that process we have reviewed the development of his independence from organic neurology, his invention and application of a new technique for the investigation of mental disorders, and the fruitful flowering of this technique into an explosion of information about the mind and its workings. Our goal has been to emphasize those aspects of his thought having immediate clinical application to the practice of intensive psychotherapy, rather than to formal psychoanalysis (a subject beyond the scope of this book). In a previous publication (1974) I have discussed at length the differences between psychoanalysis and intensive psychotherapy; however, both rest firmly on Freud's discoveries and employ his basic metapsychology, even though some of his basic metapsychological conceptions remain uncorrected.

As I see it, the essence of psychoanalysis or intensive psychotherapy begins with (1) the data of introspection by the patient; (2) communication of this data—both verbally and nonverbally—from the patient to the therapist; and (3) empathy, defined as vicarious introspection, combined with scientific rigor applied by the therapist to this data. Such a procedure generates experience-near and experience-distant theorizing by the therapist, theorizing which is then tested in the clinical situation—again using scientific rigor—to fit the observed data into a context of broader meaning and significance such as "constructions," described by Freud in his famous 1937 paper (Freud 1973D;23:256ff). This view is expanded by Kohut (1978).

Each branch of science has its natural limits, determined approximately by the limits of its basic tools of observation. The limits of psychoanalysis and intensive psychotherapy are set by the limits of potential introspection and empathy. Through introspection in ourselves and through vicarious introspection in others—defined as empathy—we are able to observe their inner world, the world of thoughts, wishes, feelings, and fantasies. We organize this observational data and proceed to develop the experience-near and experience-distant concepts—as is the procedure with any science. Some of these concepts are abstractions or generalizations; for example, we observe thoughts and fantasies introspectively, observe the conditions of their disappearance and emergence, and arrive from this at the concept of repression. This is the standard formation of inductive theories in science.

Kohut (1971) explains that the potential for the acquisition of a special talent for empathic perception is largely acquired early in life, and he offers some remarks on those who choose a career in which the empathic preoccupation with others forms the center of their professional activity. If the essence of psychoanalysis lies in the therapist's protracted empathic immersion into the observed for the purposes of data-gathering and explanation, it follows that the empirical-scientific validation of psychoanalytic propositions will have to come from the continued collection and correction of introspective data by properly trained and qualified observers with developed empathic talents, and from the application of scientific rigor to the classification of such data and the abstraction of hypotheses from them. Laboratory research and empirical observational studies such as in sociology, anthropology, psychology, and clinical medicine can at best provide only ancillary evidence and hints for future investigation, but are not useful directly in either psychoanalytic data-gathering or psychoanalytic hypothesis formation. Because it is based on the data of introspection and empathy, psychoanalysis—and intensive psychotherapy, its derivative discipline—is unique among the sciences and is clearly delineated (Kohut 1978) from other sciences that inquire into the nature of man. We owe this science to the tenacity, integrity, and creative genius of one man—Sigmund Freud.

I do not wish to deny that a certain kind of imaginative audacity characterizes the great metaphysicians—as it characterizes the great scientists. . . . I do want to say that imaginative audacity is not enough, and that the main task of what you will forgive me for calling "the ordinary *philosophers"—you and I—is something comparable to the main task of ordinary scientists or of ordinary historians. It is our job to subject the audacious speculation of our great men to the most rigorous possible critical examination, the sort of examination to which, indeed, they subjected their own ideas in the process of formulating them. And something similar applies to our own little audacities, the minor insights of which we are occasionally capable; these, too, we should think of as possibilities submitted for testing, not as deriving their value from the mere fact that they come to us as "insights". For metaphysics, or so I have suggested, is speculation controlled by close critical reasoning.*

John Passmore, "The Place of Argument in Metaphysics" [In *Metaphysics: Readings and Reappraisals*, Dennick, W., and Lazerowitz, M., eds. (Englewood Cliffs, N.J.: Prentice-Hall, Inc. 1966), p. 365]

BIBLIOGRAPHY

All references to Freud in this bibliography follow the commonly accepted cross-reference list given in the Appendix to the Abstracts of the *Standard Edition* (Rothgeb 1973).

Abraham, K. 1954. *Selected Papers on Psychoanalysis.* New York: Basic Books.

Alexander, F. 1951. *Our Age of Unreason.* Philadelphia: Lippincott.

Alston, W. 1967. Logical Status of Psychoanalytic Theories. In *Encyclopedia of Philosophy*, edited by P. Edwards, vol. 6, pp. 512–516. New York: Macmillan.

Ardrey, R. 1966. *The Territorial Imperative.* New York: Atheneum.

Arlow, J., & Brenner, C. 1964. *Psychoanalytic Concepts and the Structural Theory.* New York: International Universities Press.

Bakan, D. 1965. *Sigmund Freud and the Jewish Mystical Tradition.* New York: Schocken Books.

Balogh, P. 1971. *Freud.* New York: Charles Scribner's Sons.

Barrett, W. 1958. *Irrational Man.* New York: Garden City.

Basch, M. 1973. Psychoanalysis and Theory Formation. *Annual of Psychoanalysis* 1:39–52.

______. 1975. Perception, Consciousness and Freud's Project. *Annual of Psychoanalysis* 3:3–20.

______. 1975*a*. Toward a Theory that Encompasses Depression. In *Depression and Human Existence*, edited by E. Anthony and T. Benedek. Boston: Little Brown.

______. 1976. Psychoanalysis and Communication Science. *Annual of Psychoanalysis* 4:385–421.

______. 1976*a*. Theory Formation. In Chapter VII: A Critique. *J. of Amer. Psychoanal. Assn.*, 246:61–263.

______. 1977. Developmental Psychology and Explanatory Theory in Psychoanalysis. *Annual of Psychoanalysis* 5:229–263.

______. 1978. Psychic Determinism and freedom of will. *Internat. Rev. Psycho-anal.* 5:257–264.

Baumeyer, F. 1956. The Schreber Case. *Internat. J. Psycho-Anal.* 37:61–74.

Bellow, S. 1964. *Herzog.* Greenwich, Conn.: Fawcett.

Berkowitz, L. 1969. Simple Views of Aggression. *Amer. Scientist* 57:372–383.

Bibring, E. 1936. The Development and Problems of the Theory of Instincts. Originally published in *Imago*. Reprinted in *Internat. J. Psycho-Anal* 22:102–131, 1941.

Blanshard, B. 1969. *The Nature of Thought*. New York: Humanities Press.

Blum, H. 1974. The Borderline Childhood of the Wolf-Man. *J. Amer. Psychoanal. Assn.* 22:721–742.

Brenner, C. 1957. The Nature and Development of the Concept of Repression in Freud's Writings. *Psychoanalytic Study of the Child* 12:19–45.

______. 1973. *An Elementary Textbook of Psychoanalysis*, second edition. New York: International Universities Press.

______. 1977. Commentary from Psychoanalysis. *J. Nerv. and Mental Dis.* 165:427–441.

______; Marcovitz, E.; and Ecker, P. 1970. Chapter VII of "The Interpretation of Dreams" and "The Unconscious." *Bull. of the Phila. Assn. of Psychoanal.* 20:37–42.

Broad, C. 1975. *Leibniz: An Introduction*. Cambridge: Cambridge University Press.

Brody, E. 1969. Psychiatry's Continuing Identity Crisis: Confusion or Growth? *Psychiatry Digest*, June.

Bychowski, G. 1969. *The Evil in Man*. New York: Grune & Stratton.

Chessick, R. 1961. Some Problems and Pseudo-Problems in Psychiatry. *Psychiatric Quart.* 35:711–719.

______. 1968. The Crucial Dilemma of the Therapist in Psychotherapy of Borderline Patients. *Amer. J. Psychotherapy* 22:655–666.

______. 1969. *How Psychotherapy Heals*. New York: Science House.

______. 1969*a*. Was Machiavelli Right? *Amer. J. Psychotherapy* 23:633–644.

______. 1971. *Why Psychotherapists Fail*. New York: Science House.

______. 1971*a*. How the Resident and the Supervisor Disappoint Each Other. *Amer. J. Psychotherapy* 25:272–283.

______. 1972. Angiopastic Retinopathy. *Arch. Psychiatry* 27:241–244.

______. 1974. *The Technique and Practice of Intensive Psychotherapy*. New York: Jason Aronson.

______. 1976. *Agonie: Diary of a Twentieth Century Man*. Ghent, Belgium: European Press.

______. 1977. *Intensive Psychotherapy of the Borderline Patient*. New York: Jason Aronson.

______. 1977*a*. *Great Ideas in Psychotherapy*. New York: Jason Aronson.

______. 1977*b*. Intensive Psychotherapy for the Psychiatrist's Family. *Amer. J. of Psychotherapy* 31:516–524.

______. 1978. On the Sad Soul of the Psychiatrist. *Bull. Menninger Clinic* 42:1–9.

______. 1978*a*. Medicine, Psychotherapy, and Religion. *Bull. Menninger Clinic* 42:505–514.

Clark, L. 1966. *History of the Primates.* Chicago: University of Chicago Press.

Cohen, R., and Balikov, H. 1974. On the Impact of Adolescence upon Parents. *Adolescent Psychiatry* 3:217–236.

Colby, K. 1951. *A Primer for Psychotherapists.* New York: Ronald Press.

Compton, A. 1972. A Study of the Psychoanalytic Theory of Anxiety. The Development of Freud's Theory of Anxiety. *J. Amer. Psychoanal. Assn.* 20:3–44.

______. 1972*a*. A Study of the Psychoanalytic Theory of Anxiety. The Development of the Theory of Anxiety Since 1926. *J. Amer. Psychoanal. Assn.* 20:341–394.

Copleston, F. 1962. *A History of Philosophy*, vol. 1, part 2. Garden City, N. Y.: Image Books.

______. 1964. *A History of Philosophy*, vol. 6, part 2. Garden City, N. Y.: Image Books.

Davis, G. 1976. Depression: Some Updated Thoughts. *J. of the Academy of Psychoanal.* 4:411–424.

Deutsch, F. 1957. Footnote To Freud's "Fragment of an Analysis of a Case of Hysteria." *Psychoanal. Quart.* 26:159–167.

______. 1965. *Neuroses and Character Types.* New York: International Universities Press.

______. 1973. *Confrontations with Myself.* New York: Norton.

Durkin, E., and Bowlby, J. 1968. Personal Aggressiveness and War. In *War*, edited by L. Bramson and G. Goethels. New York: Basic Books.

D'Zmura, T. 1964. The Function of Individual Supervision. *Internat. Psychiatry Clinics* 1:381–387.

Einstein, A. 1946. The Real Problem Is in the Hearts of Men. *New York Times Magazine*, June 23.

______. 1967. Forward. In *Galileo-Dialogues Concerning the Two Chief World Systems*, translated by S. Drake. Berkeley: University of California Press.

Eissler, K. 1974. On Some Theoretical and Technical Problems Regarding the Payment of Fees for Psychoanalytic Treatment. *Internat. Review of Psychoanal.* 1:73–102.

______. 1977. Comments on Penis Envy and Orgasm in Women. *Psychoanalytic Study of the Child* 32:29–84.

Ellenberger, H. 1970. *The Discovery of the Unconscious.* New York: Basic Books.

Engelman, E. 1976. *Bergasse 19.* New York: Basic Books.

Erikson, E. 1959. *Identity and the Life Cycle.* New York: International Universities Press.

Evans, R. 1967. *Dialogue with Erik Erikson.* New York: Harper & Row.

Evans, L. 1970. *Chess Catechism.* New York: Simon & Schuster.

Ferenczi, S. 1950. Stages in the Development of the Sense of Reality. Chapter 8 in *Sex and Psychoanalysis*, vol. 1. New York: Basic Books.

Fischer, C. 1965. Psychoanalytic Implications of Recent Research on Sleep and Dreams. *J. Amer. Psychoanal. Assn.* 13:197–303.

Fischer, R. 1966. *Bobby Fischer Teaches Chess.* New York: Basic Systems.

Fischer, S., and Greenberg, R. 1977. *The Scientific Credibility of Freud's Theories & Therapy.* New York: Basic Books.

Forstrom, L. 1977. The Scientific Autonomy of Clinical Medicine. *Journal of Medicine and Philosophy* 2:8–19.

Freedman, A.; Kaplan, H.; and Sadock, B. 1976. *Modern Synopsis of Comprehensive Textbook of Psychiatry II.* Baltimore: Williams & Wilkins.

Freud, A. 1946. *The Ego and the Mechanisms of Defense.* New York: International Universities Press.

Freud, E., ed. 1960. *The Letters of Sigmund Freud.* New York: Basic Books.

Freud, E.; Freud, L; and Grubrich-Simitis, I. 1978. *Sigmund Freud.* New York: Harcourt Brace Jovanovich.

Freud, S. 1891. *On Aphasia.* London: Imago Pub. Co., 1953.

______. 1893*H*. On the Psychical Mechanism of Hysterical Phenomena. *Standard Edition* 3:26ff.

______. 1894A. The Neuro-Psychoses of Defence. *Standard Edition* 3:43ff.

______. 1895*B*. On the Grounds for Detaching a Particular Syndrome from Neurasthenia under the Description Anxiety Neurosis. *Standard Edition* 3:87ff.

______. 1895*D*. Studies on Hysteria, by J. Breuer and S. Freud. *Standard Edition* 2:21ff.

______. 1896*B*. Further Remarks on the Neuro-Psychoses of Defence. *Standard Edition* 3:159ff.

______. 1896*C*. The Aetiology of Hysteria. *Standard Edition* 3:189ff.

______. 1899A. Screen Memories. *Standard Edition* 3:301ff.

______. 1900A. The Interpretation of Dreams. *Standard Edition* 4 and 5:1ff.

______. 1901A. On Dreams. *Standard Edition* 5:631ff.

______. 1910*B*. The Psychopathology of Everyday Life. *Standard Edition* 6:1ff.

______. 1905A. On Psychotherapy. *Standard Edition* 7:256ff.

______. 1905*B*. Psychical Treatment. *Standard Edition* 7:282ff.

______. 1905*C*. Jokes and Their Relation to the Unconscious. *Standard Edition* 8:3ff.

______. 1905*D*. Three Essays on the Theory of Sexuality. *Standard Edition* 7:125ff.

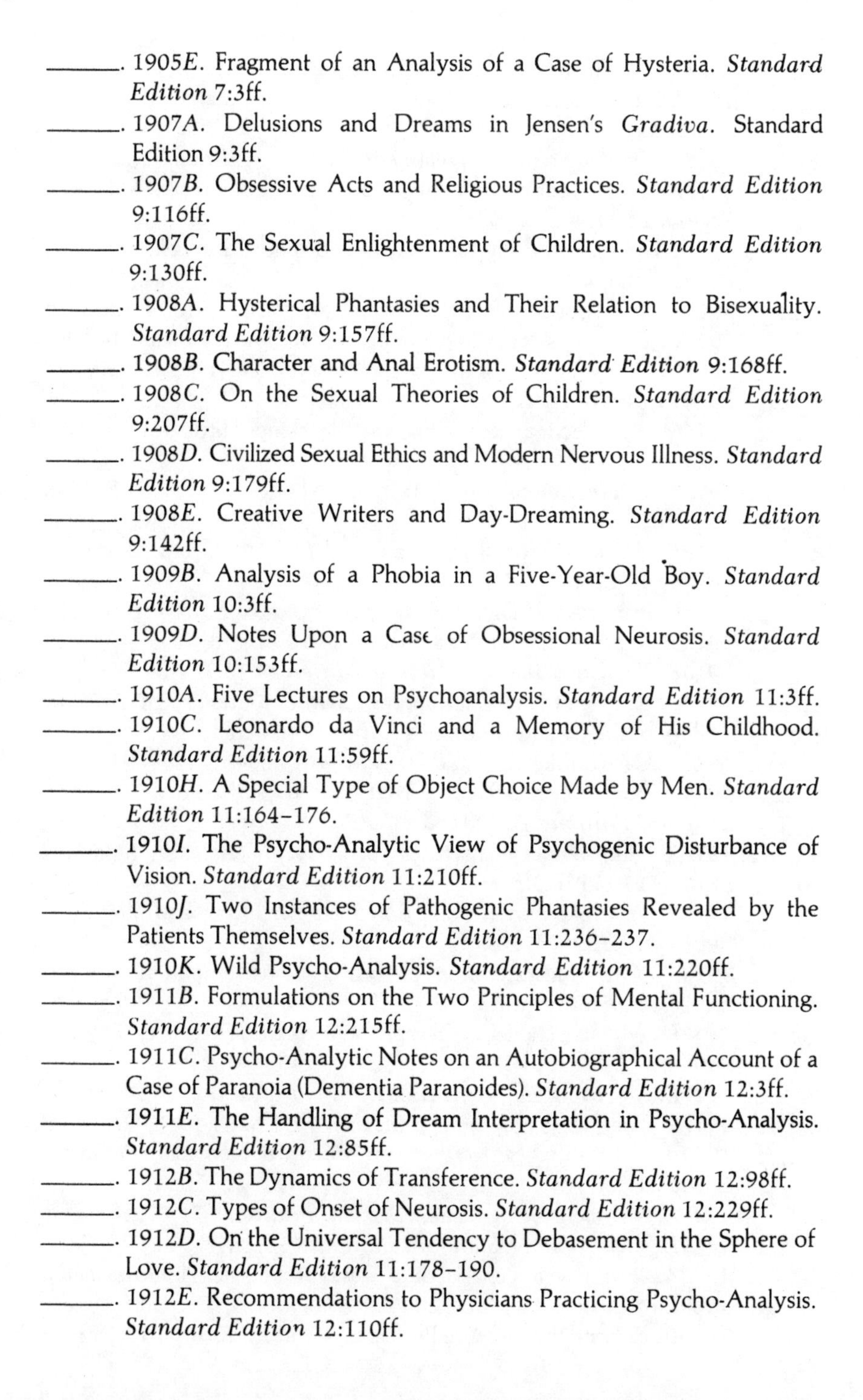

———. 1905*E*. Fragment of an Analysis of a Case of Hysteria. *Standard Edition* 7:3ff.
———. 1907*A*. Delusions and Dreams in Jensen's *Gradiva*. Standard Edition 9:3ff.
———. 1907*B*. Obsessive Acts and Religious Practices. *Standard Edition* 9:116ff.
———. 1907*C*. The Sexual Enlightenment of Children. *Standard Edition* 9:130ff.
———. 1908*A*. Hysterical Phantasies and Their Relation to Bisexuality. *Standard Edition* 9:157ff.
———. 1908*B*. Character and Anal Erotism. *Standard Edition* 9:168ff.
———. 1908*C*. On the Sexual Theories of Children. *Standard Edition* 9:207ff.
———. 1908*D*. Civilized Sexual Ethics and Modern Nervous Illness. *Standard Edition* 9:179ff.
———. 1908*E*. Creative Writers and Day-Dreaming. *Standard Edition* 9:142ff.
———. 1909*B*. Analysis of a Phobia in a Five-Year-Old Boy. *Standard Edition* 10:3ff.
———. 1909*D*. Notes Upon a Case of Obsessional Neurosis. *Standard Edition* 10:153ff.
———. 1910*A*. Five Lectures on Psychoanalysis. *Standard Edition* 11:3ff.
———. 1910*C*. Leonardo da Vinci and a Memory of His Childhood. *Standard Edition* 11:59ff.
———. 1910*H*. A Special Type of Object Choice Made by Men. *Standard Edition* 11:164–176.
———. 1910*I*. The Psycho-Analytic View of Psychogenic Disturbance of Vision. *Standard Edition* 11:210ff.
———. 1910*J*. Two Instances of Pathogenic Phantasies Revealed by the Patients Themselves. *Standard Edition* 11:236–237.
———. 1910*K*. Wild Psycho-Analysis. *Standard Edition* 11:220ff.
———. 1911*B*. Formulations on the Two Principles of Mental Functioning. *Standard Edition* 12:215ff.
———. 1911*C*. Psycho-Analytic Notes on an Autobiographical Account of a Case of Paranoia (Dementia Paranoides). *Standard Edition* 12:3ff.
———. 1911*E*. The Handling of Dream Interpretation in Psycho-Analysis. *Standard Edition* 12:85ff.
———. 1912*B*. The Dynamics of Transference. *Standard Edition* 12:98ff.
———. 1912*C*. Types of Onset of Neurosis. *Standard Edition* 12:229ff.
———. 1912*D*. On the Universal Tendency to Debasement in the Sphere of Love. *Standard Edition* 11:178–190.
———. 1912*E*. Recommendations to Physicians Practicing Psycho-Analysis. *Standard Edition* 12:110ff.

______. 1912*X*. Totem and Taboo. *Standard Edition* 13:1ff.
______. 1913*B*. Introduction to Pfister ("The Psycho-Analytic Method.") *Standard Edition* 12:327–331.
______. 1913*C*. On Beginning the Treatment. *Standard Edition* 12:122ff.
______. 1913*I*. The Predisposition to Obsessional Neurosis. *Standard Edition* 12:313ff.
______. 1913*J*. The Claims of Psycho-Analysis to Scientific Interest. *Standard Edition* 13:164ff.
______. 1914*B*. The Moses of Michaelangelo. *Standard Edition* 13:210ff.
______. 1914*C*. On Narcissism: An Introduction. *Standard Edition* 14:69ff.
______. 1914*D*. On the History of the Psycho-Analytic Movement. *Standard Edition* 14:3ff.
______. 1914*G*. Recollecting, Repeating and Working Through. *Standard Edition* 12:146ff.
______. 1915A. Observations on Transference-Love. *Standard Edition* 12:158ff.
______. 1915*B*. Thoughts for the Times on War and Death. *Standard Edition* 14:274ff.
______. 1915*C*. Instincts and Their Vicissitudes. *Standard Edition* 14:105ff.
______. 1915*D*. Repression. *Standard Edition* 14:143ff.
______. 1915*E*. The Unconscious. *Standard Edition* 14:161ff.
______. 1915*F*. A Case of Paranoia Running Counter to the Psycho-Analytic Theory of the Disease. *Standard Edition* 14:262ff.
______. 1916A. On Transience. *Standard Edition* 14:304ff.
______. 1916*D*. Some Character-Types Met with in Psycho-Analytic Work. *Standard Edition* 14:310ff.
______. 1916*X*. Introductory Lectures on Psycho-Analysis. *Standard Edition* 15 and 16:3ff.
______. 1917*B*. A Childhood Recollection from Dichtung and Wahrheit. *Standard Edition* 17:146ff.
______. 1917*C*. On Transformation of Instinct as Exemplified in Anal Erotism. *Standard Edition* 17:126ff.
______. 1917*D*. Metapsychological Supplement to the Theory of Dreams. *Standard Edition* 14:219ff.
______. 1917*E*. Mourning and Melancholia. *Standard Edition* 14:239ff.
______. 1918A. The Taboo of Virginity. *Standard Edition* 11:192–208.
______. 1918*B*. From the History of an Infantile Neurosis. *Standard Edition* 17:3ff.
______. 1919*E*. A Child is Being Beaten. *Standard Edition* 17:179ff.
______. 1919*H*. The Uncanny. *Standard Edition* 17:218ff.
______. 1920A. The Psychogenesis of a Case of Female Homosexuality. *Standard Edition* 18:146ff.
______. 1920*G*. Beyond the Pleasure Principle. *Standard Edition* 18:3ff.

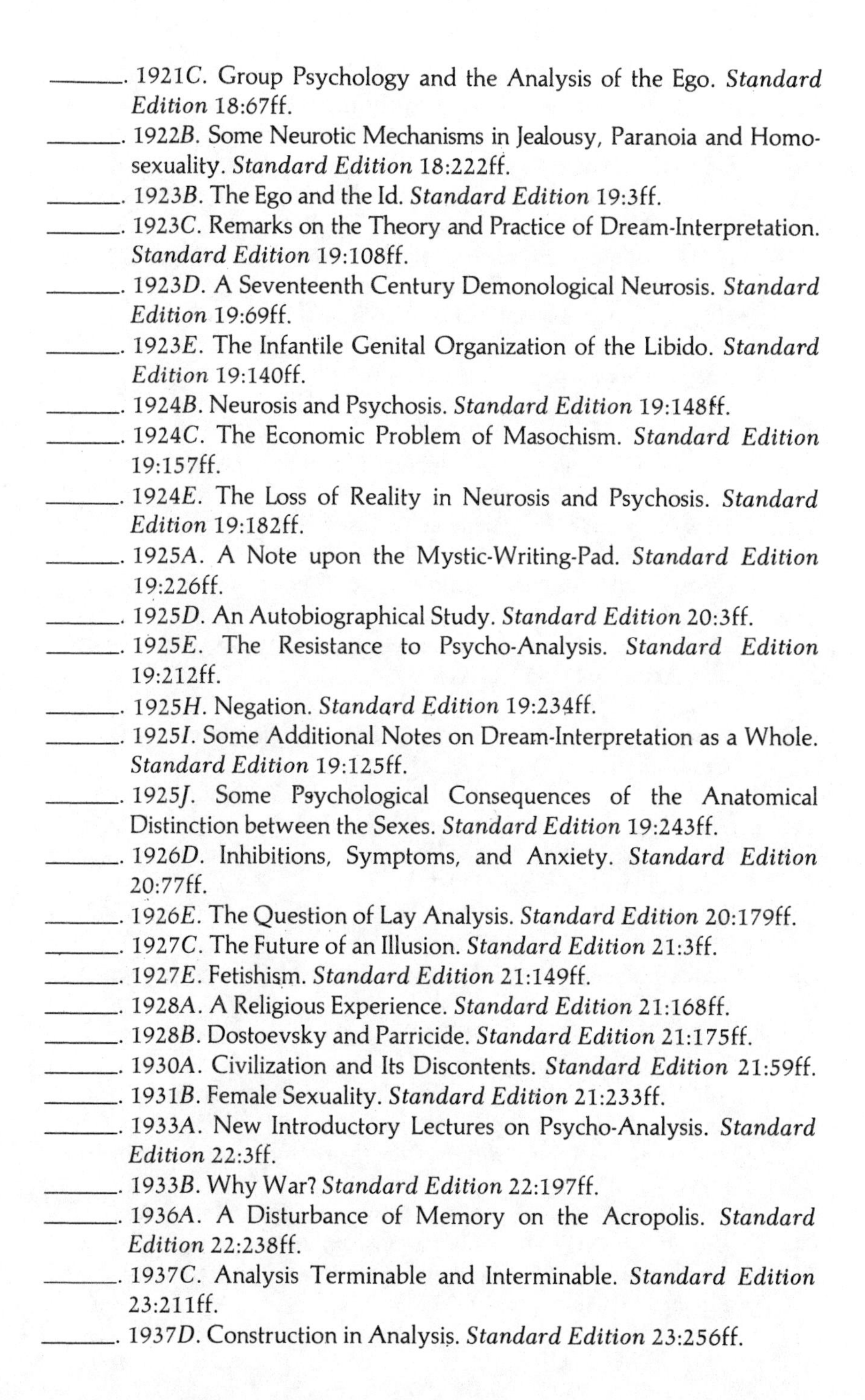

______. 1921*C*. Group Psychology and the Analysis of the Ego. *Standard Edition* 18:67ff.

______. 1922*B*. Some Neurotic Mechanisms in Jealousy, Paranoia and Homosexuality. *Standard Edition* 18:222ff.

______. 1923*B*. The Ego and the Id. *Standard Edition* 19:3ff.

______. 1923*C*. Remarks on the Theory and Practice of Dream-Interpretation. *Standard Edition* 19:108ff.

______. 1923*D*. A Seventeenth Century Demonological Neurosis. *Standard Edition* 19:69ff.

______. 1923*E*. The Infantile Genital Organization of the Libido. *Standard Edition* 19:140ff.

______. 1924*B*. Neurosis and Psychosis. *Standard Edition* 19:148ff.

______. 1924*C*. The Economic Problem of Masochism. *Standard Edition* 19:157ff.

______. 1924*E*. The Loss of Reality in Neurosis and Psychosis. *Standard Edition* 19:182ff.

______. 1925*A*. A Note upon the Mystic-Writing-Pad. *Standard Edition* 19:226ff.

______. 1925*D*. An Autobiographical Study. *Standard Edition* 20:3ff.

______. 1925*E*. The Resistance to Psycho-Analysis. *Standard Edition* 19:212ff.

______. 1925*H*. Negation. *Standard Edition* 19:234ff.

______. 1925*I*. Some Additional Notes on Dream-Interpretation as a Whole. *Standard Edition* 19:125ff.

______. 1925*J*. Some Psychological Consequences of the Anatomical Distinction between the Sexes. *Standard Edition* 19:243ff.

______. 1926*D*. Inhibitions, Symptoms, and Anxiety. *Standard Edition* 20:77ff.

______. 1926*E*. The Question of Lay Analysis. *Standard Edition* 20:179ff.

______. 1927*C*. The Future of an Illusion. *Standard Edition* 21:3ff.

______. 1927*E*. Fetishism. *Standard Edition* 21:149ff.

______. 1928*A*. A Religious Experience. *Standard Edition* 21:168ff.

______. 1928*B*. Dostoevsky and Parricide. *Standard Edition* 21:175ff.

______. 1930*A*. Civilization and Its Discontents. *Standard Edition* 21:59ff.

______. 1931*B*. Female Sexuality. *Standard Edition* 21:233ff.

______. 1933*A*. New Introductory Lectures on Psycho-Analysis. *Standard Edition* 22:3ff.

______. 1933*B*. Why War? *Standard Edition* 22:197ff.

______. 1936*A*. A Disturbance of Memory on the Acropolis. *Standard Edition* 22:238ff.

______. 1937*C*. Analysis Terminable and Interminable. *Standard Edition* 23:211ff.

______. 1937*D*. Construction in Analysis. *Standard Edition* 23:256ff.

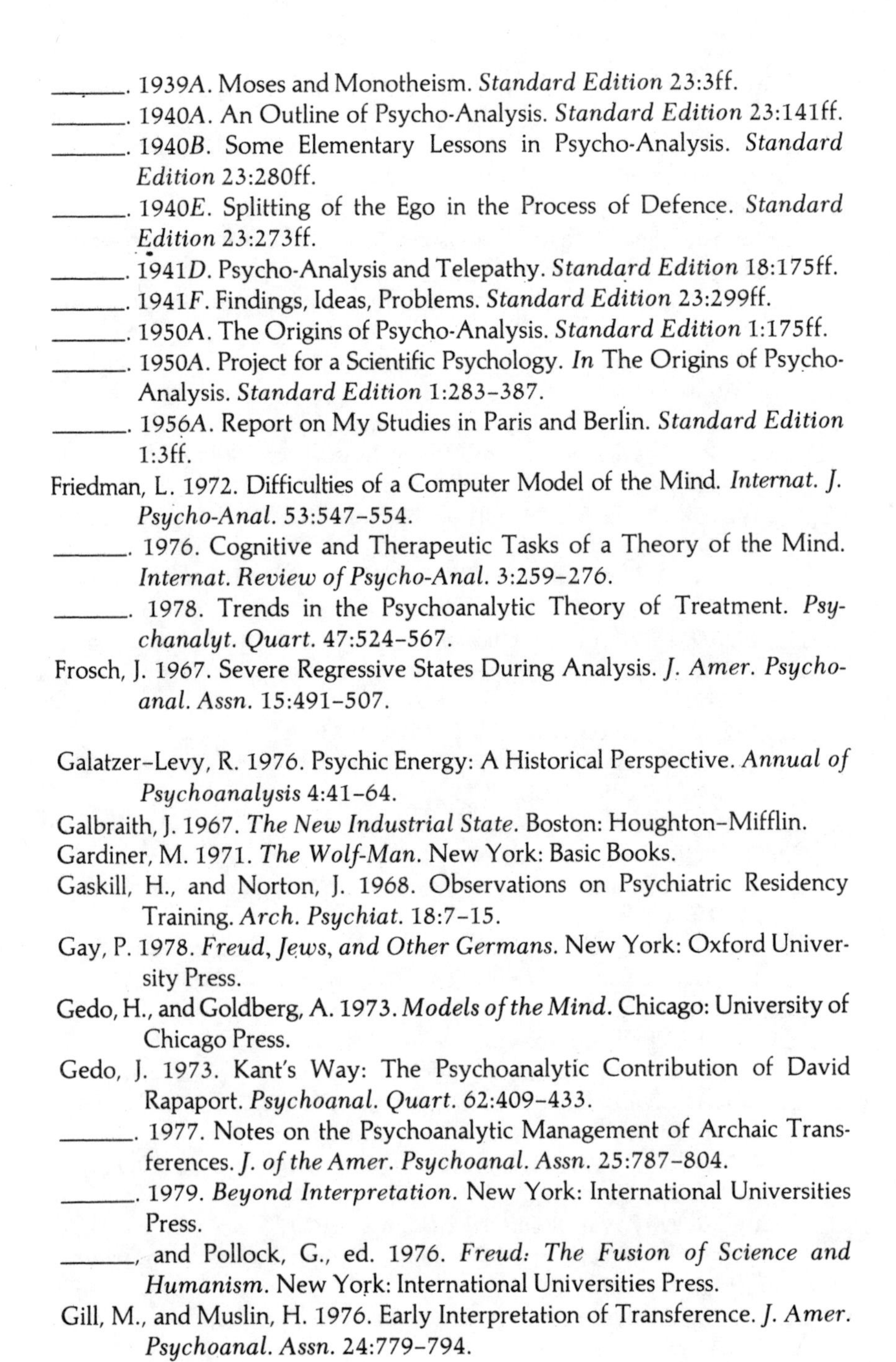

______. 1939A. Moses and Monotheism. *Standard Edition* 23:3ff.

______. 1940A. An Outline of Psycho-Analysis. *Standard Edition* 23:141ff.

______. 1940B. Some Elementary Lessons in Psycho-Analysis. *Standard Edition* 23:280ff.

______. 1940E. Splitting of the Ego in the Process of Defence. *Standard Edition* 23:273ff.

______. 1941D. Psycho-Analysis and Telepathy. *Standard Edition* 18:175ff.

______. 1941F. Findings, Ideas, Problems. *Standard Edition* 23:299ff.

______. 1950A. The Origins of Psycho-Analysis. *Standard Edition* 1:175ff.

______. 1950A. Project for a Scientific Psychology. *In* The Origins of Psycho-Analysis. *Standard Edition* 1:283–387.

______. 1956A. Report on My Studies in Paris and Berlin. *Standard Edition* 1:3ff.

Friedman, L. 1972. Difficulties of a Computer Model of the Mind. *Internat. J. Psycho-Anal.* 53:547–554.

______. 1976. Cognitive and Therapeutic Tasks of a Theory of the Mind. *Internat. Review of Psycho-Anal.* 3:259–276.

______. 1978. Trends in the Psychoanalytic Theory of Treatment. *Psychanalyt. Quart.* 47:524–567.

Frosch, J. 1967. Severe Regressive States During Analysis. *J. Amer. Psychoanal. Assn.* 15:491–507.

Galatzer–Levy, R. 1976. Psychic Energy: A Historical Perspective. *Annual of Psychoanalysis* 4:41–64.

Galbraith, J. 1967. *The New Industrial State.* Boston: Houghton–Mifflin.

Gardiner, M. 1971. *The Wolf-Man.* New York: Basic Books.

Gaskill, H., and Norton, J. 1968. Observations on Psychiatric Residency Training. *Arch. Psychiat.* 18:7–15.

Gay, P. 1978. *Freud, Jews, and Other Germans.* New York: Oxford University Press.

Gedo, H., and Goldberg, A. 1973. *Models of the Mind.* Chicago: University of Chicago Press.

Gedo, J. 1973. Kant's Way: The Psychoanalytic Contribution of David Rapaport. *Psychoanal. Quart.* 62:409–433.

______. 1977. Notes on the Psychoanalytic Management of Archaic Transferences. *J. of the Amer. Psychoanal. Assn.* 25:787–804.

______. 1979. *Beyond Interpretation.* New York: International Universities Press.

______, and Pollock, G., ed. 1976. *Freud: The Fusion of Science and Humanism.* New York: International Universities Press.

Gill, M., and Muslin, H. 1976. Early Interpretation of Transference. *J. Amer. Psychoanal. Assn.* 24:779–794.

Goble, F. 1970. *The Third Force.* New York: Grossman.
Goldberg, A. 1975. The Evolution of Psychoanalytic Concepts of Depression. Chapter 6 in *Depression and Human Existence*, edited by E. Anthony and T. Benedek. Boston: Little, Brown.
Goldstein, K. 1971. *Human Nature in the Light of Psychopathology.* New York: Schocken Books.
Graves, J. 1971. *The Conceptual Foundations of Contemporary Relativity Theory.* Cambridge, Mass.: MIT Press.
Green, R.; Carroll, G.; and Buxton, W. 1976. Drug Addiction Among Physicians. *J.A.M.A.* 236:1372–1375.
Greenson, R. 1967. *The Technique and Practice of Psychoanalysis*, Vol. 1. New York: International Universities Press.
______. 1974. The Decline and Fall of the Fifty-Minute Hour. *J. Amer. Psychoanal. Assn.* 22:785–791.
Grene, M. 1974. *The Knower & the Known.* Berkeley: University of California Press.
Groddeck, G. 1961. *The Book of the It.* New York: Mentor Books.
Grossman, C., and Grossman, S. 1965. *The Wild Analyst.* New York: Braziller.

Halleck, S., and Woods, S. 1962. Emotional Problems of Psychiatric Residents. *Psychiatry* 25:339–346.
Hartmann, H. 1958. *Ego Psychology and the Problem of Adaptation.* New York: International Universities Press.
______; Kris, E.; and Loewenstein, R. 1946. Comments on the Formation of Psychic Structure. In *Papers on Psychoanalytic Psychology*, Psychological Issues Monograph 14. New York: International Universities Press, pp. 27–55.
______; Kris, E.; and Loewenstein, B. 1949. Notes on the Theory of Aggression. *Psychoanal. Study of the Child* 3-4:9–36.
Highet, G. 1976. *The Immortal Profession.* New York: Weybright & Talley.
Hollender, M. 1970. The Need or Wish to be Held. *Arch. Psychiat.* 22:445–453.
______; Luborsky, L.; and Harvey, R. 1970. Correlates of the Desire to be Held in Women. *Psychosom. Research* 14:387–390.
______. Luborsky, L.; and Scaramella, T. 1969. Body Contact and Sexual Enticement. *Arch. Psychiat.* 20:188–191.
Holt, R. 1975. *Abstracts of the Standard Edition of the Complete Psychological Works of Sigmund Freud.* New York: Jason Aronson.

Jahoda, M. 1977. *Freud and the Dilemma of Psychology.* New York: Basic Books.

James, W. 1967. The Moral Equivalent of War. In *Essays on Faith and Morals*. New York: Meridian Books.

Jaspers, K. 1957. *Man in the Modern Age*. Garden City, N.Y.: Anchor Books.

Jones, E. 1953. *The Life and Work of Sigmund Freud*, Vol. 1. New York: Basic Books.

______. 1955. *The Life and Work of Sigmund Freud*, Vol. 2. New York: Basic Books.

______. 1957. *The Life and Work of Sigmund Freud*, Vol. 3. New York: Basic Books.

Jones, W. 1969. *A History of Western Philosophy*. 2d ed., Vol. 4. New York: Harcourt, Brace & World.

Jung, C. 1933. *Modern Man in Search of a Soul*. New York: Harcourt, Brace & World.

Kant, I. 1965. *Critique of Pure Reason*. Translated by Norman Kemp Smith. New York: St. Martin's Press.

Kanzer, M. 1952. The Transference Neurosis of the Rat-Man. *Psychoanal. Quart*. 21:181–189.

______. 1973. Two Prevalent Misconceptions about Freud's "Project." *Annual of Psychoanal*. 1:88–103.

Kaufmann, W. 1957. *Existentialism from Dostoyevsky to Sartre*. New York: Meridian Books.

Kelly, W. 1973. Suicide and Psychiatric Education. *Amer. J. Psychiat*. 130:463–468.

Kermode, F. 1976. Fighting Freud. *New York Review of Books*, Apr. 29, p. 39ff.

Kernberg, O. 1975. *Borderline Conditions and Pathological Narcissism*. New York: Jason Aronson.

______. 1976. *Object Relations Theory and Clinical Psychoanalysis*, ch. 6. New York: Jason Aronson.

Kierkegaard, S. 1946. *The Concept of Dread*. Princeton: Princeton University Press.

______. 1954. *Fear and Trembling* and *Sickness Unto Death*. New York: Anchor Books.

Klein, G. 1959. Consciousness in Psychoanalytic Theory. *J. Amer. Psychoanal. Assn*. 7:5–34.

______. 1976. *Psychoanalytic Theory*. New York: International Universities Press.

Klein, H., and Horowitz, W. 1949. Psychosexual Factors in the Paranoid Phenomena. *Amer. J. Psychiat*. 105:697–701.

Koestler, A. 1969. Man—One of Evolution's Mistakes? *New York Times Magazine*, Oct. 19.

Kohut, H. 1966. Forms and Transformations of Narcissism. *J. Amer. Psychoanal. Assn*. 14:243–272.

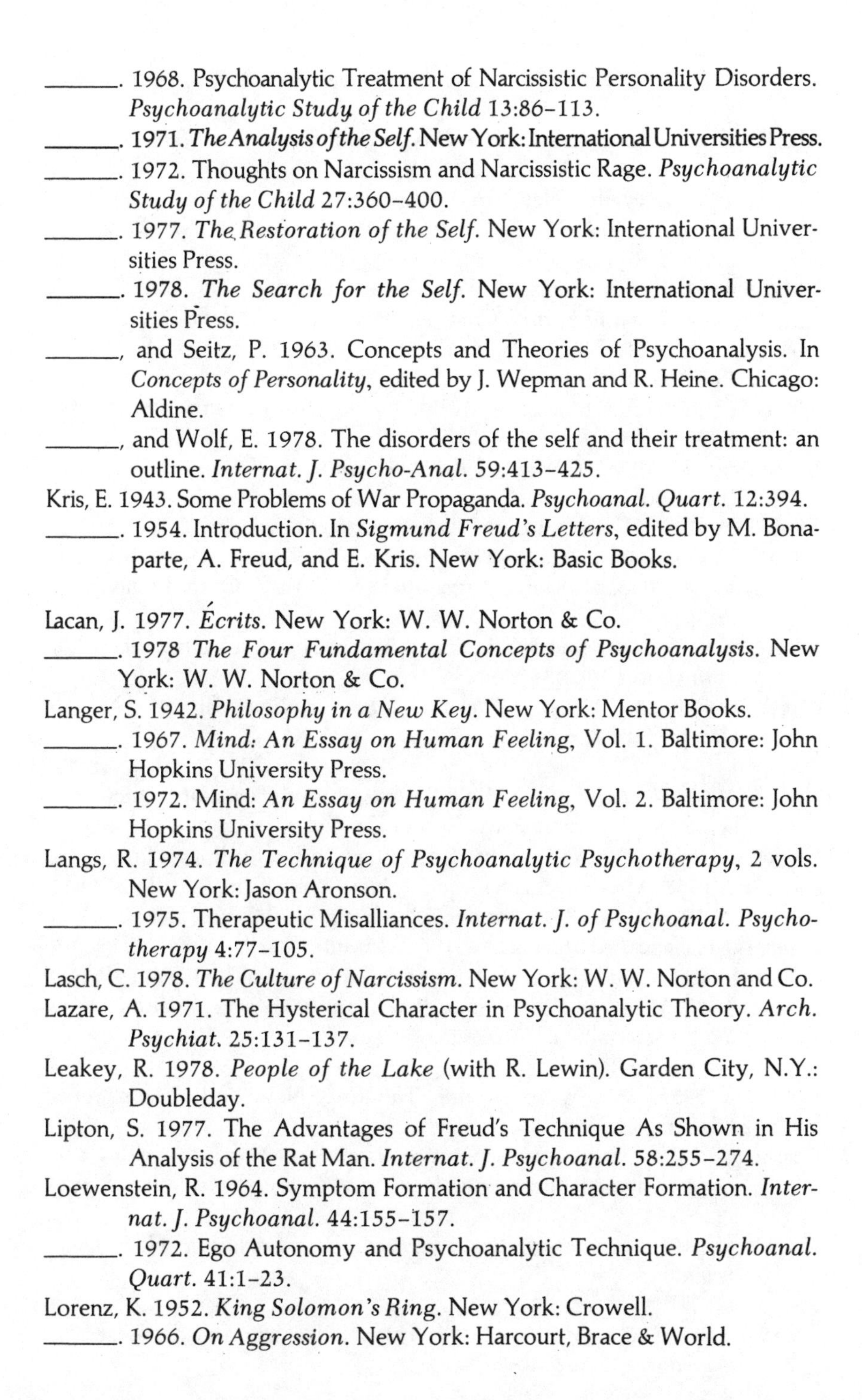

______. 1968. Psychoanalytic Treatment of Narcissistic Personality Disorders. *Psychoanalytic Study of the Child* 13:86–113.

______. 1971. *The Analysis of the Self.* New York: International Universities Press.

______. 1972. Thoughts on Narcissism and Narcissistic Rage. *Psychoanalytic Study of the Child* 27:360–400.

______. 1977. *The Restoration of the Self.* New York: International Universities Press.

______. 1978. *The Search for the Self.* New York: International Universities Press.

______, and Seitz, P. 1963. Concepts and Theories of Psychoanalysis. In *Concepts of Personality*, edited by J. Wepman and R. Heine. Chicago: Aldine.

______, and Wolf, E. 1978. The disorders of the self and their treatment: an outline. *Internat. J. Psycho-Anal.* 59:413–425.

Kris, E. 1943. Some Problems of War Propaganda. *Psychoanal. Quart.* 12:394.

______. 1954. Introduction. In *Sigmund Freud's Letters*, edited by M. Bonaparte, A. Freud, and E. Kris. New York: Basic Books.

Lacan, J. 1977. *Écrits*. New York: W. W. Norton & Co.

______. 1978 *The Four Fundamental Concepts of Psychoanalysis.* New York: W. W. Norton & Co.

Langer, S. 1942. *Philosophy in a New Key*. New York: Mentor Books.

______. 1967. *Mind: An Essay on Human Feeling*, Vol. 1. Baltimore: John Hopkins University Press.

______. 1972. Mind: *An Essay on Human Feeling*, Vol. 2. Baltimore: John Hopkins University Press.

Langs, R. 1974. *The Technique of Psychoanalytic Psychotherapy*, 2 vols. New York: Jason Aronson.

______. 1975. Therapeutic Misalliances. *Internat. J. of Psychoanal. Psychotherapy* 4:77–105.

Lasch, C. 1978. *The Culture of Narcissism.* New York: W. W. Norton and Co.

Lazare, A. 1971. The Hysterical Character in Psychoanalytic Theory. *Arch. Psychiat.* 25:131–137.

Leakey, R. 1978. *People of the Lake* (with R. Lewin). Garden City, N.Y.: Doubleday.

Lipton, S. 1977. The Advantages of Freud's Technique As Shown in His Analysis of the Rat Man. *Internat. J. Psychoanal.* 58:255–274.

Loewenstein, R. 1964. Symptom Formation and Character Formation. *Internat. J. Psychoanal.* 44:155–157.

______. 1972. Ego Autonomy and Psychoanalytic Technique. *Psychoanal. Quart.* 41:1–23.

Lorenz, K. 1952. *King Solomon's Ring*. New York: Crowell.

______. 1966. *On Aggression*. New York: Harcourt, Brace & World.

______. 1977. *Behind the Mirror*. New York: Harcourt, Brace, Jovanovich.

Macalpine, I., and Hunter, R. 1955. *Daniel Paul Schreber: Memoirs of My Nervous Illness*. London: Dawson.
May, R. 1958. *Existence*. New York: Basic Books.
McGuire, W., ed. 1974. *The Freud–Jung Letters*. Princeton, N.J.: Princeton University Press.
McNeill, W. 1963. *The Rise of the West*. Chicago: University of Chicago Press.
______. 1964. *Past and Future*. Chicago: University of Chicago Press.
Meissner, W. 1977. The Wolf Man and the Paranoid Process. *Annual of Psychoanal.* 5:23–74.
Meng, H., and Freud, E., eds. 1963. *Psychoanalysis and Faith*. New York: Basic Books.
Menninger, K. 1958. *Theory of Psychoanalytic Technique*. New York: Basic Books.
Modell, A. 1975. The Nature of Psychoanalytic Knowledge. *J. Amer. Psychoanal. Assn.* 26:641–658.
Montague, A. 1968. *Man and Aggression*. New York: Oxford University Press.
Moore, B. 1975. Toward a Classification of Narcissism. *Psychoanalytic Study of the Child* 30:243–276.
Mujeeb-ur-Ralman, M. 1977. *The Freudian Paradigm*. Chicago: Nelson Hall.

Nash, R. 1969. *The Light of the Mind: St. Augustine's Theory of Knowledge*. Lexington, Ky.: University Press of Kentucky
Niederland, W. 1974. *The Schreber Case*. New York: Quadrangle Press.
Ng, L., ed. 1968. *Alternatives to Violence*. New York: Time–Life Books.
Nisbett, A. 1976. *Konrad Lorenz*. New York: Harcourt, Brace, Jovanovich.
Nunberg, H., and Federn, E., eds. 1962. *Minutes of the Vienna Psychoanalytic Society*, Vol. 1. New York: International Universities Press.
______. 1967. *Minutes of the Vienna Psychoanalytic Society*, Vol. 2. New York: International Universities Press.

Odier, C. 1956. *Anxiety and Magic Thinking*. New York: International Universities Press.
Ornstein, P. 1968. Sorcerer's Apprentice: The Initial Phase of Training and and Education in Education in Psychiatry. *Comprehensive Psychiatry* 9:293–315.
Ovesey, L. 1969. *Homosexuality and Pseudohomosexuality*. New York: Science House.

Pasnau, R., and Russell, A. 1975. Psychiatric Resident Suicide. *Amer. J. Psychiat.* 132:402–406.

Peterfreund, E., and Schwartz, J. 1971. *Information, Systems, and Psychoanalysis*. New York: International Universities Press.
Piaget, J. 1971. *Insights and Illusions of Philosophy*. New York: World.
Popper, K. 1965. *Conjectures and Refutations*. New York: Basic Books.
Pribram, K., and Gill, M. 1976. *Freud's "Project" reassessed*. New York: Basic Books.

Rangell, L. 1959. The Nature of Conversion. *J. Amer. Psychoanal. Assn.* 7:285–298.
Rapaport, D. 1951. *Organization and Pathology of Thought*. New York: Columbia University Press.
______. 1960. *The Structure of Psychoanalytic Theory*. New York: International Universities Press.
______. 1961. *Emotions and Memory*. New York: Science Editions.
______. 1967. *Collected Papers*. New York: Basic Books.
Reichard, S. 1956. A Re-examination of "Studies in Hysteria." *Psychoanal. Quart.* 25:155–177.
Ricoeur, P. 1970. *Freud and Philosophy*. New Haven, Conn.: Yale University Press.
Roazen, P. 1968. *Freud: Political and Social Thought*. New York: A. Knopf.
______. 1975. *Freud and His Followers*. New York: Knopf.
Robert, M. 1966. *The Psychoanalytic Revolution*. New York: Harcourt, Brace & World.
______. 1976. *From Oedipus to Moses*. New York: Doubleday.
Rosen D. 1973. Suicide Rates Among Psychiatrists. *J.A.M.A.* 224:246–247.
______. 1976. The Pursuit of One's Own Healing. *Scientific Proceedings*. Washington, D.C.: American Psychiat. Assn.
Ross, M. 1975. Physician Suicide Risk. *Southern Med. J.* 68:699–702.
Rothgeb, C. 1973. *Abstracts of the Standard Edition of the Complete Psychological Works of Sigmund Freud*. New York: International Universities Press.
Russell, A.; Pasnau, R.; and Taintor, Z. 1975. Emotional Problems of Residents in Psychiatry. *Amer. J. Psychiat.* 132:263–267.
Russell, B. 1948. *Human Knowledge: Its Scope and Limits*. New York: Simon & Schuster.
______. 1951. *The Conquest of Happiness*. New York: Signet.
______. 1962. *Human Society in Ethics and Politics*. New York: Mentor Books.
Ryle, G. 1949. *The Concept of Mind*. New York: Barnes & Noble.

Sadow, L.; Gedo, J.; Miller, J:, Pollock, G; Sabshin, M.; and Schlessinger, N. 1968. The Process of Hypothesis Change in Three Early Psychoanalytic Concepts. *J. Amer. Psychoanal. Assn.* 16:245–278.

Saul, L. 1958. *Technic and Practice of Psychoanalysis.* Philadelphia: B. Lippincott.

Sawyier, F. 1973. Commentary on Freud and Philosophy. *Annual of Psychoanalysis* 1:216–228.

Schafer, R. 1968. *Aspects of Internalization.* New York: International Universities Press.

Schilpp, P. 1974. *The Philosophy of Karl Popper*, 2 vols. LaSalle, Ill.: Open Court.

Schur, M. 1966. *The Id and the Regulatory Principles of Mental Functioning.* New York: International Universities Press.

______. 1972. *Freud: Living and Dying.* New York: International Universities Press.

Semrad, E. 1969. *Teaching Psychotherapy of Psychotic Patients.* New York: Grune & Stratton.

Shaw, J. 1978. Man and the Problem of Aggression. *J. Phila. Assn. Psychoanal.* 5:41–58.

Skinner, B. 1971. *Beyond Freedom and Dignity.* New York: Knopf.

Snow, C. P. 1978. *The Realists.* New York: Charles Scribner's Sons.

Steppacher, R., and Mausner, J. 1974. Suicide in Male and Female Physicians. *J.A.M.A.* 228:323–328.

Stone, L. 1961. *The Psychoanalytic Situation.* New York: International Universities Press.

Storr, A. 1968. *Human Aggression.* New York: Atheneum.

Strupp, H. 1969. Towards a Specification of Teaching and Learning in Psychotherapy. *Arch. Psychiat.* 21:203–212.

______. 1972: On the Technique of Psychotherapy. *Arch. Psychiat.* 26:270–278.

______. 1973. *Psychotherapy: Clinical, Research & Theoretical Issues.* New York: Jason Aronson.

Sullivan, H. 1956. *Clinical Studies in Psychiatry.* New York: Norton.

Szasz, T. 1957. On the Theory of Psychoanalytic Treatment. *Internat. J. Psychoanal.* 38:166–182.

Tarachow, S. 1963. *An Introduction to Psychotherapy.* New York: International Universities Press.

Tarrasch, S. 1959. *The Game of Chess.* New York: McKay.

Thomä, H., and Kächle, H. 1975. Problems of Metascience and Methodology in Clinical Psychoanalytic Research. *Annual of Psychoanal.* 3:49–122.

Toulmin, S. 1953. *The Philosophy of Science.* New York: Harper & Row.

Toynbee, A. 1969. *Experiences.* New York: Oxford University Press.

Tuchman, B. 1978. *A Distant Mirror: The Calamitous 14th Century.* New York: Knopf.

Turkle, H. 1978. *Psychoanalytic Politics.* New York: Basic Books.

Vaughan, V. 1966. New Insights in Social Behavior. *J.A.M.A.* 198:163.

Waelder, R. 1967. Inhibitions, Symptoms, and Anxiety: Forty Years Later. *Psychoanal. Quart.* 36:1–36.

Wilkerson, T. 1976. *Kant's Critique of Pure Reason.* Oxford: Clarendon Press.

Wittgenstein, L. 1967. *Lectures and Conversations.* Berkeley: University of California Press.

Wollheim, R. 1971. Sigmund Freud. New York: Viking Press.

———. 1974. *Freud: A Collection of Critical Essays.* New York: Anchor Books.

Wolpert, E. 1975. Manic Depressive Illness as an Actual Neurosis. In *Depression & Human Existence*, edited by E. Anthony and T. Benedek. Boston: Little, Brown.

Zetzel, E. 1970. *The Capacity for Emotional Growth.* New York: International Universities Press.

Zweig, S. 1962. *The Mental Healers.* New York: Ungar.

Index

DATE DUE